CHRISTIANITY
IN THE
GRECO-ROMAN
WORLD

A Narrative Introduction

CHRISTIANITY
IN THE
GRECO-ROMAN
WORLD

MOYER V. HUBBARD

HENDRICKSON
PUBLISHERS

Christianity in the Greco-Roman World: A Narrative Introduction
© 2010 by Hendrickson Publishers Marketing, LLC
P. O. Box 3473
Peabody, Massachusetts 01961-3473

ISBN 978-1-56563-663-7

Printed in the United States of America

Hendrickson Publishers is strongly committed to sustainability and environmentally responsible printing practices. The pages of this book were printed on 30% post consumer waste recycled stock using only soy or vegetable content inks.

Art Credit: Interior design and artwork by Dana Martin.

First Printing — January 2010

Library of Congress Cataloging-in-Publication Data

Hubbard, Moyer V.
    Christianity in the Greco-Roman world : a narrative introduction / Moyer V. Hubbard.
        p. cm.
    Includes bibliographical references and indexes.
    ISBN 978-1-56563-663-7 (alk. paper)
    1. Bible. N.T. Epistles of Paul—Social scientific criticism. 2. Bible. N.T.—Social scientific criticism. I. Title.
    BS2650.52.H83 2010
    227′.067—dc22
                    2009032075

For Scott and Jeff

fellow explorers of the ancient world

CONTENTS

EDUCATION, PHILOSOPHY, AND ORATORY

CITY AND SOCIETY

HOUSEHOLD AND FAMILY

ACKNOWLEDGMENTS

This book began as a lecture series delivered at Biola University in La Mirada, California. From the time the idea for this book was first conceived, my students and colleagues at Biola University have made a steady contribution to this book's development—reading draft chapters, commenting on content, and suggesting ideas. Joanne Jung, my former teaching assistant, friend, and now colleague at Biola University, helped immensely in organizing my database of ancient sources. Joshua Carroll and Ray Lozano also assisted with indexing the final manuscript. Funding for research leaves were provided by Biola University and the Skene Trust. Without their help this book would never have been written.

My family, Heidi, Scott, and Jeff, have been a constant source of encouragement and support. Scott and Jeff, my sons, have traveled with me to Ephesus, Corinth, Athens, Rome, Pompeii, and points between. Their enthusiasm for the ancient world has kept me enthusiastic for this project.

ABBREVIATIONS AND TRANSLATIONS

OLD TESTAMENT

Gen	Genesis
Exod	Exodus
Num	Numbers
Deut	Deuteronomy
Ruth	Ruth
1 Sam	1 Samuel
Ps(s)	Psalm(s)

APOCRYPHA

1–4 Macc	1–4 Maccabees
Wis	Wisdom of Solomon

NEW TESTAMENT

Matt	Matthew
Mark	Mark
Luke	Luke
John	John
Acts	Acts

Rom	Romans
1–2 Cor	1–2 Corinthians
Gal	Galatians
Eph	Ephesians
Phil	Philippians
Col	Colossians
1–2 Thess	1–2 Thessalonians
1–2 Tim	1–2 Timothy
Titus	Titus
Phlm	Philemon
Rev	Revelation

OLD TESTAMENT PSEUDEPIGRAPHA

Apoc. Bar.	*Apocalypse of Baruch*
Apoc. Mos.	*Apocalypse of Moses*
Apoc. Zeph.	*Apocalypse of Zephaniah*
1 En.	*1 Enoch*
4 Ezra	*4 Ezra*
Jos. Asen.	*Joseph and Aseneth*
Jub.	*Jubilees*
L.A.B.	*Liber antiquitatum biblicarum (Pseudo-Philo)*
Ps.-Proc.	Pseudo-Phocylides
T. Ab.	*Testament of Abraham*

QUMRAN

1QH	(=1Q35) Thanksgiving Hymns
1QM	(+1Q33) War Scroll
1Q33	(+1QM) War Scroll
2Q23	(=2QapProph) apocryphal prophetic text
4Q186	horoscope
4Q230	catalog of spirits
4Q231	catalog of spirits
4Q291	prayers
4Q292	prayers
4Q293	prayers
4Q318	(=4QBr ar) Thunder Discourse
4Q387	(=4QpsEzek[c]) Pseudo-Ezekiel
4Q388	(=4QpsEzek[d]) Pseudo-Ezekiel

4Q389	(=4QpsMoses[d]) Pseudo-Moses
4Q390	(=4QpsMoses[e]) Pseudo-Moses
4Q408	wisdom literature
4Q409	liturgy
4Q444	incantation
4Q448	Apocryphal Psalm and Prayer
4Q503	(=4QpapPrQuot) Daily Prayers
4Q504	(=4QDibHam[a]) Words of the Luminaries[a]
4Q505	(=4QDibHam[b]) Words of the Luminaries[b]
4Q506	(=4QDibHam[c]) Words of the Luminaries[c]
4Q507	Festival Prayers[a]
4Q508	Festival Prayers[b]
4Q509	Festival Prayers[c]
4Q544	(=4QAmram[b]) Visions of Amram[b]
4Q560	Aramaic exorcistic text
4Q561	(=4QHor ar) Aramaic horoscope
11Q11	(=11QApPs[a]) Apocryphal Psalms[a]
11Q19	(=11QTemple[a]) Temple Scroll[a]

CAIRO GENIZAH

| CD | Damascus Document |

GREEK AND LATIN WORKS

Apuleius
| *Flor.* | *Florida* |
| *Metam.* | *Metamorphoses* |

Aristides
| *Or.* | *De Oratione* |

Cicero
Att.	*Epistulae ad Atticum*
Cael.	*Pro Caelio*
Dom.	*De domo suo*
Mur.	*Pro Murena*
Pis.	*In Pisonem*
Red. sen.	*Post reditum in senatu*
Verr.	*In Verrem*

Dio Cassius
  Rom. Hist.   *Roman History*

Dio Chrysostom
  Or.   *De Oratione*

Epictetus
  Disc.   *Discourses (Dissertationes)*
  Ench.   *Enchiridion*

Horace
  Ep.   *Epistulae*
  Saec.   *Carmen saecularae*
  Sat.   *Satirae (Satires)*

Ignatius
  Rom.   *To the Romans*

Josephus
  Ag. Ap.   *Against Apion*
  Ant.   *Antiquities of the Jews*
  J.W.   *Jewish Wars*

Juvenal
  Sat.   *Satirae (Satires)*

Manilius
  Astr.   *Astronomica*

Martial
  Ep.   *Epigrammaton (Epigrams)*

Maximus of Tyre
  Disc.   *Discourses*

Musonius Rufus
  Disc.   *Discourses*

Pausanius
  Descr.   *Graciae description (Descriptions of Greece)*

Persius
  Sat.   *Satirae*

Petronius
  Satyr.   *Satyricon*

Philo
  Deus   *Quod Deus sit immutabilis*
  Spec. Laws   *On the Special Laws*

Philodemus
    Epig.   *Epigrams*

Philostratus
    Vita Apoll.   *Vita Apollinii*
    Vit. soph.   *Vita sophistarum*

Plato
    Euthyd.   *Euthydemus*
    Phaed.   *Phaedrus*
    Protag.   *Protagorus*
    Soph.   *Sophist*

Pliny the Elder
    Nat. Hist.   *Natural History*

Pliny the Younger
    Ep.   *Epistulae*
    Ep. Tra.   *Epistulae ad Trajanum*
    Pan.   *Panegyricus*

Plutarch
    Mor.   *Moralia*

Quintilian
    Inst.   *Institutio oratoria*
    Res Ges.   *Res Gestae divi Augusti. Ed. J. Gagé, 1935*

Seneca the Elder
    Contr.   *Controversiae*
    Suas.   *Suasoriae*

Seneca (the Younger)
    Ben.   *De beneficiis*
    Clem.   *De clementia*
    Ep.   *Epistulae morales*

Suetonius
    Aug.   *Divus Augustus*
    Claud.   *Claudius*
    Gramm.   *De grammaticus*
    Dom.   *Domitianus*
    Rhet.   *De rhetoribus*
    Tib.   *Tiberius*

Tacitus
    Ann.   *Annales (Annals)*

Agr.	*Agricola*
Dial.	*Dialogus de oratoribus*
Hist.	*Historiae (Histories)*

Tertullian
Mart.	*Ad martyras (To the martyrs)*

SECONDARY SOURCES

AB	Anchor Bible
BDAG	Danker, F. W., W. Bauer, W. F. Arndt, and F. W. Gingrich. *Greek-English Lexicon of the New Testament and Other Early Christian Literature.* 3d ed. Chicago, 2000
BGU	*Aegyptische Urkunden aus den Museen zu Berlin: Griechische Urkunden,* 1895–
BWK	Georg Petzl, *Die Beichtinschriften Westkleinsasiens,* Epigraphica Anatolica 22 (1994)
CIJ	*Corpus inscriptionum judaicarum*
CIL	*Corpus inscriptionum latinarum*
HTR	*Harvard Theological Review*
ICC	International Critical Commentary
IGR	*Inscriptiones Graecae ad res Romanas pertinentes.* Vol. 4 Edited by R. Cagnat et al., 1927
JETS	*Journal of the Evangelical Theological Society*
JRS	*Journal of Roman Studies*
JSNT	*Journal for the Study of the New Testament*
JSOT	*Journal for the Study of the Old Testament*
LCL	Loeb Classical Library
MDAI.A	*Mitteilungen des Deutschen Archaeologischen Instituts.* Athenische Abteilung, 1876–
NIBC	New International Biblical Commentary
NICNT	New International Commentary on the New Testament
NIGTC	New International Greek Testament Commentary
NTS	*New Testament Studies*
OGIS	*Orientis graeci inscriptiones selectae.* Edited by W. Dittenberger. 2 vols. Leipzig, 1903–1905
PGM	*Papyri graecae magicae: Die griechischen Zauberpapyri.* Edited by K. Preisendanz. Berlin, 1928
PGMT	*The Greek Magical Papyri in Translation.* H. D. Betz et al. Chicago: University of Chicago Press, 1986

SIG	*Sylloge inscriptionum graecarum.* Edited by W. Dittenberger. 4 vols. 3d ed. Leipzig, 1915–1924
SNTSMS	Society for New Testament Studies Monograph Series
TDNT	*Theological Dictionary of the New Testament.* Edited by G. Kittel and G. Friedrich. Translated by G. W. Bromiley. 10 vols. Grand Rapids, Mich.: Eerdmans, 1964–1976
TynBul	*Tyndale Bulletin*
WBC	Word Biblical Commentary
WUNT	Wissenschaftliche Untersuchungen zum Neuen Testament
ZNW	*Zeitschrift für die neutestamentliche Wissenschaft und die Kunde der älteren Kirche*

Unless noted otherwise, translations of Scripture follow the NIV.

For classical authors I have used the translations of the Loeb Classical Library wherever possible. For other ancient sources (inscriptions, and so on) I have relied on the translators and editors of the works in question, which are listed in the bibliography. Quite often it was necessary to modify these translations, usually by abbreviation but also through offering clarifying glosses to aid the modern reader. These modifications are noted by an asterisk (*) preceding the reference. I have made extensive use of the inscriptional data from Corinth and Philippi. These are cited by the translator (Merrit, West, Kent, or Pilhofer, for detailed information of which see the Bibliography) and the number of the inscription assigned by the translator (e.g., Kent no. 25, Pilhofer 033/G22). Abbreviations of ancient and modern sources follow the conventions presented in *The SBL Handbook of Style* (Peabody, Mass.: Hendrickson, 1999).

INTRODUCTION

BACKGROUND AS FOREGROUND

If you have ever traveled abroad or lived in a culture other than your own, you have probably found yourself, on more than one occasion, perplexed by local customs, or unsure of local laws, or perhaps confused by an unexpected response. In addition to having specific laws that dictate who can vote, how fast one can drive, and so on, every society is governed by complex layers of unwritten codes; invisible assumptions that provide order to reality and meaning to the mundane. Often these are the result of distant historical circumstances and deeply imbedded values, which exert a powerful and enduring effect on the contemporary society. Walking into another culture, in some ways, is like landing on another planet with slightly different gravitational pull; familiar actions can have unfamiliar consequences. I remember bringing a housewarming gift to welcome new neighbors who had recently arrived from Taiwan. They warmly accepted the gift and then hastily took down one of their own wall hangings and presented it to me! This family did not understand American customs associated with welcoming neighbors, and I did not understand Taiwanese values related to reciprocity.

The world of the NT is a different world from the one in which we live. It is an ancient Mediterranean world with oligarchic political structures, primitive superstitions, and long-extinct languages. Exploring this world involves coming to grips with political, historical, economic, social, and religious realities that dominated the ancient landscape and form part of the often invisible background to the scattered writings and crumbling artifacts that remain.

This is a book about the social and historical background of the NT, and more specifically, those backgrounds as reflected in and during the time of the writing of the letters of Paul; a book where background becomes foreground. The fundamental conviction undergirding this project is that the better one understands the historical and social context in which the NT (and Paul's letters) was written, the better one will understand the writings of the NT themselves; passages become clearer, metaphors deciphered, images sharpened. If, like me, you believe that the message of the NT is as important for the modern world as it was for the ancient world, then gaining a better understanding of the world of the NT is not optional.

The particular focus of this book is on the letters and travels of the apostle Paul, arguably the most important individual in the spread of Christianity to the Greek and Roman world. His letters, together with Luke's account in Acts, are the historian's primary sources for understanding how the Jesus movement spread beyond the Jewish heartland. Although I will use words like "Christianity" and "church" frequently (they are unavoidable), it is important for the reader to understand that the primitive "Jesus movement" (another term I will use regularly) was fluid, unformed, and somewhat improvisational in its various manifestations during the first century. We need to be careful to distinguish the institutional forms of Christianity familiar to us from the small huddles of believers who met in homes in the cities of the Roman world in the first century.

LEARNING AND RELEVANCE

Two further pedagogical convictions guide this project. The first is that we learn as effectively though narrative as through discursive, informational-based treatments of a topic. Of course, we all love a good story, but the benefit of a good story is not exhausted by its entertainment value. Rather, a story can be a powerful vehicle for communicating truth, be it the facts of history or the meaning of life. A story touches a different cognitive dimension of the reader and has the potential of engaging the soul as well as the mind. The stories of the Bible contain a record of God's dealings with his covenant people and communicate both historical events and important truth. In fact, the dominant genre of the Bible is narrative, which means the Bible is more of a storybook, in the sense of a narrative history, than a textbook.

Narrative, however, has its limitations. It is not the most efficient means of disseminating large amounts of data, nor does it easily express subtle nuances of complex issues. It is also difficult, if not impossible, to critically assess differing interpretations of historical events in a narrative format, and critical assessment is one of the fundamental tasks of the historian. In this book, I want to harness both the power of narrative and the efficiency of prose in order to render the fascinating tale of the spread of Christianity a bit more engaging, interesting, and educational.

A second pedagogical conviction evident in the structure of each chapter is that learning is best achieved when practical relevance is clear and explicit. Facts isolated from relevance are not likely to be perceived as significant, that is, worth pondering and retaining. There are many fine books exploring the background of the NT—and I will recommend a few at the close of this introduction—yet rarely is there any significant space devoted to applying the facts of history to the texts of Scripture. Of course, we don't study history because it happened; we study history because it is important. My experience—bolstered by a lot of research from the social sciences—is that learning will dramatically increase when the subject matter is perceived to be relevant and significant.[1] Connecting the world of the NT to the text of the NT will be a major component of each chapter. These underlying concerns and convictions have contributed decisively to the focus and format of this book.

FOCUS AND FORMAT

Each of the following chapters focuses on a discrete area of NT background: Religion and Superstition; Education, Philosophy, and Oratory; City and Society; Household and Family. Each chapter starts with a narrative followed by an explanatory commentary and concludes with a section devoted to the NT context. Although our exploration will take us into the ancient cities of Ephesus, Thessalonica, Philippi, and elsewhere, our primary focus will be on Corinth and the Corinthian correspondence, as we have more information about Christianity in Corinth than any other first-century city.

The narratives that introduce each chapter will allow the reader to step into the world of the first century and view the cultural landscape through the eyes of first-century pagans, Christians, and Jews. These fictional vignettes also raise issues that will be addressed in the explanatory commentary that follows. The narratives are set in first-century Corinth, and each of the characters is drawn from the archaeological, biblical, or literary record related to ancient Corinth. Sospinus (ch. 3), for example, was an orator active in Corinth; Claudius Dinnipus (ch. 4) was a magistrate in Corinth in the first century; and so on. I have not knowingly contradicted any of the available facts about these historical personages, yet the narratives themselves are entirely fictional. Most of the characters can be traced to Corinth of the first century, but they were not all contemporaries. These individuals represent different genders and a variety of social classes and were selected to illustrate both the appeal of Paul's message to various groups and the challenges Christianity faced as it sought to penetrate a complex and highly stratified society like Roman Corinth.

The explanatory commentary that follows the narrative will first elaborate the Greco-Roman context of the topic under discussion (e.g., temples, sexuality, oratory) and then focus on specific NT contexts where the salient intersection of the two is vitally illuminating. The strategy of analysis in the commentary section will be to move from general to specific, describing in broad strokes the features of Greco-Roman society under consideration, then turning to context-specific explorations of these issues as we encounter them in Paul's letters and travels (Acts). Both the undisputed and the disputed letters of Paul will be subject to analysis in the New Testament Context section. Regardless of whether one considers the six disputed letters to be written by Paul (as I do) or a follower of Paul, they provide evidence of Pauline Christianity making its way in the Greco-Roman world.

The most effective means of learning another culture is to immerse oneself in that culture—its people, its literature, its ideas. *Christianity in the Greco-Roman World* is designed to provide the reader with maximum exposure to first-century culture through a generous use of ancient sources to guide and illustrate the discussion. A wide range of literary and nonliterary sources will be employed, including inscriptions, archaeology, coins, and graffiti, in order to represent a full spectrum of voices and perspectives from the ancient world. My intention in using narrative and an abundance of primary sources is to allow the ancients to tell their story with as little interruption as possible. Occasionally I have abbreviated an ancient source or offered a clarifying gloss to aid the modern reader. These are marked with an asterisk (*).

LESS IS MORE

It should be apparent that I am trying to do a lot in this book. In fact, if you have been reading this introduction carefully, you might be wondering if I have bitten off more than I can chew. I concede the point. One of the uniquenesses of this book is that it emphasizes the application of historical background studies to specific NT texts. Again, this is critical for apprehending the value of historical enquiry, but it also requires space. The resulting challenge is to concisely depict the main features of Greco-Roman society while leaving adequate room for the practical payoff, exploring the NT itself. *Christianity in the Greco-Roman World* does not attempt to be an exhaustive, encyclopedic treatment of all aspects of Greco-Roman society—as if this were possible. Rather, in this book I offer a broad overview of important features of the Greco-Roman world of the first century, selecting some issues to look at in depth, while passing over others more briefly. My primary criterion for the selection of which topics to develop more fully is their relevance to the interpretation of the NT, and Paul's letters in particular. The gymnasium, for example, was an important institution in the cities of the Greek East that Paul visited, but an in-depth discussion of the gymnasium would not yield particularly rich exegetical dividends; hence, my treatment of the gymnasium is brief. Likewise, the New Testament Context section could easily have filled several volumes, in that most passages in Paul's letters can be illuminated, in some measure with reference to the Greco-Roman context of Paul's audience or the Jewish contours of Paul's thought. For every passage or issue that I chose to discuss, there were probably a dozen others that I would have liked to discuss, but space did not permit. These issues I leave to readers to take up on their own. I hope this book serves to whet your appetite for further study! To this end, I have concluded each chapter with bibliographic resources for digging deeper. In these short supplements I offer suggestions for further reading, both important primary sources and seminal modern literature.

A WORD ABOUT CORINTH

Although the narratives in the subsequent chapters can be understood with little specific knowledge of first-century Corinth, a brief historical sketch of the city in which the stories are set may prove useful. A fuller profile of Corinth is unfolded in the following chapters.

Corinth had been an important city in ancient Greece, flourishing from the sixth century B.C.E. as a major commercial center. It was ideally situated on the narrow isthmus between the Saronic Gulf (or Gulf of Aegina) on the east and the Corinthian Gulf on the west, and the twin harbors allowed Corinth to benefit from both trade and travel. Corinth's fortunes rose and fell through the centuries, with its decisive demise occurring in 146 B.C.E. Corinth, along with other cities in the Peloponnese, rebelled against Rome's domination and soon felt the wrath of this emerging world power. The Roman general Lucius Mummius crushed Corinth and razed the city, leaving it fairly uninhabitable. Mummius tore down Corinth's walls, slaughtered its men, and sold the women and children into slavery. Plutarch relates this memorable, though probably apocryphal, story from Mummius's legendary sack of Corinth: "Best of all was the young Corinthian prisoner of war, when his city was destroyed, and Mummius, who was reviewing such free-born boys as could read and write, ordered him to write down a line of verse, he wrote this line from Homer, 'O thrice and four times as happy are the Greeks who perished then.' It is said that Mummius was affected to the point of tears and let all the boy's relations go free."[2]

Corinth's strategic location, however, meant that it would not lie abandoned forever. Julius Caesar, recognizing the commercial and military importance of developing the Isthmus, refounded Corinth in 44 B.C.E. and populated it with Roman freedmen and veterans.[3] The resulting colony was named *Colonia Laus Iulia Corinthienses,* and its architecture, street plan, and population were decidedly Roman.

By the time of Paul's first visit to Corinth (ca. 50–51 C.E.), Corinth had grown considerably and was a mixture of Roman and Greek inhabitants, though Roman influence predominated. Population estimates range between 70,000 and 100,000. Corinth, situated at one of the major crossroads of the Roman Empire and connecting Rome to the eastern portions of its empire, allowed mariners to avoid the treacherous sail to the south around the Peloponnese. Corinth's population contained a diverse assortment of nationalities. As a booming port city, Corinth had a reputation for promiscuity, though the common representation of Aphrodite's temple in Corinth as home to more than a thousand prostitutes is more mythology than reality.[4] Still, excavations from Pompeii, a similarly situated port city, though much smaller, confirm that Roman port cities like Corinth were certainly not the most family-friendly environments. The archaeological finds from Pompeii contain a surprising quantity and range of explicit material, everything from artwork to serving utensils, and Pompeii is not unique in this regard. It is no surprise that Paul has to address sexual ethics with the Corinthians (see 1 Cor 5:1; 7:2).

Paul's initial ministry in Corinth lasted eighteen months (Acts 18:11) and is outlined by Luke in Acts 18. Paul supported himself by plying his trade as a leather worker, along with Priscilla and Aquila,[5] and preached in the synagogue on the Sabbath (18:1–4). Although Paul had some success among the Jews and converted even the synagogue leader, Crispus, and a prominent God-fearer by the name of [Gaius] Titius Justus,[6] the Jewish community ultimately turned against him (18:12–17). Paul's turbulent correspondence with the Corinthians provides a window into the expansion of the Jesus movement outside of the Jewish heartland and illustrates the challenges, heartbreaks, and opportunities that accompany Christianity as it begins to take root in a religiously diverse environment.

FOR FURTHER STUDY

The following annotated bibliography contains a few of the must haves for students of the NT interested in historical background. It is highly selective and should be supplemented by the Further Study sections of the following chapters and the general bibliography.

Everett Ferguson. *Backgrounds of Early Christianity*. 3d ed. Grand Rapids, Mich.: Eerdmans, 2003. The most comprehensive survey of NT backgrounds available in English.

Albert A. Bell. *Exploring the New Testament World*. Nashville: Thomas Nelson, 1998. Not as comprehensive as Ferguson, but more readable and engaging.

Ekkehard Stegemann and Wolfgang Stegemann. *The Jesus Movement: A Social History of Its First Century*. Minneapolis: Fortress, 1999. A scholarly and technical presentation of the Jesus movement focusing on its social history.

Craig A. Evans and Stanley E. Porter, eds. *Dictionary of New Testament Background*. Downers Grove, Ill.: InterVarsity Press, 2000. Contains articles on all the important topics by specialists in the field. A treasure trove of information.

Clinton E. Arnold, ed. *Zondervan Illustrated Bible Backgrounds Commentary*. 4 vols. Grand Rapids, Mich.: Zondervan, 2002. A commentary on the entire NT that focuses solely on illuminating the text through historical, cultural, and social backgrounds. Readable, with full-color illustrations.

Jérôme Carcopino. *Daily Life in Ancient Rome: The People and the City at the Height of the Empire*. Edited by Henry T. Rowell. Translated by E. O. Lorimer. New Haven: Yale University Press, 1966. The classic treatment of daily life in the city of Rome; well written and packed with illuminating material.

Craig Steven De Vos. *Church and Community Conflicts: The Relationships of the Thessalonian, Corinthian, and Philippian Churches with Their Wider Civic Communities*. Atlanta: Scholars Press, 1999. A specialized study of the relationship between the church and the wider community in Thessalonica, Corinth, and Philippi.

Abraham J. Malherbe. *Social Aspects of Early Christianity*. 2d ed. Philadelphia: Fortress, 1983. Seminal essays on the social dimensions of primitive Christianity, including the house church.

Wayne A. Meeks. *The First Urban Christians: The Social World of the Apostle Paul*. 2d ed. New Haven: Yale University Press, 2002. A groundbreaking study of Paul and the early Jesus movement by a leading NT scholar.

J. Paul Sampley, ed. *Paul in the Greco-Roman World: A Handbook*. Harrisburg, Pa.: Trinity Press International, 2003. A collection of essays focusing on the intersection of Paul and the Greco-Roman world. Each chapter is written by a specialist and contains direct application to specific NT texts.

RELIGION AND
SUPERSTITION

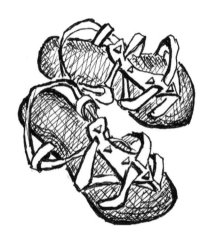

ZOE

The pale rind of the new moon hung low in the night sky as Zoe collapsed onto her bed. Her room in the stately Cornelius *domus*, adjacent to the kitchen, had one redeeming feature: a narrow window with a fitted shutter, just above her cot. The waxing crescent of *Selena* seemed strangely comforting to Zoe tonight. Memories of that evening's dinner party—the crass excess, the obligatory submission to Gaius Cornelius's advances—briefly faded beneath the demulcent beams of the goddess. Gaius Cornelius Speratus was not a tyrant, as masters go. He was, on the whole, reasonably well tempered and treated his slaves with measured courtesy. As an equestrian from a noble Roman tribe, Speratus had visions of election to the *ordo decurionum* and considered it a matter of personal *dignitas* that his slaves be known to be well-treated and well-mannered. Still, Zoe's lot as a slave was not a happy one, and she had no real hope for anything better. Dipping a towel into the amphora beside her bed, Zoe washed away the grime and sweat of another day's labor and wondered what it would be like to be *Selena*, the lunar goddess, with the power to make herself new.

The morning came with the usual abruptness of Marcus crying from his room. Marky, as he was called by the family, was the only son of Gaius Cornelius and Julia—a sturdy two-year-old with skin and hair of soft amber, a proud Roman nose, and, as all could attest, a healthy set of lungs. He was Zoe's special charge before breakfast, and while sleep was precious, her morning ritual with Marky was her only truly satisfying household duty. Pulling on her tunic, she hurried up the hall to his crib, hoisted him onto her hip, and made her way to the *peristyle*, a small inner courtyard guarded on all sides by wings of the house. The centerpiece of this botanical sanctuary was a nearly life-sized marble grouping of Apollo desperately clutching Daphne, who was already more bay tree than nymph maiden. In a few minutes, dawn would break over the roofline of the villa and illumine the god of light in all his frustrated agony; other servants would soon stir, meal preparation would begin, and the household of Gaius Cornelius Speratus would swagger into the new day like a military tribune inspecting a column of raw recruits.

Zoe was not born a slave, though she had always been little better. She was sold to Gaius Cornelius at the age of nine by the man and woman who raised her, Demetrius and Helena. Demetrius and Helena were unsavory characters to say the least. They kept themselves alive through a combination of odd jobs, pilfering, petty scams, and dumb luck. They acquired Zoe on the steps of Cybele's temple in Nemea, where unwanted newborns were regularly discarded. Raising this bloody and bawling lump to a profitable maturity was a risky investment, but it paid off handsomely. Dumb luck. Zoe's clearest memory of Demetrius, the only father she had ever known, was his squeals of excitement as Speratus's agent in Nemea counted out his asking price. She hadn't seen Demetrius or Helena in the eight years since, and hadn't wanted to.

Zoe took her breakfast of bread and cheese in the kitchen with the other servants and collected invitations to yet another *convivium* from Sisyphus, the steward. "The God Asclepius invites you to dine in the Asklepion with the friends of Gaius Cornelius," read the invitation, ". . . on the 21st day, at the 9th hour." All the usual names were included: Julius Quadratus, Babbius Philinus, Junia Theodora, and even Erastus, one of the new magistrates in Corinth. Speratus quietly despised Erastus as a mere nouveau riche—a self-made man of dubious lineage, lacking (in his view) culture and connections. But Gaius Cornelius Speratus was not so impolitic as to snub a potentially useful ally, even this "plebe-loving Greek olive picker," as he called him. Tucking the invitations into the folds of her tunic, Zoe knotted her *stola* around her shoulders and waist and made her way to the door.

A gaggle of fawning clients had already collected in the atrium, where Julia was offering a salt cake at the altar to the household spirits and exchanging pleasantries with several of those waiting to see her husband. Zoe passed unnoticed through the curtains of togas, muttered a perfunctory prayer to Janus Clusivius, the god of the doorway, and began her six-mile trek into Corinth.

A trip into the city, even on foot, was always a welcome excursion for Zoe; the sights, the sounds, the smells—the freedom. Often she would imagine herself the daughter of a nobleman, being escorted by servants for an afternoon of shopping, socializing, well-timed preening, and sundry aristocratic frivolities. But the journey from Cenchrea to Corinth offered its own magnificent distractions, especially as Zoe's first stop was in nearby Isthmia, where the games were in full swing. Athletes, spectators, merchants, peddlers, along with other, less welcome specimens of the human zoo would soon clog the arterial passages from venue to venue, and the heavy traffic meant that Zoe could travel invisibly into Corinth.

The first mile of the ascent from the harbor of Isthmia was gentle. Zoe's path ran directly in front of Poseidon's temple before striking a westward course toward the Acrocorinth. As the glimmering bronze Tritons that lined Poseidon's roof came into view, a detour through the temple precincts tempted Zoe. The statuary and artwork that filled the sanctuary—former victors at the games, deities, legendary heroes, and so on—held no allure in themselves, but this year's competitors and their attendants would certainly be loitering about the colonnades, and Zoe's pace unconsciously quickened at the thought. Reaching the open green beneath the temple, Zoe was disappointed, but hardly surprised. Instead of athletes she saw Charmenion, a garrulous sophist, bedecked in jewelry and sporting a lavish hairstyle, charming a flock of dim tourists with his oratorical wonders. Every wave of his hand, every turn of his head, every roll of his eyes was perfectly choreographed to elicit a chortle or an "Ooh" from the admiring throng. Charmenion was Julia's frequent guest at dinner, and the thought of his pretentious, ingratiating prattle, even in the background, was enough to make Zoe nearly lose her breakfast. She sighed and continued on her way.

The remainder of her trip into Corinth was uneventful. She passed the usual assortment of local farmers and artisans, philosophers, slaves, tourists, mariners, and so on. When she finally reached the base of the Acrocorinth—that rocky limestone crag towering above Corinth like a great earthen citadel—Zoe rested momentarily at a roadside shrine to Diana, goddess of the open places. Numerous prayers for protection and votive tokens lay scattered beneath a painted wooden likeness of the goddess, but Zoe's eyes were drawn upward, to the steep sides of the rugged butte looming in the foreground. The Acrocorinth was given by Helios to Aphrodite, who was still worshiped at the summit and all throughout Corinth. Scanning the road that snaked its way up the mountain side, Zoe spied the roofs and porticos of nearly a dozen other temples: to the Fates, Demeter, Hera, Isis, Serapis, to Necessity and Force, and to Cybelle, the great mother. Adjusting her tunic and mopping her forehead, Zoe rejoined the road that would take her to the gates of Corinth, beneath the shadow of the gods.

Entering through the eastern gate, Zoe strolled by monumental graves of Corinthian aristocrats. Large busts of entombed noblemen watched the young slave warily as she passed, their cold patrician eyes warning her not to linger. She was happy to oblige them. When finally she reached the sacred grove, just outside the main forum, a welcome sight met her eyes: Claudia and Varro hawking their vegetables beneath the shade of a bowing cypress.

"Zoe! *Salve!*" cried Claudia. Dropping the cucumbers she had lately been waving beneath the nose of a disinterested passerby, Claudia raced over to Zoe and lifted her off her feet in greeting. Claudia and Zoe had been friends for most of the last eight years. Claudia had also been a slave of Gaius Cornelius and Julia and was responsible for Zoe during her early years at the Cornelius household. Claudia had the terrific fortune of catching the eye of Varro, the son of a modestly successful farmer, who purchased her freedom and married her nearly three years ago. A new start, a new life, and no one deserved it more in Zoe's opinion. Not that her circumstances had improved; in many ways they were worse. Fortuna rarely smiled long on farmers, and the droughts of recent years had reduced their acreage to a dust bowl and their market share to a market stall. Still, Claudia was ever buoyant as they exchanged gossip about the town and the estate.

"Is that prig Sisyphus still in charge?" wondered Claudia.

"Oh yes—fancies he's Zeus himself when Speratus isn't around," laughed Zoe, tossing her hair and rolling her eyes in playful sarcasm.

Noticing for the first time the three inches Zoe had added to her height, her rich olive complexion, her teasing smile—her blossoming womanhood, Claudia asked in a softer tone, "and Speratus, is he . . . treating you well?"

"As well as can be expected," answered Zoe, looking away.

Squeezing Zoe's hand, Claudia broke the silence with an energetic, "Well—why don't you let me help you with those invitations? Give me those going to the Craneum, and I'll meet up with you at Media's baths, behind the amphitheatre. With Hermes' help, we should have some time left to finish catching up." Overhearing Claudia's plans and catching her pleading glance, Varro waved her off with an understanding smile. Claudia always had a way of lightening Zoe's load, and Zoe set out with a lighter step and a lighter heart.

Corinth was its usual midday bustle. Shouldering her way through the tumult of shouting merchants, bullying legionnaires, horse-drawn carts, and slave-drawn litters was harrowing, but Zoe had learned to maneuver the streets of Corinth effectively. Rounding a corner past the temple of Hercules, Zoe stopped short, finding herself facing a small crowd that had gathered to inspect a newly erected monument. The mounted figure was plainly the emperor, but Zoe stared somewhat blankly at the letters engraved on the pedestal. She could decipher the name "Tiberius Claudius Augustus," and a few of the titles, "Savior of Greece, Restorer of Peace, Father of the Country," but her letters were mostly self-taught, and so she would have to imagine the rest. Skirting the perimeter of the throng, Zoe spotted Timarchus at the bread seller and darted across the street to catch him. Timarchus, chef for the grand household of Babbius Philinus, was collecting his daily order—rather impatiently, thought Zoe as she approached. Bobbing and clanging above his head was a wind chime of engorged phalluses, a common charm protecting the shop from the daimonia and spirits that haunted the crossroads of every Roman street. This chance meeting would save her a trip to the western quarter of the city, and Zoe wondered if Hermes might indeed be with her after all!

Timarchus was an aging freedman with a perpetually brooding expression. He grunted a greeting when he saw Zoe, clearly annoyed that the chef of Babbius Philinus would be kept waiting for his bread. His annoyance only increased as Zoe gave him the invitation and explained her business.

"So, Speratus sent you all this way—on your own—to be his messenger girl? Typical." Zoe, half flattered, half bewildered by this sudden outburst of paternal indignation, said nothing.

"Well, here, take this" he grumbled, handing Zoe a crusty loaf as his order was presented. "By Zeus, Babbius can certainly spare it." His departure was as abrupt as his greeting—classic Timarchus, mused Zoe.

Zoe's rounds took her through much of the city—past pubs where wine was being quaffed by the barrel, through market stalls offering everything from linens to poultry, and by numerous brothels proffering their own sordid delicacies. More than the usual crowd was huddled around one of the leatherworker's shops. Zoe initially supposed that this was due to the influx of tourists for the Isthmian games. Many of the visitors would simply bivouac beneath the pines or in the untilled fields between Isthmia and Corinth, and so tentmakers and leatherworkers could turn a tidy profit this time of year. But more seemed to be going on here. There was Heraclitus, the schoolmaster and stoic, with his charges—a half dozen boys between nine and sixteen—engaged in an energetic discussion with . . . one of the men at the workbench? Others appeared to be hanging about just for the show. This was worth a look. Zoe gulped her last morsel of bread, along with some runt carrots she'd taken along for the journey, and cut a path towards the spectacle.

Standing under the north eve of the shop, Zoe took in the scene at a glance—a large selection of awls, knives, punches, and whatnot hung neatly in racks on the back wall, within arm's reach of the craftsmen; odd scraps of leather in various piles, together with bales of unused hide—nothing out of the ordinary, except for him. He was hunched over a table, carefully measuring and cutting what looked like a piece of goat skin, and talking philosophy with Heraclitus—and

Heraclitus was listening! When he straightened up to inspect his incision, Zoe could tell he was an Easterner, probably a Jew, though his Greek was good. As he lowered his handiwork, nodding with satisfaction, Zoe started when the leather worker suddenly addressed her: "Does it look straight to you?" he queried.

Before she had a chance to reply, Heraclitus broke in with, "But come now, Paulus! It stands against all reason and nature to argue that . . ." Zoe took the opportunity to back out of view, though she listened intently for several more minutes. Noticing the position of the sun, Zoe remembered her rendezvous with Claudia and pulled herself away from the debate. Zoe had little time for arcane philosophical wrangling, but she couldn't help thinking that this discussion was somehow important, even for a slave.

Zoe entered the north forum just as a bleating sheep was being clubbed in Athena's temple. One of the priestly underlings promptly pulled a glistening blade the length of the stunned creature's neck, and blood was now flowing everywhere. Claudia caught Zoe's arm just as a sudden gush from the dying beast sprayed the forehead and chin of the priest. "A very bad omen," Claudia whispered. "Probably won't live the year out."

Claudia and Zoe settled themselves on a grassy knoll behind Media's baths, just across from a small synagogue. A surprising mixture of people were mingling in the open courtyard: many Jews, of course, but also Greeks and Romans, mostly women. Claudia and Zoe spent the better part of an hour laughing and exchanging stories before Varro arrived and broke up their reunion. Zoe made Varro promise to let Claudia come for a visit. "Speratus will probably put her to work," he joked. "He's still mourning that sale," winking at Claudia, who blushed affectionately.

Zoe was in no hurry to return to her closet at the Cornelian villa, but she needed to be out of the gates soon in order to be home before nightfall. From her perch on the knoll across from the synagogue, Zoe could tell that some kind of ceremony was about to begin. Her curiosity, piqued perhaps by that puzzling incident with the leatherworker, compelled her to linger—this time at a safe distance. A man and a woman were standing midway up the steps, and the crowd was forming a cheerful scrum around them. The gentleman, togaed and bearded, was pronouncing a blessing on the woman, who apparently was converting to Judaism. Obviously well off, she wore an elegant purple *stola* over her linen tunic; her hair was ornately braided and hung in a ball atop her head. Bracelets and jewelry dangled here and there, including a necklace with a pendant in the shape of a gazing eye—a protective amulet warding off malicious spirits. Zoe sensed a distant and unnerving familiarity dawning within her. She had met this woman before. Was she the wife of a shopkeeper? Did she live in Cenchrea? Where had she seen her?

The woman smiled nervously (if somewhat disingenuously, thought Zoe) as the leader of the synagogue raised his hand and said:

Lord, God of Israel, powerful one of Jacob
　　who gave life to all things
　　and called them from darkness to light,
　　and from error to truth,
　　and from death to life.

You, Lord, bless this daughter,
　　make her new by your Spirit,
　　recreate her by your hidden hand,
　　give her new life through your life.
　　Let her eat your bread of life,
　　let her drink your cup of blessing,
　　and number her with your people whom you chose before all things.
　　Let her enter your rest and live in your eternal life forever.

Zoe stood pondering these words when her thoughts were interrupted by a voice right beside her. "So, we meet again." It was the leatherworker.

Completely at a loss, Zoe mumbled something like, "Meet . . . again?"

"Yes, my name is Paulus, and you are . . . ?"

"Zoe," she stammered, before she could stop herself. "And I really need be going . . . I live in Isthmia and . . ."

"Zoe," he repeated reflectively. "Life, *Chayim*, we would say." His eyes were searching her, and she felt as if she wanted to ask him something but didn't know what.

"Zoe," he said with an air of resolution, "let me walk with you as far as the city gates. I need to tell you more about your name."

THE CULTURAL CONTEXT

THE GODS OF CORINTH

Many of us have probably wondered what it would have been like to travel alongside the apostle Paul, to listen to him teach, watch him work—to see the world as he saw it. The experience would certainly be eye-opening. Perhaps the most mystifying feature of the ancient world for those of us from modern Western societies would be the all-pervasive nature of polytheism. There were gods everywhere. Gods for travelers, gods for hunters, gods for sailors, gods for warriors, gods for lovers, gods for poets; gods to help with childbirth, gods to help with baking, gods to help with treachery, gods to protect the hinges of your doors . . . the list is endless. While visiting Athens Paul himself felt confounded by the myriad of deities that surrounded him (Acts 17:16), and his opening remarks to the Athenian intellectuals were both generous and accurate: "Men of Athens! I perceive that in every way you are very religious" (Acts 17:22).

> GOOD LUCK. KAR-
> PYS, AT HIS OWN
> EXPENSE, ERECTED THIS
> ALTAR TO THE GODS
> IN THE BEEHIVE.
>
> *INSCRIPTION, CORINTH

Corinth, like Athens, Rome, Philippi, Ephesus, and every other Greco-Roman city or village was likewise "very religious." Zoe's stroll into Corinth took her past numerous temples, shrines, altars, and so on, and these were but a small portion of the rich array of deities vying for the attention of Corinthian aristocrats, townsfolk, and peasants. Inscriptions, coins, and statuary from Corinth attest to the worship of more than fifty deities in the area—including "the gods of the beehive"—and even this is only a partial listing. So crowded were the celestial realms above the Roman Empire that the second-century satirist Lucian penned "The Parliament of the Gods" in response. In this sardonic theological lampoon, Zeus summons a council of all the gods to address the heavenly population explosion. A resolution is passed, divine credentials are checked, and all pretenders are sent packing!

> GAIUS JULIUS SYRUS
> DEDICATED THIS
> COLUMN TO ISIS
> AND SERAPIS
>
> INSCRIPTION, CORINTH

The principal deities honored in Roman Corinth were Aphrodite (Venus) and Poseidon (Neptune), along with Apollo, Asclepius, Demeter and her daughter Kore, Nike (Victoria), Tyche (Fortuna), Jupiter Capitolinus, Isis and Serapis (Egyptian deities), Athena, and the imperial cult (see City and Society: Urban Landscape and Environment). Local deities and legendary heroes also figured prominently in the religious life of Corinth, such as Aphrodite Melainis (Black Aphrodite, associated with death and the afterlife), Athena Chalinitis (Athena the Bridler, who helped tame Pegasus), Bellerophon with his winged

TABLE OF PRINCIPAL GREEK AND ROMAN
GODS AND PERSONIFICATIONS

GREEK NAME	ROMAN NAME	Principal Roles in Mythology
Aphrodite	Venus	Goddess of beauty, sexal love, and fertility
Apollo	Apollo	God of music, prophecy, healing, and archery. In later mythology, associated with the sun
Ares	Mars	God of war
Artemis	Diana	Goddess of fertility, the wilderness, hunting
Asklepios	Aesclepius	God of healing
Athena	Minerva	Patron deity of Athens; goddess of wisdom, arts and crafts, and war; helper of heroes
Demeter	Ceres	Goddess of grain
Dionysus/Liber	Bacchus	God nature, wine, and merriment
Eros	Cupid	God of love
Hades	Pluto	God of the underworld and the dead
Hephaestus	Vulcan	God of fire; blacksmith of the gods
Hera	Juno	Goddess of marriage, wife of Zeus
Herakles	Hercules	Hero, worshipped as the god of strength, bravery, and victory
Hermes	Mercury	Messenger of the gods; helper of travelers and merchants
Hestia	Vesta	Goddess of hearth and home
Nike	Victoria	Goddess of victory; helper of athletes and soldiers
Poseidon	Neptune	God of the sea and earthquakes
Uranus	Uranus	God of the sky; father of the Titans
Zeus	Jupiter	Ruler of the gods

horse Pegasus, and Melicertes/Palaimon, god of harbors and patron deity of the Isthmian games (see City and Society: Festivals and Sport). In addition to these major deities, scores of lesser deities governed the affairs of everything from the household to the sheepfold.

POLYTHEISM

Polytheism, by its nature, is inclusive and tolerant, capable of accommodating new gods and absorbing innovative religious movements.[1] First-century religious shoppers could fill their baskets with any number of deities, depending on their particular needs or their occupation. The young woman in love could appeal to the goddess Peitho (Persuasion) to convince a hesitant suitor. The merchant selling his wares frequented the temple of Tyche (Success) to ensure that his business would thrive. The farmer fertilizing his field invoked Sterculius, the god presiding over the spreading of manure. Athletes flocked to Herakles (Hercules), the infirm to Asclepius, mariners to Poseidon (Neptune). The casual reader of first-century literature will stumble across heartfelt petitions to herb divinities and the goddess Earth and will hear of devout worshipers of nebulous celestial deities dutifully offering incense on the slopes of Mount Aetna in hopes of averting an eruption.[2] Some divinities of Greece and Rome are known from only a single literary reference or an obscure inscription. No wonder that Juvenal could look back wistfully on days of old when "there was no grim Pluto reigning over the gloomy underworld, no Ixion with his wheel or Sisyphus heaving his stone, no Furies, no vulture-pecked Tityus, no mob of deities as there is today."[3]

> TO THE GOD WHO
> CURES HANGOVERS
>
> *INSCRIPTION, CORINTH

And there was no reason to be exclusive in one's worship. Jews (and later, Christians) were an oddity in this regard. As the Jesus movement grew and became more noticeable, the idiosyncratic and obstinate refusal of its members to worship other deities invited sarcasm from principled Romans like Celsus, a second-century philosopher: "It is absurd that these Christians guard against serving several gods. . . . He who serves many gods does that which is pleasing to the Most High, because he honors that which belongs to Him."[4] The typical Roman might begin his day with a prayer to Ops for an abundant harvest, offer a sacrifice to Jupiter at midday, toast Serapis at dinner, and all with a good conscience—why not cover all your bases? Inscriptions from Philippi reveal individuals with dual priesthoods. Marcus Velleius Marci, for example, a resident of Philippi, erected a gravestone for his wife that proudly touts his position in both the imperial cult (see City and Society: Urban Landscape and Environment) and the cult of the great mother goddess, Cybele.[5] Lucius Apuleius, a devotee of Isis, was eager to let everyone know that he had also been initiated into the mysteries of Aesclepius and "mysteries of many a kind, rites in great number, and diverse ceremonies."[6] Polytheism, however, was not for everyone, and one group in particular remained obstinately opposed to worshiping multiple deities: the Jews.

> CONSIDER THE MAN
> WHO WORSHIPS HE-
> DONES, THE GODDESS
> OF PLEASURE, AND
> WHO IS PASSIONATELY
> DEVOTED TO THE
> BURNING MADNESS OF
> SEXUAL INDULGENCE
>
> *DIO CHRYSOSTOM

DIASPORA JUDAISM

By the first century C.E. it is probable that considerably more Jews lived outside of Palestine than inside the Jewish heartland itself.[7] The word *Diaspora* (from the Greek word meaning "scattered") is used to designate those Jews living in cities of the Gentile world. While precise population estimates are not possible, the accounts of diaspora communities from Philo, Josephus, and the NT, as well as the numerous references to Jews from Greek and Roman writers of the period, paint the picture of a visible—if not vibrant—Jewish presence throughout the Mediterranean.[8] Strabo's comments, although not without an element of hyperbole, are telling: "This people [the Jews] has already made its way into every city, and it is not easy to find any place in the habitable world which has not received this nation and in which it has not made its power felt."[9]

> INDEED, THE STREETS OF ROME ARE SO FILLED WITH DIVINITIES, THAT IT IS EASIER TO MEET A GOD THAN A MAN
>
> *PETRONIUS

Given this vast diffusion of Jews throughout the Mediterranean, it is not surprising that we find various levels of integration among Jews of the Diaspora.[10] Philo, for example, was deeply involved in Hellenistic culture, politics, and literature, while also rigorously trained in Jewish traditions. His writings present the Jewish Scriptures as the highest expression of philosophy and are noteworthy for their Platonic influence. *Psuedo-Phocylides* presents Jewish ethics in Stoic guise. *Ezekiel the Tragedian* transforms the exodus narrative into a Greek tragic drama. At the other end of the spectrum are works like *Joseph and Aseneth,* which reflect a Jewish community struggling against assimilation and loss of cultural-religious identity, particularly through intermarriage.

We can expect that some Jews abandoned their ancestral traditions, perhaps on their way up the social ladder or simply in order to negotiate life among Gentiles with fewer disruptions. Josephus reports that Antiochus, the son of a Jewish community leader in Antioch, Syria, repudiated his ancestral faith and offered sacrifices "in the manner of the Gentiles" as proof of his conversion.[11] In Philippi, a Roman named Mofius (a Latinized form of Moses) dedicated an altar to Isis: "Sacred to the queen Isis. For the honor of the divine [imperial] house and the welfare of the colony . . . has Quintus Mofius Euhemerus, the doctor, erected this altar at his own expense."[12]

> LET YOUR EMOTIONS BE MODERATE, NEITHER GREAT NOR OVERWHELMING.
>
> *PSEUDO-PHOCYLIDES

Others, however, found more creative ways to navigate a course through the expectations of their surrounding culture and the dictates of their Jewish faith. From a temple of Pan in the Thebaid (upper Egypt) come inscriptions dedicated (it would appear) to the God of the Hebrews:

> Praise (our) God. Ptolemaios the son of Dionysios, a Jew (made this).

> Praise be to God. Theodotos the son of Dorion, a Jew, saved from the sea (made this).[13]

Quite apart from these isolated, and somewhat disparate sound bites from antiquity, the surviving literary and inscriptional evidence, including the NT, depict Jewish communities in the Greco-Roman world centered around houses of worship (synagogues, see City and Society: Urban Landscape and Environment) and focused on promoting Jewish piety through adherence to authoritative religious traditions and practices. In addition to ethnicity, Jewish identity in the Greco-Roman world was reinforced through Sabbath observance, circumcision (for men), and dietary restrictions. These practices tended to separate diaspora Jews from the larger society and mark them off as Jews. Religiously, diaspora Jews were particularly distinguished by their worship of the one God of Israel. These identity markers were widely disparaged by Gentiles, and writers of the period are generally disdainful of Jews.[14]

> THE WHOLE EARTH WILL BE FILLED WITH YOU [THE JEWISH PEOPLE], AND EVERY SEA. EVERYONE WILL BE OFFENDED AT YOUR CUSTOMS.
>
> *JEWISH ORACLE, 2D CENTURY B.C.E.

Often, Jewish beliefs were misunderstood by Gentiles. For example, Jews were commonly accused of being atheists. Dio Cassius records how the emperor Domitian had the consul Flavius Clemens executed on the charge of atheism and notes that this was a charge "which many others who drifted into Jewish ways were condemned."[15] The imageless God of the Hebrews was perplexing to Greeks and Romans accustomed to statuary, painting, mosaics, and other visual depictions of the divine world. Juvenal remarks that Jews seem to worship "nothing but the clouds."[16] Others, however, supposed that Jews abstained from pork because they worshiped a pig god.[17] Similarly, observing the Sabbath was sometimes attributed to laziness.[18]

> LIKE EVERYONE ELSE, BEWARE YOU TOO OF THE JEWS
>
> *FROM A FIRST-CENTURY LETTER

In spite of this generally negative appraisal, there were Gentiles who were attracted to Judaism, frequented the synagogues, and became full proselytes. Although their numbers were probably few, it remains true that Judaism appealed to some, even if most remained God-fearers and not full converts.[19]

SUPERSTITION

Far more important for daily life than the Olympian deities or the major imports from the east like Isis and Cybele were the innumerable demons and malevolent spirits that had to be kept at bay or placated as best one could. The religion of the masses—if "religion" is the right word—was a confused conglomeration of superstition, divination, astrology, and magic. While the philosophers and academics were waxing eloquent on the nobility, grandeur, and perfection of the gods,[20] the butcher etched in lead a curse on his competitor, the farmer cleared space in his field for the divinely obscene Priapus,[21] the innkeeper trembled at the omen forecast by the stars, and the doting grandmother scrupulously enacted a dark ritual ensuring the prosperity of her progeny:

> See how the granny, fearing the gods, takes the baby out of his cradle: skilled in averting the evil eye, she first, with her rebuking middle finger, applies the charm of magical spittle to his forehead and slobbering lips; then she rocks the wizened hopeful in her arms and destines him in her prayers to . . . the mansions of a Crassus.[22]

In fact, the townsfolk, travelers, merchants, and magistrates whom Paul encountered daily were deeply superstitious and envisioned the spiritual universe as a vast, multistoried *insula* with swarms of supernatural beings occupying the floors above and below them. All throughout the Roman world the intersection of two roads was believed to be the gathering place of spirits (*daemones*) of the underworld, "the most harmful beings in the universe," according to Plutarch.[23] Shrines to Hecate, goddess of the underworld, were strategically placed at the crossroads as protection against these sinister ghouls. The Cynic philosopher sending off his disciple with the farewell, "May the gods and spirits (*daemones*) treat you well," is indicative of the metaphysical notions of the first-century milieu.[24] Lucius Apuleius's widely shared conviction that there are "divine beings holding a position . . . midway between gods and men, and that all divination and the miracles of magicians are controlled by them," forms the basis of the chilling curse he pronounces on his opponent in a crowded courtroom:

> BUT THE RIDICULOUS ACTIONS AND EMOTIONS OF SUPERSTITION, ITS WORDS AND GESTURES, MAGIC CHARMS, SPELLS, RUSHING ABOUT AND BEATING OF DRUMS, IMPURE AND OUTLANDISH PENANCES AND MORTIFICATIONS AT THE SHRINES MAKE ONE WISH THERE WERE NO GODS!
>
> PLUTARCH

> May that same god, the intermediary between the living and the dead, give you the hatred of the gods of both worlds. May he always heap up before your eyes unavoidable apparitions of the dead, ghouls, specters, ghosts, wandering spirits: all the things that you encounter in the night, all the horrors of the tomb, all the terrors of the grave.[25]

One result of such a densely layered spiritual universe was the understandable concern that the correct deity be supplicated, and in the correct manner. Ancient writers mention altars to "unknown gods" scattered throughout Greece, which stood as visible monuments to the anxiety the ancients felt concerning identifying and appeasing the appropriate divinity.[26] Among the many leaden tablets found at the oracle of Zeus at Dodona in northwest Greece comes the entreaty of one fretful soul wanting only to know where to go for help: "Nikokrateia wishes to know to which god she should offer sacrifices in order to regain her health and be rid of her disease."[27] Often the petitioner would feel compelled to add, "or by whatever name you wish to be called," after addressing the deity, in case he or she might have misdialed and an unfamiliar god picked up on the other end.[28] Another trend observable from at least the first century onwards is the fusing of several gods into one, almost as a means of reducing the clutter: "To Zeus Helios great Sarapis and his fellow gods. Is it to my advantage to buy the slave called Gaion? Grant me this!"[29] The worship of Isis and Sarapis was particularly keen to absorb deities: "As you stand there [in the temple of Serapis] say, 'One is Zeus Sarapis.'"[30]

> GREETINGS FROM YOUR SISTERS AND THE CHILDREN OF THEONIS, WHOM THE EVIL EYE SHALL NOT HARM
>
> A LETTER TO A BOY FROM HIS MOTHER

A word of clarification is necessary before proceeding. By "superstition" I mean a great variety of quasi-animistic folk beliefs and magical practices that are at variance with traditional conceptions of Greco-Roman "orthodoxy" and that were commonly disparaged by the intelligentsia of first-century society. Yet there is an implicit value judgment being made in using this term, and one that is difficult to defend when one considers that the "superstitious" would comprise the great majority of people in the NT milieu. Even the enlightened critics of popular piety held views that by modern standards would be considered comically unenlightened and tragically superstitious. The thunderous collision of our largely disenchanted universe (in the post-industrial West, at least) with the thoroughly enchanted universe of the first century is nowhere more earsplitting than when contemplating popular religiosity in its seemingly infinite permutations. Most of us, for example, would find it difficult to take seriously the idea that burying a frog at an intersection could prevent a fever[31] or that the ground where lightning strikes is sacred[32] or comprehend why a host would abruptly pour wine under the table and change the rings on his finger after hearing a cock crow.[33] Yet these beliefs and actions made sense to the ancients and were rational in the kind of universe they inhabited: an enchanted universe; a universe where the line between the spiritual and the physical was only faintly drawn and easily crossed.

> O QUEEN OF HEAVEN— WHETHER YOU BE BOUNTIFUL CERES, OR HEAVENLY VENUS, OR PHOEBUS, OR DREADED PROSERPINA—BY WHATEVER NAME, WITH WHATEVER RITE, IN WHATEVER IMAGE IT IS RIGHT TO INVOKE YOU, DEFEND ME NOW!
>
> *APULEIUS

Cicero defines superstition as "groundless fear of the Gods," and this sentiment is echoed throughout the literature of the period.[34] Seneca, Horace, Persius, Juvenal, Lucian, Plutarch, Valerius Maximus, and others besides, all cast a critical eye on the superstition of the masses and lament the sorry state of religion in their day. In mocking tones, Horace tells of the elderly freedman who, after fasting and ritual washing, runs frantically to the shrines at the crossroads in the wee hours of the morning crying "Save me! Save me!" and the distraught mother who vows that her sick son will stand naked in the Tiber on the day of the fast if Jupiter answers her prayer and heals him. With acidic wit Horace remarks that the vow is more likely to kill the poor boy than the illness, and then asks, "What is the malady that has stricken her mind? The fear of the gods."[35]

> THEN AGAIN THERE ARE THE BLACK SPECTERS AND THE PERILS OF THE "BROKEN EGG"; THERE ARE THE HUGE PRIESTS OF CYBELE AND THE ONE-EYED PRIESTESS WITH HER RATTLE, WHO WILL DRIVE DEMONS INTO YOU THAT MAKE YOUR BODIES SWELL IF YOU DO NOT SWALLOW THE PRESCRIBED MORNING DOSE OF THREE HEADS OF GARLIC.
>
> PERSIUS

The embarrassment and frustration felt by Horace and other cultured despisers of the superstition of the masses is most perfectly articulated in Plutarch's masterful *On Superstition*. Plutarch compares the lot of the superstitious with the atheist—disapproving of both—and concludes that the deluded atheist is far better off than the wretched bloke gripped by superstition who finds himself "smeared with mud, wallowing in filth, succumbing to immersions, cast down with face to the ground performing disgraceful besieging of the gods and uncouth prostrations," all at the bidding of some crone of a witch.[36] There is, no doubt, an element of playful exaggeration in Plutarch's description, but it remains true that the superstitious were at the mercy of soothsayer and sorcerer alike, and the antidotes prescribed by this rabble were limited only by their imagination and their greed.

> WHAT THEN INDUCES US TO SUCH CONSTANT USE OF DIVINATION? COWARDICE, DREAD OF THE FUTURE. THIS IS THE REASON WHY WE FLATTER THE DIVINERS, SAYING, "MASTER, SHALL I INHERIT MY FATHER'S PROPERTY?" IF HE SAYS, "YES!" WE THANK HIM AS IF WE RECEIVED THE INHERITANCE FROM HIM!
>
> *EPICTETUS

And there certainly was money to be made in the science of the supernatural. Numerous stories are told of charlatans and purveyors of snake oil preying on the phobias of the gullible:

> One man supplies magical spells; another sells Thessalian charms by which a wife may upset her husband's mind, and lather his buttocks with a slipper; thence come

loss of reason, and darkness of soul, and blank forgetfulness of all that you did but yesterday.[37]

In a letter to a friend, Pliny the Younger relates the exploits of a certain Regulus, a notorious pseudo-psychic who managed to conjure up a fortune through artfully devised astrological calculations given to wealthy widows on their deathbeds.[38] Exposing religious frauds was a favorite pastime of the satirist Lucian, and invariably money and avarice figure prominently in his tales.[39] Valerius Maximus tells of the Gallic city of Massilia, which took extreme care to bar any "who by some pretense of religion seek sustenance for sloth, holding that false and fraudulent superstition should be ousted."[40] The association of peddlers of the paranormal with rank profiteering was so commonly made that the Greek word for "sorcerer" (*goēs*) came to be a simple synonym for "swindler." Before considering more directly the crucial subject of magic and divination, a word about Jewish superstition is in order.

> WHAT CAN THEY FEAR FROM THE GODS WHEN THEY USE SUCH MEANS TO WIN THEIR FAVOR? . . . THEY SLASH THEMSELVES IN TEMPLES AND MAKE SUPPLICATION WITH THEIR OWN BLEEDING WOUNDS. ONE WILL FIND PRACTICES SO INDECENT . . . SO UNLIKE THOSE OF SANE MEN, THAT IF THEIR NUMBER WERE FEWER NO ONE WOULD HAVE ANY DOUBT THAT THEY WERE DEMENTED.
>
> *SENECA, ACCORDING TO AUGUSTINE

It was not only the Gentile world that was befogged with spirits, fair and foul. Many Jews, too, perceived the cosmos to be brimming with supernatural beings, and for them, like their pagan counterparts, this was not an altogether pleasant reality. One of the most important developments in Judaism of the Hellenistic and Roman eras was the widespread belief that the hosts of heaven were actively involved in human affairs—individual and national. These angelic forces, however, were not all benevolent; indeed, much of the speculation in the surviving extrabiblical Jewish texts focuses on the activity of the evil angelic host. A stroll through this literature takes the reader into a dark and foreboding land, a world where humanity often appears as a defenseless and expendable pawn in a vast cosmic battle. Not surprisingly, prayers for protection are commonplace:

> Save me from the hands of evil spirits which rule over the thought of the heart of man![41]

> Strengthen your servant against fiendish spirits so that he can walk in all that you love and loathe all that you hate.[42]

The apocryphal "Dream of Amram" (see Num 26:58–59), found in fragments in cave four at Qumran, describes a vision of this demon-infested universe:

And behold, two [demons] were quarreling over me. . . . And they said to me, "We have received control and we rule over all the sons of Adam. . . . Which of us do you choose to be ruled?" And I raised my eyes and saw that one of them had a dreadful appearance like the pestilence, and his clothing was colored and obscured by darkness. And the other was smiling . . . and he said to me, "This one is called King of Evil."[43]

The Jewish author of the book of *Jubilees,* written somewhere between 150 and 100 B.C.E., tries to iron out the theological wrinkles of Genesis by ascribing its problematic episodes to the shenanigans of fallen angels. According to this writer, it was not Yahweh who tempted Abraham to sacrifice Isaac, or who slew the firstborn of Egypt, or who hardened Pharaoh's heart, but Mastema, the prince of the demons.[44] These fallen angels are also held responsible for introducing humanity to astrology, disease, warfare, idolatry, slavery, murder, poverty, and all manner of evil. The writer of *1 Enoch* adds to this litany of villainy the degenerate crime of teaching women to wear makeup and jewelry![45] In fact, in much of this literature it is not the sin of Adam in the garden that led to the entrance of sin, death, and disease into the

> MOREOVER, SEND FORTH CATERPILLARS AND LOCUSTS, RUST AND GRASSHOPPERS, HAIL WITH LIGHTNING AND FURY. PUNISH THEM WITH THE SWORD AND DEATH, AND THEIR CHILDREN WITH DEMONS.
>
> 3 BARUCH 16:2

world but the sin of angelic "watchers" described in Gen 6:1–8. This is not to say that every Jew everywhere staggered through his or her day trembling, waiting for the sky to fall. Yet it is true that Jewish literature of this period—hymns, histories, testaments, apocalypses—reveals an elaborate and complex system of angelic and demonic hierarchies, ranks, divisions, and so on, and this worldview is assumed rather than argued. From this substantial body of material representing diverse theological perspectives and a variety of geographical regions we learn of the creation of angels, the classes of angels, the circumcision of angels, the number of angels, the worship of angels, the work of guarding angels, and much, much more. We are also introduced to individual angels, like Raphael, who bound the evil angel Azaz'el and buried him in the desert;[46] Jerahmeel, guardian of Hades and

> AND I, A SAGE, DECLARE THE SPLENDOR OF HIS RADIANCE IN ORDER TO FRIGHTEN AND TERRIFY ALL THE SPIRITS OF THE RAVAGING ANGELS AND THE BASTARD SPIRITS, DEMONS, LILITH, OWLS, AND JACKALS.
>
> DEAD SEA SCROLLS

the abyss;[47] Sariel, protector of Isarel's armies;[48] Purouel, the archangel who had authority over fire;[49] and the angel Repentance, who renewed the penitent Aseneth.[50] This list could go on for several pages. Among the material from

Qumran yet to be published are a handful of texts bearing the provisional title "Catalogue of Spirits."[51]

The rise of Jewish angelic speculation corresponds to a time in Israel's history when its monarchy was eradicated, its sovereignty was eviscerated, and the hopeful expectation of the prophets was fading into oblivion. This national and theological crisis was assuaged somewhat through tales of angelic intervention. To those struggling to reconcile the chaos of the present with the promises of the past, these angelic mediators revealed the mysteries of God's inscrutable purpose.[52] To those suffering under the heavy boot of foreign domination, bewildered that God's chosen people could be so oppressed, this popular folklore offered a convincing explanation: Satan and his minions were working in concert with the Gentiles to destroy, if possible, the seed of Abraham.[53]

> AND CRUEL SPIRITS LED THE SONS OF NOAH ASTRAY. AND THE PRINCE MASTEMA . . . SENT OTHER SPIRITS TO THOSE WHO WERE SET UNDER HIS HAND TO PRACTICE ALL ERROR AND SIN AND ALL TRANSGRESSION, TO DESTROY, TO CAUSE TO PERISH AND TO POUR OUT BLOOD ON THE EARTH.
>
> JUBILEES

The affinities between pagan superstition and Jewish angelic speculation are noteworthy, though the more or less rigid monotheism of Judaism provides a clear line of demarcation. Philo, Paul's Jewish contemporary in Alexandria, also noted the similarities and argued that what the Gentiles call divinities, "the sacred Scripture calls *angels*."[54] Other Jewish thinkers, like the authors of *1 Enoch*, *Biblical Antiquities,* and Paul, were less generous: "The gods of the Gentiles are demons."[55]

MAGIC

In order to understand the religious context in which primitive Christianity emerged, one must reckon seriously with the widespread practice of magic, divination, and all manner of related paranormal activities. The principal varieties of magic in Greco-Roman antiquity were protective magic (protection from evil spirits, black magic, illness), imprecatory magic (invoking curses on an enemy or competitor), and love magic (compelling affection in another). The common denominator among all these is the belief that one can manipulate the gods through the correct execution of secret rites and incantations. The practice of injurious black magic was not strictly legal, and perpetrators of such mischief could face criminal prosecution.[56] Yet traffickers in magic and the dark arts are abundantly attested in the Roman world, and this great supply implies a great demand. Horace mentions one area of Rome known for its fortune tellers[57] and another for its witches:

'Tis not so much the thieves and beasts wont to infest the place that cause me care and trouble, as the witches who with spells and drugs vex human souls . . . gathering bones and harmful herbs, as soon as the roving Moon has uplifted her beauteous face.[58]

While it would be wrong to assume that this situation was typical of every metropolis in the Roman world, it would be a greater error to assume that Rome was an anomaly. Writing from Alexandria, Philo paints a similar picture of the plethora of magical practitioners:

> But the magic practiced by wandering beggars, jesters, the most disreputable women and slaves is a disfigurement of this art. . . . They promise to achieve a purification or expiation by magical means, assuring that they can supply love potions and secret utterances. . . . They lead astray and entice above all simple and harmless persons.[59]

Both Suetonius and Horace refer to entire books devoted to sorcery and spells,[60] and understanding the abundance of such works considerably illuminates the great magical bonfire described in Acts 19:19 (see Religion and Superstition: Magic in Acts). Indeed, some of these literary productions have survived, and they reveal a world of poisons, potions, charms, incantations, curses, voodoo, amulets, and so on. Lengthy formulae are prescribed detailing the precise terminology for summoning a deity, making a request, and dismissing the deity, together with symbols to be inscribed and mysterious procedures to be enacted. Quite commonly the invocation would involve reciting nonsense words and naming scores of divinities and spirits regardless of their derivation—Greek, Roman, Pagan, Hebrew—in order to maximize the effectiveness of the petition. Knowing and employing the name of a spirit was believed to grant power over that spirit and oblige it to respond to the summons: "Hear me great god, in every ritual which I perform, and grant all the petitions of my prayer completely, because I know your signs, who you are each hour, and what your name is."[61] In the following abridged incantation, an experienced shaman offers instruction on the correct method for procuring aid from the spirit world. The role of the boy in the ritual is unclear:

> BUT YOU WHOSE PRACTICE IT IS TO LURE THE MOON DOWN FROM THE SKY AND TO PROPITIATE SPIRITS OVER THE MAGIC FIRE, COME, ALTER THE HEART OF MY MISTRESS AND SEE THAT SHE TURN PALER THAN THIS CHEEK OF MINE. THEN I SHOULD CREDIT YOU WITH THE POWER OF SUMMONING GHOSTS AND STARS WITH THESSALIAN SPELLS.
>
> PROPERTIUS

> "PROTECT HIM [NAME] WHOM SHE [MOTHER'S NAME] BORE." ATTACH THIS AS AN AMULET AROUND THE NECK.
>
> PROTECTIVE AMULET

Say, "Come to me god of the gods, the only one who appears from fire and wind . . . Loth Mouloth Pnout Ei Esioth, hail lord Lampsoure Iaao Ia. . . ." Say these things many times. If, while you are reciting the apparition delays, say, "Open up, open up, Olympus; open up, Hades; open up Abyss. Let the darkness be dispelled." If it still delays, cry out in this way and again close the eyes of the boy: "Hail holy light! Hail eye of the world . . Abra A O Na Babrouthi Bie Barache, god, come in Lord." Then ask what you wish.

Dismissal: "I give thanks to you because you came in accordance with the command of god. I request that you keep me free from terror and free from demonic attacks, Athathe Athathachthe Adonai. Return to your holy places."

> I BIND DIONYSIOS THE HELMET MAKER AND HIS WIFE ARTEMIS THE GOLD WORKER AND THEIR HOUSEHOLD AND THEIR WORK AND THEIR PRODUCTS AND THEIR LIFE.
>
> CURSE TABLET

Inscribe the magical characters. Fasten the stone to the left side of the saucer. . . . Cast in the saucer the afterbirth of a dog called "white" which is born of a white dog. On the boy's chest write in myrrh: "Karbaoth."[62]

Magic had a place among Jews as well, though the surviving evidence suggests it resided on the margins of first-century Jewish practice, at least in comparison with the Gentile world. A number of Greek and Roman writers refer to Jewish fortune tellers and sorcerers,[63] and the book of Acts records several significant encounters with Jewish exorcists and magicians (Acts 8:9; 13:6–12; 19:13–20; see 2.12). More significant is the material from Qumran dealing with exorcism, astrology, and the like,[64] and the *Prayer of Jacob,* an early Jewish magical text with striking similarities to its pagan counterparts: a summoning formula, secret names, nonsense words, and a recitation ritual. In contrast to these, however, the *Prayer of Jacob* asks for moral transformation and angelic immortality.

> I ASK FOR AND RE-QUEST YOUR POWER AND YOUR AUTHORITY. . . . BRING TERMOUTIS WHOM SOPHIA BORE, TO ZOEL WHOM DRO-SER BORE, WITH CRAZED AND UNCEASING EV-ERLASTING LOVE.
>
> MAGICAL INCANTATION

Black magic and sorcery were the grimy underside of Greco-Roman religion, and their ubiquitous presence in the first century is easily confirmed but rarely taken adequately into account when exploring the socio-religious matrix of the fledgling Jesus movement. Images of marble temples, Doric columns, and exquisite statuary of the gods can all too easily obscure the less romantic reality of curse tablets, talismans, and bizarre nocturnal rituals. Yet this is the environment from which new believers entered the church, and so it is not surprising, as we will see (see Religion and Superstition: Magic in Acts), that the residue of this worldview would occasionally become visible.

DIVINATION

Knowledge of future events, the revelation of hidden truth, supernatural guidance in pressing decisions—these have ever been the fascination of mortals, and first-century pagans had devised a great many methods for plumbing the depths of the mysterious unknown. As we have seen, spiritists, mediums, and soothsayers were in plentiful supply and, not surprisingly, there was both a low-rent and a high-rent district for psychic pursuits:

> THEN COMES THE
> JEWESS . . . A HIGH
> PRIESTESS OF THE TREE,
> A TRUSTY GO-BETWEEN
> OF THE HIGHEST
> HEAVEN. SHE TOO FILLS
> HER PALM, BUT MORE
> SPARINGLY, FOR A
> JEW WILL INTERPRET
> DREAMS OF ANY KIND
> YOU PLEASE FOR THE
> MINUTEST OF COINS.
>
> *JUVENAL

> If the woman be of humble rank, she will promenade between the turning posts of the Circus Maximus; she will have her fortune told, and will present her brow and her hand to the seer who asks for many an approving smack. Wealthy women will pay for answers from a Phrygian or Indian augur well skilled in the stars and the heavens.[65]

Of course, there's divination, and there's divination. Official divination was a venerated and hallowed form of discerning the will of the gods and occupied an important place in Rome's social and political history. It involved, principally, studying the flight patterns and eating habits of birds (augury), examining the entrails of animals (haruspicy), and observing significant cosmological phenomena (lightning, eclipses, earthquakes). In Cicero's *On Divination,* although he is doubtful of its usefulness, we see divination elevated to a science, complete with methods, rules, and procedures. Its significance in Roman history is recounted by Valerius Maximus, whose prosaic enumeration of notable portents is only thinly veiled political propaganda.[66]

> THE MANNER OF
> HER PROPHESYING
> WAS NOT THAT OF
> SO MANY OTHER
> MEN AND WOMEN
> SAID TO BE INSPIRED;
> SHE DID NOT GASP
> FOR BREATH, WHIRL
> HER HEAD ABOUT
> OR TRY TO TERRIFY
> WITH HER GLANCES.
>
> DIO CHYRSOSTOM

Divination, however, was hardly confined to cities, political aristocracy, and the leaders of the empire. Diviners were also common figures in the forums and farmlands of the Roman world, as evidenced by the casual, almost parenthetical, references to such prophetic practitioners among writers of the period: Dio tells of a fortunate chance encounter with a prophetess while lost in the countryside of the Peloponnese;[67] Horace alludes to a Sabine seer and her divining urn;[68] the mural unearthed from Pompeii depicts a common scene in the marketplace: a traveler seeking an omen from a sorceress.[69] We have numerous similar examples, but a short vignette from the Cynic epistles humorously fills out the picture. In this apocryphal anecdote, the legendary cynic Diogenes is strolling through the forum of Olympia, people watching. He passes merchants hawking their goods, poets reciting verse, philosophers discoursing learnedly on the nature of the cosmos, and finally espies a diviner:

> WHO DOES NOT KNOW THAT THIS CITY WAS FOUNDED ONLY AFTER TAKING THE DIVINATIONS, THAT EVERYTHING IN WAR AND IN PEACE, AT HOME AND ABROAD, WAS DONE ONLY AFTER TAKING THE DIVINATIONS?
>
> LIVY

He was seated in the middle of a crowd, wearing a wreath larger than Apollo's, who discovered the art of divination. So I asked him, "Are you a very good diviner, or a poor one?" When he answered that he was very good I brandished my staff and said, "Tell me then, what will I do? Will I whack you with my staff, or not?" He thought to himself for a moment and replied, "You will not." Whereupon I whacked him with a laugh, while those standing around roared.[70]

ORACLES

Oracles, dreams, and astrology were also common currency in the first century, and the surviving evidence indicates that nearly everyone made at least some use of this preternatural tender. Consulting an oracle, like that of Apollo at Delphi, or the Sybil at Cumae, or Asclepius at Epidarus, was a time-honored tradition in antiquity and considered to be a valid means of finding a divine answer to a perplexing dilemma. Although the method for obtaining a reply could be quite complex—the ritual at the oracle of Trophonius at Llebadeia took several days[71]—often the petitioner would simply scratch out his or her question on a lead tablet and await a word from the sybil or officiating priest. Another method was to sit quietly at a shrine, listening for whatever phrase might be heard from a passerby, which would constitute the response from the gods. Valerius Maximus tells of one woman whose practice it was to wait until she heard the word that suited her intention![72] Sometimes the supplicant would be required to spend the night at the shrine in the hope of receiving a nocturnal vision or healing from the deity. Dreams, in fact, were commonly held to be messages from the gods, and this not only by the superstitious and unsophisticated masses. Plutarch calls dreams "the most ancient and respected form of divination"[73] and for a time refused to eat eggs because of

> AM I TO BE SOLD? AM I TO GET A FURLOUGH? IS HE WHO LEFT HOME ALIVE? SHALL I BE AN AMBASSADOR? AM I TO BE DIVORCED FROM MY WIFE? HAVE I BEEN POISONED?
>
> FROM A LIST OF QUESTIONS TO AN ORACLE

a recurring dream.[74] Pliny the Younger relates that his friend, the historian Suetonius, feared he would be humbled in court owing to an unpleasant dream, because "dreams come from Zeus."[75] The lengthy defense of nighttime revelations offered by Valerius Maximus might give the impression that their interpretation was a safe and straightforward matter, though other voices of antiquity would beg to differ. Martial mentions those who consulted mediums to sort out their slumbering revelations,[76] and then there is this poor fellow whose vision in the temple went drastically sour:

> Apollonius to Ptolemaeus his father, greetings.

> I swear by the god Serapis that if I had not a little compunction you would never see my face again; for you utter nothing but lies, and your gods likewise, for they have plunged us into a deep mire in which we may die, and when you have a vision that we are to be rescued, then we sink outright! . . . Never again can I hold up my head in Tricomia for shame that we have given ourselves away and been deluded, misled by the gods and trusting in dreams!

> Farewell![77]

OMENS

If dreams were the common currency of popular superstition, then omens and portents were the coins exchanged by all and sundry, from peasant cobbler to provincial aristocrat. An ill omen or a favorable portent could take almost any form, and so great care was taken to recognize and interpret any premonitory sign. Ominous cosmological phenomena (lightning, thunder, comets) could forebode calamity, but so, too, could inconsequential, even trivial occurrences: a mouse eating a hole through a shoe, a donkey braying in the distance, an animal born with a deformity, even an inopportune sneeze! Superstition surrounding sneezing was still common at the time of Augustine (354–430 C.E.), who poked fun at the bedeviled soul who would return straight to bed if anyone should happen to sneeze while he dressed himself for the day.[78] Tacitus's inventory of malefic omens during the consulship of Asinius and Acilius (54 C.E.) highlights the diversity of potentially foreboding ciphers and hints at the paranoia naturally accompanying such a worldview:

> WHEN A RAVEN CROAKS INAUSPICIOUSLY, DON'T GET CARRIED AWAY! RATHER, SAY TO YOURSELF, "NONE OF THESE PORTENTS ARE FOR ME."
>
> *EPICTETUS

> In the year of the consulship of Marcus Asinius and Manius Acilius it was seen to be portended by a succession of prodigies that there were to be political changes

for the worse: the soldiers' standards and tents were set in a blaze by lightning; a swarm of bees settled on the summit of the Capitol; births of monsters, half man, half beast, and of a pig with a hawk's talons, were reported. It was accounted a portent that a quæstor, an ædile, a tribune, a prætor, and consul all died within a few months.[79]

The desire to avert an evil omen or ward off a malicious spirit generated no small industry in the Greco-Roman world, where amulets, talismans, and protective charms were common fashion accessories. Amulets were occasionally carved from gemstones but were usually fashioned from metal or papyrus. They might contain a sacred image of power (a deity or magical symbol) or be inscribed with an incantation. They could be worn as necklaces or rings or carried somewhere in one's clothing. Before donning their adult toga, Roman boys wore a *bulla* (a necklace with a small pouch) that usually contained a phallus: a small replica of the male genitalia, which was a common protective symbol. The phallus, in fact, was nearly ubiquitous in the Roman world, being found on rings, statuary, household fixtures, and other decorative knick-knacks. The excavations at Pompeii and Herculaneum have uncovered numerous phallic-shaped lamps, serving trays, wind chimes (*tintinnabuli*), and so on. The protective powers of the phallus could be found guarding the entry to a home or shop, watching over crops in the field, guiding a chariot in the races—and all this quite apart from the prominent religious use of the phallus in the worship of Dionysus or Cybele. It would probably not be an overstatement to say that if someone from our century were magically transported to the first century, the visual impact of phallic symbolism would be striking.

> HEALTH TO YOU, VIC-
> TORIA, AND WHEREVER
> YOU ARE MAY YOU
> SNEEZE SWEETLY!
>
> GRAFFITO, POMPEII

> TRUE IT IS THAT THOSE
> WHO KNOW BY HEART
> THE NAMES OF THE
> IDAEAN DACTYLS USE
> THEM AS CHARMS
> AGAINST TERRORS,
> REPEATING EACH NAME
> WITH CALM ASSURANCE.
>
> PLUTARCH

ASTROLOGY

Predicting the future by means of the stars is an ancient form of divination and one that was particularly important in the NT era. The emperors Tiberius and Nero were avid devotees of astrology, and in the case of Tiberius, Suetonius remarks that this led to "a neglect of the gods and religious matters . . . being convinced that everything was in the hands of fate."[80] Ancient writers regularly refer to superstitious stargazers and streetcorner astrologers ready to plot one's destiny or one's day according to the zodiac or some other astral phenomena.

Horoscopes were often drawn up at the birth of a child, providing the anxious parents a portent of what the future would hold.

Although the science of astrology was truly complex, involving precise calculations based on the position of the planets,[81] its popularity issued from the conviction that one's fate, fortune, character, and temperament were determined by the heavenly bodies, often conceived of as deities. In a technical manual entitled *Astronomica* (written in verse!), Marcus Manilius explains: "Nature also made the lives and the destinies of mortals dependent on the stars. . . . Every possible situation, every activity, every achievement, every skill, every circumstance that might possibly happen in human life was embraced in her lot by Nature and arranged in as many portions as there are stars placed by her."[82] Sensing the ethical implications of this determinism, Manilius goes on to offer an intriguing rationale for morality: "Let one's merits, therefore, possess glory all the greater, seeing that they owe their excellence to heaven; and, again, let us hate the wicked all the more, because they were born for guilt and punishment."[83]

A comical literary presentation of popular astrological fascination comes from the pen of Gaius Petronius Arbiter. In his *Satyricon* the pretentious parvenu Trimalchio hosts an elaborate feast in which appetizers are served on a platter depicting the twelve signs of the zodiac. Over Pisces is draped pieces of fish, over Taurus slices of beef, over Leo African figs, and so on. The entryway of the dining room is marked by a calendar depicting the course of the moon and planets, and at one point during the festivities Trimalchio attempts to give a learned discourse on providence and the zodiac but succeeds only in establishing beyond any doubt his own stupidity.[84] No wonder Cicero concluded his assessment of the claims of popular astrological lore with the frustrated cry, "What utter madness!"[85]

> THE BIRTH OF PHILOE. THE 10TH YEAR OF ANTONINUS CAESAR THE LORD, PHAMENOTH 15 TO 16, 1ST HOUR OF THE NIGHT. SUN IN PISCES, JUPITER AND MERCURY IN ARIES, SATURN IN CANCER, MARS IN LEO, VENUS AND MOON IN AQUARIUS, HOROSCOPUS CAPRICORN.
>
> HOROSCOPE

> AND IF THE YEAR BEGINS IN TAURUS: EVERYONE WHOSE NAME CONTAINS A BETH OR A YODH, OR KAPH WILL BECOME ILL, OR BE WOUNDED BY AN IRON WEAPON.
>
> JEWISH HOROSCOPE

SKEPTICISM

With so many divinities and malevolent spirits hovering about, and with all the antics and angst that could accompany their worship, it is inevitable that the snickering of skeptics could be heard outside temple precincts. Cicero's Epicurean spokesman in *On the Nature of the Gods* equates the beliefs of the common folk with the basest of ruinous delusions, "a mere mass of inconsistencies sprung from ignorance."[86] Certainly the pounding excess of *hoi polloi* produced fissures in the ancient columns of Greco-Roman piety—rumors of disbelief expressed in muffled undertones by the lettered elite: a petulant sophist mocks the oracle at Delphi;[87] a poet overhearing a prayer yields to cynicism;[88] a senator dismisses the entire religious edifice as a charade for fools.[89]

> "GOOD GOD!" EX-
> CLAIMED GALAXIDORUS.
> "HOW HARD IT IS
> TO FIND A MAN UN-
> TAINTED WITH HUMBUG
> AND SUPERSTITION!"
>
> PLUTARCH

Yet "the vitality of paganism," as Ramsay MacMullen calls it,[90] was never under serious threat, even among the literati of the ancient world. Dio Chrysostom, an orator and statesman, maintained that belief in the gods is the innate conviction of all rational beings,[91] and this sentiment is abundantly illustrated throughout the literary and archeological remains of antiquity. Pausanias, educated and enlightened, traveled through the heartland of Greece critically appraising local variations of the epic legends but never casting doubt on the gods to which they referred. Even a self-proclaimed skeptic like Cicero acknowledged that the existence of the gods "is the most probable view, and the one to which we are all led by nature's guidance."[92] Popular stoicism, itself an admixture of pantheism, polytheism, and pseudotheism, offered no consolation to the atheist and could erupt in almost psalm-like praise to the creator: "Why, if we had sense, would we be doing anything else, publicly and privately, other than praising the Deity and rehearsing his benefits? Should not we, as we dig and eat, sing hymns of praise to God? 'Great is God that He has furnished us these tools! Great is God that he has given us hands!'"[93] Not only the musings of the academy or the propaganda of imperial coinage but also graffiti, inscriptions, artwork, funerary monuments, and scores of other varieties of artifacts from antiquity bear witness to the vigor of religious devotion in the Roman world. In some quarters, failure to show proper honor to the gods was regarded as a criminal offense.[94] Still, the lengthy essay of Plutarch

> THE GOOD RULER WILL
> GIVE THE FIRST AND
> CHIEF PLACE TO RE-
> LIGION, NOT MERELY
> CONFESSING BUT ALSO
> BELIEVING IN HIS HEART
> THAT THERE ARE GODS.
> HE WILL BE ZEALOUS
> TO WORSHIP THEM.
> AND HE WILL BELIEVE
> ALSO IN DEMIGODS
> AND GOOD SPIRITS.
>
> DIO CHRYSOSTOM

on the implausibility of atheism, as well as the jeers of skeptics that occasionally rose above the din of superstition, betray a deeper, gnawing frustration; a prescient intimation of naïveté.

THE NEW TESTAMENT CONTEXT

As the previous discussion emphasizes, the philosophical conflict between paganism and Christianity would have been constant and felt at virtually every level of social engagement. The Judeo-Christian worldview that Paul introduced to Corinth, Thessalonica, Ephesus, and other communities around the rim of Aegean would have been the religious equivalent of a Copernican revolution for inhabitants of these cities, Jews excepted. At every crossroads, at every doorway, in every tavern and in every shop the new believer would be confronted with the symbols and assumptions of an unremittingly polytheistic world—and we have yet to consider the function of religion in the home and in civic institutions (see Religion and Superstition as well as City and Society). The challenge for contemporary readers (never fully attainable, granted) is to attempt to hear Paul's letters with pagan ears and so better appreciate the impact of their message on their original readers.

> **DIVINE AUGUSTUS FATHER OF THE COUNTRY.**
>
> ROMAN COIN

Most Christians today, for example, take for granted beliefs such as a bodily resurrection, divine providence, God as Father, or God as provider, but in the Greco-Roman world each of these notions was either ascribed to other deities or rejected. The Athenians scoffed at the idea of a bodily resurrection (Acts 17:32), and in Corinth even some believers had a difficult time accepting it (1 Cor 15:12). Providence and fate were believed to be determined by the stars, or perhaps the goddess Fortuna/Tyche. Stoics proclaimed Zeus as the father of humanity, and the coins jingling in first-century pockets heralded the emperor as the divine father. To the Corinthians, whose city boasted an elaborate sanctuary of Demeter, provider of grain and bountiful harvests, Paul's assurance that "he who supplies seed to the sower and bread for food will also supply and increase your store of seed" (2 Cor 9:10) might have occasioned deliberate, sincere reflection in a way that it no longer does.

> **TO DIVINE TRAJAN, CONQUEROR OF THE PARTHIANS, AUGUSTUS, FATHER.**
>
> ROMAN COIN

It would be interesting and profitable to work through all Paul's letters in this fashion, listening to each passage with "pagan ears," but this would require a much larger volume than anyone is prepared to read and rob you of the joy of discovery. Instead, The New Testament Context section of this chapter (and subsequent chapters) will look at a few key issues in central texts in Paul's letters and travels

> **WHAT DO MORTALS NEED BESIDES TWO THINGS ONLY: THE BREAD OF DEMETER AND A DRINK OF THE WATER-CARRIER.**
>
> MUSONIUS RUFUS

where the interaction between paganism and Christianity is both significant and illuminating. The broad-stroked picture of paganism in the Roman world offered above will now be nuanced with finer detail and local color as we observe first-century believers in specific settings slowly, and sometimes haltingly, realigning and reconfiguring their belief system in light of their newfound faith. We begin in Corinth.

MONOTHEISM IN CORINTH

Is it possible to be a Christian and a polytheist? The answer is no. However, a close reading of 1 Cor 8 reveals that the matter is perhaps not so simple. Paul's topic is a controversial issue among the Corinthians: dining in pagan temples and eating food sacrificed to idols (see City and Society: Urban Landscape and Environment as well as City and Society: Paul and Poverty). Paul prefaces his instruction by reminding the Corinthians that knowledge must always be tempered with love; correct belief without correct behavior is pointless (8:1–3). He then specifies the correct belief in question, monotheism: "We know that an idol is nothing in all the world and there is no God but one. For even if there are so-called gods . . . yet for us there is but one God" (8:4–6). This affirmation is quickly qualified, however: "But not everyone knows this. Some are still so accustomed to idols [pagan gods] that when they eat such food they eat it as though it were idol food, and since their conscience is weak, it is defiled" (8:7). Paul goes on to describe members of the Corinthian assembly ("brothers," 8:11, 12, 13) whose faith is "weak" and deals a serious blow by the callous insensitivity of the strong who continue to dine in pagan temples (8:10–12); yet these "brothers" do not quite understand that there is only one God (8:7). How can this be? Welcome to first-century Corinth. What we see here is the gospel taking root in a pagan environment, in a city whose heritage and culture were virtually inseparable from the polytheistic framework of the ancient world. The picture that emerges from 1 Cor 8 is of a probably small group of new believers who have put their faith in Christ but have not been divested of all their pagan notions and have not fully comprehended this novel idea of monotheism. Given their background, this is entirely understandable.

> IT IS NOT THE ABUNDANCE OF WINE OR THE ROASTING OF MEAT THAT MAKES THE JOY OF FESTIVALS, BUT THE GOOD HOPE AND THE BELIEF THAT THE GOD IS PRESENT AND GRACIOUSLY ACCEPTS WHAT IS OFFERED.
>
> PLUTARCH

However, it is important not to exaggerate the situation. Paul is not describing a group of people who have simply added Jesus to their pantheon of deities and flit happily between the temples and the Christian assembly. No.

There are too many passages in Paul's letters like 2 Cor 6:14–18 to allow us to believe that the apostle would ever tolerate that. Nor are these people who have consciously repudiated monotheism. What Paul describes in 1 Cor 8 are new believers whose knowledge is incomplete, whose embryonic faith is "weak," and for whom polytheism is so deeply rooted in their cultural-religious psyche that eating food sacrificed in the temple of Apollo constitutes eating food sacrificed to Apollo. It becomes for them a betrayal of their new allegiance, the faith they know deep in their hearts to be true.

> NEAR THE FOUNTAIN OF PEIRENE IN CORINTH ARE AN IMAGE AND A SACRED ENCLOSURE OF APOLLO; IN THE LATTER IS A PAINTING OF THE EXPLOIT OF ODYSSEUS AGAINST THE SUITORS.
>
> PAUSANIAS

Given Paul's abhorrence of polytheism (Acts 17:16; 1 Cor 6:9; 1 Thess 1:9), his approach to this problem demonstrates remarkable pastoral sensitivity. Of primary importance, Paul is clear that this lingering, hesitant polytheism is not acceptable, and these people are not where they should be. Their knowledge is incomplete, and their faith is weak. Yet he also recognizes that when people come to faith in Christ, the Apostles' Creed is not simply downloaded into their cranium; if their embryonic faith is going to develop and their knowledge is going to grow, they will need patience, nurturing, and a lot of support from the strong. Indeed, it is the inconsiderate behavior of the strong that seems to be the focus of Paul's parental scrutiny in this passage.

FAITH IN GALATIA

Galatians is unlike any other letter of Paul. Dispensing with the polite formalities that characterize his other missives—an opening prayer or expression of thanksgiving—Paul instead expresses his utter consternation: "I am astonished that you are so quickly deserting the one who called you by the grace of Christ and are turning to a different gospel!" (1:6). We soon hear the apostle calling his spiritual children "foolish" and "bewitched" (3:1), and later he calls on the Judaizing intruders who are advocating circumcision to "go all the way and emasculate themselves!" (Gal 5:12).

Paul's anger is understandable. The Galatians are tempted to embrace a very different gospel from the one that Paul preached, a gospel that "is really no gospel at all" (1:7). What is less understandable is why the largely Gentile assemblies in the province of Galatia would be tempted to add torah observance to their faith. Circumcision and dietary restrictions were hardly selling points of Judaism as far as Gentiles were concerned. Were these Jewish-Christian missionaries particularly winsome? Rhetorically persuasive? Was it the prestige and antiquity of the Jewish faith that won over some of the Galatians? In other words, what was the plausibility basis of their message? By "plausibility basis" I mean those social and cultural factors that allow a religious belief to seem obviously tenable.[95]

This puzzle has vexed generations of NT scholars, but the recent work of Clinton E. Arnold, a specialist in folk religions of Asia Minor, may have provided the missing pieces.[96] Drawing on and synthesizing a large amount of inscriptional data from these regions,[97] Arnold demonstrates that the indigenous folk religion of Asia Minor was characterized by a strong sense of obligation to fulfill cultic requirements and perform good works in order to maintain a favorable standing with the gods. The inscriptions themselves are monuments erected by individuals who have sinned in some way and who now publicly confess their sin and praise the deity, usually after experiencing severe punishment from the god or goddess.

> THE CUSTOMS OF THE JEWS ARE BASE AND ABOMINABLE. THEY SIT APART AT MEALS, AND SLEEP APART. THEY ADOPTED CIRCUMCISION TO DISTINGUISH THEMSELVES FROM OTHER PEOPLE.
>
> *TACITUS

The range of infractions that incurred the wrath of the gods included ritual misdemeanors, social offenses, and even inadvertent transgressions: a woman passes through a sacred area while ritually impure; a husband spends an evening at home with his wife instead of fulfilling his obligations at the temple; a woodsman inadvertently fells a tree belonging to a sacred grove.[98] The punishment inflicted by these regional deities (Men Axiottenos, Ainatas, Leto, Zeus Sabazios, Artemis, to name a few) depended on the nature of the offense. Images of body parts (feet, arms, eyes) on some of these monuments indicate specific bodily afflictions, and death is also meted out on occasion. Among the more heart-wrenching is the situation of Hermogenes Valerius, who, apparently out of ignorance, swore falsely to the deity:

> Then the god showed his power and punished Hermogenes, inflicting damages. He killed his ox and his donkey, and when he continued in disobedience, he killed his daughter. Then, he cancelled the vow. We, Aphias, his wife, and Alexander, Attalus, Apollonius, and Amion his children, erected this monument and on it record the power of the god and praise him from now on.[99]

Small wonder that Neis, a mother guilty of an unnamed transgression, pleads to the goddess Meter Taszene to spare her children: "Neis, who has been punished by Meter Taszene, has consecrated this monument for the preservation of her and her children."[100]

In light of the cultural context of the Galatian churches and their native religious scruples regarding adherence to all the requirements of their gods, it is not surprising that the message of the Judaizers found a hearing. Their appeal to the observance of proper rituals harmonized well with the pre-Christian sensibilities of some Galatians and made the transition to a law-oriented piety that much easier. In fact, in other inscriptions from this area, the deities Hosios (Holy) and Dikaios (Just) are pictured with scales and measuring rods preparing to weigh the deeds of their worshipers.[101]

> GREAT IS METER ANAITIS! APOLLONIUS, SON OF MENODOROS, ERECTED THIS FOR HIS BROTHER DIONYSIOS. SINCE HE UNDERTOOK A RITUAL WASHING, BUT DID NOT KEEP THE DATE APPOINTED BY THE GODDESS, SHE STRUCK HIM DEAD.
>
> INSCRIPTION, ASIA MINOR

Understanding the indigenous religious notions of the Roman provinces of Asia Minor adds definition and texture to the somewhat generic Greco-Roman polytheism outlined earlier and considerably illuminates the text and context of Paul's letter to the Galatians. For example, after reading scores of inscriptions detailing the vicious and vindictive punishments imposed by these territorial gods—often for minor transgressions—Paul's words in Gal 6:1 sound almost as if they were deliberately composed in antithesis: "Brothers, if someone is caught in a sin, you who are spiritual should restore him gently."[102]

MAGIC IN ACTS

Disabling a treacherous sorcerer, exorcising a menacing spirit, destroying a library of dark incantations—this may sound like the storyline for one of J. K. Rowling's blockbusters, but they are chapters from Paul's travels through Greece and Asia Minor. The book of Acts follows the apostle Paul as he wanders about the Mediterranean proclaiming the good news that Jesus, the Jewish messiah crucified by the Romans, had risen from the dead and now called all people everywhere to turn from their idols and serve him exclusively. If this sounds preposterous, so it was. Many of the Athenian sophisticates scratched their heads and wondered, "What is this babbler trying to say?" (Acts 17:18). But Paul remained undaunted and undeterred. His mission to proclaim God's love to the furthest reaches of the Gentile world was rooted in his own crucifying, transforming encounter with Jesus (Acts 9; Gal 2:19–20), and neither Greek skepticism nor Jewish hostility (Acts 14:2, 19; 17:5–6) could divert him from his task: "I do all things for the sake of the gospel . . . troubles, hardships,

> ALEXANDER, SON OF THALLUSA, TOGETHER WITH JULIUS AND HIS SISTER, HAVE BEEN RANSOMED FROM THEIR TRANSGRESSION—KNOWN AND UNKNOWN— BY THE GOD MEN EG DIODOTOS.
>
> INSCRIPTION, ASIA MINOR

beatings, imprisonments, riots, hard work, sleepless nights, hunger" (1 Cor 9:23 with 2 Cor 6:4–5). Small wonder that he and his companions would be accused of "turning the world upside down" (Acts 17:6 author's translation).

Although Acts is selective in what it records and focuses almost entirely on Paul (there were certainly other missionary endeavors afoot, as Philip's story below illustrates), it includes several extraordinary—even hair-raising—episodes featuring shamans, exorcists, and diviners that further illustrate the very humdrum nature of these characters in the ancient world. In each instance Luke, the author of Acts and traveling companion of Paul,[103] emphasizes the supremacy and power of the gospel over any rival claimant while quietly reminding us of the wealth, influence, and status of successful magical practitioners in the Greco-Roman world. The confrontation between paganism and Christianity had a fiscal as well as a spiritual dimension, and Luke is keen to keep both in view.

In Samaria

Simony, the ecclesiastical crime of buying or selling a sacred office, derives its name from Simon the sorcerer (Acts 8:9–24). So, what must one do in order to have a religious felony named after oneself? According to Luke, Simon had been practicing magic in Samaria, north of Judea, for some time and had succeeded in "amazing everyone, from the least to the greatest" (8:10 author's translation). He boasted of his own greatness (8:9), and the people of Samaria came to believe that he possessed a special divine power known as "the great power" (8:10), a designation that echoes many magical texts. Upon hearing Philip's preaching, Simon and many other Samaritans believed and were baptized. Simon subsequently followed Philip, "astonished by the great signs and miracles he saw" (8:13). It would seem that Simon was stalking Philip in hopes of learning some of his secrets. He is exposed, however, when he observes Peter and John bestowing the gift of the Spirit through the laying on of hands and offers them money so that he too might learn to summon this great spirit. This is how shamans operated; a price was set, an incantation was purchased, and a new power was at the buyer's disposal. Perceiving Simon's duplicity and envy, Peter's response is brutal:

> TAKE A SILVER TABLET AND ENGRAVE IT AFTER THE SUN-GOD HELIOS SETS. TAKE COW'S MILK AND POUR IT . . . ADD BARLEY MEAL, MIX AND FORM TWELVE ROLLS IN THE SHAPE OF FEMALE FIGURES. SAY [THE FORMULA] THREE TIMES, EAT [THE ROLLS] ON AN EMPTY STOMACH, AND YOU WILL KNOW THE POWER.
>
> *MAGICAL INCANTATION

May your money perish with you, because you thought you could buy the gift of God with money! You have no part or share in this ministry, because your heart is not right before God. Repent of this wickedness and pray to the Lord. Perhaps he will forgive you for having such a thought in your heart. For I see that you are full of bitterness and captive to sin. (Acts 8:20–23)

This episode is illuminating in many ways, two of which are particularly relevant for us. First, the earliest converts in Samaria were drawn from the same crowd of people who had formerly followed Simon, been amazed at his magic, and held him to be divinely empowered. These new believers brought with them a fair amount of pagan baggage that needed to be carefully unpacked and thoroughly laundered. Simon himself is able to fly under the spiritual radar of Philip for some time (we are not told how long, but the text implies a period of weeks), and it is not difficult to imagine scenarios in which people like Simon were never exposed but continued to exert influence in the community. Perhaps this is why Paul feels it necessary to add "sorcery" to the list of vices that the Galatian Christians are to take pains to avoid (Gal 6:20).

> EVERY APOSTLE WHO COMES TO YOU SHOULD BE RECEIVED AS THE LORD. . . . AND WHEN THE APOSTLE DEPARTS, HE SHOULD RECEIVE NOTHING BUT BREAD UNTIL HE FINDS HIS NEXT LODGING. BUT IF HE REQUESTS MONEY, HE IS A FALSE PROPHET.
>
> DIDACHE 11:4–6

Second, Luke's portrait of Simon (often referred to as Simon Magus, "the magician") accentuates his high standing in the community and his wealth. Simon's offer of money indicates he was a person of some means with funds at his disposal, as we would expect from an eminent magician charging fees for his expertise. If Peter has discerned correctly, Simon's motives were impure; certainly his request betrays self-interest: "Give *to me* this power so that anyone on whom *I* lay *my* hands may receive the Holy Spirit" (emphasis added). Simon does not desire the Spirit for any moral or spiritual benefit but simply to expand his clientele and enhance his reputation. It is difficult not to hear a deliberate contrast between the actions of Simon Magus, "the magician," and Simon Peter, "the rock," recorded in Acts 3:1–10. In this passage, a crippled beggar asks Peter and John for money, and Peter replies, "Silver or gold I do not have, but what I have I give you. In the name of Jesus Christ of Nazareth, walk" (3:6).[104] Lacking money, and with no prospect of compensation, Peter freely dispenses God's gift of healing. This exemplifies for Luke the correct perspective on material and spiritual benefits; both are intended for the benefit of others.

On Cyprus

We meet our next conjuror on the island of Cyprus, where Paul is beginning his first missionary tour, along with Barnabas and Mark (Acts 13:4–12).

He is called Bar-Jesus,[105] and Luke wastes no time in rendering his verdict: a sorcerer (*magos*), a Jew, and hence a false prophet (13:6). But he kept good company. Luke tells us that he was in the entourage of the Roman provincial governor, Sergius Paulus, "an intelligent man [who had] sent for Barnabas and Saul because he wanted to hear the word of God" (13:7). The scene is set for a confrontation, which quickly ensues. Bar-Jesus, realizing his position and livelihood were in jeopardy, sought to dissuade the governor from the faith, only to be humiliated by an enraged Paul:

> Then Saul, who was also called Paul, filled with the Holy Spirit, looked straight at Elymas and said, "You are a child of the devil and an enemy of everything that is right! You are full of all kinds of deceit and trickery. Will you never stop perverting the right ways of the Lord? Now the hand of the Lord is against you. You are going to be blind, and for a time you will be unable to see the light of the sun." Immediately mist and darkness came over him, and he groped about, seeking someone to lead him by the hand. (13:9–11)

Several features of Luke's narrative lead me to suspect that Bar-Jesus' magical specialty was astrology.[106] Luke's derogatory epithet "false prophet" may suggest involvement in some form of divination, and court astrologers were quite in vogue during this period. According to Suetonius, the emperors Tiberius, Nero, Otho, and Domitian all had astrologers on their payroll,[107] as did Felix, the Roman procurator of Judaea.[108] More telling, however, is Paul's added invocation, "you will be unable to see the light of the sun" (13:11), which seems both calculated and polemical. It would be a particularly well-chosen imprecation for someone who held the sun, the stars, and the moon in special reverence.

THOSE WHO CLAIM TO KNOW THE FUTURE, THE MYSTERIOUS CERTAINTIES OF FATE, ENQUIRE INTO BIRTHDAYS, THE FIRST HOUR OF LIFE AS A HARBINGER OF ALL THE YEARS TO FOLLOW: WHAT WAS THE MOVEMENT OF THE STARS? DID THE SUN STAND IN AN OMINOUS POSITION?

*SENECA THE ELDER

Certainty may elude us regarding Bar-Jesus' connection to astrology but not with regard to Luke's intention: Luke stresses the pervasive nature of magic in the Roman world and its influence at the highest level of the social and political hierarchy. The magical grandees of first-century society were provincial dignitaries with powerful allies and significant resources at their disposal. As with Simon Magus, Luke tells us nothing more of Bar-Jesus, and so we are left wondering if he ever truly saw the light. Luke does, however, provide a postscript to the story of Sergius Paulus: "When the proconsul saw what had happened, he believed, for he was amazed at the teaching about the Lord" (13:12).[109]

In Philippi

Luke's portrayal of Paul's visit to Roman Philippi, "the leading city of that district of Macedonia" (Acts 16:12), is marked by a series of intriguing episodes in which the lives of three ordinary people—a merchant woman (Lydia, 16:11–15), a prophetess (16:16–18), and a jailer (16:25–34)—are radically altered. Other literary elements add dramatic élan to the narrative—a mob scene, a public flogging, an earthquake—but the heart of the storyline is found in these transformative encounters. Although each incident contains its own fascinating set of questions, the young prophetess will be the focus of our attention.

> APPIUS COMPELLED THE PRIESTESS OF THE DELPHIC CAULDRON TO DESCEND INTO THE IN-NERMOST RECESS OF THE SACRED CAVERN, FROM WHICH SURE PREDIC-TIONS ARE SOUGHT, BUT TOO STRONG AN INTAKE OF THE DI-VINE BREATH IS FATAL TO THE MEDIUMS.
>
> *VALERIUS MAXIMUS*

Paul meets the soothsayer on his way to a Jewish place of prayer outside the city.[110] She is described as a slave girl with, literally, "a python spirit" (16:16). The python was associated with Apollo's oracular temple in Delphi, and this term came to be used of prophecy and divination generally: "a spirit of divination." Luke also informs us that her prophetic gifts netted her owners "a great deal of money" (16:16). Once again, we sense Luke building toward a confrontation, but what follows seems to belie that expectation: "This girl followed Paul and the rest of us, shouting, 'These men are servants of the Most High God, who are telling you the way to be saved.'" Is this an unlooked for ally?

To those familiar with the Old Testament, the phrase "Most High God" sounds like an authentic designation of the one true God.[111] But what if you were unfamiliar with the Old Testament? What would this phrase sound like to residents of Roman Philippi? Would they have heard it as a reference to the God of the Jews? This is very unlikely. In fact, there is an abundance of archaeological and inscriptional evidence attesting to the worship of a pagan deity in this area known as Theos Hypsistos, "Most High God," the same terminology used by this prophetess.[112] Dedicatory inscriptions to this deity, also known as Zeus Hypsistos, have been found in all quadrants of the Roman province of Macedonia, in neighboring Thracia, in Asia Minor, and else-

> MARKUS LEUKELIOS MAKLAS [DEDICATES THIS] TO THEOS HYPSISTOS AS A THANK OFFERING.
>
> INSCRIPTION, NEAR PHILIPPI

where in the Greco-Roman world. The inscriptional evidence indicates that the Macedonians in particular reverenced Theos Hypsistos, so much so that some scholars have speculated that the cult originated in this region.[113]

Nor was this diviner's reference to "the way of salvation" unambiguous. The Greek phrase could just as easily be translated "a way of salvation," and the term rendered "salvation" by English versions (*sōtēria*) quite commonly referred to well-being or rescue from hardship. In Philippopolis, north of Philippi, a certain Gaius Mailios Agathopus inscribed a dedication to Zeus Hypsistos "on behalf of the health (*sōtēria*)" of his patron.[114]

DEDICATED TO
THEOS HYPSISTOS,
GREAT SAVIOR

FIRST-CENTURY VOTIVE,
THESSALONICA

It seems most likely, then, that the residents of Philippi would have understood the declaration of the diviner to refer to a local deity, Theos Hypsistos, with whom they were familiar and whose cult was well established in the province. This also helps us understand why Paul becomes increasingly concerned about this prophetess repeating this announcement "for many days" (16:17). Not only did Paul not want a pagan diviner as his publicity agent, he also understood the ferocious ambiguity of her press release. His decision to exorcise this spirit freed the young woman from its tyranny but landed him and his coworker in jail. When the owners of the slave realized that their lucrative income had taken flight with the spirit, they determined that Paul and Silas would pay dearly for their financial ruin (16:19–24).

In Ephesus

Ephesus was the largest city in Asia Minor and became the strategic center of Paul's later missionary endeavor. It was also the scene of some extraordinary events—healings, a failed exorcism, a tumultuous riot—and will be the final stop on our magical tour in Acts. The two incidents that most illuminate the socio-religious context of the primitive Jesus movement are the conflagration of magical texts described in Acts 19:11–20 and the riot of the silversmiths in 19:21–40. In these stories Luke brings to a climax two important motifs of his historical journal: the triumph of the gospel over the spirits and the financial cost of discipleship.

AND THE WOMEN TOO
WERE WHIPPING THEM-
SELVES INTO A FRENZY
AND PROPHESYING IM-
MINENT DESTRUCTION.

TACITUS

Paul's ministry in Ephesus was both extensive, lasting at least two years (Acts 19:10), and successful. Paul's daily teaching in the lecture hall of Tyrannus ensured that his message received a wide public hearing, and the healings and exorcisms that God performed through the apostle caused his fame to spread rapidly, particularly among the magical community of Ephesus and Asia Minor (19:9–12). It was not long before a group of itinerant Jewish exorcists—with priestly credentials no less!—were trying to capitalize on Paul's notoriety and so added "Jesus" to the powers they named in their incantations: "In the name of Jesus whom Paul preaches" (19:13). In a masterful stroke of comic relief, Luke describes how one obstinate demon, far from being hurled into exile, verbally mocks these exorcists as mere pretenders and then proceeds to give them a walloping! In the end, it is the exorcists, not the spirit, who flee in terror (19:14–16).

To fully appreciate what happens next, it is important to understand that Ephesus had a reputation in antiquity as a center for magic and the occult.[115] It was from Ephesus that the infamous Ephesian Letters derived their name. The Ephesian Letters were six or so magical terms believed to impart special powers to those who uttered them or wore them as a protective amulet.[116] In other words, what Luke describes in the following verses fits comfortably in the cultural milieu of ancient Ephesus.

When word of this farcical exorcism attempt got around, the citizenry of Ephesus "were all seized with fear, and the name of the Lord Jesus was held in high honor" (Acts 19:17). But the plot continues to thicken. Under obvious conviction, many believers who had clung to their magical practices and paraphernalia confessed their clandestine sorcery, brought forth their magical scrolls and accouterments, "and burned them publicly" (19:19). Even more astounding, Luke tells us that the value of this material was fifty thousand pieces of silver. In order to account for such a colossal figure, we can only conclude that the number of Ephesian believers who continued their involvement in the dark arts was quite large and that their investment was enormous. But we should not miss the most basic observation: in the minds of these new Christians there was, initially, no obvious and necessary connection between their new faith and their former superstitious practices. There is a wealth of material, dating considerably later, mostly from the third to the seventh centuries, documenting Christian magical practices: charms, spells, curses, and incantations.[117] As far as first-century Ephesus is concerned, Luke's concluding summary implies a significant victory in the ongoing conflict between the spirits and the gospel: "In this way the word of the Lord spread widely and grew in power" (19:20).

> AND IN THE OLYMPICS, WHEN A MILESIAN AND EPHESIAN WERE WRESTLING, THE MILESIAN COULD NOT DEFEAT HIS OPPONENT BECAUSE HE HAD THE EPHESIAN LETTERS ON A KNUCKLEBONE. WHEN THIS WAS REVEALED AND THEY WERE REMOVED FROM HIM, THE EPHESIAN FELL THIRTY TIMES IN A ROW.
>
> THE SUDA

Luke's account of the riot of the Ephesian silversmiths that immediately follows (Acts 19:21–41) does not involve sorcerers, shamans, or magic, but it reinforces the connection Luke continually draws between spiritual and economic power structures, and in this respect it portrays a single, isolated scene of a much larger cultural drama slowly beginning to unfold throughout the Greco-Roman world. What was the crucial issue that prompted the uproar? Money.

Not everyone in Ephesus was thrilled with Paul's success. In particular, Demetrius the silversmith was not. His hitherto flourishing business manufacturing small silver likenesses of the goddess Artemis had noticeably declined in recent months, and he was in no doubt as to who was responsible: Paul. In an impassioned speech to his fellow artisans he articulates the issues candidly:

> MICHAEL, GABRIEL, SOULEEL! YOU MUST BRING HER AWAY BY THE METHOD OF AN ULCEROUS TUMOR. ARISE IN YOUR ANGER, BRING HER DOWN TO A PAINFUL END . . . MY LORD JESUS CHRIST, YOU MUST BRING HER DOWN TO AN END.
>
> CHRISTIAN CURSE

Men, you know we receive a good income from this business. And you see and hear how this fellow Paul has convinced and led astray large numbers of people here in Ephesus and in practically the whole province of Asia. He says that man-made gods are no gods at all. There is danger not only that our trade will lose its good name, but also that the temple of the great goddess Artemis will be discredited. (Acts 19:25–27)

Demetrius and his fellow artisans are facing a serious financial crisis, and if you have ever been a parent with mouths to feed you should be able to muster genuine sympathy for their predicament. What this incident illustrates—and what contemporary readers often miss—is the delicate interdependence of cult and economy in the ancient world. As we will explore in more detail in a later chapter (see City and Society: Urban Landscape and Environment), temples were the vital organs of a local economy, providing venues for merchants, business for craftsmen, festivals for tourists, and much more. The symbiotic relationship between civic and religious institutions is especially difficult to fully grasp for those of us whose cultural and religious heritage is based on the necessary separation of church and state.

> THIS TOMB AND THE AREA AROUND IT BELONG TO M. ANTONIUS HERMEIAS. IF ANYONE DARES TO PUT IN A CORPSE OR EXCISE THIS TEXT, HE SHALL PAY TO THE SILVERSMITHS AT EPHESUS 1,000 DENARII.
>
> FUNERARY INSCRIPTION, EPHESUS

In a letter to emperor Trajan written about 100 C.E., Pliny the Younger, then governor of Bithynia, outlines his interrogation and torture of members of a "degenerate and foolish superstition," which we know today as Christianity.[118] Pliny describes how his method of dealing with those accused of being Christians has led to many recantations and the revival of the traditional religious observances. As a result, he informs the emperor, "the flesh of sacrificial meat is being sold again, which until recently no one was buying." Here again we see the intimate connection between Christianity and the marketplace. The increase of Christianity meant the decrease in sale of sacrificial animals, which meant less meat available in local shops, which meant less income for those raising the animals, and so on. In fact, the kind of large-scale conversion to Christianity that Luke describes in Ephesus would have drastic implications for the local economy, involving everyone from village craftsmen to streetcorner astrologers to engravers of dedications—not to mention temple staff and festival tourism. As Christianity advanced, the massive economic edifice of paganism crumbled, and that collapse entailed substantial collateral damage.

DEMONS IN PAUL

"And though this world, with devils filled" is a line from Martin Luther's famous hymn, "A Mighty Fortress is Our God," but it just as easily could have been penned by Paul, because this refrain is one that the Reformer and the apostle could sing in unison. We have spent a fair amount of time considering how Paul's faith and worldview were often at odds with the polytheistic and superstitious notions of his new converts, and it is appropriate now to ask how Paul's worldview and that of his converts might be different from ours. In many ways, Paul's vision of the spiritual cosmos was identical to that of his Jewish contemporaries: congested with demons, cluttered with angels, and permeated by diabolical powers. According to Paul, Satan masquerades as an angel of light (2 Cor 11:14), ever plotting and scheming the ruin of believers (1 Cor 7:5; 2 Cor 2:11; Eph 6:11; 2 Tim 2:26). False teachers are his servants (2 Cor 11:15), false doctrine is spread by his demons (1 Tim 4:1), and apostasy is the goal of his labor (Eph 2:2; 1 Tim 5:15). He is able to successfully thwart the apostle in his ministry (1 Thess 2:18) and is eager to inflict physical pain and death (2 Cor 12:7; 1 Cor 5:5; 1 Tim 1:20). He is "the god of this age who has blinded the minds of unbelievers" (2 Cor 4:4) and whose demonic underlings the pagan world unwittingly worships at temples and shrines (1 Cor 10:20–22; 2 Cor 6:15–16). In Paul's estimation, this is not simply a case of mistaken identity; it constitutes "slavery to those who by nature are not gods" (Gal 4:8).

But we have not yet reached the conceptual nerve center of Pauline demonology. Paul's favorite manner of describing the dominion of darkness is with "power" language and terms drawn from the social sphere of governance and

> I DECIDED I SHOULD RELEASE ANY WHO DENIED THAT THEY WERE OR EVER HAD BEEN CHRISTIANS WHEN THEY HAD REPEATED AFTER ME A FORMULA OF INVOCATION TO THE GODS AND HAD MADE OFFERINGS TO YOUR STATUE . . . NONE OF WHICH THINGS, I UNDERSTAND, ANY GENUINE CHRISTIAN CAN BE INDUCED TO DO.
>
> *PLINY TO EMPEROR TRAJAN

> WE FIND NOTHING WRONG WITH THIS MAN. WHAT IF A SPIRIT OR AN ANGEL HAS SPOKEN TO HIM?
>
> ACTS 23:9

authority: "For we do not wrestle against flesh and blood, but against the rulers, against the authorities, against the cosmic lords who rule over this present darkness, against the spiritual forces of evil in the heavenly places" (Eph 6:12 ESV).[119] Again, not unlike the Jewish authors of *Jubilees* or *1 Enoch*, or *The War Scroll*, Paul envisioned ranks, divisions, and hierarchies in the demonic hosts, with Satan at the pinnacle of power, "the ruler of the kingdom of the air" (Eph 2:2). The prominence of this topic in Ephesians is hardly surprising given the description in Acts of the widespread practice of magic in Ephesus.

> AND WHAT I HAVE
> FORGIVEN—IF THERE
> WAS ANYTHING TO
> FORGIVE—I HAVE FOR-
> GIVEN IN THE SIGHT OF
> CHRIST FOR YOUR SAKE,
> IN ORDER THAT SATAN
> MIGHT NOT OUTWIT US.
> FOR WE ARE NOT UN-
> AWARE OF HIS SCHEMES.
>
> 2 CORINTHIANS 2:10–11

Fortunately, it was not only malicious spiritual forces that populated Paul's universe; the holy angelic host was also continually watching over human affairs. Angels were present at services of worship (1 Cor 11:10), observed Paul (and presumably everyone) in the routine of life and ministry (1 Cor 4:9; 1 Tim 5:21), and were particularly associated with significant events in God's program of redemption: the giving of the law (Gal 3:19), the incarnation (1 Tim 3:16), and the return of Christ (1 Thess 3:1; 2 Thess 1:7; 2:6–7).

But while this continuity is striking, the discontinuity between Paul and other Jewish thinkers of his day is equally striking. Paul was acutely aware of the spiritual battle in which he was enlisted, but he never lapses into the superstitious demonic paranoia of so many of his contemporaries, and this for two essential reasons. First and foremost, Jesus has delivered the believer from the "kingdom of darkness" (Col 1:13; cf. 2 Thess 3:3), has triumphed over the spiritual rulers and authorities by the cross (Col 2:15), and has been enthroned at God's right hand in the heavens "far above all rule and authority and power and dominion, and above every name that is named" (Eph 1:21–22 ESV)—an obvious reference to naming spiritual powers in magical incantations. This crushing, decisive victory allows Paul to assure the recipients of his letter to the Romans that no angel or ruler or power could ever separate them from God's love (Rom 8:38) and that God will soon "crush Satan under your feet" (Rom 16:20). Heard through first-century Jewish ears, this is a staggering promise.

> BUT THE LORD IS
> FAITHFUL, AND HE
> WILL STRENGTHEN
> AND PROTECT YOU
> FROM THE EVIL ONE.
>
> 2 THESSALONIANS 3:3

The second important reason for Paul's contrasting perspective is his very different analysis of humanity's plight. In Jewish literature written between, roughly, 200 B.C.E. and 200 C.E. we see the presence of evil accounted for in three primary ways: Satan, the Gentiles, and (later) the evil inclination (i.e., the flesh). However, in the literature of Paul's day, as we have already seen, it was the evil angelic host that was principally held responsible for sin, in collusion with the lawless, sinful Gentiles. Paul, by contrast, reserves his most poignant, gripping analysis of the human predicament for his discussion of the flesh (Rom 6–8; Gal 5–6). Rather than a pessimistic estimation of the historical situation, oppressed by demons and Gentiles, Paul had a pessimistic estimation of the human condition, with its bondage to sin: "O wretched man that I am! Who will deliver me from this body of death?" (Rom 7:25 ESV). Like Jeremiah and Ezekiel before him, Paul points his finger at the center of the individual, the human heart, and identifies it as the origin of sin and corruption that must be renewed and transformed. In Paul's view, again following Jeremiah and Ezekiel, it is

> AND I WILL GIVE YOU A NEW HEART, AND A NEW SPIRIT I WILL PUT WITHIN YOU. AND I WILL REMOVE FROM YOU YOUR HEART OF STONE AND GIVE YOU A HEART OF FLESH. I WILL PUT MY SPIRIT WITHIN YOU.
>
> EZEKIEL 36:26–27

only the life-giving presence of the Spirit (Rom 8:1–17; 2 Cor 3:1–18; Eph 6:16–18) that enables the believer to successfully resist both the temptations of the flesh and the enticement of the evil one.

Paul's Jewish heritage endowed him with a deeper understanding of the spiritual nature of the conflict between good and evil, though admittedly, the demon-saturated world of the first century may strike us moderns as an alien and terrifying place. The crucial question for us is this: Which is closer to reality, the worldview of the first-century writers of the New Testament or the worldview of its twenty-first-century readers?

PAUL THE VISIONARY

The apostle Paul was a visionary. His letters are full of travel itineraries, expansion plans, fund-raising, and so on. They bear witness to all the requisite skill sets, personality traits, and ambitions of a man determined to change the world—an entrepreneur par excellence. His mission statement was "to preach the Gospel where Christ is not known" (Rom 15:20), and his impact strategy was as shameless as it was effective: "I have become all things to all people so that by all possible means I might save some" (1 Cor 9:22). In the course of his lifetime, the Jesus

> THE HEART IS DECEITFUL ABOVE ALL THINGS AND DESPERATELY SICK; WHO CAN UNDERSTAND IT?
>
> JEREMIAH 17:9

movement snowballed from a tiny, frightened huddle in Palestine to an empire-wide phenomena. History leaves no doubt as to who was primarily responsible: Paul of Tarsus.

But Paul was a visionary in another important sense, one that is inextricably linked to his vocational calling: he was the recipient of numerous revelatory visions that changed the course of his life and altered the path of his travels. Essential for understanding the pivotal function of visionary experiences in Paul's life and ministry is Luke's account in the book of Acts. In fact, if it were not for Acts, the heading "Paul the Visionary" might seem applicable only in terms of Paul's role in the globalization of Christianity.

The central vision of Paul's life—indeed, the central event of Paul's life—was his dramatic encounter with the risen Christ on the road to Damascus. Luke goes out of his way to keep this event in front of the reader, recounting it in detail in Acts 9 and allowing Paul to reiterate it in Acts 22 and Acts 26. Luke is clearly making a point regarding the divine origin of Paul's mission, and this agenda is further promoted by his inclusion of other revelatory events known only from his record of Paul's travels. According to Luke, Paul's vision on the Damascus Road is followed shortly by a second vision. In a remarkable set of circumstances, Luke describes how a Christian in Damascus by the name of Ananias has a vision in which the Lord tells him that Saul (Paul) has had a vision of him!

> AND NOW, CONCERN-
> ING MY VISIONS AND
> REVELATIONS FROM
> THE LORD . . .
>
> 2 CORINTHIANS 12:1
> AUTHOR'S TRANSLATION

> Now there was a disciple at Damascus named Ananias. The Lord said to him in a vision, "Ananias." And he said, "Here I am, Lord." And the Lord said to him, "Rise and go to the street called Straight, and at the house of Judas look for a man of Tarsus named Saul, for behold, he is praying, and he has seen in a vision a man named Ananias come in and lay his hands on him so that he might regain his sight." (Acts 9:10–12 ESV)

This particular vision is unusual in its detail ("he has seen a man named Ananias come and lay hands on him") but does not differ in kind from other revelations granted to Paul that Luke records, especially in imparting knowledge concerning the future. Soon after returning to Jerusalem, Paul is in the temple praying when he enters an altered state of conscience ("I fell into a trance," Acts 22:17)[120] and is told by the Lord that the Jews of Jerusalem are not going to accept his message and that he must leave Jerusalem immediately. It is highly significant that it is in Jerusalem, the city of David, and in the temple, the symbol of God's abiding presence with Israel, that Paul is clearly told, "I will send you far away to the Gentiles" (22:21).

Unlike the temple vision and the Damascus Road appearance, the other revelations given to Paul recorded by Luke occurred at night, presumably as dreams. While in Troas, Paul has a nocturnal vision of a Macedonian pleading for help and so concludes that God was calling him to preach the gospel in Macedonia (Acts 16:9–10). In Corinth, the Lord appears to Paul during the night and encourages him to keep preaching, promising him that "no one is going to attack and harm you" (18:10). Paul then stays in Corinth for another eighteen months. During his imprisonment in Jerusalem and subsequent journey to Rome, Paul twice received nighttime visitations assuring him that he would indeed reach Rome and urging him, "Take courage!" (23:11; cf. 27:24).

> WHETHER I WAS IN THE BODY, OR OUT OF THE BODY, I DO NOT KNOW; GOD KNOWS.
>
> *2 CORINTHIANS 12:3 AUTHOR'S TRANSLATION

Based on the material in Acts, the visions granted to Paul were intended to provide crucial direction in his mission, vital encouragement in his ministry, and critical information regarding impending events. Divination in the Greco-Roman world was pursued for largely the same reasons, but especially for direction and knowledge of the future. The chief difference between Paul and his divining pagan counterparts is that we have no indication that Paul ever deliberately sought out any of his visionary experiences. There are no mysterious ceremonies, no dark rituals, no complicated formulas, no manipulative techniques.

A more important contrast, however, is found when we compare Luke's presentation of Paul the visionary with Paul's own presentation in his letters. As noted earlier, if it were not for the book of Acts we would know nothing of Paul's vision of Ananias, his temple ecstasy, his frequent nighttime revelations, and so on. Moreover, quite unlike Paul in Acts, Paul the letter writer never provides an account of his experience on the Damascus Road. To be sure, his letters contain tantalizing allusions to this event, but even these are only reluctantly offered and seem calculated to conceal as much as they reveal. For example, each of the generally agreed upon allusions in Paul's letters to his bolt

> THEN, FOURTEEN YEARS LATER I WENT UP TO JERUSALEM AGAIN . . . IN RESPONSE TO A REVELATION.
>
> GALATIANS 2:1–2

from the blue on the Damascus Road (1 Cor 9:1; 15:8; 2 Cor 4:4–6; Gal 2:16) is found in contexts where Paul is defending himself; his back is up against the wall, and he finds it necessary to remind his readers of his apostolic credentials. We learn very little of the Damascus Road apocalypse from Paul himself; the information is meager and given almost involuntarily. The same is true of Paul's extraordinary journey to paradise described in 2 Cor 12—an entirely different episode from his conversion vision. Paul is bullied into mentioning this incident by the boasting of his rivals ("I must go on boasting, though there is nothing to be gained by it," 2 Cor 12:1), and after doing so he refuses to relate what he saw (12:4).

Yet, what we do learn from these veiled allusions to Paul's initial encounter with Christ is that, as a result, Paul's cognitive world was turned inside out and upside down. What is striking about these passages is that each features a prominent Christological title which, taken together, provides a synopsis of Paul's highly elevated Christology.[121] In 1 Cor 9:1, Jesus is designated "Lord" (*kurios*); in 15:8, he is called "Messiah" (*christos;* literally, "Anointed One"). In Gal 2:16, he is revealed as God's "Son" (*huios*). Finally, in 2 Cor 4:4–6, he is called "the image of God" (*eikon tou theou*). This accumulation of lofty titles is indicative of the massive reorientation that occurred on the Damascus Road; Paul left Jerusalem with a mandate to persecute Christians and entered Damascus on a mission to proclaim Christ.

The difference in perspective between Luke and Paul allows us to draw one further inference concerning Paul's studied reticence to speak in detail of his revelatory experiences in his letters. While Paul seems willing to tell his story in the defense and proclamation of the gospel, as in Acts 22 and Acts 26, he is keenly aware of the propensity of his new converts to fixate on the flashy and flamboyant side of religious experience rather than on issues of ultimate significance.[122] In fact, Paul is frank about the matter: "But I refrain [from boasting of such experiences] so no one will think more of me than is warranted by what I do or say" (2 Cor 12:6). In his letter to the church at Colossae, Paul openly mocks the man who would "go on in detail about visions he has seen," describing such a person as "puffed up without reason by his sensuous mind" (2:18 ESV). Paul's guarded comments are not primarily evidence of personal modesty but of a pastoral strategy aimed at fostering maturity and perspective in new believers. In a world in which diviners, mediums, and visionaries could command the attention of a large portion of the populace (particularly the uneducated masses) and revelatory experiences were eagerly pursued, Paul refuses to draw attention to such matters, insisting on the priority of the internal over the external: "And if I have prophetic powers and can divine all mysteries and knowledge . . . but do not have love, I am nothing" (1 Cor 13:2 author's translation).

> WE FIND NOTHING WRONG IN THIS MAN. WHAT IF A SPIRIT OR AN ANGEL SPOKE TO HIM?
>
> ACTS 23:9

FURTHER READING

Primary Sources

Plutarch (first century C.E.). *On Superstition.* A treatise comparing the atheist and the superstitious, featuring vivid depictions of the superstitious excesses of the first century. Available in the LCL.

Lucius Apuleius (second century C.E.). *Metamorphoses (The Golden Ass).* The story of Apuleius, who attempts to transform himself into a bird through witchcraft but succeeds only in becoming an ass. He wanders through most the narrative in this form and is finally transformed back into a human by the goddess Isis. *Metamorphoses* contains many picturesque magical scenes and portraits of daily life. Also illuminating is his *Defense against the Charge of Sorcery.* This is Lucius Apuleius's brilliant and successful refutation of the charge that he induced a wealthy widow to marry him by sorcery. The *Metamorphoses* is available though the LCL; the *Defense* is available online at http://ccat.sas.upenn.edu/jod/apuleius/.

Cicero (first century B.C.E.). *On Divination.* Cicero's assessment of the validity of divination, in which he first carefully presents the evidence in support of the art and then thoroughly demolishes that evidence. Available in the LCL.

Philostratus (second-third century C.E.). *The Life of Apollonius of Tyanna.* An account of a first-century charismatic wonder worker, Apollonius, widely revered for his miracles and healings. Available in the LCL.

Valerius Maximus (first century C.E.). *Memorable Doings and Sayings* 1.1–8. A handbook of notable historical incidents containing a wealth of material related to the first-century Roman religious and moral conceptions. Available in the LCL.

Jubilees (second century B.C.E.). The rewriting of Genesis and parts of Exodus by Jews of the period in light of their present domination by Hellenistic kingdoms. An important resource on Jewish demonology and eschatology of the Maccabean era. Available in the *Old Testament Pseudepigrapha,* Edited by James H. Charlesworth. 2 vols. Garden City, N.Y.: Doubleday, 1983.

Songs of the Sabbath Sacrifice (first century B.C.E.). Also known as *Angelic Liturgy,* this hymn from the Dead Sea Scrolls invokes angelic hierarchies and depicts them as present at the worship of the community. It offers an illuminating picture of mysticism and angelology at Qumran. Available in *The Dead Sea Scrolls Translated: The Qumran Texts in English.* Edited by Florentino Garcia Martínez. Translated by W. G. E. Watson. Leiden: Brill Academic Publishing, 1994.

The Greek Magical Papyri in Translation. Edited by Hans Dieter Betz. Chicago: University of Chicago Press, 1997. A collection of ancient magical texts, translated with annotations.

Secondary Sources

Les Adkins and Roy Adkins. *Dictionary of Roman Religion.* Oxford: Oxford University Press, 2001.

Clinton E. Arnold. *Powers of Darkness.* Downers Grove, Ill.: InterVarsity Press, 1992.

Mary Beard. *Religions of Rome,* vol. 1, *A History.* Cambridge: Cambridge University Press, 1998.

John Gager, ed., *Curse Tablets and Binding Spells from the Ancient World.* New York: Oxford University Press, 1992.

Hans-Josef Klauck. *The Religious Context of Early Christianity: A Guide to Graeco-Roman Religions.* Minneapolis: Fortress, 2003.

Georg Luck. *Arcana Mundi: Magic and the Occult in the Greek and Roman Worlds.* 2d ed. Baltimore: John Hopkins University Press, 2006.

Ramsay MacMullen. *Paganism in the Roman World.* New Haven: Yale University Press, 1981.

Jon D. Mikalson. *Ancient Greek Religion.* Oxford: Wiley-Blackwell, 2009.

EDUCATION, PHILOSOPHY, AND ORATORY

HERACLITUS

"But come now, Paulus! It stands against all reason and nature to argue that this very flesh, this paltry body, will rise from the dust. What is death but release from our mortal shackles and a return to God, whence we came? Surely Homer spoke correctly: 'There is no regaining your life, when once your soul escapes through the guard of your teeth.' Even vengeful Achilles understood that! Paulus . . . are you even listening?"

"Yes, I am listening, Heraclitus," came the reply, "and your poet has spoken correctly, in part." The leatherworker turned slowly, pausing to scan the street behind the onlookers who had gathered around the shop. "True enough," he continued, "when death comes, life in this paltry body cannot be regained, but the body that is raised is not like the body that is buried. Does not the cycle of seasons and the harvest teach you this? The paltry seed becomes a stalk of wheat; the acorn becomes an oak. What is sown with the hand is gathered in bushels. Death, Heraclitus, is transformation."

Heraclitus considered this novel line of thought somewhat skeptically, his eyes narrowing in pointed reflection. His own views on the afterlife were far from settled. He had difficulty accepting the notion of Epicurus and his followers that death meant extinction, but neither could he see much sense in the idea that a decrepit body would one day crawl out of the tomb or magically reassemble itself from ashes in a funerary urn. These superstitions of the Jews utterly baffled him—special foods, an imageless god, circumcision, and other nonsense. Still, there was an admirable cogency to this argument that impressed Heraclitus, especially the appeal to the natural order.

Increasingly aware that the eyes of the crowd—including his students—were now fixed on him, Heraclitus pulled himself out of his ruminations and quipped, "So, you imagine yourself Herakles in the next life, do you? Complete with club and lion's mane, I suppose!" The chuckles from the bystanders came as a relief to the schoolmaster, though Heraclitus knew his recourse to sarcasm, albeit mild, was more rhetorical maneuver than philosophical rejoinder. At least one of his students was also unimpressed. Heraclitus noted Phillip's failure to join in the laughter and was not surprised. Phillip, son of Stephanas and Theodora, was not one to be diverted by rhetoric devoid of substance, which was one of the reasons Heraclitus liked him. Phillip reminded Heraclitus of himself.

"What I imagine is hardly relevant, Heraclitus. What I have seen, however," Paulus hesitated, as if considering carefully how to finish his thought, "could never be imagined." An initial snicker from someone in the crowd was smothered by the obvious seriousness of the speaker and the studied silence of Heraclitus, who seemed unwilling to challenge this patently self-authenticating claim.

"'The sky thundered, the cloud descended, and Romulus was snatched away to heaven in the whirlwind,'" mused Heraclitus audibly, though addressing no one in particular. He was looking directly at the leatherworker, though it was not at all clear to those standing nearby what precisely Heraclitus meant or how the rapture of Romulus, the legendary co-founder of Rome, was relevant to the present debate. For Heraclitus's students, however, the far-off gaze, the pondering tone, the obscure literary allusion, were the telltale signs that their *grammaticus* was poised to embark on a philosophical excursus. In the classroom, these were always a welcome reprieve from the drudgery of recitation and the tedious dissection of arcane literary tropes in the tragic poets and comic playwrights—their daily educational fare.

"As for your visions, Paulus," sighed Heraclitus, returning once again to the workshop and the topic at hand, "I'll hear more about that tonight. Right now, the Muse beckons—as you can see, my students are eager to explore metonymy in Menander and litotes in Livius!" Heraclitus's droll wit was not lost on the six or so moppets bobbing around his elbows and shoulders, who heaved a collective groan as their tutor motioned for them to follow promptly.

The sight of Heraclitus parading a troupe of adolescents through the streets of Corinth was a familiar scene to the townsfolk. Cordial nods greeted him as he passed through the forum, under the marble archway leading to the Laeceum Road, and settled his band of toga-clad, wax-tablet-toting youths in the shade of one of the vaulted apses within the courtyard of the fountain of Peirene. Heraclitus preferred the cool enclosure of the Peirene for his late-morning lessons. Although his flat above the north forum was well ventilated and possessed an enviable balcony, it grew uncomfortably warm by mid-morning. The Peirene, by contrast, provided him with a splendid platform to advertise his talents. The fountain of Peirene, the mourning nymph, was regularly filled with a generous assortment of people—townsfolk and tourists seeking a drink, merchants discussing their trade, or city officials grousing about the state of the empire. Whoever they were and for whatever reason they happened to be there, all would see Heraclitus the scholar querying, scolding, cajoling, and occasionally even praising his pupils. With students bent over their scrolls, Heraclitus would answer questions with bravura and erudition, ever mindful of the watchful gaze of potential patrons. Since he had moved to the Peirene, his class size had nearly doubled.

Heraclitus's vocation as a grammaticus was more necessity than preference. His first love was for philosophy, and he even had the good fortune of sitting under the great Musonius Rufus in Rome for nearly a year. But Roman disdain for anything deemed impractical or without obvious political or economic return forced Heraclitus to seek gainful employment as an educator of youth. The real money, as everyone knew, was in oratory; competent teachers of rhetoric could command a handsome salary. Yet Heraclitus's deep suspicions of the inflated pretensions of the sophists, coupled with his somewhat overdramatic temperament, led him to reject the persuasive arts wholesale, even their more noble practitioners. Eventually Heraclitus came to understand his vocation as a providential bestowment of the gods. As opportunity afforded him, he prodded those under his tutelage in the direction of philosophy, denouncing vice and extolling the virtues of a life free from the cares of money, possessions, and concern for reputation. He remembered Musonius saying, "Train yourself to be satisfied with what you have been given." He felt he was finally beginning to appreciate the wisdom of this advice.

Heraclitus and his flock were halted just before the entering the Peirene by a rather outlandish spectacle, but one that was emblematic of the cultural landscape of this cosmopolitan provincial capital: a procession of Isis devotees cavorting and merrymaking through the heart of the city on their way to the goddess's temple at Cenchrea. Leading the religious revelers was a collection of absurdly costumed characters playfully parodying the social hierarchy of Corinth: one came as a gladiator, another as a philosopher, complete with staff, tattered cloak, and beard. Next there was a ghastly fellow in a silk dress and a curly wig, swinging his hips suggestively in every direction. His thick makeup and gaudy jewelry suggested a wealthy—and wanton—matron. A plump mock-magistrate in a purple toga followed, pinching the "woman's" posterior at regular intervals, to the great delight of the onlookers. Heraclitus's students were also snickering and guffawing; his attempt to scowl them into indifference failed miserably, and so he had to content himself with glaring disapprovingly at the passing charade. Next came a centurion, then a fowler, and then an ass with wings strapped to his back in a deliberately feeble impersonation of Pegasus, the winged companion of Belleraphron.

As this burlesque revue concluded, the formal procession of the savior goddess advanced, arranged in ascending order of importance. First came a large company of women dressed in gleaming white gowns, their hair crowned with colorful spring garlands. Some held ivory combs and were adoringly stroking the air as if combing the goddess's divine locks. Others sprinkled perfume and flowers along the parade route; still others had polished bronze mirrors fastened to their backs so as to magnify the image of the approaching goddess. Next came the lightbearers, toting lamps, torches, and candles, symbolic of Isis' role as the source of the heavenly luminaries and enlightener of the soul. Musicians and singers followed closely behind, performing traditional hymns of Isiac worship.

Striking a more solemn tone, but sill celebrative, the new initiates came into view, their linen robes sweeping the marble pavement as they passed. Each held a sistrum, a small metal timbrel that clanged and rattled as the neophytes shook them in praise to the goddess. The female novitiates had their hair wrapped tightly in sheer gauze, while the men were completely shaven, their bald heads glistening in the morning sunlight.

Finally came the priests, carrying the sacred symbols of their faith. The first clutched a golden lamp shaped like sailing vessel. The second bore an altar symbolizing the deity's eagerness to help any who approach her sanctuary. Another carried a golden jar shaped like a swollen breast, from which he poured libations of milk. He was greeting the townsfolk as he passed, chanting, "Isis is the eternal mother of the universe, from whom the milk of new life flows in abundance." As a climax came a priest in the guise of Anubis, the jackal-headed Egyptian god of the underworld. Walking on two feet but wearing an exquisitely crafted likeness of the canine deity on his shoulders, he held aloft a golden statuette of the goddess. Heraclitus mustered a patient smile as the jackal god turned in his direction; as soon as his gaze moved on, however, the schoolmaster snapped his fingers in front of his distracted students and pointed across the street to the courtyard of the Peirene. They moved quickly down the steps and into the fountain square.

"Why do you waste your time with that grubby, circumcised beltmaker," scoffed Julius, just as the rest of the group had settled into their places. Julius's timing was impeccable. One moment later and Heraclitus would have begun his lesson; one moment earlier and the challenge would not have been heard above the chatter of the younger boys. As always, his tone was laced with contempt. Julius, along with Phillip, was one of the older boys and would soon be advancing to the study of rhetoric under Sospinus, who happened to be at the Peirene as well, deep in conversation with Erastus, a local magistrate. Both boys were from wealthy families, but they could hardly be more different in temperament, attitude, and predilections. Oddly, Erastus and Sospinus grew noticeably silent at Julius's comment, almost as if they were interested in hearing Heraclitus's reply.

"And do you suppose that knowledge is confined to the Greeks and Romans, Julius?" countered the grammaticus, unruffled. "Did not Pythagorus travel the world seeking wisdom from wherever he could find it? And what of Simon the shoemaker? He was a mere 'grubby' cobbler, yet even Socrates took notes as Simon mended sandals and discoursed on the nature of truth. Do you imagine yourself more learned than Pythagorus or wiser than Socrates?"

Flustered but not yet spent, Julius retorted, "Of course not, grammaticus, but can anyone claim to be wise who does not also possess eloquence? Is not sound speech the surest index of sound understanding? Cicero and the handbooks make that plain enough. I've heard this Jewish sandal stitcher before, and no one would ever mistake him for anything more than a bungling amateur." He glanced quickly in the direction of Sospinus, who was nodding in agreement. Buoyed by this show of support, Julius added, "And when is eloquence ever found beneath a shabby coat? This Paulus spends most of the day hunched over his workbench like a slave and then has the cheek to address freeborn Romans in the forum. Ridiculous!"

"Your error, young Julius, is that you cannot distinguish between appearance and reality, and thus between form and content." Heraclitus's labored forbearance issued, in part, from his knowledge that Julius had two younger siblings who would soon be requiring a tutor. "Would you discard a pearl because it was presented in a grimy, misshapen oyster? And is it not Hephaestus, the lame, disfigured god, exiled from Olympus, whose forge produces the mightiest and most exquisite weaponry? Externals, you see, are a matter of indifference. Wealth, beauty, health, freedom, lineage, and the like are not intrinsic to moral advance, and so one should not place undue value on possessing them." Julius, who had heard this sermon before, merely stared back incredulously.

Searching the bewildered faces of the younger boys, Heraclitus folded his hands beneath his chin, stooped to eye level, and took his case to those who were still capable of being influenced. "Who is truly free except the one who has mastered his passions and so is free to grow in virtue?" he asked with genuine concern in his expression. "Who is truly rich except the one who possesses courage, honesty, and discernment? Such a man may own nothing and yet possess all things. It is your parents who make you citizens of Corinth or Rome, but it is your integrity that makes you a citizen of the world and a child of Zeus. And which is really the greater kingdom? Which is the more noble lineage?"

The faint lines of a smile that had started to form beneath Erastus's closely-trimmed beard disappeared when his companion, Sospinus, abruptly took up Julius's cause: "Well spoken, grammaticus, but certainly you don't mean to imply that a noble birth and a respectable education are irrelevant to the public good? How does one persuade the assembly of the correct course of action if not through well-chosen words? And how does one acquire the ability to persuade if not through proper study? And how can one receive such training without adequate means? Or are you now offering your lessons for free?"

The bystanders in the fountain precinct had naturally taken an interest in this unexpected entertainment, and, once again, Heraclitus felt the eyes of a watching public bearing down on him. Evincing no little disdain, Heraclitus replied coolly, "Oh yes, I still charge fees, Sospinus, but not nearly as much as some, I'm told." The clear reference to Sospinus's higher fee scale was not lost on the locals in the know, and their audible silence palpably increased the mounting expectation for Sospinus to demonstrate his rhetorical prowess and so vindicate himself and his profession.

Rising to the occasion, Sospinus gathered his toga in his left hand, sauntered forward several steps, and waved his right hand in feigned surrender. "Touché, my dear Heraclitus. I stand guilty as charged. I train the future leaders of our great city in the skills of public leadership and am duly compensated. But isn't this as it should be? Gladiators obtain wealth, honor, and praise in the arena fighting mere men and beasts; how much more should the man who prevails in the public assembly! It is a small matter to vanquish one man with a gladius or a trident. I train men to conquer a thousand. The power of persuasion, Heraclitus, is truly the most formidable force in the universe, rivaling even the bolts of thundering Zeus, and is capable of moving an entire nation. It was not for love of Thessaly that Athens dared to defy Phillip, but because of the flaming tongue of Demosthenes; a fire ignited and fanned by the goddess Peitho herself." Sensing the approval of the onlookers, Sospinus gazed at the admiring crowd and blinked back tears produced especially for his rousing climax: "Without a grammaticus, our city might be bereft of the classics, but without a rhetor, we would have no passion, no direction, no soul! And which would be the greater loss?" His arms, outstretched toward the spectators, now collapsed to his side as if overcome by exhaustion. Applause erupted spontaneously from around the courtyard. Sospinus bowed his head in acknowledgment of their appreciation. Satisfied he had the final word on the subject, the silver-haired orator walked slowly back towards Erastus, pausing to shake several hands that were thrust out from among those stationed nearby.

"A fine peroration, Sospinus, as we have all come to expect." The crowd, which had all but forgotten about Heraclitus, turned to find him nonchalantly adjusting his cloak, seemingly indifferent to Sospinus's verbal wizardry and the verdict rendered by those assembled at the fountain that morning. "No doubt you spent many hours choreographing your gestures, selecting your words, and choosing just the right intonation in case such an occasion should ever arise. And your time was not wasted; no one here would deny it, least of all me—a humble grammaticus schooled only in literature and philosophy. Yet even this modest education is sufficient to make me deeply suspicious of your intentions. Your goal, Sospinus, is to make an impression, and that you do quite well. As for me, I pity the man who seeks to make an impression rather than an impact—the wretched soul who would entertain the world rather than change the world." Turning his back on Sospinus, Heraclitus once again focused his attention on his students. "And when *you* address the court, or the forum, do not strive for applause, and do not expect it. Rather, your goal should be to hear silence—complete, unbroken, earsplitting silence. Only then can you be certain that your message has pierced the hearts of those who heard it. Only then will you have any hope that vice has been uprooted and folly rebuffed. Only if the audience is left examining themselves rather than admiring you will you have any reason to think that the world is a better place because you are in it."

Heraclitus straightened himself upright, deliberately ignoring the crowd that stood mute around the courtyard. As he did so he noticed Phillip to his left, his eyes fixed on Heraclitus, beaming with admiration. Genuinely touched by Phillip's approval, the grammaticus choked back the emotion he felt unexpectedly rising in his breast, cleared his throat, and barked, "Enough dawdling—back to Homer! We left the windy city just as Patroclus fell before Hector. Alexander, begin reciting from, 'and. . . .' enunciating each syllable clearly!"

THE CULTURAL CONTEXT

LITERACY

If you are reading this book, chances are you graduated from high school or an equivalent secondary school and may well have attended a college or university. Statistically, you are one of the most fortunate individuals who has ever lived. Universal and mandatory public education as we find it in the West today is, historically speaking, a relatively recent phenomena and is confined largely to affluent, industrialized societies with stable systems of governance and generous amounts of public funds to devote to the cause. Yet most of the world's population today do not live in such societies, and so many countries around the globe struggle with illiteracy rates as high as 50, 60, and even 70%.[1]

> I, ZOLIUS SON OF HORUS HAVE WRITTEN THIS CONTRACT FOR PTOLEMAEUS, BECAUSE HE IS ILLITERATE.
>
> APPRENTICESHIP CONTRACT

Literacy and education in the ancient Mediterranean world were similar in many respects to the situation of some of the poorest nations today. Secondary and tertiary education was virtually the exclusive privilege of the elite establishment: wealthy, enfranchised, freeborn males. The economic, social, and ideological conditions necessary for widespread literacy did not exist in ancient societies,[2] as they still do not exist in many contemporary societies. Economically, there was no middle class; the vast majority people lived at or below the poverty level (see City and Society: Class and Status). Writing materials could be expensive, and even the nominal fees charged by most tutors were beyond the reach of many. Socially, the world of first-century Rome had little enthusiasm for the democratic, egalitarian ideals of modern Western societies. The scrupulously observed social hierarchy of the Roman Empire necessitated the marginalization of the unlettered masses, who had little opportunity to improve their lot. Moreover, the ancient world was not a textual world, as is ours. Our world is bulging with newspapers, magazines, journals, flyers, mailings, bestsellers, and landfills, but this was not the world of the first century. Gutenberg's press was still fourteen hundred years away,

> NOR CAN THE PHILOSOPHER TRUST THE MASSES, FOR THEY ARE UNEDUCATED.
>
> *CYNIC EPISTLES

> THE REASON WHY MORE HERBS ARE NOT FAMILIAR IS BECAUSE THEIR USE IS CONFINED TO ILLITERATE COUNTRY FOLK, WHICH IS THE ONLY TYPE OF COUNTRY FOLK THERE ARE.
>
> PLINY THE ELDER

and mass printing was not even a fantasy that could be imagined.

Ideologically, the most important factor in promoting literacy in the West was the Protestant Reformation, with its emphasis on the common folk being able to read the Bible in their own language. Yet Greco-Roman religions were not centered around a sacred text; there was no holy writ to be studied, copied, memorized, and transmitted.

> BUT YOU KNOW THAT TIMOTHY HAS PROVED HIMSELF, BECAUSE AS A SON WITH HIS FATHER HE HAS SERVED WITH ME IN THE WORK OF THE GOSPEL.
>
> PHILIPPIANS 2:22 ESV

EDUCATION

Any overview of education in the Greco-Roman world is obliged to simplify and synthesize the varied practices of nearly fifty million people from dozens of nations on several continents—obviously a Herculean task. Yet the Hellenization, and later Romanization, of the ancient world helped promote a widespread educational model that can be depicted at least in its ideal form, even if the ideal was rarely perfectly applied, especially the further one ventured outside the major population centers. Comum, for example, a town in northern Italy, did not even have a school until Pliny urged parents to pool their resources to hire a teacher, pledging his own financial support to the cause.[3] We moderns must bear in mind that most children in antiquity had little or no formal schooling. Boys learned a trade from their father or were apprenticed to a local tradesman. Girls were taught to manage a household and were married young (see Household and Family: The Family).

> AS A BOY PERTINAX WAS TAUGHT BASIC LITERATURE AND ARITHMETIC, AND WAS ALSO ENTRUSTED TO A GRAMMATICUS AND THEN TO THE SCHOLAR SULPICIUS APOLLINARIUS. PERTINAX THEN SET HIMSELF UP AS A GRAMMATICUS, BUT WHEN THE INCOME PROVED TOO LITTLE, HE APPLIED FOR A COMMISSION AS A CENTURION.
>
> FROM THE AUGUSTAN HISTORY

The Roman educational ideal is best articulated by the vainglorious Apuleius as he enumerates but a few of his thousand perfections:

> The first cup of the Muses is given by the master who teaches you to read and redeems you from ignorance; the second is given by the teacher of literature and equips you with learning; the third arms you with the eloquence of the rhetorician. Of these three cups, most men drink. I, however, have drunk yet other cups at Athens—the imaginative draught of poetry, the clear draught of geometry, the

sweet draught of music, the more austere draught of dialectic, and the nectar of philosophy, of which no person drinks enough.[4]

Apuleius, writing from the second century, identifies three stages in what he considers to be the typical educational curriculum, portraying each as successive cups of wine given at a dinner party hosted by Muses, the goddesses of literature and the arts. The first represents "the master" (*ludi magister*), who teaches reading, the second the *grammaticus,* who teaches grammar and literature, and the third the *rhetor,* who teaches eloquence. These stages correspond roughly to what we would call primary, secondary, and tertiary (higher) education. The true renaissance man, exemplified by Apuleius, adds to these the refinements of the arts and, most importantly, philosophy.

Primary and Secondary Education

Formal primary education began at about age seven and concentrated on reading, writing, and basic computation.[5] Families with means might hire a private tutor.[6] Those with little means, who were the majority, would either teach their children themselves (if they were literate) or place them under the tutelage of a local schoolmaster. The typical school day would start at dawn and would continue, with breaks for sport at the gymnasium or palaestra, till evening. A household slave known as a *paedagogus* (literally, "child guide," see Gal 3:24) would accompany the student to and from class to ensure he arrived on time and got into no mischief.

> THIS FATE, TOO, AWAITS YOU, THAT STAMMERING AGE WILL COME UPON YOU AS YOU TEACH BOYS THEIR A, B, Cs AT THE ENDS OF THE CITY STREETS.
>
> HORACE

A wide variety of venues were used for instruction, including temples, public squares, rented accommodation, or the private apartment of the teacher. Martial complains bitterly of his neighbor, the "cursed schoolmaster," who held class in his apartment and robbed Martial and his neighbors of sleep with all the clamor and shouting:

> The cocks have not yet broken silence and already you make a din with your savage roaring and your thwacks. . . . We your neighbors ask for sleep—not all night through; to lie awake is nothing much, but to lie awake all night is a cross. Dismiss your pupils![7]

The cramped living quarters of all but the very well-off, coupled with the mild climate of the Mediterranean, meant that the public squares, temples, fountains, and the like were frequently used for primary and secondary education. Suetonius's description of the *grammaticus* Lenaeus, who set up shop "near the temple of Tellus" in Rome, or Dio's passing reference to "elementary teachers who sit in the streets with their pupils,"[8] give the impression that this was a typical scene in the cities of Greece and Rome. A fictitious yarn from the Cynic epistles has Diogenes wandering into the marketplace in Corinth, where he encounters a group of students who, in his opinion, "were reciting rather poorly." Diogenes takes it upon himself to wait for their teacher, Dionysius, the former ruler of Syracuse, whom he hails with the greeting, "Dionysius, how awful that you are teaching!"[9] The biting double entendre was lost on the dim-witted ex-tyrant.

By the age of eleven or twelve, once the requisite skills of literacy had been mastered, the student was ready for more serious study of literature with the *grammaticus.* According to the historian Suetonius, who wrote a short but informative treatise on the *grammaticus,* many of the early *grammatici* in Rome were freedmen (former slaves) who found their way into the profession after manumission. One formerly held a priesthood, and another had been a soldier.[10] Lucius Crassicius left the theater for the schoolhouse, Pomponius Marcellus hung up his boxing gloves, and Remmis Palaemon sold his weaver's loom.[11] The common denominator in these biographies is that each was able to obtain an education and was then able to leave a less desirable vocation—usually involving physical labor—and don the mantle of a schoolmaster. Petronius tells similar tales of slaves who bettered themselves through schooling and concludes with the maxim, "Education is a treasure."[12]

Some *grammatici* did become successful and gained fame. Quintus Remmius Palaemon, the erstwhile weaver, attained an annual income of four hundred thousand sesterces from his school.[13] This, however, was exceptional and could occur only in large, densely populated cities like Rome, Ephesus, or Alexandria. Suetonius more often speaks of dire poverty. Marcus Pomplilius Andronicus was forced to sell his library to make ends meet; Lucius Orbililus lived in an attic; Gaius Julius Hyginus survived on handouts from wealthy friends; Publius Valerius Cato died destitute, "buried in a little hovel."[14] This corroborates the picture painted by other writers and illustrated in the lament of a later epigrammist:

> Teaching "the wrath of Achilles" was the cause of pernicious poverty to me too, since I adopted the profession of a *grammaticus.* Would that that "wrath" had killed me with the Greeks, before the bitter hunger of teaching grammar had put an end to me.[15]

As alluded to in this epigram, the curriculum of the *grammaticus* gave special attention to Homer but also included a healthy assortment of other poets and playwrights: Menander, Aesop, Euripides, and others. Lessons concentrated on grammatical analysis of nouns and verbs, recitation and memorization of texts, and correct enunciation of words.[16] The purpose of this curricular focus was to equip the budding orator with a repository of apposite illustrations that he could articulate with elegance and ease. As one might expect from this approach, the childhood *grammaticus* was most often remembered for his punctilious concern for grammatical trivialities and his hypercritical treatment of even the most acclaimed writers and orators. Typical of this censure is the epigram of Antiphanes, quoted here with my own explanatory glosses:

> AS FOR NECESSARY READING, HOMER COMES FIRST AND IN THE MIDDLE AND LAST, IN THAT HE GIVES TO EVERY BOY AND ADULT AND OLD MAN JUST AS MUCH AS EACH OF THEM CAN TAKE.
>
> DIO CHRYSOSTOM

Idly curious race of grammarians, you who dig up by the roots [critically examine] the poetry of others; unhappy bookworms that walk on thorns [delight in difficult passages], defilers of the great [criticizing renowned writers], proud of your Erinna [a sophisticated poet], bitter and dry dogs set on by Callimachus [another poet], bane of poets [on account of the grammarian's criticism], darkness to little beginners [dreaded by students], away with you bugs that secretly bite the eloquent [disparage their betters].[17]

For Lucilius, another writer of epigrams, simply the memory of his *grammaticus* was enough to induce stammering and grammatical gaffes: "If I only think of the grammarian Heliodorus, my tongue at once commits solecisms and I suffer from a speech impediment."[18] Not even the emperor was exempt from the nitpicking scrutiny of the *grammaticus,* as Suetonius relates: "Once, when a noted grammarian criticized a word in one of Tiberius' speeches, Ateius Capito declared, 'It is perfectly good Latin. And if not, it surely will be from now on!'"[19]

Hand in hand with this penchant for faultfinding were the harsh methods employed by the *grammaticus.* While one occasionally runs across fond recollections of school days,[20] and Horace even mentions one *grammaticus* who used sweets as an incentive,[21] more common by far is the painful memory of rods, verbal abuse, and caning. Horace's nickname for his own teacher was "the flogger."[22] Quintilian, perhaps the most successful rhetorician of his day, roundly condemns the "shameful abuse" of young students through corporal punishment so common among Roman schoolmasters.[23] The "rod of school days,"[24] which Apuleius refers to, is vividly illustrated by a wall painting from Pompeii that shows a young lad held in position by his classmates in front of his teacher and fellow students while being thrashed by his

> ZEONIS KEEPS MENANDER THE BEARDED GRAMMATICUS, AND SAYS SHE HAS ENTRUSTED HER SON TO HIM; BUT HE NEVER STOPS AT NIGHT MAKING HER PRACTICE CASES, CONJUNCTIONS, FIGURES, AND CONJUGATIONS.
>
> GREEK ANTHOLOGY

paedagogus on his bare buttocks—and this in a public portico with onlookers strolling by.[25]

The bad-tempered *grammaticus* became a common stereotype in first-century literature. Martial's description of the "savage roaring" of the schoolmaster that was "hateful to girls and boys"[26] is echoed by many and epitomized in the epigram, "None of the grammarians can ever be moderate, as from the very beginning he has 'wrath,' and 'spite,' and 'bile.'"[27] It is no wonder that Seneca marveled, "It is the hottest-tempered schoolmaster who contends that one should never lose one's temper."[28]

> WORK HARD, BOY, LEST YOU BE THRASHED.
>
> A WARNING COPIED FOUR TIMES BY THE STUDENT

Tertiary Education

The final phase of Greco-Roman education (for the small minority who continued) began around the age of fifteen or sixteen and consisted of training in rhetoric and oratory. The rudiments of public speaking had already been introduced by the *grammaticus*. His attention to proper diction and elocution was always with an eye to the future orator. It was the *rhetor*, however, who was charged with transforming the literate, pubescent teen into the articulate, eloquent citizen.

With this lofty goal in mind, the *rhetor* placed before his pupils a series of "preliminary training exercises" (*progymnasmata*) intended to develop the requisite skills of composition, invention, argumentation, and critical analysis.[29] These exercises gradually developed into a set curriculum of fourteen types of speeches that prepared the student for public declamation and, eventually perhaps, a career in politics or litigation. A sampling of these include Fable (*mythos*), which consisted of retelling an ancient myth; Narration (*diēgēma*), narrating real or fictitious events; Refutation (*anaskeuē*), refuting an untenable argument; Praise (*enkōmium*), commending admirable people, deeds, or virtues; and Comparison (*synkrisis*), comparing two persons or things for the purpose of praise or censure.

> IF CICERO PAINS YOU, YOU'LL TAKE A BEATING!
>
> SCHOOLHOUSE GRAFFITO, POMPEII

Once these rudiments were thoroughly mastered, the students graduated to declamation, where they were charged with the construction of complete orations on specified themes. These speeches were of two types: *suasoriae* and *controversiae*. The *suasoriae* were considered easier for the beginning pupil and addressed dilemmas faced by an ancient or mythological character.[30] Should Alexander sail into the unknown in search of further conquests?[31] Should the Spartans give up the pass at Thermopylae in the face of Xerxes' Persian horde?[32] Should Cicero capitulate to Antony and burn his own writings, thus saving his life?[33] And so on. The historicity of the proposed quandary was not important. What mattered was the inventiveness and rhetorical prowess of the pupil. Dio

Chrysostom delivered a declamation in which he "proved" to his audience that the Greeks did not defeat and sack Troy—a proposition accepted by no one among his listeners.[34]

The *controversiae* dealt with complicated legal questions and were usually contrived in such a way as to be almost wholly unrelated to common judicial proceedings. For example: Ostian fishermen agree to sell their catch to certain fishmongers from Rome. The money is paid, the fishermen pull in their nets but find no fish; instead, there is a chest of gold. To whom does it belong?[35] Even more preposterous: a father refuses to ransom his son who has been captured by pirates. The pirate chief's daughter intercedes for the captive, and the chief agrees to free the young man on the condition that he marry his daughter, which he does. When he returns home, his father insists that he divorce the girl for a more advantageous match of the father's choosing. The son refuses. Who is in the right?[36]

> THE CONTROVER-
> SIAE ARE ASSIGNED
> TO RIPER SCHOLARS
> AND, GOOD HEAV-
> ENS! WHAT STRANGE
> AND ASTONISHING
> PRODUCTIONS—SUB-
> JECTS REMOTE FROM
> ALL REALITY ARE AC-
> TUALLY USED FOR
> DECLAMATION.
>
> *TACITUS

Many of the principled literati objected to these absurd concoctions as useless for training men for real litigation. Quintilian held the rhetoricians responsible for the declining standards of the profession: "The actual practice of declamation has degenerated to such an extent owing to the fault of our teachers. . . . For we shall hunt in vain among actual court cases for magicians and plagues and oracles and cruel stepmothers, and other subjects more unreal than these."[37] Petronius is even more blunt:

> I believe that college makes complete fools of our young men, because they see and hear nothing of ordinary life there. Yes, its tyrants writing edicts ordering sons to cut off their father's heads, or oracles in time of pestilence demanding the blood of three virgins, or more—flowery, honey-coated nonsense. People who are fed of this diet can no more be sensible than people who live in a kitchen can smell good.[38]

Despite the far-fetched and artificial nature of these standard themes—and many more could be cited—this type of declamation became extremely popular in the late republic and early empire, and not just among students and their teachers. The elder Seneca's collection of *suasoriae* and *controversiae* probably derive from public gatherings of rhetors sparring with each other in their treatment of these familiar, if improbable, scenarios.[39] From these schoolroom exercises evolved recreational and professional declamation in which orators and legal practitioners would declaim for display in order to attract students or clients. Declamation became an end in itself, reveling in its own beauty and opulent loquacity. One predictable result is that the courtroom sometimes became merely an exhibition of the mental and verbal agility of the orator, as this client complains concerning his hired counsel:

> I lost a little pig and a cow and a nanny-goat, and on account of them you received your little fee, Menecles [a lawyer]. But what have I to do with Othryades, or the three-hundred from Thermopylae? My suit is against Eutychides, so how can the Xerxes and the Spartans help me? I beg of you, mention my name just for the sake of good form![40]

These conditions created an optimal environment for the revival of an ancient and controversial form of oratory which, in its original manifestation, aroused the ire of Plato himself: sophistry.

THE SECOND SOPHISTIC

The sophists of Plato's day (fifth-century B.C.E. Athens) were teachers of rhetoric and argumentation who trained young men for a career in politics. Many were itinerant, collecting fees for their services from the students they gathered around them. They were extremely popular and could attain great wealth. Plato's objections to the sophists, usually placed on the lips of his teacher, Socrates, were numerous.[41] He mocked their pretensions to wisdom (the Greek word for *sophist* is derived from Greek word meaning "wise"),[42] he ridiculed their choice of verbose speechifying over dialectical debate,[43] and he was appalled at their practice of charging fees for their "wisdom."[44] Yet Plato's most fundamental objection was their employment of oratory not in pursuit of justice and truth but in order to please the crowd, line their own pockets, and enhance their reputation.[45] Indeed, if Plato can be trusted, the sophistic orators of his day did not need to be convinced of the truth of the position they were advancing or even possess in-depth knowledge of their subject matter. Their sole concern was to persuade, and so their knowledge need not extend beyond discovering the necessary means of persuasion. Plato, however, believed that all speech should aim at "nurturing the soul"[46] and that the speaker should be motivated not by what is expedient but by what is "pleasing to the gods."[47] Anything short of this, reasoned the great philosopher, is the blind leading the blind.[48]

> ALAS, WE LEARN OUR LESSONS, NOT FOR LIFE, BUT FOR THE LECTURE-ROOM.
>
> SENECA

> SOCRATES: IF A SPEECH IS TO BE GOOD, MUST NOT THE MIND OF THE SPEAKER KNOW THE TRUTH ABOUT THE MATTERS OF WHICH HE IS TO SPEAK? PHAEDRUS: ON THAT POINT, SOCRATES, I HAVE HEARD THAT ONE WHO IS TO BE AN ORATOR DOES NOT NEED TO KNOW WHAT IS REALLY JUST, BUT WHAT WOULD SEEM JUST TO THE CROWD.
>
> PLATO

Although roughly five centuries had passed between the sophists of ancient Greece and the sophists of first-century Rome, little had changed in terms of their manners and methods, nor had they managed to gain the respect of the high-minded philosophers.[49] Yet, the opinion of establishment philosophy mattered little to the sophists when compared with the adoration of the masses who flocked to admire their florid oratorical arrangements. This sophistic renaissance has come to be known as "the second-sophistic," a designation originally given by Philostratus in his third-century biographical work, *Lives of the Sophists.*[50] The popularity of sophists and other virtuoso orators in the ancient world would be comparable to movie stars or pop-music icons in the modern world. Indeed, Dio Chrysostom lumps entertainers and sophists together when he speaks of the crowds that hang about "sophists, flute-players, and choir-masters."[51] Philo's contemptuous description of "the vast number of those called sophists" who were "winning the admiration of city after city . . . drawing nearly the whole world to honor them for their crafty argumentation"[52] betrays more than professional resentment; it reveals a society fixated on rhetorical prowess and beguiled by expert practitioners of the art.

> REJOICE THAT A THOUSAND EYES SURVEY YOU AS YOU SPEAK.
>
> HORACE

It is difficult to fully appreciate the reputation, wealth, and power of those orators who were at the top of their profession. Marcus Aper, himself a highly sought-after courtroom pleader, speaks with authority when he says, "It is impossible to imagine [any career] richer in advantages, more splendid in its prospects, more attractive in fame at home, more illustrious in celebrity throughout our whole empire and all the world."[53] Lucian's tongue-in-cheek advice to the aspiring orator hardly overstates the matter: "Just see how many who were previously nobodies have come to be accounted men of standing, millionaires, even gentlemen, because of their eloquence."[54] Philostratus corroborates this appraisal as he recounts intercity rivalry over local sophists, statuary erected in honor of prominent orators, political appointments and embassies awarded to sophists, and especially the cozy relationships that often existed between sophists and emperors. In one story, the emperor Trajan turns to Dio Chrysostom and gushes, "I do not understand what you are saying, but I love you as myself!"[55] Even the sophist Favorinus's infamous quarrel with the emperor Hadrian only under-

> YOU HAVE SO MANY DELIGHTFUL SPECTACLES TO BEHOLD: ORATORS, WRITERS, POETS, AND, LIKE GORGEOUS PEACOCKS, SOPHISTS IN GREAT NUMBERS, MEN WHO ARE LIFTED ALOFT AS ON WINGS BY THEIR FAME AND THEIR DISCIPLES.
>
> *DIO CHRYSOSTOM

scores the influence and impact of this man in the inner precincts of power in the Roman world.[56]

The crowds that would attend the declamations of notable orators and sophists, cooing their approval and shouting "How divine!" or "Spoken like a god!"[57] reinforced the speaker's high opinion of himself and provided vivid proof of the voracious appetite of the general public for the verbal delicacies these rhetoricians served up. Lucius Apuleius, scanning the eager faces of a packed theater in Carthage, begins his declamation by modestly observing, "You have come in such numbers to hear me that I feel I ought to congratulate Carthage for possessing so many friends of learning among her citizens!"[58]

> GIVEN BY GREAT HERODES ATTICUS, [AN ORATOR] PREEMINENT ABOVE OTHERS, WHO HAD ATTAINED THE PEAK OF EVERY KIND OF EXCELLENCE . . . FAMOUS AMONG THE HELLENES AND FURTHERMORE A SON [OF GREECE] GREATER THAN THEM ALL, THE FLOWER OF ACHAIA.
>
> *INSCRIPTION, CORINTH

As Lucius Apuleius too perfectly illustrates, the doting throngs, the heady political connections, the celebrity status, and the red-carpet treatment so inflated the ego of the orator that conceit became an occupational hazard of sophistry. Such was Apuleius's confidence that he could assume that there must be many among his listeners who either envied him or hated him because "there are always those who prefer to abuse rather than imitate persons better than themselves."[59] Not that Lucius Apuleius was overly concerned about his detractors: "It is not that I lack praise," he informs his audience, "for my glory has long bloomed fresh and bright."[60] Lucius's boasting was hardly atypical, as Favorinus's speech to the Corinthians illustrates. After discovering that a statue the Corinthians had erected in honor of his eloquence had been removed, Favorinus reminds the Corinthians of his superior lineage, athletic prowess, wisdom, and eloquence, and concludes, "Ought [I] not have a bronze statue here in Corinth? Yes! And in every city!"[61] Aelius Aristides, in defending oratory against its most formidable ancient critic, Plato, compared orators to rulers and concludes,

> THE SERIOUS STUDENT SHOULD REGARD FLOWERY, LAVISH LANGUAGE AND THEATRICAL AND SPECTACULAR SUBJECT MATTER AS THE DOMAIN OF DILETTANTES AND SOPHISTS, AND STEER CLEAR OF IT.
>
> PLUTARCH

"All rulers are by nature superior to those beneath them."[62] No wonder that Philostratus, in a rare moment of unpartisan candor, labels the entire sophistic vocation "a profession prone to egotism and arrogance."[63] This was the verdict of many philosophers and social critics who were utterly baffled at the appeal of these pretentious showmen.

THE PHILOSOPHIC CRITIQUE OF SOPHISTRY

As noted ealier, the feud between philosophy and rhetoric was at least as old as Plato, yet the main lines of the battle had changed remarkably little in the intervening centuries. The essential philosophic criticism of sophistry and sophistic-styled oratory as practiced in the first and second century was its orientation toward the superficial and the ephemeral. Its practitioners were more concerned with hearing the applause of the audience than improving the character of the audience; their declamations had become the ultimate example of form dominating over content. In the words of Persius, so much oratory was simply "frothy inflated stuff, like an old bough smothered under the weight of its bloated bark!"[64]

> BY JUPITER! ONE MAN ACTUALLY ASKS TO READ PLATO, NOT IN ORDER TO BETTER HIS LIFE, BUT TO DECK OUT HIS DICTION AND STYLE—NOT TO GAIN IN DISCRETION BUT IN PRETTINESS!
>
> AULUS GELLIUS

Impression versus Impact

Epictetus, a stoic philosopher and younger contemporary of Paul, was one voice among many conscientious objectors to sophistic oratory as merely a public display of the orator's vanity. In a discourse entitled "For Those Who Read and Discuss for Display," Epictetus decries those who have perfected "the art of selecting trivial phrases . . . who recite them gracefully, and then in the midst of the delivery shout out, 'There are not many people who can follow this, by your lives, I swear it!'"[65] Knowing full well, however, that verbal communication was the stock in trade of both the sophist and the philosopher, Epictetus enjoined his students to continually inquire of themselves whenever they addressed a crowd, "Do I wish to do good, or to be praised?"[66]

> JUST LOOK AT OUR BUDDING ORATORS . . . BRAIDING THE HAIR, REFINING THE VOICE TILL IT IS AS CARESSING AS A WOMAN'S, COMPETING IN BODILY SOFTNESS WITH WOMEN, BEAUTIFYING THEMSELVES WITH FILTHY FINERIES.
>
> SENECA THE ELDER

The philosopher, Epictetus argues, is like a physician, and his lecture room is a hospital: "You should not walk out of it in pleasure, but in pain."[67] Far from marveling over the cleverness of the speaker, the listener should leave examining his own soul, convinced of his "evil plight" and "self-conceit,"[68] saying to himself, "I must not act like this any longer!"[69] With delicious mockery Epictetus lampoons these cheap peddlers of eloquence who compete with each other for the attention of the crowds and with every rehearsed intonation and contrived emotion implore their listeners, "Just praise me . . . cry out to me 'Bravo!'

or 'Marvelous!'"[70] Indeed, Aelius Aristides is remembered as one "who could not control his anger against those who did not applaud his lectures."[71] Epictetus urges his students to soberly weigh their motives: "When you are in such a state as this, gaping for men to praise you and counting the number of your audience, is it your wish to do good to others?"[72]

This shameless craving for admiration led to the practice of hiring, as Pliny calls them, "bravo-callers," who, for a fee, would attend their patron's lecture and applaud on cue.[73] The philosopher, however, cares nothing for the approval of the masses, insists Epictetus; on the contrary, he scorns their applause.[74] His sole aim is "to show to the individual, as well as to the crowd, the warring inconsistency in which they are floundering. . . . For they want what leads to happiness, but they are looking in the wrong place."[75]

Equally disturbing to Epictetus and many others was the flamboyant manner of dress and meticulous personal grooming that was so in vogue among the sophists. Epictetus addresses the issue in a lecture entitled "On Personal Adornment."[76] Here he describes a young orator from Corinth who was "elaborately dressed . . . and whose attire in general was highly embellished."[77] Flashy jewelry and a perfect coif completed his ensemble, that was draped over skin plucked of any bodily hair.[78] Obsessive attention to appearances was not confined to the ranks of the sophists but was prevalent among orators generally, who daily faced the scrutiny of the watching public. In Tacitus's *Dialogue on Oratory*, a work discussing the declining standards of first-century oratory, Vipstanus Messala advises, "It is better for an orator to wear drab clothing than to glitter in multi-colored and gaudy attire . . . which is adopted by many of the speakers of our age."[79] Lucian's tongue-in-cheek checklist of what one needed to become a truly successful orator is summarized in the exhortation, "First of all, you must pay especial attention to outward appearance."[80] As for the particulars of Lucian's guide to fashion chic:

> "YOU ARE A THIEF!" SAYS THE ACCUSED TO [THE ORATOR] PEDIUS. HOW DOES PEDIUS REPLY? HE BALANCES THE CHARGES AGAINST EACH OTHER IN SMOOTH ANTITHESES, AND IS PRAISED FOR HIS ARTISTIC TROPES . . .
>
> PERSIUS

> Let your clothing be gaily-colored, or else white, a fabric of Tarentine manufacture, so that your body will show through; and wear either high Attic sandals of the kind that women wear, with many slits, or else Sicyonian boots, trimmed with strips of white felt.[81]

Lucius Apuleius's portrayal of Apollo as the ideal orator is the look to which many aspired: "a fair and smooth body . . . his hair smoothed and plastered into tufts and curls that fall about his brow . . . eloquent in prose or verse."[82] No wonder that Dio Chrysostom could caricature the lot as "gorgeous peacocks,"[83] and Juvenal could ask without fear of being gainsaid, "When is eloquence ever found under a shabby coat?"[84] Indeed, it was the plain garb of the philosopher that distinguished him from the sophist, which is why the prosecutor in Apuleius's trial for sorcery disputed his claim to be a philosopher—he looked too good![85]

Form versus Content

The conceits of the sophists might have been tolerated had they applied their talents to noble causes and sought to improve the masses who flocked to hear them. More often than not, however, their orations were merely "the jingle of empty words,"[86] pleasing to the ear but of little ultimate consequence. Consider, for example, the twenty-six partial orations of Lucius Apuleius that have survived in his *Florida* (Latin for "flowery"). This corpus includes such meaningful themes as "Ode to a Wayside Shrine," "In Praise of a Theater," "The Beauty of the Parrot," and "A Eulogy for the Proconsul." Only two of these twenty-six orations might be construed as socially or morally beneficial,[87] and at least four of them could be accurately entitled "In Praise of Me."[88]

> THOSE WHO DO COME BEFORE YOU CLAIMING TO BE MEN OF CULTURE DECLAIM SPEECHES INTENDED MERELY FOR DISPLAY—AND STUPID ONES TO BOOT.
>
> *DIO CHRYSOSTOM

The sophist's addiction to the approval of the crowds resulted in syrupy orations confected to please the adolescent tastes of the crowds, with more attention given to style than to substance. Philostratus's candid assessment of the sophist Antipater as one who "let the rhythmic effects of his style dissipate the vigor of his ideas"[89] identifies a problem endemic to the profession. Tacitus, recording the criticism of Messala, warns against "the style which is being adopted by many speakers ... with its idle redundancy of words, its meaningless phrases and license of expression, imitates the art of the actor."[90] This is certainly what Pseudo-Plutarch had in mind in advising, "One should always be careful to avoid the theatrical and melodramatic style ... and avoid triviality and vulgarity in style."[91]

> SO THERE FLARED UP AMONG THE SOPHISTS THAT USELESS AND SUPERFLUOUS "WISDOM" OF THEIRS—IN THEIR OWN OPINION INVINCIBLE—THOSE CLEVER BAFFLING ABSURD REPLIES AND PERPLEXING MAZY QUERIES.
>
> LUCIAN

The concern underlying much of this criticism is well articulated by Pliny, who recognized that even intelligent listeners can be "seduced by the pleasures of the ear" and the "charm and skill" of the delivery and abandon their critical faculties.[92] In lamenting the popularity of sophistry over philosophy, Plutarch complains that the naïve and undiscerning "do not keep in view the life, the actions, and the conduct of a man who follows philosophy, but rate as matters for commendation points of style, phrasing, and a fine delivery—whether it be useful or useless."[93] The potential for self-serving manipulation was a real danger in Plutarch's view, especially as "most sophists not only use words to conceal their thoughts, but they so sweeten their voice by certain harmonious modulations and softenings and rhythmic cadences to ravish away and transport their hearers."[94] The sophists' use of "words to conceal their thoughts" highlights another common objection to sophistry, and one which constitutes the chief legacy of its ancient practitioners: trickery and deceit.

Duplicity versus Sincerity

One contemporary dictionary defines sophistry as "plausible but fallacious argumentation" and a sophist as "one skilled in elaborate and devious argumentation."[95] The harshly negative overtones of contemporary usage are rooted in the historical reality of sophists as those who delighted in convoluted and crafty reasoning. In fact, trickery and guile could, arguably, be considered the defining characteristics of first-century sophistry, so much so that by the second century the orator Titus Castricius considered deception a professional prerogative:

> It is the orator's privilege to make statements that are untrue, daring, crafty, deceptive and sophistical, provided they have some semblance of truth and can by any artifice be made to insinuate themselves into the minds of the persons who are to be influenced.[96]

The criticism of sophists as intellectual charlatans who relied more on wiliness than wisdom is so widespread in the ancient sources it hardly needs to be established.[97] No one, however, was more vociferous in voicing this complaint than Philo, Paul's contemporary in Alexandria. Not unlike the dictionary entry above, Philo defines a sophist as "one who labors to devise what is persuasive for establishing a false opinion"[98] and sophistry as "studying the art of words in opposition to truth."[99]

Philo and the Sophists

The sophists in Philo's writings are emblematic of everything amiss in the world. They are hypocrites who preach virtue while practicing vice,[100] they are quarrelsome and contradict one another,[101] they are verbal exhibitionists who

FOR THE NAME "AMORITES" MEANS "TALKERS," BEING A SYMBOL OF THOSE WHO TALK TOO MUCH. THEIR LEADER IS THE LECTURER OR SOPHIST, SKILLED AT SEARCHING AFTER VERBAL ARTIFICES, BY WHICH THOSE WHO TRANSGRESS THE BOUNDARIES OF TRUTH ARE DECEIVED.

PHILO

parade their knowledge when, in fact, they know little.[102] The irony of the sophists for Philo is that, although their name means "wisdom," they embody its opposite.[103] The sophists provide for Philo a convenient cipher representing all the antagonists of the Jewish Scriptures: Ishmael, Baalam, the Amorites, the Egyptian sorcerers, and even the serpent in the garden.[104]

> HE NEVER WENT TO SCHOOL, BUT I EDUCATED HIM BY SENDING HIM AROUND TO THE PHILOSOPHERS HANGING ABOUT IN THE MARKET.
>
> PETRONIUS

Yet for all this, Philo's most consistent criticism of the Alexandrian sophists is deceit and trickery, especially evidenced by their crafty argumentation. The "sophistries of deceitful speech"[105] is a Philonic refrain that quickly begins to grate. The sophist is a "lover of disputations" whose arguments are designed only "to deceive and perplex people."[106] Not only in Alexandria, but "everywhere," sophists "annoy the ears of those whom they meet by discussing with minute accuracy, and expounding precisely all expressions of a double and ambiguous character."[107] As one who "rejoices in disputatious arguments", the reasoning of the sophist is characterized by the "adulteration of the truth."[108] So vile were the sophists to Philo that he could include sophistry without comment in his catalog of vices relating to dishonesty: "deceit, cajolery, trickery, *sophistry*, pretence, and hypocrisy."[109]

While many more texts could be adduced to illustrate Philo's disdain for all things sophistic, we needn't belabor the point. One might argue that Philo's histrionics represent an idiosyncratic obsession that borders on sensationalism. Perhaps. It remains true, however, that the portrayal of the sophists in the surviving literature is overwhelmingly negative, and Philo's somewhat cartoonish caricature finds numerous echoes in other first- and second-century writers.

PHILOSOPHICAL SCHOOLS

Philosophy was born in Greece, and the cities in which Paul lived, worked, and traveled to and from had rich philosophic traditions and significant opportunities for advanced study in all the major schools of philosophy. The picture painted by the writers of the period is that of the philosopher as a familiar figure in the markets, squares, and public life of town and city. The crowded lecture halls, the streetcorner cynics, together with the abundance of philosophic pretenders, provided ample fodder for the satirists and gave rise to such proverbial sarcasm as recorded by Lucian: "It would be easier for a man to fall into a boat without hitting a plank than for his eye to miss a philosopher wherever he looks."[110] Luke's portrayal of Paul debating with Stoics and Epicureans in Athens (Acts 17:18) allows us a glimpse at what was probably a routine feature of Paul's public ministry.

The philosophical schools prominent in the first century represented complex systems of cosmology, religion, logic, and ethics, and each had a long and venerable history, beginning in the classical age, developing through the Hellenistic period, and continuing into the Roman era.[111] Two important developments, however, should be noted with respect to philosophy in the first century. First, the rise of peripatetic Cynic and Stoic philosophers, along with the popularity of sophists, led to the diffusion and democratization of philosophical concepts, themes, and terminology vis-à-vis the masses. Philosophical discourse was no longer confined to the aristocratic academies of Athens but could be heard in the porticoes of local temples. Second, while the accessibility of philosophy broadened, the focus of philosophy narrowed. The speculative cosmological theories of the various schools remained as dogmatic tenets, but ethics—the attainment of virtue and the avoidance of vice—became the dominant concern of Roman-era philosophers. As it trickled down to the common folk, philosophy grew more practical and utilitarian, becoming virtually absorbed with "how to live rightly."[112] It is crucial to remember that in the first century questions concerning how one ought to live were not the domain of organized religion and its priestly caste but of philosophers:

> JULIUS EUTECNIUS, NATIVE OF LAODICIA . . . WHEN HE ADDRESSED THE GAULS PERSUASION FLOWED FROM HIS TONGUE. HE CIRCULATED AMONG VARIOUS RACES, HE KNEW MANY PEOPLE AND AFFORDED TRAINING TO THE SOUL AMONG THEM.
>
> INSCRIPTION, GAUL

> For only through philosophy and in company with philosophy it is possible to attain knowledge of what is honorable and what is shameful, what is just and what is unjust, what, in brief, is to be chosen and what is to be avoided, how a man must bear himself in his relations with the gods, with his parents, with his elders, with the laws, with strangers, with those in authority, with friends, with women, with children, with servants.[113]

The religions of the Greco-Roman world offered instruction on how to avoid and appease the wrath of the gods and how to win their favor, but it was philosophy that determined "the boundaries of good and evil."[114] Philosophers became spiritual directors who guided the neophyte in moral progress.[115] Indeed, philosophy could be defined by no less a luminary than Musonius Rufus as "training in nobility of character, and nothing else."[116] One contemporary scholar uses the word "therapeutic" to summarize the goals of philosophy in the Roman era,[117] and this is a fair description of so much of what first-century

> AND THOSE FOLLOWING ME OFTEN LISTENED TO ME DISCUSSING PATIENT ENDURANCE . . . AND MANY INVITED ME TO DINNER . . . BUT I ONLY DINED WITH THOSE IN NEED OF THERAPY.
>
> CYNIC EPISTLES

philosophers were doing. In many respects, they were the ancient equivalent of our self-help gurus—physicians of the soul promising happiness to all who enrolled in their program. Seneca's words to Lucilius, his friend, disciple, and pupil, illustrate well the all too familiar message of these spiritual guides:

> The path to which I am leading you is not different from that on which your nature leads you; you were born to such conduct as I describe. Hence there is all the more reason why you should increase and beautify the good that is in you.[118]

IT LOOKS AS IF THE NOTABLE MEN OF THE FORUM ARE LINING UP IN GREAT NUMBERS TO SEE THIS STOIC.

*LUCIAN

What follows is a brief outline of the major schools of philosophy prominent in the first century, focusing only on issues important for understanding the intellectual milieu of the first century and particular NT contexts. Subsequent chapters will explore the social setting of philosophers and the influence of the philosophical schools on a variety of issues—marriage, slavery, ethics.

Stoicism

Stoicism was probably the most influential philosophical school of the first and second centuries. It derived its name from the painted porch (*stoa poikile*) in Athens where its founder, Zeno, began lecturing at around 300 B.C.E. Among the philosophical schools prominent in the first century, Stoicism is notable for its remarkable ethical affinities to Christian teaching. As early as Tertullian (ca. 160–225) we see the Stoic Seneca positively noted,[119] and by the time of Jerome (ca. 345–419), who refers to Seneca as *"our* Seneca,"[120] many believed that the similarities between Paul and this Stoic philosopher constituted decisive evidence that Seneca had been converted by the apostle.[121] Stoicism illustrates well the democratization of philosophy in that its leading figures spanned the social spectrum—from the former slave Epictetus (late first century) to the emperor Marcus Aurelius (late second century). Seneca makes this point particularly well:

IF, HOWEVER, YOU DESIRE A PATTERN, TAKE SOCRATES.

SENECA

> But a noble mind is free to all men; according to this test, we may all gain distinction. Philosophy neither rejects nor selects anyone; its light shines for all. Socrates was no aristocrat. Cleanthes worked at a well and served as a hired man watering a garden. Philosophy did not find Plato already a nobleman; it made him one.[122]

Stoics, like most of the philosophical schools we will survey, had a deep admiration for Socrates.[123] For the Stoics, however, this admiration could almost be described as veneration. Dio Chrysostom refers to Socrates as "the wisest of all" and does not blush in calling himself "an admirer of Socrates . . . filled with wonder at the man."[124] Although Socrates founded no school of philosophy, the Stoics saw themselves as Socrates' true heirs and looked to him as their guide and paradigm:

> GOD IS ONE AND THE SAME WITH REASON, FATE, AND ZEUS; HE IS ALSO CALLED BY MANY OTHER NAMES.
>
> DIOGENES LAERTIUS

> The good and excellent man neither contends with anyone, nor as far as he has the power, does he allow others to contend. We have a paradigm before us of this also, as in everything else, in the life of Socrates.[125]

The imitation of Socrates is a common theme among Stoics, so much so that Epictetus could define Stoics as "followers of Socrates."[126]

While Stoic ethics were similar in many respects to those of Christians, its theology and ontology could not have been more different. Stoicism was essentially pantheistic, believing God and the cosmos to be coterminous: "the world is god."[127] Yet Stoic pantheism did not result in an impersonal deity. Rather, they conceived of universe as a vast rational being with intelligence and volition. This ultimate reality could be designated God, Zeus, Reason, Logos, Spirit, Fire, and so on, and they also accepted other divinities as part of this great cosmic deity—stars, planets, and the traditional Olympian gods. Moreover, first-century stoics like Musonius Rufus, Epictetus, and Dio Chrysostom could refer to God as "father" and humanity and lesser gods as his "children." Their language at times was so affectionate and personal that one could be forgiven for suspecting them of being monotheists.[128] That Paul could cite the Stoic Aratus in Acts 17:28 is a perfect illustration of this ambiguity: "For we are indeed his offspring."

> THE PALTRY BODY MUST BE SEPARATED FROM THE BIT OF SPIRIT, EITHER NOW OR LATER, JUST AS IT EXISTED APART FROM IT BEFORE . . . WHY? SO THAT THE CYCLE OF THE UNIVERSE MAY NOW BE ACCOMPLISHED.
>
> EPICTETUS

Stoics held to a cyclical view of history in which the world moved ineluctably toward a cosmic conflagration, from which a new world emerged. This cycle was infinitely repeated, and each subsequent world was identical to the previous, hence the fatalism of Epictetus: "Lead me on, Zeus and Destiny, to wherever I have been allotted by you; I will go without faltering. And if I become evil and unwilling, nevertheless, I will follow."[129] At death the constituents of the individual were "restored to those elements from which it came"[130] and would reappear in the next

> ALL THE VIRTUES MAKE IT THEIR GOAL TO BE HAPPY, WHICH DEPENDS ON LIVING IN AGREEMENT WITH NATURE.
>
> ARIUS DIDYMUS

cosmic cycle. Although some Stoics entertained the possibility that the soul of the deceased would survive until the next cosmic conflagration, the afterlife and personal immortality were little discussed by the Stoics.

The primary relevance of Stoicism to the nascent Christian movement is the Stoic image of the virtuous person and the means by which virtue is attained. The ideal sage is someone who could face hardship, calamity, fame and fortune with casual indifference: "Hunger, exile, loss of reputation and the like have no terrors for him; nay he holds them as mere trifles."[131] The Stoic arrived at this state of sublime transcendence by learning to distinguish what is necessary for true happiness from what is unnecessary:

> FURTHER, THIS YOUNG STOIC BELIEVED THAT TORTURE, BODILY PAIN AND DEADLY PERIL COULD NEITHER INJURE NOR DETRACT FROM THE HAPPY STATE AND CONDITION OF LIFE WHICH, IN HIS OPINION, HE HAD ATTAINED.
>
> AULUS GELLIUS

> Of the things which exist, some are good, some are bad, and some are indifferent. These are examples of good things: intelligence, self-restraint, justice, bravery. . . . These are examples of bad things: stupidity, lack of self-restraint, injustice, cowardice. . . . These are examples of indifferent things: life, death, reputation, lack of reputation, toil, pleasure, riches, poverty, sickness, health, and things of this sort.[132]

Moral progress was made by consistently choosing the good, rejecting the bad, and wisely using the indifferent things to advance in virtue: "If good health, rest, and freedom from pain are not likely to hinder virtue, shall you not seek these things? Of course I shall seek them, but not because they are goods,—I seek them because they are according to nature."[133] Living according to nature, an idea ubiquitous in Stoic writings,[134] would lead to *eudaimonia,* "happiness," and would render the valiant Stoic completely self-sufficient, impervious to the vicissitudes of fortune and the cussedness of life: "Who then is a Stoic? . . . Show me a man who though sick is happy, though in danger is happy, though dying is happy, though condemned to exile is happy, though in disrepute is happy. Show him! By the gods, I would fain see a Stoic!"[135]

> JUST AS THE LOSS OF LEAVES IS A LIGHT THING, BECAUSE THEY ARE BORN AFRESH, SO IT IS WITH THE LOSS OF THOSE WHOM YOU LOVE AND REGARD AS THE DELIGHT OF YOUR LIFE; FOR THEY CAN BE REPLACED.
>
> SENECA

The Stoics were also notorious for their disdain of emotion, which is chiefly how they are remembered today: in contemporary usage *stoic* refers to someone "not affected by or showing passion or feeling."[136] Technically, this is not an accurate representation of ancient Stoicism. In principle Stoicism distinguished between good, healthy emotions, and inappropriate, unhealthy emotions:

> [The Stoics] also say that there are three emotional states which are good, namely, joy, caution, and wishing. Joy, the opposite of pleasure, is rational elation. Caution, the opposite of fear, is rational avoidance. For while the wise man will never feel fear, he will use caution. And they say that wishing is the opposite of desire, or craving.[137]

Yet because the Stoics so severely restricted the range of appropriate emotion, the modern caricature of Stoicism as cold and impassive is probably not wildly inaccurate. In fact, it was a stereotype that first-century Stoics battled as well.[138] Moreover, it is not difficult to find passages in which Stoics do sound as if they are rejecting emotions entirely, as in Seneca's advice in *Epistle* 116:

> The question has often been raised whether it is better to have moderate emotions, or none at all. Philosophers of our school reject the emotions; the Peripatetics keep them in check. I however, do not understand how any half-way disease can either be wholesome or helpful. . . . Let us therefore resist these faults when they are demanding entrance, because, as I have said, it is easier to deny them entrance than to make them depart.[139]

Stoics were particularly scornful toward grief and romantic love. Epictetus, for example, agrees that familial affection is proper and in accord with nature[140] but argues that the wise man should be able to abandon home, family, wife, and children "without groaning or yearning."[141] To the one who countered that, according to Homer, Odysseus wept over his wife, Epictetus retorted, "Do you believe everything you read in Homer? Odysseus was an excellent man, and it is impossible for an excellent man to weep."[142] Seneca counsels that one's affection for a friend should be like one's affection for a flower; when it dies, find a new one.[143] As for romantic love, it was a regarded as a distraction that ultimately led to the lover being enslaved to his or her beloved.[144]

> DO NOT BE UPSET, FATHER, THAT I AM CALLED A DOG. . . . FOR I AM HEAVEN'S DOG, NOT EARTH'S, SINCE I LIKEN MYSELF TO IT, LIVING AS I DO, NOT IN CONFORMITY WITH POPULAR OPINION, BUT ACCORDING TO NATURE.
>
> CYNIC EPISTLES

Cynicism

Cynics shared many of the concerns of Stoics, and their preaching reflected similar themes: moral advance through living in accordance with nature and enduring hardship. This would lead to detachment from material things and complete self-sufficiency.[145] The Cynics, however, radicalized these values into a way of life that was intended as a visible affront to the status quo, especially those at the top of the social pyramid. In the words of the Cynic Demonax: "What men ought to do, then, is to reduce and cheapen the ranks of the rich by erecting in the face of their wealth a breastwork of contempt."[146]

Many Cynics advocated a lifestyle of extreme asceticism as a way of confronting and condemning the luxury and vice of society. Their model was their founder, Diogenes, who, legend has it, lived in a barrel in the outskirts of Corinth. His rough living and snarling rebukes led to his nickname, "the Dog," *kyōn*, from which we derive our word "cynic." The oft-told but fictitious tale of his meeting with Alexander the Great illustrates the contempt for status and material goods that came to characterize the movement. The powerful king visits Diogenes in his barrel and bids him, "Ask whatever you want, and it will be granted." Diogenes replies coolly, "Move out of the way; you are blocking my sun."[147]

> YOU OFTEN SEE HIM BY THE THRESHOLD OF THE NEW TEMPLE, HIS UNKEMPT BEARD FALLS ON HIS CHEST, A THREADBARE CLOAK COVERS HIM, AND THE CROWD THAT COMES HIS WAY GIVES HIM THE FOOD HE BARKS FOR. HE IS NO CYNIC, HE IS A DOG!
>
> *MARTIAL

The Cynics took the idea of "living in accordance with nature" to mean acquiring nothing more than what was absolutely essential for survival. They rejected the Stoic idea that wealth and property could be neutral "indifferents," believing that anything beyond "bread, water, a bed of straw and a coarse cloak"[148] was a sign of weakness and enslavement to pleasure. Herakles, who spent his life overcoming hardship by his own brute strength and ingenuity, was held up as the ideal Cynic: "Consider your ragged cloak to be Herakles' lion's skin, your staff his club, and your wallet the land and sea from which you are fed. For thus would the spirit of Herakles, mightier than every turn of fortune, stir in you."[149] The more extreme Cynic was perfectly happy to perform any act in public that he regarded as "natural," for example, intercourse or defecation: "'This solid adamant of virtue, this rebuker of everyone, this cynic who battles the elements has been caught!' 'At what?' 'It is not proper to say.'"[150]

> I AM SATISFIED TO HAVE THE PLAINEST FOOD AND THE SAME GARMENT SUMMER AND WINTER, AND I DO NOT WEAR SHOES AT ALL.
>
> CYNIC EPISTLES

It was not only this radical lifestyle that separated the Cynics from most Stoics. Cynics were doctrinally more eclectic. Diogenes passed on to his followers not primarily a dogma but a lifestyle. The Cynics entertained a variety of conceptions of the afterlife, and they were more critical of traditional religion. Their harsh confrontational style was more severe than that of the Stoics, and they supported themselves through begging and handouts:

> Be bold, not only in your dress, name, and way of life, but also in begging people for sustenance, for it is not at all disgraceful. . . . It is all right to beg, if it not for a free gift or for something worse in exchange, but for the salvation of everyone. . . .

Socrates used to say that sages do not beg, but demand back, for everything belongs to them, just as it does to the gods.[151]

Although Diogenes was admired by later generations, his first-century disciples were more often regarded as charlatans, or at least infiltrated by pretenders: "No one denies, Menestratus, that you are a cynic, and bare-footed and that you are shivering. But if you shamelessly steal loaves and broken pieces on the sly, I have a stick, and they will call you a dog."[152]

Epicureanism

In contemporary usage "epicurean" denotes the pursuit of sensual pleasure, a connotation already associated with Epicureans in the first century. Epicurus (341–270 B.C.E.), the founder of Epicureanism, did advocate a life devoted to pleasure but not one of unbridled self-indulgence and carnal excess. Rather, Epicurus sought to attain a state of tranquility, free from pain and anxiety: "For the goal of all our actions is that we have no pain and trouble."[153] Seeking pleasure was intuitive, in his view, the most basic instinctual drive: "All animals from the moment of their birth are delighted with pleasure, and are offended with pain by their natural instinct, and without the employment of reason."[154] Epicurus's brand of hedonism maintained that "the pleasures of the soul are greater than those of the body,"[155] and so he argued that not all pleasures should be embraced and not all pains should be avoided:

> And since pleasure is our first and native good, for that reason we do not choose every pleasure whatsoever, but sometimes pass over many pleasures when a greater annoyance results from them. And sometimes we consider pains superior to pleasure, when submission to the pain ... brings us as a consequence a greater pleasure.[156]

In fact, Epicurus advocated a life of moderation, simplicity, and virtue, as this was most likely to result in true tranquility: "Plain fare gives as much pleasure as a costly diet. . . . It is not an unbroken succession of drinking bouts and of revelry, not sexual love, not the enjoyment of fish

> WHEN WE SAY THAT PLEASURE IS A CHIEF GOOD, WE ARE NOT SPEAKING OF THE PLEASURES OF THE DEBAUCHED MAN, OR THOSE WHICH LIE IN SENSUAL ENJOYMENT, AS SOME THINK . . . BUT WE MEAN THE FREEDOM OF THE BODY FROM PAIN, AND THE SOUL FROM CONFUSION.
>
> EPICURUS

> IT IS IMPOSSIBLE TO LIVE A LIFE OF PLEASURE WHICH IS NOT A LIFE OF PRUDENCE, HONOR, AND JUSTICE.
>
> EPICURUS

> EPICURUS HIMSELF, THE FATHER OF TRUTH, COMMANDED WISE MEN TO BE LOVERS, AND SAID THAT THIS IS THE GOAL OF LIFE.
>
> PETRONIUS

and other delicacies of a luxurious table which produce a pleasant life; it is sober contemplation."[157] It is no small irony then, that Epicurus was not, in the modern sense of the word at least, an Epicurean.

Epicurus's later followers, however, were commonly accused of carousing and licentiousness: "These men despise all things divine and have set up the image of one single female divinity . . . representing a kind of wantonness or self-indulgent ease and unrestrained lewdness, to which they gave the name 'Pleasure.'"[158] The frequency of these kinds of accusations leads one to suspect that where there's smoke there's fire and that the ideals of the founder dissipated as they were applied by men of weaker moral fiber. Philodemus (ca. 110 B.C.E.–ca. 35 B.C.E.) is a perfect example of this dissipation. As a leader of the Epicurean school he wrote a ponderous assortment of books on theology, ethics, rhetoric, and so on, but his amatory epigrams betray the firsthand experience of a soul clenched in the vise of sexual desire: "My soul, knowing my earlier tears and desires, tells me in advance to flee passion for Heliodora. It speaks, but I have not the strength to flee; for shamefully indeed the same (soul) both foretells and, while foretelling, desires."[159] Feasting and carousing seem to have been somewhat routine as well:

> FIRST, BELIEVE THAT GOD IS A LIVING BEING, IMMORTAL AND BLESSED . . . FOR THERE ARE INDEED GODS, AND KNOWLEDGE OF THEM IS SELF-EVIDENT, BUT THEY ARE NOT LIKE THE MASSES SUPPOSE THEM.
>
> EPICURUS

> To have white-violet wreaths yet again, harp songs and Chian wine again, and Syrian myrrh yet again; to revel again and to enjoy a drunken whore—this is what I do not want. I hate these things that lead to madness. But bind my brow with narcissus and give me a taste of cross-flutes and anoint my limbs with saffron, myrrh and wet my lungs with wine of Mytilene and wed me to a stay-at-home girl.[160]

Epicureans faced opposition on other fronts too. Epicurus was particularly concerned with the negative affects of popular superstition (the fear of the gods' wrath, punishment in the afterlife, etc.) and so developed a theology that maintained that the gods have no involvement in human affairs and are unconcerned with happenings on earth.[161] Although Epicurus believed in the gods, his denial of divination, providence, and the intervention of the gods led to the widespread belief that Epicureans were atheists—a serious allegation in antiquity: "It is doubtless therefore truer to say . . . that Epicurus does not really believe in the gods at all, and that he said what he did about the immortal gods only for he sake of deprecating popular odium."[162]

One further Epicurean doctrine worth noting is its complete materialism. Epicurus taught that body and soul are composed of atoms that, upon death, are reunited to the material cosmos from which they came. There is no afterlife, no punishment or rewards, no sensation: "Death is nothing to us; for the body, when it has been resolved into its elements has no feeling, and that which has no feeling is nothing for us."[163] Epicureanism, then, was very much a this-worldly philosophy. With nothing at stake in terms of future bliss or pain, it is little wonder that Epicurus's followers had difficulty implementing the ethical standards of their master.

Skeptics, Eclectics, and Others

An exhaustive (and exhausting!) account of first-century philosophical currents would include entries on Neo-Platonism, Peripatetics, Phyrrhonism, Neo-Pythagoreanism, and others.[164] Perhaps the most relevant finding of a complete survey would be to underscore how varied Hellenistic-Roman philosophy was, and how blurred the lines between schools had become. Many, if not most, of the prominent writers of the period were somewhat eclectic in their philosophical musings, picking and choosing what they liked from the intellectual smorgasbord: Horace's poetry is Epicurean with Stoic accents; Philo was a Jewish Neo-Platonist; Dio Chrysostom, converted from sophistry, became Stoic in theology and Cynic in lifestyle; Cicero represented the skeptical Academy but with strong Stoic affinities, and so on.

Most of the common folk would not have identified with any school or even been aware of such neat divisions. Their worldview would have been formed by both local superstition and popular philosophy. This is not to say, however, that these philosophical currents were irrelevant to *hoi polloi*. Ideas have consequences, and the NT was written within a world of ideas that at times collided and at other times coincided with

> THE TRUE CYNIC MUST KNOW THAT HE HAS BEEN SENT BY ZEUS TO MEN PARTLY AS A MESSENGER, IN ORDER TO SHOW THEM THAT IN QUESTIONS OF GOOD AND EVIL, THEY HAVE GONE ASTRAY.
>
> EPICTETUS

its message and aims. In his determination to "take every thought captive for Christ (2 Cor. 10:5), Paul was engaged in a battle of worldviews. His campaign to win hearts and minds took place on a crowded battlefield in which many combatants struggled for the same goal: the conversion of the undecided and the unsatisfied.

CONVERSION

For the modern reader, it might seem odd to treat the subject of conversion in a chapter dealing with philosophy and education. It is important to remember, however, that because exclusivity in worship was not a requirement of the gods of the Greco-Roman world, one didn't convert from the worship of one to the worship of another. The pious pagan devoutly honored his or her ancestral gods, dutifully offered sacrifices to the deified Caesars, and might also participate in whatever mystery religions were represented in his or her locality. The closest parallel in antiquity to religious conversion in the modern sense—usually defined in terms of a reorientation of beliefs and behavior within the context of a supportive community—would be the often dramatic stories of conversion to philosophy.

Conversion to Philosophy

A survey of philosophical conversion narratives reveals three common elements: Moral exhortation (preaching) that induces psychological guilt and an existential crisis; followed by a radical change of lifestyle; leading to a life characterized by moral renewal and the pursuit of virtue.

The writings of Dio Chrysostom, Epictetus, and Musonius Rufus provide numerous examples of Stoic-Cynic preaching, which aimed at producing deep conviction. Lucian's experience represents the ideal for which the philosopher strived: "When he stopped speaking . . . I dripped with sweat, I stumbled . . . my voice failed, my tongue faltered, and finally I began to cry in embarrassment; for the effect he produced in me was not superficial or casual. My wound was deep and vital."[165] Converts to philosophy, especially of the Cynic variety, were known to leave their professions, sell their possessions, abandon their families, and lead a life of radical simplicity.[166] The story is frequently told of Crates, who, after hearing the preaching of Diogenes, rushed into the market, bequeathed all his earthly possessions to the city, and shouted, "Crates sets Crates free!"[167]

> PHILOSOPHY, HOWEVER, IS THE ONLY POWER THAT CAN SHAKE OFF OUR DEEP SLUMBER.
>
> SENECA

The moral transformation that accompanied conversion to philosophy is often described in terms of "freedom"—be it from vice or from material possessions[168]—but also in terms of inner renewal. According to Lucian, philosophy claimed to "wash away the scars of the soul."[169] Seneca's words to his disciple Lucilius are equally effulgent: "I am not only being improved, I am being transformed."[170] The inwardness of the transformation is emphasized by Valerius Maximus, who speaks of "receiving philosophy into the heart,"[171] and Horace goes so far as depict philosophic conversion in terms of the new creation of the convert. Likening the study of philosophy to the magical arts, Horace persuades his readers that philosophy cures all the vices of the soul:

> Is your bosom fevered with avarice and sordid covetousness? There are spells and sayings where by you may soothe the pain and cast much of the malady aside. Are you swelling with ambition? There are fixed charms which can fashion you anew (*recreo*) if with cleansing rites you read the booklet thrice.[172]

Conversion to Judaism

It would be a mistake to attempt to delineate typical elements involved in converting to Judaism, not least because there was a spectrum of adherence to Judaism among Gentiles, ranging from sympathetic "God-fearers" (using Luke's term) to full converts.[173] Circumcision was required of male converts, which was an obvious hurdle, and then there was the problem of how the newly converted Gentile related to the ethnic Jewish community. Were they full members of the family or only stepbrothers and stepsisters? More practically, could a good Jewish boy or girl marry a converted Gentile? While this question was, no doubt, variously answered, the Jewish community responsible for the novella *Joseph and Aseneth* responded with an emphatic yes. In the course of providing a rationale for this answer, *Joseph and Aseneth* provides a remarkable window into the status of converts to Judaism and perhaps into the rituals involved in Gentile conversion.

> IT IS NOT FITTING FOR A MAN WHO WORSHIPS GOD, WHO WILL BLESS WITH HIS MOUTH THE LIVING GOD . . . TO KISS A FOREIGN WOMAN WHO WILL BLESS WITH HER MOUTH DEAD AND DUMB IDOLS.
>
> JOSEPH AND ASENETH

Joseph and Aseneth, a first- or second-century romance of diaspora Judaism, tells the story of the marriage of Joseph to Aseneth, mentioned in Gen 41:45. The marriage of a venerated patriarch to the daughter of a pagan priest would have raised a few Jewish eyebrows and invited explanation. The author of *Joseph and Aseneth* solves this impropriety by explaining that Aseneth converted to Judaism prior to her marriage. In a wonderful tale of love, longing, intrigue, and vengeance, the author describes how the convert to Judaism (in this case, Aseneth) is recreated by God's Spirit, so all prior idolatrous involvements are irrelevant. This clears the way for marriage between ethnic Jews and pagan converts. The blessing offered by the synagogue leader to the new convert and overheard by Zoe (ch. 1) repeats verbatim the prayer of Joseph concerning the yet-to-be converted Aseneth:

> IF ANYONE IS IN CHRIST, THEY ARE A NEW CREATION! THE OLD THINGS HAVE PASSED. LOOK, THE NEW HAS COME!
>
> 2 CORINTHIANS 5:17

> You lord, bless this daughter, make her new by your Spirit, recreate her by your hidden hand, give her new life through your life. Let her eat your bread of life, let her drink your cup of blessing, and number her with your people whom you chose before all things. Let her enter your rest and live in your eternal life forever.[174]

Whether this prayer represents a formulaic blessing routinely pronounced over proselytes is uncertain, but what is clear is that it presents conversion to Judaism as new creation by God's Spirit. This imagery is not only relevant to converts to Judaism; thanks to Paul, a diaspora Jew, it also becomes relevant to converts to Christianity (2 Cor 5:17; Gal 6:15).

Conversion among Mystery Religions

Mystery religions of antiquity—and there were a substantial number—offered initiates a more personal form of religion than that available through the worship of the major Greco-Roman deities and promised a blissful eternal afterlife to their devotees. The initiation process often involved ceremonies similar to those of the primitive Jesus movement (ritual washing, ritual meals), and the event is sometimes interpreted as a kind of dying and rising, or rebirth.

Apuleius's *Metamorphoses* provides an illuminating picture into a significant mystery religion, the worship of Isis, from an insider's perspective. The main character of the story is a fellow named Lucius, who, through dabbling in magic, gets himself turned into an ass. He is restored to human form by the goddess Isis, which is symbolic of the transformation this mystery religion promised. Lucius's initiation is explained to him by the officiating priest as follows: "He said that both the gates of death and the guardianship of life were in the goddess's hands, and the act of initiation was performed in the manner of voluntary death and salvation obtained by favor."[175]

> HOW FORTUNATE HE IS, BY HERCULES, AND THRICE BLESSED! . . . FOR HE WAS IN A MANNER REBORN AND IMMEDIATELY ENGAGED TO THE SERVICE OF ISIS.
>
> APULEIUS

Although mystery religions did not require the exclusive worship of their followers, some, like the mysteries of Isis, evinced an evangelistic tendency. The followers of Isis regarded her to be the supreme deity who embodied all the gods. In this context, "initiation" took on connotations normally associated with "conversion." The public parade of Isiac worshipers that halted Heraclitus and his wards before entering the Peirene is taken from Apuleius's story, and these spectacles were intended to attract the attention of potential followers. Unlike the typical portrayal of the gods of Greece and Rome, Isis is described by Apuleius as beneficent, loving, and deeply concerned about humanity:

> Finally I prostrated myself before the goddess and wiped her feet with my face for a long time. Tears welled up in me . . . as I spoke to her: "O holy and eternal savior of mankind, you who ever bountifully nurture mortals, you apply the sweet affection of a mother. . . . The fullness of my voice is inadequate to express what I feel about your majesty. . . . I shall store your divine countenance and sacred godhead in the secret places of my heart."[176]

The fervency of this devotion may represent literary hyperbole, but it is still a far cry from anything we see in the worship of the traditional Roman gods.

The personal nature of the deity and the salvation offered is what set the mystery religions and Christianity apart from other first-century religions and is one of the reasons that the mysteries of Mithras nearly eclipsed Christianity in the fourth century.

THE NEW TESTAMENT CONTEXT

PAUL THE LETTER WRITER

Paul is remembered in many ways—an apostle, a missionary, a pastor, and a theologian, to name just a few. Yet fundamental to all of this—and often overlooked—is that Paul wrote a lot of letters. Not just the one-page sort that you and I occasionally write, but tremendously long and sometimes cerebral letters. If a hand-written copy of Romans were sitting before us, it would take up nearly forty pages of standard writing paper. When was the last time you wrote a letter like that?

> I, PAUL, WRITE THIS GREETING WITH MY OWN HAND. THIS IS THE SIGN OF GENUINENESS IN EVERY LETTER OF MINE; IT IS THE WAY I WRITE.
>
> 2 THESSALONIANS 3:17

Paul's letters were not simply personal notes of greeting intended to stay in touch. Romans reads like a theological treatise, 1 Corinthians like a lengthy FAQ, 1 Timothy like a minister's manual, and so on. The production, dispatch, and collecting of Paul's letters is a fascinating subject,[177] but my concern here is to emphasize something even more obvious: Paul was literate. This fact alone put Paul in a very select group of privileged individuals. If contemporary estimates of ancient literacy are correct, and between 80 and 90 percent of the population of the first-century Mediterranean world were functionally or completely illiterate, then Paul, educationally speaking, was among the most privileged people in antiquity.

And Paul was not semi-literate or moderately literate. Far from it. His letters contain complex rabbinic argumentation, sophisticated rhetorical conventions, numerous Old Testament citations—which he apparently had memorized—all in well-crafted and intentionally chosen epistolary formats.[178] In fact, for all the Corinthians' complaints about Paul, even they acknowledged his letters packed a wallop: "His letters are weighty and forceful" (2 Cor 10:10).

> TIMOTHY, WHEN YOU COME . . . BRING MY BOOKS, AND ABOVE ALL THE PARCHMENTS.
>
> 2 TIMOTHY 4:13 ESV

The details of Paul's education remain obscure, though Acts tells us that Paul was trained under the leading Jewish scholar of his day, Gamaliel.[179] Given the caliber of his letters, this comes as no surprise. Paul admits that he was something of an overachiever: "I was advancing in Judaism beyond many Jews of my own age and was extremely zealous for the traditions of my fathers" (Gal 1:14). It would also appear that Paul had training in forensic (judicial) rhetoric, perhaps in the school of Gamaliel.[180] Bruce Winter observes that in defending himself before Festus in Acts 24, Paul was able to downgrade the criminal charge to a theological issue, restrict the arraignment to focus only on his activities in Jerusalem, and eliminate the accusations of Asian Jews not present at the hearing. All this was done within the formal forensic structure of an *exordium* (introduction), *narratio* (presentation facts), *confirmatio* (confirmation of facts), *refutatio* (refutation of charges), and *peroratio* (conclusion).[181] This is not the work of an amateur. We can also safely conclude that Paul was trilingual, speaking Greek, Aramaic, and Hebrew. It is also very probable that Paul was at least conversant in Latin, the lingua franca of his day. That such linguistic ability was unusual for a Jew is evident from the surprised response of the military tribune in Jerusalem when Paul asked to speak to him: "You know Greek?" (Acts 21:37).

> "YOU ARE OUT OF YOUR MIND, PAUL!" FESTUS SHOUTED. "YOUR GREAT LEARNING IS DRIVING YOU INSANE!"
>
> ACTS 26:24

We will explore Paul's social status in more detail later, though even this brief résumé of Paul's educational and literary achievements indicates that Paul was a formidable intellect. Indeed, prior to his conversion, it would appear that Paul was on a career path headed toward the religious academy in Jerusalem: "a Hebrew of Hebrews . . . a Pharisee" (Phil 3:5). Understanding this background should inform our reading of Paul's letters generally and shed light on specific texts. Who better could say, "knowledge puffs up, but love builds up" (1 Cor 8:1) than someone who had drunk deeply of the heady draft of religious intellectualism and academic privilege? In defending his practice of supporting himself through working with his hands, Paul inadvertently betrays his perspective on the matter: "Was it a sin for me to lower myself in order to elevate you by preaching the gospel of God to you free of charge?" (2 Cor 11:7). In referring to his deliberate "lowering" of himself by laboring with his hands, Paul confirms that this was not a lifestyle he was born to or trained for. It was a lifestyle he was called to: "I make myself a slave to everyone, to win as many as possible. . . . I do all this for the sake of the gospel" (1 Cor 9:19, 23).

> OUR LORD'S PATIENCE MEANS SALVATION, JUST AS OUR DEAR BROTHER PAUL ALSO WROTE YOU WITH THE WISDOM THAT GOD GAVE HIM. . . . HIS LETTERS CONTAIN SOME THINGS THAT ARE HARD TO UNDERSTAND . . .
>
> 2 PETER 3:15–16

PAUL AND POPULAR ORATORY

As alluded to above, the Corinthians had many difficulties with Paul. They balked at his teaching about the resurrection (1 Cor 15), they chafed under his ethical strictures (1 Cor 5–6), they were embarrassed by his manual labor (2 Cor 11:17), and they were having second thoughts about contributing to the collection (2 Cor 8–9). The Corinthians had many complaints, but Paul cites only one of them directly: "For some are saying, 'His letters are weighty and forceful, but his physical appearance is unimpressive and his speaking is miserable'" (2 Cor 10:10 author's translation). Paul echoes this complaint again in the next chapter where he concedes, "I may be an amateur in speech, but not in knowledge" (11:6 author's translation). His parting warning to the Corinthians exposes the heart of the matter: "When I come again, I will spare no one, since you seek proof that Christ is speaking in me" (13:3 author's translation).

The Corinthians were clearly unimpressed with Paul's oratory. Yet Paul's continued insistence that God (2 Cor 5:20) or Christ (2 Cor 2:17; 12:19) was speaking through him would have only provided his detractors with fuel for their fire. First-century orators commonly attributed their eloquence to divine giftedness. Favorinus, for example, in a speech to the Corinthians, declares that his wisdom and eloquence are evidence that he had been "equipped by the gods" for oratory.[182] Philostratus opens his history of the sophistic movement by comparing its practitioners with divine oracles and mouthpieces of the gods.[183] Even so sober-minded a person as Pliny could offhandedly refer to the orator as "divinely inspired."[184] Paul's claim to be a divine spokesman would have created some very high expectations.

> FOR WHAT MAN AMONG YOU WOULD PARDON ME ONE SOLECISM OR CONDONE THE BARBAROUS PRONUNCIATION OF SO MUCH AS ONE SYLLABLE? . . . BUT YOU SUBJECT EVERY WORD I UTTER TO THE CLOSEST EXAMINATION.
>
> APULEIUS

We have to remember that the Corinthians, like average citizens of any first-century Greco-Roman city, relished oratory, having been fed a rich diet of rhetoric from birth. They erected statues to their favorite orators and became the beneficiaries of public buildings from the wealthier practitioners of the art.[185] Dio Chrysostom's description of Isthmia, some six miles from Corinth, is illuminating. He speaks of "crowds of wretched sophists around Poseidon's temple."[186] Moreover, from the earliest days of their formal education the Corinthians were taught to scrutinize every word choice and turn of phrase employed by a speaker. Hence, Maximus of Tyre laments the fate of the orator as "a slave of vindictive judges,"[187] and Plutarch feels compelled to urge listeners "not to rigorously examine the speaker's little slips, applying criticism to every word and action."[188]

Corinth was also known for producing dapper dandies, orators more intent on making a fashion statement than engaging in serious litigation. Martial describes Charmenion, a Corinthian orator, as one who "goes around looking smart with hair in curls . . . smoothed daily with hair-removal."[189] Juvenal caricatures "the whole tribe" of Corinthians as "perfumed with shaven legs."[190] It was no accident that Epictetus's essay "On Personal Adornment" (4.4) was prompted by a foppish sophist from Corinth. In short, the Corinthians were accustomed to polished, professional, well-groomed orators, and Paul, whose "physical appearance is unimpressive" (2 Cor 10:10), did not measure up.

> BECAUSE OF HIS UP-
> RIGHT CHARACTER AND
> GENERAL EXCELLENCE,
> THE CITY COUNCIL AND
> THE CITIZENS SET UP
> THIS MONUMENT TO
> HONOR PUBLIUS AELIUS
> SOSPINUS, THE RHETOR.
>
> INSCRIPTION, CORINTH

Paul, by contrast, had intentionally and explicitly rejected the gaudy, manipulative, sophistic-styled oratory so popular in his day, and he had already offered the Corinthians a complete theological rationale for his decision: "When I came to you, brothers and sisters, I did not come in eloquent speech. . . . My message and my preaching were not in persuasive words of wisdom, but with the demonstration of the Spirit's power, so that your faith might not rest in human wisdom, but God's power" (1 Cor 2:1–5). Paul understood that when form dominates over content, the result is misplaced faith; faith that focuses on the preacher rather than the one being preached. Paul also realized that it was possible to present the gospel in a form that robbed it of its most potent dynamic, the cross: "For Christ did not send me to baptize, but to preach the gospel; not in words of wisdom, lest the cross of Christ be emptied of his power" (1 Cor 1:17). To resort to the manipulative, self-serving techniques of popular oratory would be to reject the power of the cross. Paul would have

> YOU ARE DEVOTED TO
> ORATORY . . . AND YOU
> TOLERATE AS SPEAK-
> ERS ONLY THOSE WHO
> ARE VERY CLEVER.
>
> DIO CHRYSOSTOM

fully agreed with what James Denny said over a century ago: "No man can give the impression that he himself is clever, and that Christ is mighty to save."[191] The Corinthians, however, saw matters differently, and it remains uncertain if Paul ever managed to silence his critics on this point.

PAUL AND THE RESURRECTION

As is clear from our survey of the philosophical schools, the intellectuals of Paul's day were hardly in agreement on the question of the afterlife. Stoics and Epicureans were skeptical about any postmortem existence, while Cynics entertained a wide spectrum of beliefs.[192] Popular conceptions of what lay beyond the grave were equally varied. Quite apart from Epicurean influence, the notion of extinction was widespread, commonly expressed on gravestones in the epitaph "I was not, I was, I am not, I care not." The Massalians are labeled "fools" by Valerius Maximus for their belief in the immortality of the soul.[193] On the other hand, funerary monuments from Philippi and environs often contain symbolic representations of continued existence after death.[194] In Corinth and elsewhere, we find evidence of the primitive but enduring notion that the spirit of the deceased somehow lived on in the tomb. Some tombs had openings through which food and drink could be supplied; others were equipped with clothing and items for meal preparation; some were stocked with charms to ward off evil.[195] A literary representation of this idea is preserved in Petronius's satire, *The Satyricon,* where Trimalchio defends his plans for an elaborate mausoleum by reasoning, "It is quite wrong for a man to decorate his house while he is alive, and not to trouble about the house where he must make a longer stay."[196] The popular Homeric legends spoke of the dreary underworld of Hades, to which all mortals are destined, while mystery religions, like the Isis cult, promised their devotees immortality in the Elysian fields,[197] and so on.

> WHEN YOU ARE DEAD, YOU ARE NOTHING.
>
> GRAFFITO, POMPEII

While vastly different from each other, these pagan belief systems were united in their rejection of a bodily resurrection: "Similar also is the vanity about preserving men's bodies, and about Democritus' promise of our coming to life again. . . . Plague take it, what is this mad idea that life is renewed by death?"[198]

The idea of a postmortem physical rejuvenation was absurd to most Greeks and Romans. The Athenians and Corinthians openly scoffed at the notion (Acts 17:32; 1 Cor 15), and it is constantly being defended by the second-century apologists.[199] The incredulous reply of the judge at the trial of the martyr Phileas (d. 305 C.E.) may be regarded as typical of the pagan reaction: "This very body will rise?"[200] Yet neither was first-century Judaism in complete agreement on this issue. Some Jewish thinkers, influenced by Hellenistic ideas, affirmed the immortality of the soul apart from any physical resurrection.[201] Others, including Jesus, Paul, and the Pharisees, vigorously defended the notion of a bodily resurrection: "My brothers, I am a Pharisee, the son of a Pharisee. I stand on trial because of my hope in the resurrection of the dead" (Acts 23:6).[202]

> I, THE WELL-KNOWN AND FAMOUS PRIMUS, AM IN THIS TOMB. YET AMONG THE SPIRITS, THE PHOENIX, WHICH RUSHES TO RENEW ITSELF ALONG WITH ME, SAVES ME ON THE ALTAR.
>
> *FUNERARY INSCRIPTION, OSTIA

Within a culture that had no clear conception of the afterlife, it is no wonder that Paul could refer to unbelievers who mourned the loss of friends and relations as "those who have no hope" (1 Thess 4:13). Regardless of popular conceptions of the afterlife, the sheer cacophony of voices and conflicting speculations would have stifled any whisper of assurance that those in grief desperately needed to hear. We can be certain that a man of Pliny's education, travel, and experience was familiar with all the views of the afterlife outlined here, yet when faced with death, despair was his only companion: "What I need is something new and effective which I have never heard or read about before. For everything I have heard or read . . . is powerless against grief like this."[203] Paul's unyielding proclamation of the resurrection of Jesus and the future resurrection of believers, while greeted with skepticism, offered hope to the discouraged (1 Thess 4:13–18; 1 Cor 15:17–19; 2 Cor 5:1–6) and contained a clear warning against the ethical relativism of Epicureans and other annihilationist philosophies: "For we must all stand before the judgment seat of Christ, that each one may receive what is due him for the things done while in the body, whether good or bad" (2 Cor 5:10; cf. 1 Cor 15:32).

> WELL, WELL, IF WE KNOW WE MUST DIE, WHY SHOULD WE NOT LIVE AND ENJOY OURSELVES?
>
> PETRONIUS

PAUL AND THE PHILOSOPHERS

The letters of Paul provide so many fruitful points of comparison and contrast with the philosophical schools that narrowing the topic to fit within a few pages is a formidable task in itself. The importance of the Stoic-Cynic tradition—both in the first century and in contemporary NT scholarship—justifies focusing here, especially given the striking continuity (at points) between Paul and the Stoics. Because ethics were central to both Paul and the philosophers, the following discussion looks at the place of hardships and the role of the mind in moral advance, as well as Paul's emphasis on love as the epitome of the virtuous life.

> IF THE DEAD ARE NOT RAISED, "LET US EAT AND DRINK, FOR TO-MORROW WE DIE."
>
> 1 CORINTHIANS 15:32

Hardship Catalogs

Paul's hardship catalogs, those lists of trials we find in 2 Cor 4:8–19, 6:3–10, and 11:22–33, constitute perhaps the most obvious literary parallels to the Stoic-Cynic tradition in the entire NT. Every Stoic and Cynic writer of the era has at least one discourse devoted exclusively to this theme, to say nothing of the countless references to enduring hardships that occur throughout their writings.[204] The motif is very nearly ubiquitous. And not only is the subject matter between Paul and his philosophic contemporaries analogous, but the literary form of the hardship catalog could bear remarkable correspondence, as this comparison with Plutarch illustrates:

2 CORINTHIANS 4:8–9 (AUTHOR'S TRANSLATION)	PLUTARCH, MOR. 1057E	2 CORINTHIANS 6:9–10 (AUTHOR'S TRANSLATION)
"Afflicted in every way, but not crushed; perplexed, but not despairing; persecuted, but not abandoned; thrown down, but not vanquished."	"Confined, but not hindered; thrown down, but not constrained; tortured, but not in pain; maimed, but not injured; pinned down, but not beaten; surrounded, but not defeated; enslaved, but not captive."	"Unknown, yet well known; dying, but look! we live; punished, but not killed; sorrowful, but always rejoicing; poor, but making many rich; having nothing but possessing all things."

Although Plutarch is mocking the Stoics, he provides us with an illuminating parody of what must have been a stereotypical manner of Stoic expression. The Stoic's penchant for rehearsing his adversities was intended to demonstrate three primary virtues: fortitude, self-sufficiency, and indifference to external circumstances. The ideal sage, according to popular Stoic-Cynic reckoning, was the person who relied solely on their own inner resources to face whatever deprivation and calamity life supplied. According to Arius Didymus, the noble Stoic is "great, powerful, eminent and strong . . . because he has possession of the strength which befalls such a man, being invincible and unconquerable."[205] Musonius Rufus is equally candid: "He makes the whole matter [of happiness] depend upon himself."[206]

Like the Stoics, Paul believed hardships strengthened character and promoted virtue (Rom 5:3–5; 1 Cor 9:24–27; 2 Cor 4). Also like the Stoics, Paul's references to his suffering were made with a view to offering his converts a model

NOW SOCRATES COMMANDED US BEFORE HE DIED THAT NO CARE WAS TO BE TAKEN FOR HIS BODY, SINCE IT WAS WORTHLESS AND NO LONGER USEFUL AFTER THE SOUL HAD LEFT IT.

CYNIC EPISTLES

WE TRAIN BOTH BODY AND SOUL WHEN WE DISCIPLINE OURSELVES TO COLD, HEAT, THIRST, HUNGER, MEAGER RATIONS, HARD BEDS, AVOIDANCE OF PLEASURES, AND PATIENCE UNDER SUFFERING.

*MUSONIUS RUFUS

to emulate. Yet far from parading Stoic bravado and claiming personal invincibility, Paul inventories his adversities in order to demonstrate his weakness: "But he said to me, 'My grace is sufficient for you, for my power is made sufficient in weakness' . . . That is why, for Christ's sake, I delight in weaknesses, in insults, in hardships, in persecutions, in difficulties. For when I am weak, then I am strong" (2 Cor 12:9–10). This line of thinking would have baffled Paul's Stoic contemporaries and exposes the most fundamental difference between the valiant Stoic and the follower of Jesus Christ. Paul's sufficiency was not his own achievement, but was entirely derivative: "Not that we are sufficient to claim anything as coming from us, but our sufficiency is from God" (2 Cor. 3:5 ESV). Nor was his ability to endure hardships evidence of personal fortitude but of self-confessed dependence: "I can do all things, through him who strengthens me" (Phil 4:13).

> "TO THIS END I LABOR, STRUGGLING WITH ALL HIS ENERGY WHICH SO POWERFULLY WORKS IN ME."
>
> COLOSSIANS 1:29

Mental Renewal

Both Paul and the Stoics placed a high value on the role of the mind in character development and spiritual formation. In many ways they anticipated contemporary cognitive therapy in emphasizing the link between correct thinking and correct behavior.

In Stoic thought, the mind is the supreme gift of God. It is what enables mere mortals to assess external sense impressions and come to a judgment regarding their validity and benefit.[207] According to Seneca, it is this capacity that separates humanity from animals and Stoics from Epicureans![208] Vice, then, is considered to be a "disease of the mind"[209] whose cure is right thinking. According to Dio, "For all these maladies [lust, greed, ambition, etc.] one remedy and cure has been provided by the gods, namely, education and reason."[210] Likewise, worry and anxiety are primarily the result of faulty thinking: "It is not things themselves that disturb men," reasons Epictetus, "but their judgments about things. For example, death is nothing terrible . . . what is terrible is the judgment that death is terrible."[211]

> TO RELAX THE MIND, IS TO LOSE IT.
>
> MUSONIUS RUFUS

Epictetus in particular emphasizes throughout his discourses the importance of correct thinking for coping with the circumstances of life, be they hardships or temptations. His philosophy for moral development was predicated on the assumption that one has the ability to choose what one thinks about. Our external circumstances may not be within our control, concedes Epictetus, "but as to thinking or not thinking, that is in our power and not in externals."[212]

Epictetus's strategy for mental renewal involved training one's mind to focus only on what is beneficial for the soul's progress: "Let others think about lawsuits, problems, and syllogisms. You labor at thinking about death, chains, the rack, exile . . . then you will prove what the rational governing power can achieve."[213] For those overly fond of ephemeral comforts, Epictetus counseled an incremental divestiture:

> This is what you ought to practice from morning till evening. Begin with the most trifling things . . . like a pot, or a cup, and then advance to a tunic, a paltry dog, a mere horse, a bit of land; thence to yourself, your body and its members, your children, wife, brothers. Look about on every side and cast these things away from you. Purify your judgments![214]

> AND WHAT IS THIS GOOD? IT IS A CLEAR AND FLAWLESS MIND, WHICH RIVALS THAT OF GOD, RAISED FAR ABOVE MORTAL CONCERNS. . . . YOU ARE A REASONING ANIMAL. WHAT GOOD, THEN, LIES WITHIN YOU? PERFECT REASON.
>
> SENECA

Sexual attraction, too, could be overcome by withdrawing oneself from the temptation and contemplating more sublime desires: "Make it your wish to appear beautiful in the sight of God. Set your desire upon becoming pure in the presence of your pure self and God. . . . If you confront your external impression [the object of desire] with such thoughts, you will overcome it."[215] Most importantly, Epictetus warns not to linger on the attractive image and let yourself daydream: "Do not let it [the object of desire] lead you on by picturing to you what will follow. Otherwise, it will take possession of you. . . . Rather, introduce and set over against it some fair and noble impression, and throw out this filthy one."[216]

Paul, too, has much to say about the role of the mind in spiritual formation:

Be transformed by the renewing of your mind. (Rom 12:2)

Clothe yourselves with the Lord Jesus Christ, and do not think about how to gratify the desires of the flesh. (Rom 13:14)

Be of the same mind toward one another, do not be haughty in mind . . . do not be wise in your own estimation. (Rom 12:16 author's translation)

Whatever is true, noble, just, pure, lovely, admirable . . . think about such things. (Phil. 4:8 author's translation)

> ONE WHO HAS LEARNED AND UNDERSTOOD WHAT HE SHOULD DO AND AVOID IS NOT A WISE MAN UNTIL HIS MIND IS TRANSFORMED.
>
> SENECA

You were taught with regard to your former way of life, to put off our old self . . . and to be made new in the attitude of your minds. (Eph 4:22–23)

Set your mind on things above. (Col 3:2)

Many more such texts could be added. In fact, whenever Paul says things like, "Consider yourself" or "Do you not know that . . . ?" he is affirming the importance of correct thinking for correct living.

Yet while Paul and Epictetus would see eye to eye on many points regarding the role of the mind in moral progress, there remains a vast chasm that separates the two. For Paul, moral transformation was not primarily accomplished through the strength of one's will (although that is crucial), but through the empowering of the Spirit:

We serve in the new life of the Spirit. (Rom 7:6 author's translation)

The Spirit is life for righteousness. (Rom 8:9 author's translation)

The mind set on the flesh is death; the mind controlled by the Spirit is life and peace. (Rom 8:6)

The Spirit helps us in our weaknesses. (Rom 8:26)

The fruit of the Spirit is love, joy, peace, patience, kindness. (Gal 5:22)

I pray that . . . he may strengthen you with power through his Spirit. (Eph 3:16)

Again, many more such texts could be adduced, but that would be to belabor the obvious. According to Paul, it is the Spirit which both gives new life (2 Cor 3:6; Gal 5:25; Titus 3:5) and enables moral growth (Rom 7:6; 8:9; 2 Cor 3:17–18, etc.). Stoics taught that "the wise man is self-sufficient,"[217] while Paul taught that the wise person is radically dependent, and this notion would have been greeted by Epictetus, Seneca, and the Stoics with unmitigated derision.[218]

Love

So far I have compared Paul and Stoicism on points where both strong continuity *and* discontinuity exist between the two. Yet this is not true of the present topic. In fact, while it is difficult to imagine a summary of Christian ethics that did not emphasize the primacy love, I have yet to see any representation of Stoic ethics—ancient or modern—that even lists love as a topic to be discussed. Arius Didymus, for example, presents his "Epitome of Stoic Ethics" without any discussion of love as a virtue. This is not to say that love is absent in Stoicism, but it is true that Christianity and Stoicism had different ethical priorities.

> AND OVER ALL THESE VIRTUES PUT ON LOVE, WHICH BINDS THEM ALL TOGETHER IN PERFECT UNITY.
>
> COLOSSIANS 3:14

The ethical priorities of Hellenistic philosophy were strongly influenced by the Platonic-Socratic emphasis on justice, along with the three other primary virtues: courage, prudence, and moderation.[219] Further, love was considered a somewhat dangerous virtue by the Stoics in that it was closely associated with inappropriate and excessive emotion, for example, grief, or sexual passion.

The primary reason, however, for the radically different evaluation of love in the ethical systems of Stoicism and Christianity relates directly to their radically different interpretations of the deaths of their founders, Socrates and Jesus, respectively.[220] Early Christian literature regularly interprets the death of Jesus as an act of sacrificial love. This hardly needs defense, but here are a few illustrative texts:

> Greater love has no one than this, that he lay down his life for his friends. (John 15:13)

> The life I live in the body, I live by faith in the Son of God, who loved me and gave himself for me. (Gal 2:20)

> This is how we know what love is: Jesus Christ laid down his life for us. And we ought to lay down our lives for our brothers. (1 John 3:16)

> and from Jesus Christ . . . who loves us and has freed us from our sins by his blood. (Rev 1:5)

> Because of the love he had for us, Jesus Christ our Lord . . . gave his blood for us, and his flesh for our flesh, and his life for our life. (*1 Clem.* 49.6)

> Arm yourselves with gentleness and regain your strength in faith (which is the flesh of Jesus) and in love (which is the blood of Jesus). (Ignatius, *To the Trallians* 8.1)

Not surprisingly, Paul's letters contain some one hundred occurrences of "love" (in verbal and nominal forms), and on several occasions the apostle ascribes to love a place of preeminence as the paramount virtue: "And now these three remain: faith, hope and love. But the greatest of these is love" (1 Cor 13:13; cf. Rom 13:8–10; Col 3:14; 1 Tim 1:5).

The Stoics, by contrast, looked to Socrates as their exemplar and model. In fact, the death of Socrates exerted a powerful influence on the Stoic imagination and became a common theme of Stoic and Cynic reflection. Space does not permit an extensive survey of this important topic, but what captured the Stoic imagination most was the manner of Socrates' death as a dutiful, determined, even defiant resolve to remain obedient to the will of Zeus and the laws of the state, which had condemned him.[221] This image of the noble sage marching fearlessly to his death so inspired the Stoics that dying well became as important to them as living well.[222] While Stoic writers do, on occasion, reflect on the nature of Socrates' death as intentionally undertaken for the benefit of others,[223] it is never presented as motivated by love but by a dutiful commitment to justice.

TAKE COURAGE,
XANITHIPPE, AND
DO NOT DISCARD
ANY OF THE GOOD
INSTRUCTIONS OF
SOCRATES . . . MEDI-
ATE ON HOW HE LIVED
AND HOW HE DIED.

CYNIC EPISTLES

Paul's perspective on the death and resurrection of Jesus, the "good news," as he called it, is
that it represents the ultimate expression of the
"justice of God" (Rom 1:17).[224] But when Paul
describes what motivated him to share this good
news with others, he does not recount the justice
of God but the love of Christ: "For the love of
Christ compels us, recognizing this: one died for
all, therefore, all died" (2 Cor 5:14).

FURTHER READING

Primary Sources

Suetonius, *The Grammaticus* (second century C.E.) is an anecdotal but informative survey of notable grammarians of Rome. A translation and commentary by Robert Kaster is available from Oxford University Press; an older
translation can be found online at www.gutenberg.org/etext/6398.

The orations of Aelius Aristides (second century C.E.) provide splendid examples
of sophistic oratory at its zenith. These have been translated by C. A. Behr
and are available through Brill Academic Publishers. Dio Chrysostom's orations (late first to early second century) are equally valuable and shed light
on popular Stoic-Cynic philosophy. Dio's orations are found in the LCL.

Philostratus, *Lives of the Sophists* (early third century), represents an apprecia-
tive and sympathetic biography of the important sophists of the first and
second centuries. Informative, if read critically. It is found in the LCL.

The *Discourses* of Epictetus and Seneca's *Moral Epistles* (both from the first century C.E.) are the best representatives of mature, well-reasoned Stoicism.
They provide many useful insights into the world of the NT and will nour-
ish both mind and soul. They are available from the LCL.

The *Cynic Epistles,* edited by Abraham Malherbe, is a collection of Cynic writings ranging from the first century B.C.E. to the second century C.E. They
represent both radical and moderate Cynic viewpoints and are published
by Scholars Press.

Diogenes Laertius's *Lives of Eminent Philosophers* (LCL) preserves a wealth of
material on Epicurus, including several of the philosopher's letters. The
works of Philodemus are slowly being translated. Especially useful is David
Sider's *The Epigrams of Philodemos* (Oxford University Press).

Cicero's *Nature of the Gods* provides an extensive summary and evaluation of
the major schools of philosophy in Rome just prior to the Christian era.
As one of the true luminaries of antiquity, Cicero's assessment repays close

scrutiny. On the lighter side is Lucian's "Philosophies for Sale." Both are found in the LCL.

Joseph and Aseneth (first century B.C.E. to first century C.E.). A Hellenistic romance of diaspora Judaism depicting the conversion of Aseneth, a pagan priestess, to Judaism, and her subsequent marriage to Joseph, the Jewish patriarch. This is available in *The Old Testament Pseudepigrapha,* edited by James H. Charlesworth (2 vols.; Garden City, N.Y.: Doubleday, 1983).

Secondary Sources

Troels Engberg-Pedersen. *Paul and the Stoics.* Louisville, Ky.: Westminster John Knox, 2000.

John T. Fitzgerald. *Cracks in an Earthen Vessel: An Examination of the Catalogues of Hardships in the Corinthian Correspondence.* Atlanta: Scholars Press, 1988.

William V. Harris. *Ancient Literacy.* Cambridge, Mass.: Harvard University Press, 1989.

Moyer V. Hubbard. *New Creation in Paul's Letters and Thought.* SNTSMS 119. Cambridge: Cambridge University Press, 2002.

Duane Litfin. *St. Paul's Theology of Proclamation: 1 Corinthians 1–4 and Greco-Roman Rhetoric.* SNTSMS 79. Cambridge: Cambridge University Press, 1994.

Abraham J. Malherbe. *Moral Exhortation: A Greco-Roman Sourcebook.* Philadelphia: Westminster Press, 1986.

Henri Irénée Marrou. *A History of Education in Antiquity.* Wisconsin Studies in Classics. Madison: University of Wisconsin Press, 1982.

Arthur Darby Nock. *Conversion: The Old and the New in Religion from Alexander the Great to Augustine of Hippo.* Oxford: Clarendon, 1952.

Bruce W. Winter. *Philo and Paul among the Sophists: Alexandrian and Corinthian Responses to a Julio-Claudian Movement.* Grand Rapids, Mich.: Eerdmans, 2002.

CITY AND SOCIETY

SPERATUS

Speratus eyed appreciatively the young slave Claudius Dinippus had brought with him to the baths that afternoon. He was carefully scraping his master's back with a small *strigil* while Claudius complained vociferously of the management of the games, the demands of the baker's association, the temperature of the caldarium, and almost anything else that came to mind. This was not making his slave's work any easier, and more than once the boy was threatened with flogging or crucifixion if his master was nicked in the course of his blustering. Claudius was mostly sound and fury, but Speratus knew the slave had reason to fear Claudius's rod, no matter how handsome he was.

Speratus listened patiently to Claudius, feigning deep interest by occasionally nodding in agreement or chiming in with, "Quite right," or "Absolutely." As one of the chief magistrates of Corinth and former president of the Isthmian games, Claudius Dinippus was an important friendship for Speratus to cultivate as he planned his own political career.

"Did you hear the council asked me to supervise the grain supply for the coming year?" remarked Claudius casually.

"No, I hadn't," replied Speratus, "but in view of the recent shortages, I'm not surprised. We need someone of your abilities in control— and we certainly don't want Athens or Epidaurus poaching our corn."

"Exactly. There were riots in Rome last month when the bakers failed to produce their quota of loaves, and we must not think we are immune to such troubles here. Empty stomachs lead to clenched fists, and that's not good for business. I expect I will have to cough up a fortune to keep the city in good supply."

"Perhaps," mused Speratus, "but I'm sure the citizenry will show their appreciation in due course—monuments, plaques, perhaps even a statue."

"They had better!" Claudius grunted.

Claudius was a stout, barrel-chested, ex-military man with a weathered face and strong hands. Now in his mid-fifties, his once formidable physique had gone slightly to seed, though he looked as if he could still handle himself in a scuffle. He had distinguished himself as a tribune of the sixth legion under Claudius and returned from the campaigns against the Britons with a curious sickle-shaped scar above his left eye. The tale that Claudius told about the scar involved flying arrows, glinting steel, and a dozen or so barbarians in close combat. The truth, however, was far less glorious. After several flagons of wine at a dinner party the previous spring, Claudius had blearily confessed to Speratus that he got the scar when he fell asleep on his mount and tumbled off his horse.

Speratus and Claudius were now back in the changing room, carefully wrapping their togas around their waists and over their shoulders, with their slaves attentively assisting with the folds and knots. A properly draped toga was a matter of singular importance to a Roman aristocrat, and both were fastidiously inspecting each crease, while trying not to let the other notice their own vain preoccupation. Claudius wore his *toga trabea* today, a priestly vestment with purple and scarlet stripes near the hem. As an augur and priest of a local religious association, Claudius donned this toga whenever he had business in one of the temples, and today's dinner at the Asklepion was just such an occasion.

"I'll be needing some help with my new responsibilities, Speratus, and I've been thinking you might want a little more exposure among the citizenry and the council. Are you interested?"

"Definitely," replied Speratus, perhaps too eagerly, he immediately thought. Although Speratus understood that this kind of opportunity was precisely why he pursued Claudius as a patron, he did not want to be classed with those unctuous sycophantic clients from the lower orders. He himself was a patron with many clients, and he preferred to think of his relationship to Claudius as a mentoring friendship.

"Excellent. Help me out, and this time next year you'll be wearing the *toga candida*," remarked Claudius brightly.

Leaving the bath complex, Speratus and Claudius were met by Claudius's retinue of clients who had been loitering near the entrance waiting for their patron to emerge. They were a mixed lot: a few fresh-shaven faces and well-laundered togas, but most looked as if they had but one toga and little surplus; some were positively shabby.

"*Ave!* Greetings!" declared one of the more smartly attired attendees, obviously trying to attract Claudius's attention amid the throng. "The sun shines brighter now that it has such a worthy object of its rays!"

"Oh please!" thought Speratus, though he was careful not to express his disdain visibly.

"I don't recall seeing you this morning, Flavius," replied Claudius brusquely. The young man shuffled uncomfortably. Apparently he had hoped that Claudius would not have noticed his absence at the *salutatio*.

"*Domine*, my sincerest apologies . . . important matters, very urgent . . . kept me from this most agreeable task—*opportunity*—to wait on you . . . terribly sorry . . ."

"If you have more important matters to attend to, then off you go—attend to them. I have more important clients to attend to as well," was Claudius's retort.

Deservedly rebuked and deflated, the young man bowed sheepishly toward Claudius and hastily backed out of view.

Claudius dismissed most of the rest his clients with a smile and a piece of silver, retaining a small handful to clear a path through the crowds as the pair made their way to the sanctuary of Asklepios, where they would dine.

"'Important matters' my *clunis!*" scoffed Claudius under his breath as he and Speratus started toward the Asklepion. "More important *patrons* is the real reason. If Flavius wants to court Babbius Philinus, good riddance. But what can you expect? His grandfather was a mason, you know—a bricklayer! The old man happened to be in the right place at the right time and profited handsomely from Corinth's rebuilding, but there's still sand in Flavius's hair and gravel in his tunic, if you ask me. You can't cover up that lineage with a toga."

Speratus and Claudius crossed the street, passed the crossroads shrine, and proceeded down a narrow lane that would eventually open up into the forum. Claudius had wisely chosen the sturdiest of his clients to serve as his advance guard, and they did their best to clear a way through the congestion, but with children tossing knucklebones, merchants hawking their wares, and idlers hanging about everywhere, the going was slow. A bucket of some kind of fetid gruel was tossed from a window overhead and dowsed an old woman who was begging on the corner. Some of the street rabble doubled over in paroxysms of mirth, while the buskers and shopkeepers shouted profanities at the window above. A surly women peeked through the opening, noted the commotion, cursing, and glaring, and simply waved hello with her middle finger.

"This is why I prefer my villa in Cenchrea," observed Speratus. Claudius, however, wasn't listening. His gaze was still fixed above, but not on the now vacant window. His eyes had caught sight of a flock of geese.

". . . five, six, seven—yes! Notice the very tight formation, Speratus, and the southerly direction; this bodes well. I think we can expect a close partnership, and grain supplies from the south."

"Oh . . . uh, very good," replied Speratus, trying to muster convincing enthusiasm for Claudius's prediction.

"So, you think augury is for the birds, do you?" queried Claudius.

Embarrassed that his skepticism was so transparent, Speratus added in apologetic overtones, "No, no—it's not my expertise, of course, so I must leave the matter to those endowed with such gifts, like yourself." Speratus was painfully aware of his pathetic response and was relieved to see Claudius was amused at his squirming.

"Not to worry," chuckled Claudius. "I have enough faith for both of us."

There was that word again, *fides*, faith. Speratus had heard it quite a lot in recent weeks, and his thoughts meandered back to Julia. . . .

"What do you mean you want a new fresco in the atrium? Mars embracing Venus was *your* idea, Julia, remember?" Speratus was becoming increasingly concerned with his wife's new interests, tastes, and friendships. Every week for the last month she had absconded with Zoe and spent the evening with Phoebe, a prominent widow in Cenchrea who was hosting a religious association of some kind. On the one hand, Speratus had noticed a new civility, even kindness, in Julia's demeanor; on the other hand, some of her behavior was strange to say the least. She had been neglecting the household shrines—something unthinkable for the Julia he had always known—and he had even caught her and Zoe huddled together in the *tablinum* as if in prayer—with Zoe, a slave!

"*Meum mel*, dearest," cooed Julia, "wouldn't you prefer a hunting scene or perhaps Scipio victorious over Hannibal?"

"What I would *prefer* is not to dishonor the gods—and you know how important Aphrodite is to the city. I've spent much of the last two years entertaining members of the council and other prominent citizens as I prepare for a seat on the council. They have all admired this fresco and toasted Aphrodite in our *triclinium*. Why would you want to jinx it all and arouse unnecessary suspicions?"

"Speratus," Julia's mood was suddenly more serious, "do you really *believe* that Aphrodite sprung from the froth of the sea, that Cronus swallowed his children whole, and that if we climbed Olympus we might see Zeus resting on a cloud?"

Speratus stared at Julia with a mixture of bewilderment and disbelief. Julia knew full well that Speratus was not particularly religious, but to question the existence of the gods was to ridicule the *mos maiorum* itself, the traditions of the ancestors.

"What if," Julia continued, not waiting for Speratus to regain his equilibrium, "what if there was only one God who made everything, and who loves everyone equally, and who always acts justly, with true *sanctitas*, holiness—wouldn't such a god be more deserving of our *fides*?"

"Deserving of faith? Loving? What are you talking about?" Speratus sputtered, still looking somewhat disoriented. "If this god existed he would have shown himself to the Romans by now!"

"But he has!" interjected Julia. "He appeared . . ."

"Enough of this nonsense!" Speratus's expression was now severe and determined. "I'll be damned if I am going to let you and your god ruin my political career. You are no longer to see Phoebe," Speratus announced in a tone that brooked no objection. His eyes were fixed on his wife as though he were unsure of the person who stood before him.

"Sisyphus!" Speratus summoned his steward abruptly. Always eavesdropping, Sisyphus appeared practically before his name had left his master's lips.

"Yes, *kurie*." Sisyphus often lapsed into Greek when nervous. The steward's eyes passed quickly between Speratus and Julia as he assessed the situation.

"You are to make preparations immediately to sell Zoe at the next auction," ordered Speratus, still staring at his wife.

"Sell Zoe? But *domine*, she . . ."

"Immediately!" barked Speratus.

Sisyphus nodded compliantly, shooting Julia a pleading expression as he exited. Julia stood motionless and silent. The *pater familias* had spoken. The matter was closed.

When they finally reached the Asklepion, Claudius and Speratus were greeted heartily by a dozen or so local dignitaries—prominent citizens, members of the city council, and other wealthy notables. A table had been prepared for them in an open courtyard adjacent to the sacred grove, and Speratus observed with satisfaction that passersby could not help but notice the party, and of course him, toasting the gods with the local elite.

Claudius Dinnipus's words were endued gravitas as he led the party in an offering to Asclepius, the healing savior, and poured libations to the emperor and the imperial family. It was apparent that Claudius relished these rituals, performing even the most trivial components with ceremonious flair. The temple attendants were cheerful and quick to oblige, and the food was ample. The conversation predictably centered around victories at the recent games and likely sources of grain for the coming year. Claudius announced his choice of Gaius Cornelius Speratus as co-curator, which was met with enthusiasm, backslapping, and jokes about Claudius's age.

The only noteworthy gossip, as far as Speratus was concerned, involved Erastus, of all people. Maecius inquired about his absence, and Claudius was insistent that Erastus had been invited. After several members of the party compared notes, it became apparent that Erastus had not been seen at any of the recent functions, not even the sacral procession of Apollo.

"But I see him in the forum every day, objected Maecius. "He is quite conscientious about his duties."

"Well, we'll need to look into the matter," intoned Claudius. "An aedile needs to give attention to more than just the markets and the buildings; *pietas*, reverence toward the gods is every magistrate's responsibility."

Speratus and his slave trotted home at a brisk pace and arrived as the sun westered beyond the horizon. Dismounting, Speratus remembered that today was auction day and that Zoe would no longer be waiting on him and Julia that evening or coddling little Marky in the morning. His confrontation with Julia the previous week was still a source of pain for Speratus, not least because he didn't really want to sell Zoe. However, Claudius's sober reminder of the importance of *pietas* reinforced for Speratus the hard line he took with his wife. He didn't want to end up like Erastus—the subject of gossip and innuendo.

Entering the atrium, Speratus spotted Julia seated in the courtyard *peristyle*, humming softly. Her mood seemed surprisingly serene for having just lost a faithful servant. Gaius Cornelius knew that a good master was just as hard to come by as a good servant, and he marveled that Julia wasn't consumed with anxiety or tears. Sisyphus emerged from the opposite hallway and immediately began to help his master with his traveling cloak.

"How did it go at the auction today, Sisyphus?" whispered Speratus. His steward, noting Julia in the courtyard, followed his master's cue and replied in hushed tones, "Very good. You received full price, and then some!"

"Excellent," replied Speratus, half-heartedly. "And, the buyer— what was he like?"

"Not he, *domine*, she."

"She?"

"Yes, *domine*, a local woman bid fifty denarii more than your already steep asking price right at the start, and after that nobody else even bothered."

"Amazing," said Speratus, this time with sincerity. "A local woman, you say? Did you recognize her?

"Yes, *domine*. Her name is Phoebe."

"Phoebe?" echoed Speratus, turning in the direction of his wife, a look of dawning comprehension in his eyes.

Speratus stood pondering his wife, and after a few moments of contemplation he mused audibly, "Well, she may not believe in the gods, but she's as cunning as any daughter of Hera."

Sisyphus offered no response, but Speratus was almost certain he detected a guilty expression flash across his steward's face. Speratus's eyes darted quickly back to his wife, still humming in the courtyard, and realized that Julia had a partner in this little domestic conspiracy.

"That's all for tonight, Sisyphys," said Speratus, eyeing his steward warily.

"Yes, *kurie*."

THE CULTURAL CONTEXT

PAUL AND THE CITY

Jesus was a man of the village. Much of his ministry took place in rural areas, and his stories are full of images drawn from provincial life: fishermen, farmers, mustard seed, and sheep. Paul, by contrast, was very much a man of the city. He was born in a city, raised in a city, and spent most of his adult life traveling between cities.[1] When we read his letters, we hear of ambassadors, orators, magistrates, athletes, and merchants. His images recall the gymnasium and the tribunal (Rom 14:10; 2 Cor 5:10), and he was not above boasting of this heritage: "I am a Jew, from Tarsus in Cilicia, a citizen of no ordinary city" (Acts 21:39). One gets the impression that Paul was much more comfortable teaching in the "lecture hall of Tyrannus" (Acts 19:9) than he ever would have been in the hill country of Galilee (cf. Matt 5:1). Yet while Paul and Jesus spoke from within, and to, different contexts, their lives and ministries both took shape in the shadow of imperial Rome. They both walked on Roman roads, conversed with Roman officials, carried Roman coins, sat in Roman shackles, and died as Roman criminals.

> PAUL RESOLVED TO GO TO JERUSALEM, PASSING THROUGH MACEDONIA AND ACHAIA. HE SAID, "AFTER I HAVE BEEN THERE, I MUST ALSO SEE ROME."
>
> ACTS 19:21

The focus of this chapter is the urban centers of the Roman world because it was here that Christianity took root, grew, and became clearly distinguished from Judaism, as Luke informs us: "The disciples were first called Christians in Antioch" (Acts 11:26). Paul in particular seemed intentionally to target key cities in his evangelistic endeavors, and so we know more about urban Christianity in the first century than any other form—assuming other forms existed. The addressees of Paul's letters read like a who's who of major cities of the Greco-Roman world: to the saints in Ephesus, to the church of God in Corinth, to the church of the Thessalonians, to all those in Rome.

TRAVEL IN ANTIQUITY

The Feasibility of Travel

Moving about from city to city or country to country had become more feasible in the first century than at any other time in the history of Greek and Roman civilizations. Two related circumstances led to this state of affairs: the establishment of the *Pax Romana* ("Roman peace") and the construction of a vast network of roads that connected Rome to its distant provinces and far-flung cities. Prior to Octavian's victory at Actium (31 B.C.E.) and the subsequent consolidation and centralization of imperial power, the Roman world convulsed with civil wars, rebellious provinces, and internal power struggles. The end of this reign of chaos was such a relief to the general populace that poets like Virgil announced the advent of "the golden age,"[2] and cities and provinces erected monuments declaring Augustus to be "a savior who has put an end to war."[3] The advance and maintenance of the Roman Empire necessitated a means for the rapid deployment of troops, which resulted in a system of roads whose durability was unequalled until modern times.

> TO L. CALPURNIS PRO-
> CLUS, CURATOR OF
> THE TRAJANIC ROADS,
> PROCONSUL OF THE
> PROVINCE OF ASIA. . . .
> HIS FRIENDS ERECTED
> THIS AT THEIR OWN
> EXPENSE, WITH THE PER-
> MISSION OF THE CITY
> COUNCIL OF CORINTH,
> BECAUSE OF HIS JUSTICE.
>
> *INSCRIPTION, CORINTH

The Dangers of Travel

Yet for all this, travel was still a difficult and often dangerous endeavor in the first century. It is true that Augustus and subsequent emperors had made great strides in reducing banditry and piracy, yet the relative ease and safety of travel that we moderns enjoy was not the experience of the first-century traveler.[4] While Epictetus, for example, extolled the relative peace achieved by imperial Rome, where there was "no brigandage on a large scale, nor piracy, but at any hour we may travel by land or sail from the rising of the sun to its setting,"[5] he also described roads "infested with robbers" and commended the prudent traveler as one who waits for a passing diplomat and travels with his retinue rather than proceeding alone.[6] In a similar vein, Plutarch remarks that the only people who don't fear the highwayman are those who never leave their homes.[7] This explains the scene in the Satyricon where two travelers suddenly reveal their swords to settle a dispute: the wise traveler prepared for the worst.[8]

> IT IS APPROPRIATE FOR
> THE GOOD GOVERNOR
> WHO TAKES HIS JOB
> SERIOUSLY TO SEE THAT
> HIS PROVINCE IS QUIET
> AND PEACEFUL. HE WILL
> HUNT OUT TEMPLE
> ROBBERS, HIGHWAY
> ROBBERS, KIDNAP-
> PERS, AND THIEVES.
>
> *ULPIAN

Modes of Travel

Quite apart from the perennial concern of brigands, travel in antiquity was also rendered difficult by the limited modes of transport available and, in the case of longer journeys, the lack of suitable accommodation. When undertaking an overland journey, most people had little choice but to travel on foot.[9] Horses were expensive and used mainly by the military and imperial couriers.[10] Merchants and farmers transporting goods might use a cart drawn by a mule or a team of oxen. The wealthy elite could travel in grand style: wagons hauled by horses, carriages drawn by slaves, a huge entourage. Wheeled transport, however, was not a realistic alternative for most. In explaining why he is thankful to be man of modest means, Horace remarks that otherwise, "I should have to enlarge my means, welcome more callers, take one or two in my company so as not to go abroad or into the country alone; I should have to keep more pages and ponies and a train of wagons. As it is, if I want, I may go on a bob-tailed mule as far as Tarentum."[11] The biblical phrase "a day's journey" (e.g., John 3:4; Luke 2:44) is generally taken to mean around twenty miles on foot,[12] though inclement weather would dramatically reduce this distance.

> WHAT A LOT OF TRICKS YOU USE TO DECEIVE, INNKEEPER! YOU SELL WATER BUT DRINK UNMIXED WINE.
>
> GRAFFITO, POMPEII

Accommodation

For accommodation travelers relied on the hospitality of local residents, on the availability of inns, or the necessity of sleeping in the open. Horace described a trip that involved all three at various points.[13] Inns, however, were notorious for bedbugs, brawling, and promiscuity.[14] Graffiti from Pompeii attest to the availability of barmaids at inns for the lonely traveler,[15] and this confession scribbled near the door at the Inn of the Muledrivers in Pompeii must have surely turned away a few patrons: "We have wet the bed, innkeeper. I confess we have done wrong. If you want to know why, there was no chamber pot."[16] In addition, innkeepers were notorious for swindling their guests. Josephus includes the innkeeper in a list of dishonorable trades (along with prostitutes and slaves) as one who connives to cheat.[17]

> . . . DO WE NEED, AS SOME DO, LETTERS OF RECOMMENDATION TO YOU OR FROM YOU?
>
> 2 CORINTHIANS 3:1

The preferred option was to stay with a relative or friend. Letters of recommendation were used when the journeyer was personally unknown to the host. These letters might be sent along ahead or carried by the traveler:

> Theon to the most honored Tyrannus very many greetings. Heraclides, the bearer of this letter is my brother, wherefore I entreat you with all my power to take him under your protection. I have also asked your brother Hermias by letter to inform you about him. . . . Above all else I pray that you may have health and the best of success, unharmed by the evil eye. Goodbye.[18]

Cynics, who took pride in "living according to nature," required much less attention from their host—or so they liked to boast: "To Rhesus, Greetings. Phrynicus the Larissaean, a disciple of mine, is anxious to see Argos, 'where horses graze.' And he will not require much from you since he is a philosopher."[19]

Travel by Sea

Sea travel was sometimes an expedient option, though it was very different from what we are accustomed to today.[20] Passenger ships were not in existence, so those wishing to travel by sea would have to find a merchant ship sailing in the direction they wished to go, book passage, and wait for favorable winds. Sailing during the winter months (November through April) virtually ceased due to storms and limited visibility; navigation was by the stars and visible landmarks. Passengers passed the day and the night on the open deck, as cabins were available only for the captain and, on larger ships, VIPs. Seafaring travelers were also expected to provide their own food and covering sufficient for the journey. Horace's description of an overnight trip on a canal boat depicts the minor annoyances of such conditions: "Cursed gnats and frogs of the fens drive off sleep; the boatman, soaked in sour wine, singing the while of the girl he left behind, and a passenger taking up the refrain. . . ."[21] These minor annoyances might be considered a fair exchange for the ordeals of traveling overland, if it were not for the major annoyance that sea travel offered: shipwrecks.

> DINIS DEFCILA, A MARINER AND GAIUS RASININUS VALENS DEDICATE THIS MONUMENT TO THE GOD NEPTUNE AND THE SACRED DIOSCURI, BECAUSE THEY APPEARED TO US AND RESCUED US.
>
> *INSCRIPTION, PHILIPPI

The frequency with which ancient sources mention shipwrecks, stranded sailors, and the hazards of sea travel attests to the primitive conditions and technology (comparatively speaking) of even nautically advanced societies in antiquity. While first-century mariners possessed considerable knowledge of tides and winds in well-traveled routes, they lacked our modern detailed navigational charts that display currents, depths, hazards, and the like. When squalls arose, there was no radio to call for help and no Coast Guard to offer help. First-century vessels were not equipped with lifeboats or life vests,[22] so the best one could hope for in desperate situations was to run the ship aground.[23] Failing this, passengers and crew scrambled for a plank to float on or attempted to swim to shore as best they could.[24] The *Greek Anthology* preserves this tragic dedicatory epigram:

> AS FOR ME, I WOULD BE AMAZED TO SEE A SKIPPER LIVE TO OLD AGE.
>
> PLUTARCH

> Dionysius, the only one saved out of forty sailors, dedicates here the image of a *cele* [part of the ship's rigging], tying which close to his thighs he swam to shore. So even a *cele* brings luck on some occasions.[25]

Military vessels could make use of slaves working oars to supply propulsion, but most merchant ships had to rely on a single mainsail, with possibly a smaller sail on the bowsprit. This significantly reduced maneuverability and inhibited tacking (sailing in a zigzag pattern against the wind) and meant that ancient mariners were left largely at the mercy of prevailing winds.

It is no wonder, then, that maritime disaster was one of the most common fears of the ancients[26] and that the stranded sailor (often begging in the forum) became a literary cliché among writers of the period.[27] Lucian describes "crowds" of former sailors in the temple spinning yarns of "waves, tempests, headlands, strandings, masts carried away, rudders broken. . . ." The very real perils involved in seafaring explains Juvenal's contempt for the merchant who weighs anchor in less than ideal conditions, allowing greed to trump good judgment: "Poor wretch! On this very night he may well be cast out amid broken timbers and engulfed by the waves, clutching his money-belt with his left hand or his teeth."[28] Such was the fear and risk of seafaring that Petronius advises that anyone "who would not haste to die" should keep their feet on dry land.[29]

> PITY THE SHIPWRECKED, FOR NAVIGATION IS UNSURE.
>
> PSEUDO-PHOCYLIDES

Superstition and Travel

Sailors have always been superstitious, and this was even more true in the first century. The wary skipper always had one eye peeled for favorable or unfavorable omens, and they were careful to have their vessels equipped with sacred objects to ward off calamity.[30] Travelers, whether by land or sea, would take vows and pray for safe travel:

> Melikertes son of Ino Leukothea the grey ruler of the open sea and divine averter of troubles, choruses of Nereids, Waves, and you Poseidon, and Thracian Zephyros the gentlest of the Winds, graciously may you bear me safely across a calm sea in my flight to the sweet shore of Peraeus.[31]

At the end of the journey a dedication or sacrifice of thanksgiving might be made, as this example found near the temple of Pan in Egypt illustrates: "Praise our God. Theodotus the son of Dorion, a Jew, saved from the sea made this."[32]

CIVIC AND PROVINCIAL ADMINISTRATION

The cities that Paul traveled to and from were all connected to Rome, be they in Syria, Asia, or Macedonia. Philippi and Corinth, for example, were Roman colonies; Iconium was a Roman provincial capital. Even so-called free cities like Thessalonica were granted this status only at the pleasure of Rome. The general structure of Roman imperial rule (the emperor, the senate, proconsuls) does not require extended comment here; my focus will be on local government. It should be remembered, however, that the world in which Paul lived and died was the Roman world, and the cities he visited belonged to Roman provinces governed by Roman administrators.

This is not to say that these cities were identical—far from it. Municipalities in Syria differed significantly from those in Galatia in culture, ethnicity, and, to a lesser extent, in organization. Focusing on the Greco-Roman world, the Hellenistic cities of the East were subject to Roman taxation (with a few exceptions) and to direct intervention by Rome in their local affairs if Rome deemed it in their interests. Administratively, Greek cities were historically more democratic in their organization than their Roman counterparts, with elected magistrates, a city council (the *boule*), and some forum for input from the populace (the *demos*).[33] Roman cities outside the Italian peninsula, like Philippi and Corinth, maintained a traditional form of Roman civic administration: *Aediles* controlled the markets and public buildings, *quaestores* functioned as city treasurers, and the *duoviri* were the chief judges and senior members of the city council (*ordo decurionum*).

> EACH OF THE PERSONS WHO SEEK ELECTION TO THE DUOVIRATE OR THE QUAESTORSHIP . . . IS TO PROVIDE SURETIES TO THE PUBLIC FUNDS OF THE CITIZENS OF THE MUNICIPALITY.
>
> INSCRIPTION, BAETICA

The democratic ideals of Greek cities were undermined by Rome, which demanded significant income and property requirements for those considering public office in both Hellenistic and Roman cities.[34] This ensured that power remained in the hands of the wealthy elite.[35] There was also the expectation that elected officials would bestow benefactions on the community, whether in the form of athletic competitions, gladiatorial shows, or some needed public work. Apuleius's fictional account of the gladiatorial games sponsored by a Corinthian *duumvir* represents nothing out of the ordinary.[36] Paul's companion and aedile of Corinth, Erastus (Rom 16:23), paved the area near the lower theater and left the following inscription commemorating his gratitude: "Erastus, in return for his aedileship, laid the pavement at his own expense."[37]

URBAN LANDSCAPE AND ENVIRONMENT

Unlike modern cities, cities in antiquity would be enclosed within a wall for protection against enemies and would contain several gates that would close after dark. Tombs and mausoleum-like graves of illustrious residents would often be placed along the main roads leading into the city, between the outer wall and the city center. Excavations from Pompeii have provided splendid examples of these funerary monuments. Many of the structures found in modern cities would naturally be found in ancient cities as well: government buildings,

AS ONE GOES UP TO CORINTH THERE ARE TOMBS, AND BY THE GATE IS BURIED DIOGENES OF SINOPE, WHOM THE GREEKS CALL "THE DOG."

PAUSANIUS

theaters, inns, pubs, brothels, and the like. These public and private buildings would be arranged around large open plazas, or forums (Greek *agorai*), which would serve as markets and areas for public assembly. From the standpoint of the NT, several civic institutions in particular are worth looking at in more detail: temples, baths, synagogues, and prisons. The former two are crucial because of their centrality to daily life in a Greco-Roman city; the latter are crucial because of their importance to Paul's letters and travels. Synagogues were Paul's first stop in the cities he evangelized. Prisons require special comment because so much of Paul's time was spent in, and many of his letters written from, Roman confinement.

Temples

Temples were easily the most prominent feature of any civic landscape, particularly the city center. A visitor standing in the main forum of Corinth would be, quite literally, surrounded by the gods: Hermes, Fortuna, Poseidon, Apollo, Herakles, the Pantheon, the imperial cult, and others. The same would be true of Pompeii, Ephesus, Philippi, or any city of the Greco-Roman world. Pausanias, a second-century tourist who took notes on his visits to notable cities in Greece, describes temples, shrines, and altars on virtually every corner of the cities he visited. No wonder that Paul's stroll through Athens caused him so much distress as he observed that "the city was full of idols" (Acts 17:16).

MELITE AND MACEDON, BECAUSE THEY STOLE SOME ITEMS FROM THE SANCTUARY, HAVE BEEN PUNISHED. THEIR PARENTS HAVE INTERCEDED FOR THEM WITH THE GOD APOLLON AZYROS. THEY INTERCEDED, AND THIS OFFERING IS PRESENTED WITH GRATEFULNESS.

INSCRIPTION, BITHYNIA

Temples varied in size, function, and significance. Some were little more than semi-enclosed shrines. Every city, however, had its grander temples, even if they did not rival the temple of Artemis in Ephesus as one of the wonders of the ancient world. Few, however, of these great temples have survived the ravages of time; wars, earthquakes, and locals needing building material have taken their toll. What we moderns see as we gaze at the columns and porticos that still stand are vestiges of ancient polytheism. What we ought to see as well are centers of commerce, art, entertainment, and social networking.[38]

It is common to run across references to robbing temples in ancient literature. From tyrants plundering foreign temples to enrich their own treasury to peasants pilfering local shrines to line their pockets,[39] burglary was a perennial problem for temple staff and local magistrates, as Cicero acknowledges: "For we have often seen temples robbed and images of gods carried off from the holiest shrines by our fellow-countrymen."[40] The practice even warrants mention by Paul (Rom 2:22). At the risk of stating the obvious, temples were robbed because temples possessed wealth.

THE SANCTUARY OF ASCLEPIUS IS WORTH SEEING BOTH FOR ITS PAINTINGS AND FOR THE STATUES OF THE GOD AND HIS CHILDREN.

PAUSANIAS

Temples often served as banks, taking deposits and extending loans.[41] They were also used to display plunder taken from enemies[42] and to house artwork, gilded statuary, and other utensils made from precious metals. Pausanias's travelogue provides a virtual catalog of artwork from the temples of second-century Greece.[43] As objects of civic pride, temples were adorned to appeal to locals and tourists alike; paintings were commissioned, walls were frescoed to herald the excellencies of the deity, and attractions were added to encourage frequent visits.[44] These might include exotic animals, extensive gardens, and even theaters. The sanctuary of Demeter and Kore in Corinth had a theater attached with a capacity of nearly one hundred. Some temples contained libraries and provided venues for poets to read their work or philosophers and educators to hold lectures.[45]

AND ON THE NEXT DAY OF THE FESTIVAL HONORING ISIS THE SMALL TRADERS MAKE THEMSELVES BOOTHS OF REEDS OR OTHER IMPROVISED MATERIAL. ON THE LAST OF THE THREE DAYS THEY HOLD A FAIR, SELLING SLAVES, CATTLE OF ALL KINDS, CLOTHES, SILVER AND GOLD. AFTER MID-DAY THEY TURN TO SACRIFICING.

* PAUSANIAS

Music was also important to temple life. Flute players, pipers, and the like sometimes accompanied a sacrifice to muffle background noise, as Pliny the Elder tells us, "so that nothing but the prayer is heard."[46] A sacrificial altar from the temple of Vespasian in Pompeii depicts a priest with his attendants, the bull to be sacrificed, and a flutist providing musical accompaniment.[47] Temples regularly employed singers and chorales to chant hymns to the deity and troupes of dancers to perform cultic dances. In Ephesus the chief priest was commanded to ensure that worshipers "sing songs of praise at the sacrifices, at the processions, and at the night festivals."[48] Mystery religions, like those of Isis, Dionysus, and Cybele, were notorious for pious revelry, as Lucian explains:

I forebear to say that not a single ancient mystery-cult can be found that is not without dancing. . . . At Delos, indeed, even the sacrifices were not without dancing, but were performed with that and with music. Choirs of boys came together, and while they moved and sang to the accompaniment of flute and lyre, . . . [they] performed an interpretive dance.[49]

Temples could be lively places indeed! In a letter to Christians in Rome, Ignatius, bishop of Antioch, traveling under armed guard to Rome where he would be martyred (107 C.E.), pictures himself a sacrifice upon an altar with believers gathered around as a chorus chanting praise—an image drawn from the daily routine at pagan temples.[50]

> APHRODITE'S TEMPLE WAS PROLIFIC WITH GARDEN FRUITS. THESE TREES, LUXURIANT FAR AND WIDE WITH FRESH GREEN LEAVES ROOFED IN THE AIR AROUND THEM. UNDER THE PARTICULARLY SHADY TREES WERE JOYOUS COUCHES. ALL THE CITY RABBLE FLOCKED THERE ON HOLIDAYS.
>
> *PSEUDO-LUCIAN

Another important function of temples was to provide dining facilities for private parties, be they local guilds, political clubs, or family events.[51] The meager size of the typical Roman domicile (see Household and Family: The Home) made renting facilities a necessity for gatherings of more than fifteen or so.[52] Funerals, weddings, and rites of passage typically involved at least a sacrifice at a temple, if not a meal. In Troezen, south of Corinth, Pausanias tells us that "every maiden before marriage cuts off a lock for [the god] Hippolytus and, having cut it, she brings it to the temple and dedicates it."[53] Archaeological remains of dining facilities in the sanctuary of Asclepius in Corinth and the Temple of Demeter and Kore confirm what was a standard feature of the larger temples,[54] as the Corinthian correspondence also confirms (see City and Society: The Temple of God and the Idols in Corinth). Some temples had outdoor dining facilities available in the sacred groves adjacent to the temple compounds.[55] According to Pausanias, at the Asklepion in Epidaurus there was a rule that "all the offerings . . . are entirely consumed within the bounds [of the temple precinct]."[56] Dining in a temple would typically involve drinking a toast or pouring a libation to the deity, who was believed to be present at the table. In some cases the invitation to such a banquet would come from the deity: "The god calls you to a banquet being held in the Thoereion tomorrow from the ninth hour."[57]

Temples also hosted regular festivals in commemoration of the patron deity and were integral to the success of other city-wide celebrations as well. Dio gives us a glimpse of the energy and bustle associated with these events:

> Many, too, bring in merchandise of all sorts, the trades people, that is; and some display their own arts and crafts; while others show off their accomplishments, many of them declaiming poems, both tragedies and epics, and many others prose works.[58]

Plutarch's perspective is probably representative of most: "The pleasantest things that people enjoy are festal days, and banquets at the temples, initiations and mystic rites, and prayer and adoration of the gods."[59]

Banquets and dinner parties—in private homes or public venues—were commonly the scene of sexual liaisons, drinking, and other unseemly behavior.[60] Quintilian complains that children see their parents' vice and luxury at dinner parties and their father's mistresses and are corrupted before they reach adulthood.[61] Martial's numerous epigrams on the subject may intentionally exaggerate the matter,[62] but other voices from antiquity corroborate the sordid picture he depicts.[63] Exquisite murals from Pompeii and Herculaneum portray both indoor and outdoor banqueters, perhaps in a temple grove, with scantily clad courtesans, flagons of wine, amorous foreplay, and so on.[64] One can always count on the Cynics to play the role of the party pooper:

> And you, blockheads . . . deserve greater punishment. Whenever the so-called festival of Hermes or the Athenaean games are held, both in the gymnasia and right in the market place, you eat and drink, get drunk, have intercourse, and act effeminately . . . in the open and in secret.[65]

HOWEVER, MARRIAGE IS VERY STRICT AMONG THE GERMANS. THEIR WOMEN LIVE THEIR LIVES WITH THEIR CHASTITY FIRMLY GIRDED, CORRUPTED BY NO LURES OF EXTRAVAGANZAS, NO UNSETTLING EXCITEMENTS OF DINNER PARTIES.

*LIVY

Even this broad-stroked depiction of the role of temples in community life is sufficient to reveal an institution at the nexus of social discourse. A vibrant temple supplied work for musicians, sculptures, farmers, food venders, and many others. It was the setting for significant family celebrations, it provided a means for strengthening social and professional connections, and—importantly—it provided an avenue for political advancement.

Digging Deeper: The Cursus Honorum

To be elected to a priesthood was a substantial boon to any political résumé and could be an important rung on the ladder an aspiring aristocrat had to climb. The Romans called this ladder of success the *cursus honorum,* succession of honors, referring to the established sequence of public offices in one's ascent of the socio-political pyramid. All throughout the Greco-Roman world the political grandees etched their curriculum vitae in stone and erected them in prominent places for all to see. These monuments regularly boast of priestly appointments. Babbius Philinus, a contemporary with Paul, built a fountain in the Corinthian forum on which he inscribed the following inscription twice:

Gnaeus Babbius Philinus, aedile and pontifex [priest], had this monument erected at his own expense, and he approved it in his official capacity as duovir.[66]

From Cisalpine Gaul (now northern Italy) comes the *cursus honorum* of Calpurnius Fabatus, which includes an important priestly appointment:

Lucius Calpurnius Fabatus: Member of the board of six; twice military tribute with the Twenty-First Legion; prefect of the Seventh Cohort of Lusitanians and of the six tribes of Gaetulians in Numidia; priest of the deified Augustus; patron of the municipality: erected in accordance with his will.[67]

Although his name is lost, the achievements of this magistrate from Philippi are not: "Pontifex, Priest of the divine Augustus, Duumvir *iure dicundo,* twice Duumvir *quinquennalis.*"[68]

Even emperors boasted of priestly appointments:

Tiberius Claudius Caesar Augustus Germanicus, Supreme Pontif, in the sixth year of his tribunician power, designated consul for the fourth time, hailed Imperator for the eleventh, Father of his country, constructed this road.[69]

FOR GAIUS JULIUS SPARTIATICUS, PROCURATOR OF CAESAR AND THE AUGUSTA AGRIPPINA, MILITARY TRIBUNE, PRIEST OF THE DEIFIED JULIUS, TWICE QUINQUENNIAL DUOVIR, PRESIDENT OF THE ISTHMIAN AND CAESAREAN SEBASTEON GAMES, HIGH PRIEST IN PERPETUITY OF THE HOUSE OF AUGUSTUS.

*INSCRIPTION, CORINTH

These *testimonia*—and countless more could be added—illustrate more than the typical career track of ambitious noblemen and the prestige of sacerdotal investiture. They also highlight the inextricable connection between politics and religion in antiquity. A priestly office was a political appointment, and a politician was, to some extent, a religious functionary. The separation of religion and the state that undergirds modern Western democracies would have struck the ancient as absurd, even dangerous. The primary duties of elected officials were to oversee their area of responsibility. The *curator viarum* maintained the roads, the *agonothetes* supervised the games, the *curator annonae* monitored the grain supply, and so on. Yet it was also the duty of politicians to ensure that the gods were properly honored and that no offense was given to any deity that might adversely affect the prosperity of the city. Atheism was such a serious offense in antiquity not primarily because it was a sacrilege but because it was treason; it constituted a religio-political betrayal that endangered the entire community.

So, the oaths that magistrates took as they entered office typically involved a sacrifice to the gods and a promise of religious fealty:

As each of the candidates seeking election to the duovirate, aedileship or quaestorship wins the majority of the total number of voting units, before the person holding the elections declares that man a successfully elected candidate, he is to cause him in public at an assembly to take an oath by Jupiter, the Deified Augustus, Claudius, and Vespasian Augustus and Titus Augustus and by the Genius of Imperator Domitian Augustus and by the gods of the household that he will perform those things which are incumbent upon him.[70]

Local magistrates were expected to participate in religious feasts and acts of piety toward the gods, in addition to the secular affairs of their office. The city council of Gytheion, the port of Sparta in Laconia, proposed to Tiberius a celebration of his divinity that involved theatrical performances, festal processions, incense, and a sacrifice, all to be supervised by the magistrate in charge of the market, the aedile.[71]

The Imperial Cult

The most important temples and priesthoods in many cities of the Roman world belonged to a new arrival on the celestial scene, a god who was declared to be "the savior of all men"[72] and "the world's glory,"[73] who brought "good news" (*euangelion*) to the world,[74] the Roman emperor. Emperor worship began in earnest sometime after the posthumous deification of Julius Caesar in

> SACRED TO THE DEIFIED AUGUSTUS
>
> INSCRIPTION, CORINTH

42 B.C.E. Octavian, Julius Caesar's successor and adopted son, was then able to claim the title "Son of [a] God," and assumed the name *Augustus*, which is difficult to render in English: "highly revered," "sacred one," or "most majestic" are imperfect attempts. Octavian's successors happily followed his example, and the phrase *Divi Filius*, "son of [a] god" was inscribed on coinage for generations to come. In Egypt, with its long history of the divinization of pharaoh, and in the East, with its tradition of accommodating the ruler within the pantheon, worship of the emperor as a god was embraced. In Rome, however, such divine claims were more muted and subtle, at least by most emperors.[75] Nonetheless, by the middle of the first century the imperial cult was firmly established in Rome and the provinces.[76]

> NERO CLAUDIUS, SON OF GOD, CAESAR AUGUSTUS GERMANICUS, IMPERATOR, WITH TRIBUNICIAN POWER, CONSUL.
>
> ROMAN COIN

The voices heralding the new god and the new age were many and varied. The literati curried favor with the emperor through grand epics like the *Aeneid* (Virgil), which legitimized imperial rule, and through shorter poems and epigrams flattering the emperor by affirming his divinity.[77] Calpurnius Siculus, a Roman poet under Nero, proclaimed the advent of the "Golden Age of untroubled peace" and unbounded prosperity.[78] In messianic overtones he beseeches Nero:

Thou too, Caesar, whether thou art Jupiter himself on earth in altered guise, or one other of the powers above concealed under an assumed mortal semblance (for thou art very God)—rule, I pray thee, this world, rule its peoples forever! Abandon not, O Sire, the peace thou hast begun.[79]

More important for spreading the imperial gospel than the highbrow literature of the poets were the coins, statues, inscriptions, and temples, which were part and parcel of the daily routine of first-century urbanites. Coins not only bluntly proclaimed the emperor's deity; they also more subtly implied his divine status through images of gods and goddesses on one side and the image of the emperor on the other. Divine personifications on coins (e.g., the goddesses Peace, Security, Justice, Prosperity), suggested the emperor ruled with the blessings of the gods, while investing that rule with divine sanction. Representations of the emperor with a globe under foot graphically depicted his conquest of and dominion over the world.

Because of the significant benefits that accrued to cities with a vibrant imperial cult, local assemblies scrambled to show their devotion to the imperial house. Busts of the ruling monarch were added to temples dedicated to the traditional gods,[80] artwork and statuary portrayed the emperor in the guise of a deity, and sometimes surnames were added to shrines and altars: in Suel (modern Spain) we hear of Neptune Augustus,[81] in Philippi of Mercury Augustus,[82] in Corinth of Apollo Augustus,[83] in Rome of Pax Augustus,[84] and so on. The most conspicuous change, however, was the transformation of civic space that occurred in many localities throughout the Roman world. Old sanctuaries were remodeled and given imperial additions, new temples to the emperor and his family were built, and city centers were gradually refurbished to give due homage to Augustus, "the sacred one."[85] The worship of the emperor was carried out not only in rituals performed within his temples but also in citywide festivals and athletic competitions given in his honor. Some cities made the emperor's birthday, "Augustus Day," a public holiday.[86] The ruling assembly of Asia went even further, issuing a decree that the calendar would be revised to begin the new year on Augustus's birthday:

> TIBERIUS CLAUDIUS GREETS THE COUNCIL OF AEZANI. KNOWING YOUR DEVOTION TO ME, I GLADLY RECEIVED YOUR ENVOYS AND THE DECREE DEMONSTRATING YOUR GOOD WILL TOWARD ME. I WILL ENDEAVOR TO DO MY PART TO SUPPORT YOUR INTERESTS.
>
> *LETTER FROM TIBERIUS

Whereas the providence which has regulated our whole existence, and which has shown such care and liberality has brought our life to the climax of perfection in giving us Augustus, who, being sent to us and our descendants as a savior, has put an end to war and set all things in order and, having become manifest, Caesar has fulfilled the hopes of earlier times and, whereas the birthday of the god [Augustus] has been for the whole world the beginning of good news [*euangellion*] concerning him, [therefore let a new era begin from his birth and let his birthday mark the beginning of the new year.][87]

The language found in this inscription is remarkably similar to language found in the NT and foreshadows an inevitable conflict between the followers of Caesar and the followers of Jesus. Many early Christians refused to acknowledge the emperor as "savior of the world" and paid a costly price for their defiance (see City and Society: Paul's Counter-Imperial Gospel in Thessalonica as well as City and Society: Erastus and the Imperial Cult).

The Synagogue

As noted earlier (Religion and Superstition: Superstition), Jews were well established throughout the Mediterranean by the first century, with most cities having a significant Jewish presence. Paul seems to expect to find a Jewish place of worship in the cities he visited, and he leveraged this opportunity to great effect as he sought to gain a hearing for his message (e.g., Acts 13:13–52). The most common designation in the NT for this place of worship is *synagogue*. Another common term outside the NT, particularly in Philo of Alexandria, is *prosueché*, "place of prayer." Luke uses this term to describe the gathering of Jews in Philippi (Acts 16:13).

SYNAGOGUE OF
THE HEBREWS

INSCRIPTION, THIRD
CENTURY C.E., CORINTH

The NT writers often use expressions like "entering the synagogue," "teaching in the synagogue," and so forth, which in many instances seems to denote a building set apart for worship and other activities.[88] This was probably the situation in most larger cities of the Diaspora, like Ephesus, Corinth, and Rome, where the Jewish community had sufficient funds and political favor to either build or acquire a structure specifically for the Jewish communal services. In first-century Ostia, near Rome, there existed an elaborate synagogue complex complete with a water supply, dining facilities, and stately architectural features.[89] Philo notes that there were many synagogues in all quarters of Alexandria.[90] Tacitus refers to the Jewish places of worship as "temples," apparently because he thought they were roughly analogous to pagan structures used for worship.[91] Other archaeological and literary evidence confirms this picture and suggests that private homes may have been used as places of gathering for Jews in some locales.[92] While firm archaeological evidence for house-synagogues is necessarily meager—there would be little archaeologically to distinguish them as such—an inscription from Stobi in the present-day Republic of Macedonia dating to the second or third century C.E. details how one Jewish patron donated his home for religious use:

[Claudius] Tiberius Polycharmus, also [called] Achyrius, the father of the synagogue at Stobi, having lived my whole life according to the (prescriptions of) Judaism, in fulfillment of a vow (have donated) the rooms(?) to the holy place, and the *triclinium* with the *tetrastoa*, out of my personal accounts without touching the sacred (funds) at all.[93]

The most widely attested office in the first-century synagogue is the synagogue ruler (*archisynagogue*). This official is mentioned in the NT, in inscriptions, and elsewhere. In the NT and other literary sources, the ruler of the synagogue is clearly a religious functionary. For example, in Luke 13:10–17 the synagogue ruler takes Jesus to task for healing on the Sabbath; in Acts 18:12–18 the synagogue ruler is part of the delegation accusing Paul of violating the Jewish law. The inscriptional evidence, however, points to the synagogue ruler as a benefactor and patron to the Jewish community. One of the most important and frequently cited first-century synagogue inscriptions, the Theodotus inscription from Jerusalem, illustrates the philanthropic contributions of a synagogue ruler:

> [AUGUSTUS] KNEW THEREFORE THAT THEY [THE JEWS] HAVE HOUSES OF PRAYER AND MEET TOGETHER IN THEM, PARTICULARLY ON THE SACRED SABBATHS WHEN THEY RECEIVE AS A BODY A TRAINING IN THEIR ANCESTRAL PHILOSOPHY.
>
> PHILO

Theodotos son of Vettenus, priest and archisynagogos, son and grandson of archisynagogoi, built the synagogue for reading the law and teaching the commandments, and the guest-house and the rooms and the water provisions, as accommodation for those who need it from abroad. His fathers and the presbyters [elders] and Simonides founded the synagogue.[94]

There is no need to pit the literary evidence against the inscriptional evidence. Inscriptions tend to honor benefactors, so it is not surprising that philanthropy is emphasized by the inscriptional material. While the exact function of synagogue rulers no doubt varied somewhat from place to place, it is reasonable to assume they may have had religious, administrative, and financial responsibilities.[95]

> P. RUTILIUS JONES THE MOST RESPECTABLE ARCHISYNAGOGOS FOR LIFE, WITH BISINNIA DEOM HIS WIFE [BUILT IT] FROM THE FOUNDATIONS, FROM HIS OWN MONEY.
>
> INSCRIPTION, SECOND TO THIRD CENTURY C.E.

Other officials associated with the synagogue are the "rulers" (*archons*), elders, and occasionally the "father" or "mother" of the synagogue (as in the inscription from Stobi, earlier). The latter two were probably honorific titles granted to faithful supporters of the Jewish community. The distinction between elders and rulers is not entirely clear, nor can we assume that there was uniform nomenclature and responsibilities for these officials from city to city.[96] A later inscription from the synagogue in Dura Europos refers to Samuel, son of Yeda'ya, as an "archon" in the Aramaic portion and as an "elder" in the Greek portion.[97] Elders were important community leaders in Jewish antiquity (Deut 21:3; Ruth 4:2; 1 Sam 8:4; Ps 107:32), and it follows that they would be prominent in the synagogue as well. However, whether the community elders were a separate body from the synagogue elders is difficult to determine. Moreover, it seems that the title "elder" was used commonly in some regions (e.g., Asia Minor, southern Italy) but rarely or not at all in other regions (Rome, Egypt, Syria, Palestine).[98] Indeed, Lee Levine's study of the ancient synagogue, one the most comprehensive ever produced, concludes that not only was there "no fixed nomenclature for synagogue leadership" but also that "diversity is the dominant characteristic of synagogue leadership in antiquity."[99]

> TO THE WELL-DESERV-
> ING STAFYLUS, ARCHON
> AND ARCHISYNAGO-
> GUS, WHO HELD ALL
> THE HONORS. RESTI-
> TUA HIS WIFE MADE
> [THE MONUMENT]. IN
> PEACE YOUR SLEEP.
>
> FUNERARY INSCRIPTION,
> SECOND TO FOURTH
> CENTURY, ROME

The most important activity of a Sabbath gathering at a synagogue was the reading of, and instruction in, the sacred texts, particularly the Torah.[100] All the sources underscore this point, and Josephus and Philo are particularly emphatic concerning the centrality of torah reading. According to Josephus,

> He [Moses] appointed the law to be the most excellent and necessary form of instruction, ordaining, not that it should be heard once for all or twice, or on several occasions, but that every week men should desert their other occupations and assemble to listen to the Law and obtain a thorough and accurate knowledge of it.[101]

Philo offers an illuminating description of what this looked like in the synagogues of Alexandria:

> There [in the synagogue], arranged in rows according to their ages, the younger below the elder, they sit decorously as befits the occasion with attentive ears. Then one takes the books and reads aloud and another of especial proficiency comes forward and expounds what is not understood.[102]

Philo's portrayal of reading, followed by teaching, corresponds to the Theodotus inscription cited earlier. Moreover, there is archaeological evidence indicating that some synagogues were equipped with a special chamber to house the scrolls of the law. An inscription from the synagogue in Ostia probably indicates such an architectural feature: "For the safety of the Emperor. Mindius Faustus with his family built and made it from his own gifts and set up the ark for the holy law."[103]

Prayer and worship also figured prominently in synagogue gatherings. The term *proseuchē,* "place of prayer," so prominent in designating a synagogue in the Diaspora, attests to the importance of communal prayer at synagogal gatherings. While it was not a synagogue per se, the abundance of liturgical prayers found in the scrolls from Qumran further illustrate the importance of prayer in a Jewish communal setting.[104] Jesus' censure concerning the religious showmanship of his day is also telling: "And when you pray, do not be like the hypocrites, for they love to pray standing in the synagogues and on the street corners to be seen by men" (Matt 6:5). Philo preserves a memorable scene in which the Jews of Alexandria were both singing and praying. The occasion of this spontaneous communal worship was the removal of the Roman governor Flaccus, who had led a pogrom against the Jews, which included the destruction of their places of worship (*proseuchai*). Because of this, their worship took place outdoors, in the city streets and near the beaches:

> FOR MOSES HAS BEEN PREACHED IN EVERY CITY FROM THE EARLIEST TIMES AND IS READ IN THE SYNAGOGUES ON EVERY SABBATH.
>
> ACTS 15:21

> ... with hands outstretched to heaven they sang hymns and led songs of triumph to God who watches over human affairs. ... "We give thanks to Thee because Thou has taken pity and compassion on us and relieved our unbroken and ceaseless affliction." All night long they continued to sing hymns and songs of praise and at dawn pouring through the city gates, they made their way to the parts of the beach near at hand, since their meeting-houses [*proseuchas*] had been taken from them.[105]

> THE HIGH PRIEST WILL TAKE UP POSITION, AND HIS BROTHERS THE P[RIESTS] AND THE LEVITES AND ALL THE MEN OF THE ARRAY WITH HIM, AND HE WILL SAY IN THEIR HEARING THE PRAYER FOR THE TIME OF WAR ... WITH ALL THE WORDS OF THEIR THANKSGIVINGS.
>
> DEAD SEA SCROLLS

Another important synagogal activity was communal dining.[106] We noted earlier that the synagogue at Ostia included a *triclinium* (dining room), and a decree by Julius Caesar preserved by Josephus confirms that communal dining was a widespread practice among the Jews:

> The Jews in Delos and some of the neighboring Jews, some of your envoys being present, have appealed to me and declared that you are preventing them by statute from observing their national customs and sacred rites. Now it displeases me that such statutes should be made against our friends and allies and that they should be forbidden to live in accordance with their customs and to contribute money to common meals and sacred rites, for this they are not forbidden to do even in Rome.[107]

Josephus also mentions a decree regarding the Jewish right to assemble in order to "decide their affairs and controversies with one another," which points to the broader use of the synagogue as a community center.[108] Scattered references to public assemblies, business transactions, legal actions (divorce warrants, property disputes), and so forth, within the context of the synagogue indicate that in some places the synagogue functioned almost as a town hall for the local Jewish population.[109] The juridical function of Palestinian synagogues is underscored by the NT writers as well. The Synoptic Gospels contain a tradition in which Jesus warns that his followers will be "beaten in the synagogues,"[110] a punishment to which Paul's letters and speeches in Acts also refer.[111]

The Baths

No society in the ancient world was cleaner than that of the Romans. Pausanias's remark that "Corinth has many baths"[112] would have been true of most Roman cities, especially under the emperors. In the words of one modern scholar, "The baths embodied the ideal Roman way of urban life."[113] In 33 B.C.E., Rome had at least 170 public baths, and by the end of the third century this number had swollen to nearly a thousand.[114] The baths were typically open from mid-morning until sunset and were especially crowded in the early afternoon, the close of the Roman work day.[115] Some baths were small and privately owned, but others were large complexes covering several city blocks and were subsidized by the state. Such was the Roman enthusiasm for bathing that the wealthy elite were known to equip their villas with private bathing facilities.[116]

> SMYRNA HAS SO MANY BATHS THAT YOU WOULD BE AT A LOSS TO KNOW WHERE TO BATHE.
>
> AELIUS ARISTIDES

The grander public baths featured facilities for exercise or sport (the *palaestra*) and contained a series of rooms and baths that one would enjoy in progression, as Lucian explains:

> When you enter the baths you are received into a large hall with plenty of rooms for servants and bath attendants. Next are the locker rooms to undress in. In the hall between are three swimming pools of cold water. On leaving this hall you come into another room slightly warmed instead of meeting you with a fierce blast of heat. Next is the hot room and in the room beyond three hot tubs. When you have bathed, you need not go back through these rooms, but you can go straight into the cold room.[117]

These ancient spas were used for more than personal grooming and fitness; business and social contacts were made at the baths,[118] poets and rhetors recited at the baths,[119] and outside the baths merchants hawked their goods. In his description of all the sights and sounds associated with the baths, Seneca notes the food venders in particular:

> Then there are various cries of the pastry cooks, the sausage-sellers, and all the hawkers from the cook-shops, who advertise their wares with a sing-song all their own.[120]

There is also considerable evidence of sexual promiscuity associated with bathing. Mixed bathing was common, as was complete nudity.[121] Martial takes for granted that bathing was *au naturel* and provided an opportunity to meet sexual partners,[122] whatever one's sexual orientation.[123] A host of inscriptions attest to sexual activity in and around bath complexes, and in Ephesus a brothel was conveniently located next door.[124] The magical papyri contain formulae for attracting a lover while at the baths:

> BATHS, WINE, AND
> SEX CORRUPT OUR
> BODIES—BUT THESE
> ARE LIFE ITSELF!
>
> FUNERARY INSCRIPTION,
> ROME, FIRST CENTURY

> Love spell of attraction: . . . Take a pure papyrus and with the blood of an ass write the following names and figure, and put in the magical material from the woman you desire. Smear the strip of papyrus with moistened vinegar gum and glue it to the dry vaulted vapor room of a bath, and you will marvel.[125]

We can assume that public bathing was usually done without any sexual fraternization, yet the environment of the baths was particularly conducive to such cavorting. Writing at the end of the second century, Clement of Alexandria confirms this sordid picture, focusing especially on the opulence and lasciviousness associated with the baths:

> The baths are opened promiscuously to men and women; and there they strip for licentious indulgence—for from looking, men get to loving—as if their modesty had been washed away in the bath.[126]

In the end, Clement counsels Christians to use the baths only for health and hygiene. Bathing for pleasure is strictly forbidden.[127] Given the dodgy atmosphere of public bathing, Clement's strictures were probably more prudent than prudish.

Prisons

Quite unlike the temples or baths, Roman prisons were not a noteworthy feature of the civic landscape. In fact, Pausanias fails to mention a single prison in his chronicles of the cities he visited throughout Greece.[128] This is not surprising. The Greeks and Romans did not build prisons for the long-term incarceration of convicted prisoners as a form of punishment. Rather, jails were used as temporary holding tanks while the accused was awaiting trial. Indeed, "holding tank" is an apt description for a Roman jail, as many were simply converted cisterns.[129] Sallust's description of the infamous Tullianum prison in Rome is probably somewhat typical of the *carcer* (jail; cf. the English in*carcer*ated)—virtual dungeons:

> In the prison . . . there is a place called the Tullianum, about twelve feet below the surface of the ground. It is enclosed on all sides by walls, and above it is a chamber with

a vaulted roof of stone. Neglect, darkness, and stench make it hideous and fearsome to behold.[130]

The conditions of these *carcer* were particularly horrid: overcrowded, lice-infested, unsanitary, lightless hovels. Darkness is ubiquitous in depictions of Roman prisons as they rarely were constructed to allow the entrance of natural light: "Lastly there is the darkness, the chains, the prison, the tortures of being shut up, of being shut off . . . from drawing free breath and looking upon the common light of day."[131] References to the "stench" and "foul air" are also commonplace.[132] With little opportunity for personal hygiene, prisoners routinely contracted illness through incarceration.[133] Lucian describes a visit to a prison where the inmate had become unrecognizable due to his emaciated appearance and his "unkempt and matted hair," which had grown over his face.[134]

> A FEW DAYS LATER WE WERE LODGED IN THE PRISON—I HAVE NEVER SEEN SUCH A DARK HOLE! WITH THE CROWD, THE HEAT WAS STIFLING, THEN THERE WAS THE THREATS BY THE SOLDIERS.
>
> MARTYRDOM OF PERPETUA AND FELICITAS

Other, less severe, types of incarceration were also at the disposal of the magistrate, depending on the status of the accused (citizen or non-citizen, slave or freeborn) and the severity of the crime.[135] The prisoner might be turned over to military custody or placed under guarded home confinement. The martyr Perpetua looked forward to transferral to military custody as a reprieve from the squalor of the *carcer*.[136] Paul was able procure his own accommodation during his imprisonment in Rome, though under the constant watch of a Roman guard (Acts 28:16–31). Although chains were particularly associated with imprisonment in a *carcer*, manacles were used in other forms of confinement as well. These heavy iron shackles were extremely uncomfortable and produced both pain and lacerations. Antiphilus, a character from Lucian's *Toxaris*, was robbed of sleep due to his grating chains and his cramped conditions.[137] According to Philostratus, philosophical contemplation allowed the imprisoned Apollonius to take his mind off of the agony of his chains.[138] Paul and Silas used singing and prayer to the same effect (Acts 16:25–26). Long-term incarceration in such conditions inevitably resulted in the picture described in one of the elder Seneca's *Controversiae*: "You would have seen my body clothed in rags, all my limbs burdened under chains, my eyes sunken in my emaciated state, my hands worn

> SLEEP MAKES LIGHT THE CHAINS OF PRISONERS AND THE INFLAMMATIONS SURROUNDING WOUNDS.
>
> PLUTARCH

> WHAT, YOU MAY OBJECT, IS A SHOW WITHOUT AN IDOL? WHO PLAYS SPORT WITHOUT A SACRIFICE?
>
> PSEUDO-CYPRIAN

with shackles and useless."[139] This was the common lot of those who fell afoul of the law and of the magistrates.

FESTIVALS AND SPORT

Holidays and athletics are an important part of every society, and the cultures of Greece and Rome were no exceptions. The obvious difficulty in broaching this subject is that the Roman Empire was a vast conglomeration of numerous civilizations, societies, and people groups, each with its own traditions, particularly related to civic festivals. The festivals of the Greeks were centered around the cycles of nature, fertility, honoring the gods, or celebrating the founding of a city, and *agonistic* festivals related to athletic and artistic competition. The athletic events included running, boxing, wrestling, and other sports, while the artistic competitions were comprised of singing, dancing, poetry, and drama. Suetonius and Tacitus report Nero's fondness for entering such competitions, and no matter if his voice cracked or he fell off his chariot, he still managed to take home the victor's wreath.[140]

THE VICTORS
BOYS' BOXING:
D. PTOLEMY OF
ALEXANDRIA
YOUTH BOXING:
A. ASCLEPIUS OF
ALEXANDRIA
MEN'S BOXING:
S. TYRANNUS OF
ALEXANDRIA
BOYS' PANCRATIUM:
DRAW

INSCRIPTION, CORINTH

The four major competitive festivals were celebrated in either two- or four-year cycles and were dedicated to one of the Olympian deities: the Olympic and Nemian games to Zeus, the Pythian games to Apollo, and the Isthmian games to Poseidon. Athletics were particularly important to the Greeks, where training in the gymnasium was a crucial part of the educational curriculum. By the time of the first century, the Roman calendar was packed with festivals and holidays, and many of these included accompanying games. Romans preferred gladiatorial exhibitions and chariot races to the more traditional fare of Greek athletics, but the Pan-Hellenic competitions in Olympia, Isthmia (Corinth), Nemea, and Delphi drew hordes of Greeks and Romans alike.

Digging Deeper: Corinth and the Isthmian Games

Although the games at Olympia held pride of place among the agonistic festivals in the Greco-Roman world, coming in a close second were the games held in Isthmia and managed by nearby Corinth. The Isthmian games were staged every two years and attracted athletes from all over the empire, along with huge numbers of spectators. They featured musical, literary, oratorical, and athletic competitions and had divisions for boys, youths, men, and women. The

Isthmian games originated in sixth century B.C.E. and were vital to the culture and ethos of Corinth. Lucius Castricius Regulus, a Corinthian benefactor, aristocrat, and sports enthusiast, was an important figure in modernizing the games in the early first century:

> For Lucius Castricius Regulus, aedile, prefect, duovir, quinquennial duovir, agonothete [president] of the Tiberea Caesarea Sebastea games, agonothete of the Isthmian and Caesarean games, who was the first to preside over the Isthmian games at the Isthmus under the sponsorship of the Colony of Corinth. He introduced poetry, a contest for girls, and after all the buildings of the Caesarean games were renovated he quickly completed the construction of other facilities and gave a banquet for all the inhabitants of the colony. His son erected this monument in his honor, in accordance with a decree of the city council.[141]

This inscription mentions two other series of competitions that were added to the Isthmian games in alternating years: one honoring imperial rule (the Caesarean games) and one honoring the reigning emperor, in this case Tiberius. This confirms both the popularity of these games and the importance of imperial politics in Corinth. Among the inscriptions and artifacts unearthed from Corinth and Isthmia are plaques and columns listing victors in the competitions, statues of famous athletes, engraved panels depicting victors' wreaths, and other athletic paraphernalia. In Corinth, the victor's wreath was made of celery, which Paul alludes to when referring to the "perishable wreath" awarded to the victor in the games (1 Cor 9:25).

Dozens of inscriptions also attest to the prominence of the *agonothetes,* or president, of the games among the elite aristocracy of the colony. Lucius Castricius Regulus, who probably financed the renovations described in the inscription above, was obviously a man of great wealth and status.[142] In fact, unlike most cities, whose highest political office was that of the *duumvir,* in Corinth the most prestigious political appointment was the *agonothetes.*[143] In Corinth, when local dignitaries heralded their progress on the *cursus honorum,* the final rung to be noted was *agonothetes,* president of the games:

> For Tiberius Claudius Dinippus, duovir, duovir quinquennalis, augur, priest of the Brittanic Victory, military tribune of Legion VI Hispanesis, chief engineer, curator of the grain supply three times, agonothetes of the Neronean, Isthmian, and Caesarean games.[144]

While Corinth today is remembered primarily as a promiscuous port city, in antiquity it was considered one of the premiere sport centers of the empire:

> But the noble man considers his hardships to be his greatest antagonists, and enjoys battling them night and day. Not for a sprig of celery [as in Corinth] or Olive [as in Olympia], or pine [as in Delphi], and not merely when the Olympians, or Corinthians, or Eleans announce the honors, but to win happiness.[145]

VOLUNTARY ASSOCIATIONS

Voluntary associations, as the name implies, were assemblies of individuals freely joining themselves together for a particular purpose. In other words, they were clubs. Not unlike their modern counterparts, voluntary associations were extremely diverse in the interests they represented but can be loosely categorized under three headings: funerary, religious, and professional.[146] Funerary associations were particularly concerned for the proper burial and continued funerary rites of their members; religious associations were organized for the worship of a particular divinity; professional associations were comprised of members of a guild or trade: bakers, tanners, mariners, and the like. This traditional taxonomy is useful, as long as the lines are not drawn too firmly. For example, most associations worshiped a patron deity, and associations across all three categories provided burial rites.[147]

> I ORDER THE BAKERS NOT TO MEET AS AN ASSOCIATION AND NOT TO BECOME THE RINGLEADERS IN RECKLESS BEHAVIOR.
>
> EDICT OF THE PROCONSUL OF ASIA

There were many appeals of voluntary associations, both social and religious. Voluntary associations would meet in a public building, such as a temple, or in a private home and would often share a meal, drink, and socialize. In Philo, voluntary associations are virtually synonymous with rowdy partying: "They are united by wine, drunkenness, and revelry, and the offspring of these indulgences, insolence."[148] While these social gatherings were known to get out of hand, there was also a very real concern for order during the meetings and polite behavior. Some associations posted lists of rules that spelled out the terms and obligations of membership and addressed behavior during the meetings:

> THE MEMBERS OF THE ASSOCIATION OF THE GOD SYLVANUS DURING THE PRIESTHOOD MAGIUS BICTOR ARE INSCRIBED BELOW. . .
>
> INSCRIPTION, PHILIPPI

> It was voted further that any member who becomes *quinquennalis* in this society is exempt [from obligations related to banquets] and that he shall receive a double share in all distributions. It was further voted that if any member desires to make any complaint or bring up any business, he is to bring it up at a business meeting, so that we may banquet in peace and good cheer on festive days. It was voted further that any member who moves from one place to another so as to cause a disturbance shall be fined four sesterces. Any member, moreover, who speaks abusively of another or causes and uproar shall be fined 12 sesterces. Any member who uses any abusive or insolent language to a *quinquennalis* at a banquet shall be fined 20 sesterces.[149]

As this excerpt illustrates, voluntary associations elected ranks of officers, which were patterned after the provincial government. One social historian speaks of the "positive exuberance" evident in assigning officers in these clubs,[150] which points to an important need these societies met in providing status denied by the larger society (see City and Society: Class and Status). The roster of a typical voluntary association was drawn mostly from the lower orders: freedmen, shopkeepers, working-class artisans, slaves. Becoming a member of a voluntary association provided a sense of belonging, as well as an avenue to status and social standing. Every chance to trumpet this status was, quite understandably, taken full advantage of. One can only imagine the satisfaction gained by Titius Flavius and Tiberius Claudius at the opportunity of seeing this column set up in the forum in Corinth:

> This monument was erected by the decision of the Association of the Lares of the Imperial House. Those who had charge of its erection were the two most outstanding members of the association, Titius Flavius Antiochus, a freedman of the Emperor, and Tiberius Claudius Primignenius.[151]

POPULATION DENSITY

A city, of course, contains people—lots of people. Cities in the ancient world contained large numbers of people in considerably less space, proportionately, than do their modern counterparts. Rome was the true megapolis of the first century, with a population of nearly 1,000,000 people, followed by Alexandria and Antioch with about half that many, and then Ephesus with approximately 250,000. Lesser cities, but still large by ancient standards, were Corinth, Thessalonica, and Jerusalem, which hovered around 100,000. Historically informed artistic reconstructions of these cities found in books and on the Internet capture well their architecture, street plans, and general layout but fail to convey perhaps the most brutal reality of life in a major metropolis of the Roman world: overcrowding comparable to only the bleakest of modern urban slums. A crowded North American city like New York has a population density of approximately 41 inhabitants per acre; Chicago has 20, and Los Angeles 12.[152] First-century Rome had a population density of nearly 300 inhabitants per acre; Jerusalem contained 188 per acre, Antioch 117 per acre, and Ostia 158 inhabitants per acre.[153] Corinth would have been positively spacious with 65 persons per acre, fully three and a half times the urban density of Chicago. These staggering demographics provide the background for Juvenal's description of his trip home through the streets of Rome:

NOVIUS IS MY NEIGHBOR AND CAN BE TOUCHED BY HAND FROM MY WINDOWS. IN ALL OF ROME THERE IS NOBODY SO NEAR ME AND SO FAR AWAY.

*MARTIAL

> THERE'S DEATH IN EVERY OPEN WINDOW AS YOU PASS ALONG AT NIGHT. . . . YOU CAN BUT HOPE, AND PUT UP A PITEOUS PRAYER IN YOUR HEART THAT THEY MAY BE CONTENT TO POUR DOWN ON YOU THE CONTENTS OF THEIR SLOP-BASINS.
>
> JUVENAL

Hurry as we may, we are blocked by a surging crowd in front, and by a dense mass of people pressing in on us from behind: one man digs an elbow into me, another a hard sedan pole; one bangs a beam, another a wine cask, against my head; soon huge feet trample on me from every side, and a soldier plants his hobnails firmly on my toe.[154]

While satirists like Juvenal had some license to exaggerate, this description of the streets of Rome was probably close to a snapshot of the swarming congestion of most major urban centers in the ancient world. Plutarch's description of a summer evening in Lachaeum, near Corinth, gives a similar picture of a much smaller township: "It was summer time, and the whole length of the street even to the water's edge was one mass of dust and confusion by reason of the great crowd of vehicles and people."[155]

The practical difficulty of accommodating the needs of such large numbers of people is evident from inscriptions like these from Pompeii:

> Anyone who wants to defecate in this place is advised to move along. If you act contrary to this warning, you will have to pay a penalty. . . .[156]

> To the one defecating here. Beware of the curse. If you look down on this curse, may you have an angry Jupiter for an enemy.[157]

Of course, if you had connections to the imperial house, you could not only ignore such proscriptions, you could sign your name: "Apollinaris, the doctor of the emperor Titus, defecated well here."[158]

While allowance must be made for varying conditions, the cumulative evidence is clear: narrow streets packed with pedestrians and merchants, winding alleys where one dodged rubbish flung from the windows above, and rows of tenement slums bursting with occupants were as much a part of the civic landscape as were temples, theaters, and the villas of the aristocracy.

URBAN UNREST

The cramped living conditions of most of the populace coupled with the mild climate of the Mediterranean meant that leisure time was spent outside the domicile, in the streets, markets, and public squares.[159] We have already mentioned such forum fixtures as philosophers, orators, diviners, and schoolmasters, who regularly conducted business in public venues; to these we could add merchants, vendors, buskers, and the large number of unemployed.[160] Because education was neither mandatory nor feasible for the masses, children were free to loiter or play where they found room, carving their game boards in the forum pavement.[161] The combination of high poverty levels and high population density led, predictably, to a high incidence of urban unrest and mob violence. This is particularly relevant as one follows Paul's travels in the book of Acts (see City and Society: The Perils of Carrying the Name). In the words of one first-century observer, "Whenever a blast of turbulence falls upon the assembly . . . we find jibes and brawling and laughter."[162]

THE CITY BLOCK OF THE ARRII POLLII IN THE POSSESSION OF GNAEUS ALLEIUS NI-GIDIUS IS AVAILABLE TO RENT FROM JULY 1ST. THERE ARE SHOPS ON THE FIRST FLOOR, UPPER STORIES, HIGH-CLASS ROOMS AND A HOUSE. CONTACT PRIMUS, THE SLAVE OF GNAEUS AL-LEIUS NIGIDIUS MAIUS.

PUBLIC NOTICE, POMPEII

CLASS AND STATUS

Like many societies, Rome and its provinces were characterized by a hierarchical class structure divided along economic lines. These lines were more rigidly drawn than in most contemporary Western societies, though some upward (and downward) mobility was possible. In addition to wealth, Roman society pivoted on the axes of aristocracy versus plebe, male verse female, slave versus free, citizen versus non-citizen, Roman versus provincial, and Roman/Greek versus "barbarian." More subtle distinctions also applied.

Economic Disparity

At the top of the social pyramid was the senatorial order, representing six hundred families. In order to qualify for the senate one had to have a net worth of 250,000 denarii, a denarius being approximately one day's wage for a laborer. Senators wore a toga with a broad purple stripe and sandals with a crescent-shaped clasp, announcing at the same time their rank and their wealth. The equestrian order—so called because in the early republic they could afford to ride into battle on a horse—was much larger and had a property requirement of 100,000 denarii—still an enormous sum. Membership into these elite groups generally followed the successful completion of lesser posts and could be the crowning

GAIUS JULIUS, SON OF GAIUS, FROM THE TRIBE OF VOLTINA, HONORED WITH THE BROAD PURPLE STRIPE BY THE DEIFIED PIUS

*FUNERARY INSCRIPTION, PHILIPPI

achievement of one's *cursus honorum* (see City and Society: Urban Landscape and Environment). Decurions, aediles, and other members of provincial and municipal aristocracy round out this upper echelon of society, and on the whole would be much less well off. The imperial family possessed wealth almost beyond imagination, though they would be a statistically insignificant portion of the population. All together, these groups possessed most of the wealth, land, and goods, yet comprised only about 3% of the entire population of the Roman Empire.[163]

YOUR CHEST GLEAMS WITH COUNTLESS DINNER SUITS, AND YOUR WHITE GOWNS ARE ENOUGH TO CLOTHE A TRIBE. YET YOU GAZE IMPASSIVELY AT YOUR FREEZING CLIENT, YOUR THREADBARE ESCORT.

*MARTIAL

Beneath the elite aristocracy would be a narrow band of modestly successful artisans, merchants, freedmen, military veterans, and others who were fortunate enough be able to acquire a small surplus but were still relatively poor by modern standards. This group would comprise about 7% of the population. The vast majority of people in the Roman World—estimates range from 70 to 90%—survived at or below the subsistence level.[164] They lived hand to mouth, hoping to earn or scrounge enough food each day to fill themselves and their dependents. In this group we would find most craftsmen and shopkeepers, farmers, fishermen, day laborers, slaves, and many (if not most) clients of patrons. Apuleius refers to this unfortunate lot as "the lowborn masses" (*vulgus ignobile*) who were "forced by ignorant poverty . . . to seek the filthiest of supplements and free meals for the shrunken bellies."[165]

The crucial difference between ancient Mediterranean societies and contemporary Western societies is the absence of a middle class. An economic class is generally understood as a group of people with shared socio-economic characteristics forming a significant and integral part of the economic system.[166] In this sense, there was no middle class in the Greco-Roman world.[167] Quite unlike many affluent economies today, where the middle class is pandered to as the largest economic force, in the milieu of the NT the few who did manage to achieve a modest surplus would have little impact on the economy as whole. The prospects for socio-economic advancement were so bleak that some were willing to sell themselves into slavery in order to procure adequate food and shelter.[168] The grim reality of life in the first century was abject poverty on a monumental scale. It was not so much a collection of societies consisting of the haves and the have-nots but simply of the have-nots.

ALL THE MEN IN THE WORKSHOPS TOILING AND MOILING FROM MORNING TILL NIGHT, DOUBLED OVER THEIR TASKS, THEY MERELY EKE OUT A BARE EXISTENCE.

*LUCIAN

Social Stratification

Roman society was extremely status conscious, and the distinction between the various strata was scrupulously observed. The most fundamental distinction in the Greco-Roman world was between slave and free. Even to be of servile lineage (i.e., a freedman or the child of one) entailed an insurmountable social stigma no matter how far up the social ladder one subsequently climbed. In his biography of Roman grammatici and rhetors, Suetonius is careful to comment if any were slaves or freedmen, illustrating the long memory of highborn Romans regarding such things. Horace lauds his patron who, "unlike the rest of the world, does not turn up his nose at men of unknown birth, men like myself, a freedman's son."[169] According to (Pseudo-) Plutarch, those who lacked citizenship and a respectable lineage "have an indelible disgrace in their low birth which accompanies them throughout their lives and offers to anyone ... a ready subject of reproach and insult."[170] This represents the perspective of the wealthy elite; no doubt those among the lower orders saw things differently.

> FOR ALL PERSONS WHO HAVE PASSED THROUGH THEIR TRAINING I PRESERVE INTACT THEIR ALEXANDRIAN CITIZENSHIP, WITH THE EXCEPTION OF ANY PERSONS WHO HAVE INSINUATED THEMSELVES AMONG YOU IN SPITE OF HAVING BEEN BORN OF SLAVE WOMEN.
>
> *EMPEROR CLAUDIUS TO THE ALEXANDRIANS

Roman deference to rank took innumerable forms, proper seating arrangements being prominent among them. Equestrians and senators were granted premier seating in the theaters while "the baser sort," notes Calpunius Siculus, "viewed the show in dingy garments near the women's benches."[171] In Philippi, similar arrangements were made for the *Seviri Augustales,* a priesthood of freedmen devoted to promoting the imperil cult.[172] Apuleius describes a typical scene at a public hearing where magistrates took their seats "in order of rank," duly acknowledging peers of higher status. In a display of almost comical fastidiousness but written with utmost seriousness, Aulus Gellius weighs the delicate issue of who should be seated first, a father or his son who is a magistrate.[173]

> "OUT YOU GO! FOR SHAME!" SAYS THE MARSHAL. "OUT OF THE EQUESTRIAN SEATS, YOU WHOSE WEALTH DOES NOT SATISFY THE REQUIREMENT!"
>
> JUVENAL

This attention to status was also played out at dinner parties; guests were seated according to social standing and allowed to comment on the after-dinner recitation of poetry according to rank, more prominent guests first:

> See, now, the sons of Romulus [Romans], having dined well, are asking over their cups, 'What has divine poetry to say'? Whereupon some fellow with a purple mantle round his shoulders [i.e. of senatorial rank] lisps out with a snuffle some insipid trash ... the great men signify their approval ... the lesser guests chime in with their assent.[174]

The social pyramid was also reinforced by serving higher-quality food and drink to more distinguished guests. Pliny's account of one such affair is worth citing at length:

WHY IS NOT THE SAME DINNER SERVED TO ME AS TO YOU? YOU TAKE OYSTERS FATTENED IN THE LUCRINE LAKE, I SUCK A MUSSEL THROUGH A HOLE IN THE SHELL. . . . WHY DO I DINE WITHOUT YOU PONTICUS, ALTHOUGH I AM DINING WITH YOU?

MARTIAL

I happened to be dining with a man whose "elegant economy," as he called it, seemed to me a sort of stingy extravagance. The best dishes were set in front of himself and a select few, and cheap scraps of food before the rest of the company. He even put the wine into tiny little flasks, divided into three categories, not with the idea of giving his guests the opportunity of choosing, but to make it impossible for them to refuse what they were given. One lot was intended for himself and for us, another for his lesser friends (all his friends are graded) and the third for his and our freedmen.[175]

Although Pliny disapproved of the somewhat extreme lengths taken by his miserly host, he goes on to observe that when he dines with his own freedmen, all get the same fare, but it is not of the same quality as he normally eats himself. It is difficult to tell how far down the social ladder such practices were maintained, though the numerous references to socially graded dining incline me to believe it was widespread.[176] Among the multitude of impoverished clients (see below) who depended on their patrons for an occasional meal, Juvenal's rhetorical question was probably asked frequently enough: "Is a dinner worth all the insults with which you have to pay for it?"[177]

Benefaction and Patronage

Given the economic inequities of the Roman world and the huge proportion of impoverished and unemployed, cities and individuals relied on the largesse of the upper classes for survival. The wealthy were expected to finance public works (benefaction) and to support as many of the needy lower classes as possible (patronage).

THE PEOPLE OF CLAUDICONIUM HONOURED LUCIUS PUPIUS PRAESENS, SON OF LUCIUS OF THE SABATINA TRIBE, MILITARY TRIBUNE, PREFECT OF THE PICENTINE CALVARY SQUADRON . . . THEIR BENEFACTOR AND FOUNDER.

INSCRIPTION, PHRYGIA

All manner of public works would be funded by the wealthy, from temples to libraries to public festivals and athletic competitions. Even the scanty inscriptional remains from Corinth show benefactors providing fountains, temples, shops, apartment buildings, paved streets, and so on.[178] This is the backdrop to Dio's remark that "time and again . . . there may be seen in our cities one group of men spending, handing out largesse, adorning their city with dedications."[179] Such eager generosity was motivated by the expectation of receiving public honor in return. Fundamental to both benefaction and patronage was reciprocity. The benefactor or patron contributed to the needs of the citizenry and would receive honor from the recipients in exchange, in the form of esteem, political support, honorific monuments, and the like. Although time has obscured identity of this benefactor, his generosity to the city of Philippi remains evident:

> THOSE WHO HAVE LOST THE TRUE FAME THAT DERIVES FROM VIRTUE. . . . FLEE TO THE FAME WHICH RESULTS FROM FLATTERY, AND INVITE THE ACCLAMATION OF THE MASSES BY MEANS OF DISTRIBUTIONS AND PUBLIC FEASTS.
>
> PSEUDO-SOCRATES

> A decree of the assembly: Since [Da]rit[us] [?], a friend of the city of Philippi, has not ceased to be continually well disposed to the city, and where able provides materially according to his means, and has promised to loan money interest free, the assembly thought it good to praise him and to post this decree next to the city hall.[180]

The patron-client system involved people of unequal social and economic status in a mutually beneficial relationship. The higher-status patron assisted the lower-status client materially and otherwise in return for support in the political sphere, honor in the public arena, and a variety of other services. Refusing the offer of patronage could result in animosity on the part of the rejected patron. A person might refuse a benefaction if the giver were deemed unworthy or if accepting the offer of patronage might put the recipient in a difficult situation with respect to another party, perhaps another patron.[181] Religious organizations and voluntary associations (see City and Society: Voluntary Associations) also benefited from patronage. The patron might receive special privileges from the organization, such as larger portions at meals,[182] and of course

> CLIENTS YOU SAY? NOT ONE OF THEM WAITS ON YOU, BUT RATHER WHAT HE CAN GET OUT OF YOU.
>
> SENECA

honorific monuments: "The initiates of the mysteries Botrus Dionysus have given to Rufus Zipas, their benefactor and chief initiate [this monument]."[183] The generosity of a patron always entailed an obligation, as Martial, himself a client, understood well: "Whoever gives much, wants much in return."[184]

The duties of a client often began with greeting the patron at his residence early in the morning (the *salutatio*),[185] where the client would receive a small stipend (in the form of food or money) and instructions regarding any other help the patron might need for the day. Clients were received not in order of arrival but in order of rank: "Praetor first, and after him the Tribune," shouts the patron's steward.[186] Failure to address the patron with due respect could cost the client his daily wage, as Martial learned:

> By chance I greeted you this morning by your real name, Caecilianus, instead of calling you, "my lord." Do you want to know how much such freedom costs me? It robbed me of a hundred farthings.[187]

A client might have several patrons, and the patron would have as many clients as he could reasonably afford. The patron, too, might be the client of someone higher up the social pyramid. Occasionally the client would be required to attend the patron throughout his daily activities. To be surrounded by a troupe of clients was one way the patron could display his status and wealth, and some would even borrow money to keep themselves supplied with clients and to ensure that their stroll through the city was noticed by all.[188]

WHEN SELIUS IS SPREADING HIS NET FOR A DINNER, TAKE HIM WITH YOU TO APPLAUD, WHETHER YOU ARE RECITING OR ACTING AS A COUNSEL: "A GOOD POINT! WEIGHTY, THAT! HOW READY! A HARD HIT! BRAVO!" THAT IS WHAT I WANTED. YOU HAVE NOW EARNED YOUR DINNER; HOLD YOUR TONGUE.

MARTIAL

The obvious danger of becoming a client is summarized by Publilius Syrus: "To accept a benefaction is to sell one's freedom."[189] In the context of a lopsided distribution of captial, the inevitable consequence of the patron-client system was to produce a sizeable caste of groveling, servile, parasites who were forced to flatter and connive to fill their stomachs every day. Imagine a client loitering about the public latrines hoping to receive a dinner invitation from his patron,[190] or shouting gratuitous flattery as his patron delivers a speech,[191] or being forced to escort the patron's litter through the muddy streets to massage the patron's ego.[192] These were common sights in the major cities of the Roman world. Horace, a successful literary client to a wealthy patron devoted two essays to the topic of how to court a patron without appearing as a parasite. His advice amounts to, "Be compliant and full of compliments."[193] Plutarch wrote the corresponding essay from the perspective of a patron: "How to Tell a Flatterer from a Friend."[194]

Manual Labor

As is true today, cities in antiquity contained a full assortment of all the vocations necessary to sustain a community: butchers, bakers, barbers, shopkeepers, carpenters, tradesmen, teachers, clerics, and so on. Also similar to today, some trades and professions were held in greater esteem than others. Slave traders, for example, were widely despised, and Martial lumps the small tradesman together with embezzlers, political informants, and gladiator trainers.[195]

Martial's perspective was hardly unique. In fact, the utter disdain of the elite toward artisans, merchants, and manual labor is one of the chief differences between contemporary Western societies and the values of ancient Rome. The most often cited representative of the elitist perspective is Cicero:

> Now concerning trades and other means of livelihood . . . unbecoming to a gentle-men and vulgar are the means of livelihood of all hired workmen whom we pay for mere manual labor, not for artistic skill. For in their case the very wage they receive is a pledge of their slavery. . . . And all workmen are engaged in vulgar trades, for no workshops can have anything honorable about them. Least respectable of all are the trades which cater to the appetites: fishmongers, butchers, cooks, poulterers, and fishermen.[196]

The slavish appearance of manual labor is also one of the reasons why Lucian, in choosing his profession, opts for the "dignified appearance" of the orator rather than the "servile" appearance of the sculptor, with his garments covered in marble dust, toting chisels in his calloused hands.[197] Moreover, there was a generational component to this snobbery; your parents' occupation mattered too:

> Pay no heed to those idle objectors who like to sneer not only at a person's employment, but even that of the parents, if the mother was a hired servant, or a wet-nurse, or grape-picker; or if the father was a schoolmaster or a tutor. Let them feel no shame![198]

The pervasiveness of this prejudicial attitude among the wealthy elite is undeniable and is one of the reasons why some Stoics championed the opposite view, arguing that working with one's hands was good.[199] The upper classes, however, constituted only a tiny fraction of the population as a whole, and there is ample evidence that the working classes themselves were pleased with their contributions to society and felt no embarrassment over their "vulgar trade." Funerary monuments, for example, depict shoemakers proudly displaying the tools of their trade, poulterers in their shops, knife makers surrounded by their blades, and so on.[200] Clearly these were folks who were proud of their vocations and trades, regardless of whether Cicero might pass by with his nose in the air. Yet the values of the nobility were deeply entrenched and, as Paul discovered in Corinth, could prove to be a difficult obstacle for an apostle who supported himself by making tents (see City and Society: Paul the Leatherworker).

> IN ORDER FOR A GIRL TO BE CHOSEN AS A VESTAL VIRGIN, SHE MUST BE FREE FROM EVERY BODILY DEFECT. NOR MAY SHE SERVE IF EITHER OF HER PARENTS WERE SLAVES OR ENGAGED IN BASE OCCUPATIONS.
>
> *AULUS GELLIUS

THE NEW TESTAMENT CONTEXT

PAUL'S COUNTER-IMPERIAL GOSPEL IN THESSALONICA

"Why, what harm is there in saying 'Caesar is Lord,' and offering incense, and thereby saving yourself?" This question, posed to the aged Polycarp by the magistrates of Smyrna about 155 C.E., is one that many Christians faced in the first three hundred years of the Christian movement. Surrounded by imperial propaganda that hailed Caesar as savior, lord, god, and son of god, the followers of Jesus were confronted with a dilemma whose outcome ranged from social ostracism to public execution. Not only divine titles but also divine attributes were ascribed to the emperor, portraying him as the supreme world sovereign, bringer of peace, and inaugurator of a new age: "For long have I been pondering verses fit to celebrate the golden age, to praise even that very god who is sovereign over nations and cities and toga-clad peace."[201] In some quarters of the empire the accolades could be particularly fulsome:

> SINCE THE ETERNAL AND DEATHLESS NATURE OF THE UNIVERSE HAS PERFECTED ITS BENEFITS IN GIVING US CAESAR AUGUSTUS, SAVIOR OF THE WHOLE HUMAN RACE, IT IS FITTING TO HONOR THE GOD WITH PUBLIC GAMES, STATUES, SACRIFICES, AND HYMNS.
>
> *INSCRIPTION, HALICARNASSUS

> The beautiful Youth [Augustus], the Prince of Princes, chosen by Ptah and Nun . . . Autocrat, son of the Sun, Lord of the diadems, Caesar, Ever-living, beloved of Ptah and Isis.[202]

> The emperor [Augustus], ruler of oceans and continents, the divine father among men, who bears the same name as his heavenly father—Liberator, the marvelous star of the Greek world, shining with the brilliance of the great heavenly Savior.[203]

Paul's letters call on Christians to live as good citizens (Titus 3:1), to be at peace with everyone (2 Cor 13:11), and to submit to the governing authorities as God's servants on their behalf (Rom 13:1–7). However, it is also possible to detect undercurrents that might have been deemed politically subversive, if not outright seditious. Paul applied all the standard imperial slogans (Lord, savior, son of God) to Jesus and spoke of his present (Eph 1:19–23) and future world dominion (1 Cor 15:25–28). This in itself would have raised Roman eyebrows. In 1 Thessalonians, however, Paul's language almost certainly would have been interpreted as assault on the imperial order, whether he intended it to be read that way or not. On four different occasions Paul speaks of the impending "coming" of Jesus, using a term, *parousia,* commonly associated with the visit of the emperor or other royal dignitary (2:19; 3:13; 4:15; 5:23). In the context of a letter that describes Jesus as Lord (seventeen times) and the son of God (1:9–10) who brings salvation (5:9), this language is unguarded to say the least. Even more troublesome, from the Roman point of view, is Paul's teaching that the "coming" of this Jesus will mean destruction for all those boasting of "peace and safety" (5:3).

> TIBERIUS CLAUDIUS CAESAR AUGUSTUS, PONTIFEX MAXIMUM, HOLDER OF TRIBUNICIAN POWER, EMPEROR FOR THE PEACE OF AUGUSTUS
>
> ROMAN COIN

As we have already seen, the peace that Augustus and his successors brought to the empire, the *Pax Romana,* was a popular theme among poets, who were especially fond of contrasting the present prosperity with the turmoil of the past: "Your age, Caesar, has brought back rich harvests to the field.... With Caesar in charge, peace will not be driven out by civic madness or violence, or the anger that beats out swords."[204] As common as this type of flattery is, more pervasive and accessible was the coinage minted by Rome and disseminated throughout the empire. This imperial propaganda reinforced the association of the emperor with peace and stability by portraying him with various goddesses, personifications of these virtues. Emperors of the NT era (from Augustus to Trajan) are depicted with *Pax* (peace), *Securitas* (safety, security), *Constantia* (stability, unchangeableness), *Felicitas* (fortune, happiness), along with many others. The message was clear and read by all: Rome brought peace. Equally clear was Rome's response to anyone who threatened that peace: "But if [any] venture to cause a disturbance, swift is that anger and vengeance visited on them by you [the Roman authorities]."[205]

> THE COUNCIL AND PEOPLE OF THE EPHESIANS AND THE OTHER HELLENIC CITIES WHICH DWELL IN ASIA ACKNOWLEDGE GAIUS JULIUS AS HIGH PRIEST AND AUTOCRAT AND CONSUL FOR THE SECOND TIME, THE GOD MANIFEST BORN OF ARES AND APHRODITE, AND THE COMMON SAVIOR OF HUMAN LIFE.
>
> INSCRIPTION, EPHESUS

In describing the imminent destruction of those boasting of "peace and safety," Paul may not have intended an allusion to the imperial order. It is difficult to imagine, however, that his message would not have been interpreted politically, as it already had been on his initial visit to Thessalonica: "These men who have caused trouble all over the world have now come here.... They are all defying Caesar's decrees, saying that here is another king, one called Jesus" (Acts 17:6–7). A first-century observer reading Paul's letters and listening to him preach might have concluded that Rome would eventually kill this man, which it did.

ERASTUS AND THE IMPERIAL CULT

Archaeology and other voices from antiquity are unanimous in attesting to the importance of the imperial cult in the cities and municipalities that Paul evangelized in the Mediterranean basin. As Roman colonies, places like Corinth and Philippi have yielded huge numbers inscriptions related to the imperial cult. Asia Minor also proved to be fertile soil for the growth of emperor worship, with some 180 imperial cult centers by the end of the third century.[206]

The vitality and pervasiveness of the imperial cult is not difficult for us to grasp. Combine ambitious provincials with egocentric emperors, and the rest is axiomatic. What we may need to be reminded of, however, is that unlike today, religion was not confined to the realm of personal conscience and private faith. The rituals and festivals related to the imperial cult permeated civic life and incorporated the entire citizenry in the worship of the emperor and the gods.[207]

In Laconia, not far from Corinth, a weeklong imperial festival was instituted upon Tiberius's succession that involved theatrical performances, games, singers, and a festal procession, culminating with the sacrifice of a bull at Caesar's temple. The decree calls for full participation ("young men, virgins, married women, and the rest of the citizenry") and ends with proscriptions against any violators.[208] The festal calendar from Philippi held about ten separate imperial dates.[209] Athletic competitions were also used to celebrate the ruling emperor. Inscriptions from Corinth attest to imperial games dedicated to Claudius, Nero, Vespasian, and Trajan.[210]

Another important means of expressing devotion to the emperor—religious and political—was through the annual oaths taken by provinces and municipalities throughout the Roman world. The practice of swearing oaths to the emperor had a long tradition in the military establishment, beginning with Octavian and his forces prior to the battle at Actium, and continued as a ritual of accession throughout the principate.[211] These vows become annual events in the provinces, often celebrated on the emperor's birthday or the anniversary of his accession. An oath of loyalty might seem a harmless civic right, perhaps even patriotic. All of these vows, however, were religious in nature and involved an explicit connection to the imperial cult and other deities.[212] The residents of Paphlagonia and neighboring Phazimon, near Bithynia on the Black Sea, swore by "Zeus, Earth, Sun, [and] all the gods and goddesses" that they would be loyal to the emperor Augustus, invoking grim curses on themselves and their children if they failed. These vows were taken by "all the inhabitants of the countryside

> YOU CAN BE SURE [O TRAJAN], THAT EVERYWHERE THE OATH IS BEING TAKEN FOR YOU . . . FOR NO ONE WOULD DENY HIMSELF THIS PLEASURE.
>
> PLINY

. . . in the shrines of Augustus."[213] In a letter to Trajan, Pliny reports rather perfunctorily on his annual administration of the rite:

> We have celebrated with appropriate rejoicing, Sir [*dominus*], the day of your accession whereby you preserved the Empire; and have offered prayers to the gods to keep you in health and prosperity on behalf of the human race, whose security and happiness depends on your safety. We have also administered the oath of allegiance to your fellow-soldiers in the usual form, and found the provincials eager to take it too, as proof of their loyalty.[214]

Pliny's offhand reference to the locals who took the oath "as proof of their loyalty" speaks volumes concerning both the expectations of Roman governors and the strategies of politically savvy provincials. Conspicuous indeed would have been the absence of any prominent citizens at such ceremonies, particularly elected magistrates. The city-wide nature of imperial festivals and rituals made demands on every segment of society and could not be easily avoided, especially in Roman colonies like Philippi and Corinth whose founding involved a large influx of military veterans. Christians certainly would have had a difficult time negotiating a path through pagan, imperial society.

PUBLIUS MARIUS VALENS, HONORED WITH THE DISTINCTION OF A DECURION, AEDILE, AT THE SAME TIME DECURION OF PHILIPPI, PRIEST OF THE DEIFIED ANTONINUS PIUS, DUUMVIR, SUBSIDIZER OF THE GAMES.

*INSCRIPTION, PHILIPPI

More puzzling still is how Erastus, an elected magistrate (*aedile*) of Corinth and companion of Paul (Rom 16:23), could have fulfilled the duties of his office without compromising his faith. Magistrates were expected to participate in the festivals, sacrifices, and vows made to the emperor, and often they were responsible for officiating at such events. In Laconia, southeast of Corinth, the aedile was in charge of setting up the cult statues of the emperors prior to the festival, leading the procession, and supervising the sacrifice at the imperial shrine.[215]

Erastus's faith would have also derailed his climb up the *cursus honorum,* which usually entailed priestly appointments in imperial and local religious orders. Titus Claudius Dinippus, a contemporary of Erastus in Corinth, is one of many Corinthian magistrates whose career illustrates this:

> To Tiberius Claudius Dinippus, who was duovir, augur, priest of Britannic Victory, military tribune of Legion VI Hispanesis, chief engineer, agonothetes [superintendent] of the Neronian and Isthmian games.[216]

The dilemma of Christians in public service was so intractable that Tertullian (c. 160–220 C.E.) felt compelled to address the matter directly in chapter 17 of a treatise entitled *Concerning Idolatry.* His conclusion is that the magistrate's duties are so extensively and inextricably involved with idolatry that it is scarcely conceivable that a Christian could hold public office. How Erastus managed to discharge the duties of his office without compromising his faith remains one of the unsolved mysteries of NT studies.[217] It may not be mere coincidence that Erastus's name is not found in any other inscription or elsewhere in the historical record. It is possible that Erastus's faith necessitated an early retirement from public life.

THE TEMPLE OF GOD AND IDOLS IN CORINTH

It was not only aspiring politicians like Erastus who had to balance faith with professional and social obligations. We have seen how central temples and pagan religiosity were to communal life in a Roman city (see City and Society: Urban Landscape and Environment), and it goes without saying that the functions, celebrations, and rituals associated with civic religion would regularly make demands on the citizenry. In Magnesia, south of Ephesus, property owners and businesses were required to contribute to the upkeep of the temple of Artemis, under the threat of a curse:

> And it is good for the owners of houses or for those who have built workshops to provide according to [their] means for the decorations of the altars before the [temple] entrance, and for those who make inscription[s] for Artemis Leukophryene Nikephoros. And if someone should fail to accomplish [these things], it will not be good for him.[218]

A PUBLIC FEAST IS A GLAD AND MERRY DAY, WITH ALL THE DELIGHT OF GRAND BANQUETS, WITH TABLES SET OUT AT EVERY TEMPLE AND EVERY CROSSWAY, AND WITH NIGHT-LONG FEASTS, AND WITH COUCHES SPREAD ALL DAY AND ALL NIGHT.

*JUVENAL

We should not be surprised, then, that Paul has to address such matters with the Corinthians. What may surprise us is that he has to do so in three separate contexts (1 Cor 8:1–13; 10:1–30; 2 Cor 6:15–7:1). In 1 Cor 8, Paul chides the "strong" who continue to dine in pagan temples without consideration of their "weaker" brothers and sisters (see Religion and Superstition: Monotheism in Corinth). In 1 Cor 10, the sin is more egregious, participating in pagan celebrations and eating meat sacrificed to idols.[219] By the writing of 2 Corinthians, Paul's patience has worn thin and his approach is confrontational:

> Do not be inappropriately yoked with unbelievers! . . . What harmony is there between Christ and Belial? What does a believer have in common with an unbeliever? What agreement is there between the temple of God and idols? . . . Come out from among them and be separate! Touch no unclean thing! (2 Cor 6:15–17)

Paul's concern that believers separate themselves from idols, along with his reference to Belial (Satan), hearkens back to his admonitions in 1 Corinthians where similar issues are addressed, and 10:14–22 in particular, where he urges the Corinthians to "flee from idolatry" (v. 14), reminding them that pagan sacrifices are offered to demons: "You cannot participate in both the Lord's table and the table of demons!" (v. 21). Further, his concern for maintaining purity and abstinence from "everything that contaminates the body and spirit" (7:1) remind us of the sexual license that was common in banquets within temples. The dilemma of the early followers of Jesus is clear: temple activities were an integral part of Roman society and were connected to many important community and family rituals—puberty rites, marriage ceremonies, and civic celebrations. Moreover, since only the elite had homes large enough for entertaining a party of any size, the numerous temples in Corinth provided the facilities, with the fees naturally being used to support the temple and cult.

Yet Paul was not insensitive to the difficulties of negotiating a path through pagan society, and in 1 Cor 10 he suggests a pragmatic approach to the problem of meat sacrificed in temples and sold in the market. Essentially, he advises believers in Corinth to enjoy the meat they are served without asking questions about its provenance (vv. 25–26). However, if they are invited to a dinner and their host goes out of his or her way to point out that the meat being served was offered in a sacrifice, and so includes his or her guests in that sacrifice, believers should abstain (vv. 27–28).

In a culture where pagan religion and the social order walked hand in hand, the separation that Paul demanded was a delicate and dangerous task—too much so for many. Withdrawing from idolatry often meant withdrawing from society. Within decades of Paul's letters to Corinth Nero felt justified in executing "an immense multitude" of Christians on the charge of anti-social behavior, "hatred against mankind," as Tacitus puts it.[220]

PAUL AND POVERTY

A Pauline scholar recently argued that "neither the appropriate use of riches nor the plight of the economically deprived are dominant concerns for Paul." To be blunt, this is a woefully inadequate appraisal. It is true that in the letters of Paul that have survived we find only two extended discussions of wealth, poverty, and issues related to the economically disadvantaged, 2 Cor 9:6–14 and 1 Tim 6:3–10, 17–19. It is also true, however, that from the letters of Paul that have survived we know that the apostle spent nearly two decades of

> SEE THAT YOU EXCEL IN THIS GRACE OF GIVING. I AM NOT COMMANDING YOU, BUT I WANT TO TEST THE SINCERITY OF YOUR LOVE.
>
> 2 CORINTHIANS 8:7–8

his life engaged in an economic relief effort for the poor in Jerusalem; it was a project that he cared about deeply.

We first hear of the collection for the poor in Jerusalem in Gal 2:10, where Peter, James, and John request that Paul "continue to remember the poor," referring to "the poor among the saints in Jerusalem" (Rom 15:26). To this Paul comments, "this is the very thing I have always been eager to do," indicating that even prior to this request he had been involved in some type of poverty relief. This is verified by his famine relief ministry to Jerusalem described in Acts 11:27–30. True to his word, as Paul made his way around the Mediterranean his promised relief campaign began in full force.

The next explicit reference is in 1 Cor 16:1–4, where we learn that the Corinthians were aware of the project and wanted to participate, and that "the churches in Galatia" (16:1) were on board.[221] Paul's most extensive discussion of this charitable venture is found in 2 Cor 8–9, where Paul spends fully two chapters prodding, needling, and persuading the believers in Corinth to fulfill their promise to contribute. Obviously this was an important matter for Paul. Along the way we hear that the Macedonian churches (Philippi, Berea, and Thessalonica) have also made a generous donation (2 Cor 8:1–5). In Rom 15:26, Paul confirms that the churches of Achaia (Corinth and neighboring communities) have indeed made a contribution and that his plans are to visit Rome on his way to deliver the aid to "the poor among the saints in Jerusalem."

> AT THE PRESENT TIME YOUR PLENTY WILL SUPPLY WHAT THEY NEED, SO THAT IN TURN THEIR PLENTY WILL SUPPLY WHAT YOU NEED. THEN THERE WILL BE EQUALITY.
>
> 2 CORINTHIANS 8:13

In his instructions to the Corinthians, Paul explained that delegates from the contributing Gentile churches would accompany him to Jerusalem with the funds (1 Cor 16:3–4; 2 Cor 8:19–20), which is what Luke records in Acts 20:4. In this verse Luke mentions representatives from Derbe, Lystra, Berea, Thessalonica, and Ephesus—apart from those we know of from Corinth and Achaia—who are journeying with Paul to Jerusalem. The scale of this endeavor was massive, by ancient standards, and clearly took a great deal of planning and effort on the part of Paul and his companions. I think it would be fair to call it a "dominant concern."

The reason(s) for the poverty of the believers in Jerusalem are not clear, though we know of both persecution (Acts 8:1–3) and famine affecting believers in Jerusalem (Acts 11:27–30). In the course of discussing his relief program with the Corinthians, Paul divulges that one result would be an increased unity between the Jewish and the Gentile portions of the church: "In their prayers of thanksgiving for your generosity, their hearts will go out to you"

(1 Cor 9:12–13). The consistent emphasis throughout Paul's letters and Acts, however, is to relieve the economic distress of the destitute in Jerusalem:

> Now, I am on my way to Jerusalem . . . to make a contribution for the poor among the saints in Jerusalem. (Rom 15:25–26)

> Our desire . . . is that there might be equality. At the present time, your plenty will supply what they need, so that in turn their plenty will supply what you need. (2 Cor 8:13–14)

> This service . . . is supplying the needs of God's people. (2 Cor 9:12)

> I came to Jerusalem to bring my people gifts for the poor. (Acts 24:17)

Paul's relief effort was very different from benefaction as exercised in Roman society. Benefaction was not aimed at poverty relief but at gaining status. According to Pliny, the typical benefactor would "bestow their gifts on those best able to make a return."[222] Nor did the patron support clients who had no social standing or citizenship. The rank of the client enhanced the status of the patron.[223] In contrast to those motivated by ambition and status, Paul expects generosity to be motivated by love and based on the sacrificial example of Christ (2 Cor 8:7–9).

It is true that Paul's primary mission was to spread the message of the death and resurrection of the Messiah. It is equally true, however, that along with being a missionary and a theologian, Paul was a relief worker trying to make a difference in one corner of a poverty-stricken world, Jerusalem.

WEAKNESS AND STRENGTH

It goes without saying that Paul's letters offer unique insights into the social setting of their addressees and the problems—as Paul perceived them—faced by his original audience. For example, power language in Ephesians alerts us to the prevalence of magic in that community (see Religion and Superstition: Magic), political language in 1 Thessalonians and 2 Thessalonians signals a potential conflict with the imperial order in Thessalonica

> GOD HAS AP-
> POINTED STRENGTH
> OVER WEAKNESS.
>
> DIO CHRYSOSTOM

(see City and Society: Paul's Counter-Imperial Gospel in Thessalonica), and so on. Second Corinthians is home to one of Paul's most theologically weighty ideas, penetrating to the heart of his apostleship:

> Therefore I will boast all the more gladly about my weaknesses, so that Christ's power may rest on me. That is why, for Christ's sake, I delight in weaknesses, in insults, in hardships, in persecutions, in difficulties. For when I am weak, then I am strong. (2 Cor 12:9–10)

Although not stated explicitly until 2 Cor 12, this idea of strength cloaked in weakness lies behind Paul's presentation of himself as a conquered foe being led to his death while simultaneously spreading the knowledge of Christ (2 Cor 2:14–16), or as an earthen vessel concealing great treasure (4:7), as one who is wasting away outwardly but being renewed inwardly (4:16–17), or as one who has nothing yet possesses everything (6:10). Paul is engaged in a long and difficult struggle with the Corinthians over their value system and their superficial evaluation of him, his ministry, and his preaching, and he crystallizes this censure in a paradox of profound magnitude: weakness is strength. Given the audience Paul was addressing, it would be difficult to formulate a more counterintuitive and countercultural thesis.

> HE WAS CRUCIFIED IN WEAKNESS, YET HE LIVES BY GOD'S POWER. LIKEWISE, WE ARE WEAK IN HIM, YET BY GOD'S POWER WE WILL LIVE WITH HIM TO SERVE YOU.
>
> 2 Corinthians 13:4

For Corinth, a city whose traditions, perspectives, and identity were decisively shaped by athleticism and the conquest of strength over weakness, Paul's message of a savior "crucified in weakness," and his insistence that weakness is strength, certainly would have confused many. As the sponsor of the celebrated Isthmian games, Corinth's most deeply held civic values were personified by the triumphant athlete. On a stroll through the streets of Corinth a first-century tourist would pass elegant statues depicting boxers sparring or champions wearing their wreaths; they would admire inscriptions heralding victors; and of course they could visit the sanctuary of the goddess of victory herself, Nike/Victoria. Coins, pottery, and other artwork bore similar athletic imagery, and an imposing bust of Herakles/Hercules would bid travelers farewell as they left the city along the Laechaeum road. In fact, Hercules, the "savior of the earth and humanity," as Dio Chrysostom calls him,[224] performed many of his famous labors in the vicinity of Corinth and was widely venerated throughout the Peloponnese. His muscular profile is depicted on scores of artifacts from Corinth, and his temple was located near the heart of the city. Pitted against Hercules or the heroes at the games, Jesus the crucified criminal surely would have come in a distant third, and Paul's strenuous campaign in 2 Corinthians to redefine strength and weakness was an exercise in resocialization. In fact, this aspect of Paul's argument in 2 Corinthians is so firmly rooted in the unique cultural profile of Corinth that if the letter lacked any

> DEDICATED TO THE GODDESS VICTORY."
>
> Inscription, Corinth

> SOME ARE SAYING OF ME, "HIS LETTERS ARE WEIGHTY AND STRONG, BUT HIS BODILY PRESENCE IS WEAK."
>
> 2 Corinthians 10:10

reference to its destination or its recipients, we would probably still be able to trace it to this city.

PAUL THE LEATHERWORKER

When we attempt to imagine a day in the life of the apostle Paul, we might find ourselves lingering on images of Paul preaching the public forums, or teaching in the lecture hall of Tyrannus, or perhaps traveling with Timothy along the Via Egnatia to the next stop on their itinerary—all of which were certainly regular features of his missionary endeavors. Yet if we look at Paul's description of his daily routine, a fuller, less glamorous picture emerges of a hardworking artisan who labored with his hands "night and day" (2 Thess 3:8) in order to offer the gospel "free of charge" (1 Cor 9:18) to his listeners.[225]

Manual Labor as a Missionary Strategy

When Paul arrived in Corinth he met two fellow Jews recently expelled from Rome, Aquila and Priscilla, and because they were leatherworkers like him he set up shop with them (Acts 18:1–3). The Greek word often rendered "tent-maker" in Acts 18:3, *skēnopoios*, should probably be translated more broadly as "leatherworker."[226] This would include the production and repair of tents but also a large assortment of related goods. Although we do not know with certainty that Paul plied his trade as a leatherworker in every city he evangelized, the evidence of Acts and his letters suggests that something close to this scenario is the most likely. During his solemn, tearful farewell to the elders in Ephesus Paul reminds them, "You yourselves know that these hands of mine have supplied my own needs and the needs of my companions. In everything I did, I showed you that by this kind of hard work we must help the weak" (Acts 20:34–35). Similar comments are made to the Corinthians (1 Cor 4:12–13; 9:3–18) and to the Thessalonians: "For you yourselves know how you ought to follow our example. We were not idle when we were with you.... On the contrary, we worked night and day, laboring and toiling so that we would not be a burden to any of you" (2 Thess 3:7–8).

> WE WERE NOT IDLE WHEN WE WERE WITH YOU, NOR DID WE EAT ANYONE'S FOOD WITHOUT PAYING FOR IT. ON THE CONTRARY, WE WORKED NIGHT AND DAY, LABORING AND TOILING SO THAT WE WOULD NOT BE A BURDEN TO ANY OF YOU.
>
> 2 THESSALONIANS 3:7–8

Paul's determination to finance his missionary work through his skills as a leatherworker seems to be fundamental to his missionary strategy, and for good reason. Every city and village required leather products—tents, awnings, satchels, belts, and so on—and the tools of the trade were easily portable. While at his workbench the apostle could make contacts, establish friendships, exchange ideas, and gain familiarity with the city. It was a shrewd entrée into a local community and provided a stable platform for the proclamation of the gospel, without burdening those to whom he was preaching.

Manual Labor and Patronage in Corinth

Not everyone, however, perceived the wisdom of Paul's missionary strategy. The Corinthians in particular seemed to have taken offense at Paul's refusal to accept their money and at his principled determination to engage in manual labor to support himself. Paul addresses their concerns on several occasions,[227] but his comments in 2 Cor 11 are especially illuminating. He asks, "Was it a sin to lower myself . . . in order to preach the gospel of God to you free of charge?" (v. 7). In speaking of "lowering himself" Paul probably echoes a complaint circulating among some of the Corinthians who were appalled at the sight of Paul hunched over his workbench in the forum like a slave. That Paul's work as a tentmaker is in view is made certain by Paul's insistence that this lowering takes place so that he can preach the gospel "free of charge" and not be "a burden" on any of them (11:9; 12:15–16). Lest we be tempted to think that the Corinthians are exaggerating the situation and that Paul's working conditions must not have been so demeaning as to warrant such embarrassment, listen to Paul's description in verse 27: "I have labored and toiled and have often gone without sleep; I have known hunger and thirst and have often gone without food; I have been cold and naked." On only two other occasions does Paul use this exact phrase, "laboring and toiling" (*kopos kai mochthos*), and in both instances it refers explicitly to his manual labor "night and day" in order not to be a burden to others (1 Thess 2:9; 2 Thess 3:8); it is not a reference to his evangelistic ministry more generally. This candid picture of a poorly clad artisan laboring into the wee hours of the morning to make ends meet, often lacking sufficient food and shelter, echoes numerous descriptions of the working classes in antiquity and is precisely the kind of image that many in the elite orders of Corinth would have found so distasteful.

In justifying his determination not to accept the support the Corinthians had offered, Paul inadvertently divulges their perspective on his refusal: "Is it

> SIMILARLY WITH ALL WORKMEN AND CRAFTSMEN, TOILING DAY AND NIGHT . . . STAYING UP LATE TO GET THE WORK DONE. NO CITY COULD DO WITHOUT THEM, BUT YOU WILL NOT FIND THEM ON THE COUNCIL, NOR DO THEY SIT WITH MEN OF RANK.
>
> *SIRACH 38:27–33

because I do not love you? God knows I do!" (11:11; cf. 12:15–16). Paul's rejection of their patronage is being interpreted as a rejection of their friendship, which is entirely in keeping with the politics of patronage and benefaction in the Roman world (see City and Society: Class and Status). In refusing their offer of support Paul has violated certain cultural conventions related to giving and receiving financial support, and at least some in Corinth have taken grave offense.[228]

> I COMMEND TO YOU OUR SISTER PHOEBE, A DEACONESS OF THE ASSEMBLY IN CENCHREA. HELP HER IN WHATEVER SHE NEEDS, FOR SHE HERSELF HAS BEEN A BENEFACTOR TO MANY PEOPLE, INCLUDING ME.
>
> *ROMANS 16:1–2
> AUTHOR'S TRANSLATION

Although Paul does not explain why he was willing to accept money from the Macedonians (2 Cor 11:9; Phil 4:14–19) and assistance from Phoebe of Cenchrea (Rom 16:1–2) but not from the Corinthians, he is clear as to why he engaged in manual labor:

To not financially burden his congregations (2 Cor 11:7–9; 12:15–16; 1 Thess 2:9)

To set an example of hard work (Acts 20:34; 1 Thess 2:9–10; 2 Thess 3:7–9)

To allow him to contribute to the needs of others (Acts 20:34–35; Eph 4:28)

To distinguish himself from religious charlatans (2 Cor 2:17; 11:12, 23–27)

We can reasonably surmise that Paul was uncomfortable with the motivation behind the Corinthian offer of support. Perhaps he perceived patron-client strings attached, which would limit his freedom and keep him from being "all things to all people" (1 Cor 9:19–23). Additionally, it may be that the Corinthians were trying to avoid the embarrassment of seeing their founding apostle toting his awls and knives through the streets each morning and setting up shop in one of the forums next to slaves, shopkeepers, and other peasant artisans. If this was the case, Paul may have determined that offending patrician sensibilities was less important than modeling the servanthood of Christ (Phil 2:6–11), who made himself poor so that others might become rich (2 Cor 8:9). In his long-running struggle to invert the Corinthians' value system, Paul's principled stand on supporting himself through manual labor constituted a daily assault on a status-conscious society that honored form over content, style over substance, and status over character.[229]

> ONE SHOULD ENDURE HARDSHIPS AND SUFFER THE PAINS OF LABOR WITH HIS OWN BODY, RATHER THAN DEPEND UPON ANOTHER FOR SUSTENANCE.
>
> MUSONIUS RUFUS

THE PERILS OF CARRYING THE NAME

Paul's encounter with the risen Jesus on the road to Damascus not only effected a profound inner transformation (see Religion and Superstition: Paul the Visionary), it also cast a foreboding destiny over the erstwhile Pharisee's life, which his letters and Luke's account in Acts unfold in poignant detail. In the vision given to Ananias, who is instructed to lay hands on the still blind-struck Paul, Ananias's reservations are dismissed by God with the solemn pronouncement, "Go! This man is my chosen instrument to carry my name before the Gentiles and their kings and before the people of Israel. I will show him how much he must suffer for my name" (Acts 9:15–16).

Travel

No passage better illustrates the fulfillment of these ominous words than 2 Cor 11:23–30, where Paul recounts in short staccato salvos the occupational hazards of an itinerant evangelist, many of which center on the dangers of travel in the first century: shipwrecks, fording rivers, bandits, exposure to the elements, and being "constantly on the move" (v. 26). As perhaps the most well-traveled person in the NT, Paul's calling as a missionary-evangelist entailed a lifetime of hardships due to his obligation to travel (see City and Society: Travel in Antiquity), quite apart from other sources of difficulty. It is estimated that Paul's journeys described in Acts—which is not comprehensive—comprised nearly 10,000 miles of travel.[230] Most of this would have been on foot along roads constructed by Roman soldiers.

> I PLAN TO VISIT YOU ON MY WAY TO SPAIN. I HOPE TO VISIT YOU WHILE PASSING THROUGH AND TO HAVE YOU ASSIST ME ON MY JOURNEY THERE. . . . NOW, HOWEVER, I AM ON MY WAY TO JERUSALEM.
>
> *ROMANS 15:24

While Paul employs a host of images to portray the Christian life (an athlete, a soldier, a laborer, a slave), it should not surprise us that his favorite image is that of a traveler, someone whose life is spent walking.[231] Thirty-two times Paul exhorts his readers to walk (*peripatein*) in a particular manner. Believers are to walk in love (Rom 14:15), to walk according to the Spirit (Rom 8:4), to walk by faith (2 Cor 5:7), to walk worthy of their calling (Eph 4:1). This metaphor dominates Paul's ethical instruction, and so it is not surprising to hear Paul describe sin as stumbling (Rom 9:32; 11:11; 1 Cor 8:9; 2 Cor 11:29). Although the walking metaphor is found eight times in John's epistles, no other NT writer uses it as extensively or as imaginatively as Paul.[232] In a somewhat jarring mix of images, Paul can even speak of "walking in good works" (Eph 2:1)! Paul might have picked up this idiom from his Hebrew Bible[233] or perhaps from the usage of his contemporaries,[234] but his fondness for this metaphor almost certainly derives from the fact that he spent so much of his life on the road, determinedly putting one foot in front of the other as he sought to fulfill God's calling on his life. It is hardly an overstatement to say that Paul's walk-commands provide as much insight into the apostle's biography as his ethics.

> YOU, [TIMOTHY] HOWEVER, KNOW ALL ABOUT MY TEACHING, MY WAY OF LIFE . . . MY PERSECUTIONS, SUF-FERINGS—WHAT KINDS OF THINGS HAPPENED TO ME IN ANTIOCH, ICONIUM AND LYSTRA, THE PERSECUTIONS I ENDURED. YET THE LORD RESCUED ME FROM ALL OF THEM.
>
> 2 TIMOTHY 3:10–11

Prison

Paul also speaks of being "in prison more frequently" than his rivals in Corinth (2 Cor 11:23; 6:5). When we correlate this statement with the information provided by Acts we see again the selective nature of Luke's account. Luke records only one imprisonment prior to the writing of 2 Corinthians (55–56 c.e.), in Philippi (Acts 16:16–40); Paul's incarceration in Jerusalem, Caesarea, and Rome were later events.

The imprisonment in Philippi followed a mob action and a severe flogging, and we are told that Paul and Silas were placed in stocks in an "inner cell." In all likelihood this was a room with no natural light, no latrine, and no sanitation. The "frequent imprisonments" mentioned in 2 Cor 11:23 were probably also the result of Paul's evangelistic work and would have led to similar types of confinement. In Jerusalem, Paul was bound with two chains and held in a military barracks (Acts 21:37; 23:16). We know nothing of Paul's situation in Caesarea beyond the location of Paul's confinement, Herod's residence (Acts 23:35). In Rome, Paul was kept under house arrest at his own expense (Acts 28:30), guarded by a soldier and bound with a chain (Acts 28:16, 20), where he was able to continue teaching and preaching (Acts 28:17–31).

Readers of the NT would do well to be attentive to the circumstances in which Paul's letters were produced. Five of the thirteen letters ascribed to Paul were written from Roman confinement: Ephesians, Philippians, Colossians, Philemon, and 2 Timothy. Paul's many references to his "chains" (e.g., Col 4:18; Phil 1:14; 2 Tim 1:16) remind us that these missives were penned or dictated in circumstances of psychological duress and physical pain. In light of this, it is striking that certain themes in these letters seem to belie these harsh conditions; for example, joy in Philippians (1:4, 18, 25–26; 2:2, 17–19; 3:1; 4:1–2, 4) or peace in Ephesians (2:14–15; 4:3; 6:15, 23). It is also striking that

> I, PAUL, WRITE THIS GREETING IN MY OWN HAND. REMEMBER MY CHAINS. GRACE BE WITH YOU.
>
> COLOSSIANS 4:18

Paul never speaks of himself as a prisoner of Rome or any other human authority. Rather, he is "a prisoner of Christ Jesus" (Phlm 1, 9; Eph 3:1) or of "the Lord" (Eph 4:1; 2 Tim 1:8) or "of the Gospel" (Phlm 13). This unique perspective allowed Paul to reason that even though he may be "bound like a criminal . . . God's word is not bound" (2 Tim 2:9). So, when free, Paul could refer to himself as "an ambassador for Christ" (2 Cor 5:20), and when imprisoned, "an ambassador in chains" (Eph 6:20), but in either case he remained Christ's ambassador. Once again one cannot help but sense the divine irony of Paul's life, as he went from imprisoning Christians (Acts 8:3; 22:4; 26:10) to proclaiming Christ while in prison: "I appeal to you, Philemon, for my child Onesimus, whom I have begotten while in chains" (Phlm 10; cf. Acts 16:25–34; 28:17–30; cf. Phil 4:22).

> THEY STONED PAUL AND DRAGGED HIM OUTSIDE THE CITY, THINKING HE WAS DEAD.
>
> ACTS 14:19

Riots

Along with imprisonments, 2 Cor 11 mentions flogging, stoning, and, more vaguely, "dangers in the city" (vv. 23–24, 26). To be beaten with rods (v. 25) was a distinctively Roman form of punishment, while "forty lashes minus one" (v. 24) was a penalty meted out by the synagogue. Stoning was the result of mob violence, as in Lystra (Acts 14:19). In fact, harassment from the market rabble seems to be a routine feature of Paul's evangelistic endeavors; Luke records mob violence against Paul and his companions in Iconium (Acts 14:1–7), Lystra (14:8–20), Philippi (16:19–24), Thessalonica (17:5–9), Berea (17:13–15), Corinth (18:12–17), and Ephesus (19:23–41). Some, however, claim that the picture sketched by Acts of riots and stoning is simply a tendentious creation of Luke, who followed a stereotypical storyline.[235] On closer inspection, however, Luke's portrayal seems firmly rooted in the social setting of the densely populated urban centers of the ancient world.[236]

Civic disorder in the Roman world, both east and west, was a widespread and common occurrence, associated with everything from grain shortages to sporting events to shabby rhetorical displays. According to Cicero, stampeding and stone throwing could erupt as "a mere spontaneous expression of popular indignation."[237] Almost anything could uncork the bottle: an unwelcome verdict from a judge;[238] an annoying poet reciting his verse;[239] a teacher suspected of fraud and chicanery.[240] Even children could be found joining in the fun of a vigilante-style stoning.[241] Civic officials were also vulnerable, as well as the emperor. The historian Suetonius tells us that Claudius was once cornered in the forum by a mob of angry commoners, verbally abused and pelted with pieces of bread. He barely escaped with his life.[242] To be sure, these were not everyday occurrences, but neither was Plutarch's assessment wildly overstated: "Men engaged in public affairs [are] compelled to live at the caprice of a self-willed and licentious mob."[243]

To be involved in public service was to make oneself a target for the disgruntled masses; philosophers and moralists in particular often bore the brunt of public discontent. According to Dio Chrysostom, one measure of a true philosopher, the philosopher determined to extol virtue and condemn vice, is whether he is willing to endure the "cruel and unruly" public assembly.[244] Dio warns that the noble philosopher must "steel himself against the crowd, for they may become suddenly angry and seek to abuse him."[245] Writers of this era describe ridicule, heckling, jeering, stoning, and so on, as the occupational hazards of philosophers,[246] and public life generally, which explains Petronius's depiction of the lawyer whose nightmare consists of "looking with terror upon the tribunal surrounded by a throng."[247]

These voices from antiquity bear witness to the very real risks involved in exposing oneself to the volatile and unforgiving masses in the public arenas of the Roman world and considerably illuminate the social setting of the mob scenes depicted in Acts. The highly flammable nature of public gatherings achieved proverbial status among writers of the period. In Dio's scathing denunciation of "the ridicule, disorder, and uproar of the mob"[248] he is able to cite Homer and the epic poets as his authority: "Unstable and evil is the public assembly, and wholly like the sea . . . a little puff can rouse it."[249] Similar sentiments are expressed by Jewish writers. Pseudo-Phocylides hands down the maxim, "Do not trust the people; the mob is fickle."[250] Philo is equally cynical: "For the multitude is unstable in everything—intentions, words, and deeds."[251]

> PHILOSOPHERS MUST KEEP VIGILS, WORK HARD, OVERCOME DESIRES, ABANDON THEIR FRIENDS, BE LAUGHED AT AND SCORNED BY EVERYONE THEY MEET. IN EVERY WAY WE GET THE WORST OF IT!
>
> *EPICTETUS

The high incidence of social unrest during this period issues predictably from the urban conditions described earlier, poverty and overcrowding in particular (see City and Society: Population Density as well as City and Society: Urban Unrest as well as City and Society: Class and Status). Apulieus's description of the common folk who were "forced by ignorant poverty . . . to seek the filthiest supplements and free meals for their shrunken belly" provides substantiation for Dio's insistence that the two greatest evils facing the empire were "idleness and poverty."[252] Day laborers, beggars, the unemployed, and the bored congregated in the markets and forums where the dole was distributed, which meant there was usually a crowd in the center of the city with too much time on their hands. When Luke describes the Jews of Thessalonica "rounding up some bad characters from the market" and starting a riot (Acts 17:5),[253] he provides further confirmation of the dismal social and economic conditions prevalent throughout the Mediterranean in this era. High population density combined with high unemployment created an environment in which urban unrest not only flourished; it was probably a welcome diversion for a large portion of the urban poor. With this background in mind, Luke's later description of the riot in the theater at Ephesus, in which "some were shouting one thing, some another; and most of the people did not even know why they were there" (Acts 19.32), sounds entirely plausible.

> MOST PEOPLE SIT
> ABOUT IN PUBLIC
> PLACES GOSSIPING
> AND WASTING TIME.
>
> PLINY

FURTHER READING

Primary Sources

Pausanius (second century C.E.) was a traveler and cultural geographer. His *Descriptions of Greece* contains his firsthand observations of Athens, Corinth, Olympia, and many other urban centers of Greece. He comments on architecture, mythology, art, and numerous aspects of the urban landscape. Available in the LCL.

Martial (late first century C.E.) is perhaps our most important primary source for daily life in the city of Rome in the first century. His *Epigrams* are pithy, humorous, and sometimes raunchy glimpses of the important features of Roman life: the baths, patrons and clients, morality, social status, and much more. Available in the LCL.

Lucian (second century C.E.), *Toxaris* 24–34. A brief account of a judicial proceeding and subsequent incarceration that illuminates the dark world of Roman prisons. Available in the LCL.

Martyrdom of Polycarp (second century C.E.); *The Martyrdom of Perpetua and Felicitas* (third century C.E.). Moving accounts of two early Christian martyrs that illustrate the clash between Christianity and pagan religion, including emperor worship. Perpetua's story also contains a gripping depiction of a Roman imprisonment. Equally important is Pliny's correspondence with Trajan concerning what to do with Christians who refuse to pay homage to the emperor (*Letters* 10.96–97). Pliny's *Letters* and the *Martyrdom of Polycarp* are available in the LCL. Several reliable versions of the story of Perpetua and Felicitas can be found online.

Musonius Rufus (first century C.E.), "What means of livelihood is appropriate for the Philosopher." This discourse by Musonius, "the Roman Socrates," sheds light on first-century values concerning manual labor from the perspective of an enlightened Stoic. Also important on this theme are Lucian's

"The Dream" and Arius Didymus's *Epitome of Stoic Ethics* 11m. Musonius's *Discourses* is edited by Alfred Bellinger and is available from Yale University Press. A translation of Arius Didymus edited by Arthur Pomeroy is published by the Society of Biblical Literature.

Secondary Sources

Richard S. Ascough. *Paul's Macedonian Associations: The Social Context of Philippians and 1 Thessalonians*. WUNT 2.161. Tübingen: Mohr Siebeck, 2003.

Lionel Casson. *Travel in the Ancient World*. Baltimore: Johns Hopkins University Press, 1994.

Stephen K. Catto. *Reconstructing the First-Century Synagogue: A Critical Analysis of Current Research*. Library of New Testament Studies 363. London: T&T Clark, 2007.

Ronald F. Hock. *The Social Context of Paul's Ministry: Tentmaking and Apostleship*. Philadelphia: Fortress, 1980.

A. H. M. Jones. *The Greek City from Alexander to Justinian*. Oxford: Clarendon, 1998.

Ramsay MacMullen. *Roman Social Relations, 50 B.C. to A.D. 284*. New Haven: Yale University Press, 1974.

S. R. F. Price. *Rituals and Power: The Roman Imperial Cult in Asia Minor*. Cambridge: Cambridge University Press, 1984.

John Stambaugh. *The Ancient Roman City*. Baltimore: Johns Hopkins University Press, 1988.

HOUSEHOLD
AND FAMILY

HELENA

Helena sat impatiently as her maidservants massaged perfumes into her shoulders and neck, knotted and embroidered her hennaed tresses into small ringlets using ivory beads, and prepared her *peplum* to drape over her linen tunic. Believers from all the surrounding communities would be gathering at her house that afternoon, as they did monthly, and Helena was keen to ensure that her position and status were not easily overlooked.

In truth, Helena didn't care a fig about her husband's new friends or his new faith. She had endured his attachment to the synagogue prior to their marriage and even "converted" to cement their relationship and dispel any doubts Titius Justus might have about her intentions, but his devotion to this new Jewish sect had gone too far. He was even ready to donate a sizeable sum to that indigent pseudo-philosopher Paulus to help "the poor in Jerusalem." A likely story! Fortunately she had dissuaded the gullible idiot from that lunacy. Gaius Titius Justus had been a carefully selected prey: aged, wealthy, and naïve. Helena was determined that not one obol of her legacy would be lost or purloined by some religious charlatan.

But, not to worry, Helena thought to herself as she inspected her wardrobe for the evening. Titius Justus was nearly dead anyway, and if Thanatos, the reaper of souls, didn't fetch the old man soon she would take matters into her own hands again. Her first husband, Demetrius, had swallowed the honeyed wolfsbane greedily enough—he rarely paused before gulping—and croaked in a convulsive heap on the floor within an hour. Titius Justus's fondness for mushrooms, however, would make the job much easier this time. Helena had become very cozy with Titius Justus's son, Quintus, a man her own age, and with the father out of the way they would no longer have to sneak around the city. If all went according to plan, Helena would be the *domina domi*, the lady of the house, till Charon ferried her across the Styx.

Gaius, of course, knew nothing of Helena's past. After burying Demetrius, Helena sold the plot of land they had managed to acquire and moved from Nemea to Corinth. Posing as a refugee from the famines in the south, Helena shrewdly positioned herself in the forum and the theater so that she would attract attention from the right sorts of people, which didn't take long.

Rising from her dressing table, Helena gathered her floor-length *peplum* in her hand and descended the stairs into the atrium. The walls of the stairway were frescoed with geometric panels of azure and crimson; medallions of Gaius's three children were spaced evenly throughout the passage; Quintus in the guise of Mercury, Calliana as Athena, and Secundus as Apollo. Only Quintus survived. Calliana had died of malaria just before her tenth birthday, and Secundus succumbed to pneumonia not long after donning his *toga virilis*. Their mother died in childbirth along with their fourth child.

The atrium was constructed in the classic Greek style, with a square opening in the slanted roof above and a large sunken *impluvium* in the center of the room to catch the rainwater. Helena gazed at her reflection in the water with satisfaction. Hebe, the goddess of youth, had treated her kindly. Although she was nearly forty, there were few visible creases under her eyes, and her figure still turned heads in the marketplace. But Aphrodite's jealousy would not long be held in check, and Helena understood that the day was fast approaching when her reflection would frown back at her in disgust. But Helena had planned for this as well. Her marriage agreement with Titius Justus was carefully drawn up to ensure that her fate would not be that of so many undowered widows and divorcées: shoeless, penniless, draped in rags, and begging for spare change on temple steps.

Against the far wall was the *lararium*, which contained a small likeness of the *genius*, the guardian spirit, of Gaius Titius Justus, and was framed by two crested serpents. Since his baptism by Paulus, Gaius no longer maintained the shrine, but neither did he remove it. It was one thing to worship only one god; it was quite another to dismantle an altar. The opposite wall depicted several chubby cupids playing hide and seek, and the tiled floor beneath Helena's feet displayed a splendid mosaic of Poseidon and Amphitrite frolicking with nereids and dolphins. Gaius might not be the shrewdest at spotting a con—and thank the gods! Helena chuckled in her thoughts—but he was a true aesthete, with exquisite tastes in décor, furnishings, and art. The walls of the upstairs bedrooms were all adorned with scenes from nature and mythology, and the downstairs *cubicula*, which surrounded the atrium, were frescoed with columns and niches that gave the impression of depth and dimension.

Helena's attention was momentarily diverted by the coo of a pigeon, which had fluttered into the atrium through the open roof, quickly darted through the tablinum, then into the *peristyle*, and now rested on one of the granite columns outlining the courtyard. From its perch this intruder surveyed the garden and surrounding rooms as if it were claiming the *domus* as its own. Five minutes ago it had been meandering haplessly from treetop to rooftop, and now it posed as the mistress of a grand estate. Clever bird, thought Helena.

A loud crash from behind her jolted Helena back into the moment, and she pivoted around toward the *vestibulum,* the long entry hall that connected the atrium to the street, to ascertain the source of the disruption. Moving quickly to the thick wooden doors at the end of the entryway, Helena slid the bolt and walked out into street. A fractured barrel of olives lay to the left of the doorway bleeding its innards down the gutter. Several grimy street urchins had already begun scavenging its contents, while the owner of the cart off of which the barrel had fallen was desperately trying to calm the donkey hauling the load.

Eumolpos, the olive merchant who managed one of the shops flanking the entry to the home of Gaius Titius Justus, rushed to shoo the imps away from his merchandise and to salvage what he could. He halted mid-stride and cowered visibly when Helena emerged from the doorway. Eumolpos was a freedman of Titius Justus who rented his property from Gaius and represented his former master's interests among the merchants as his client. Eumolpos's shop, and that of Statius, the neighboring wine merchant, fronted the *domus* of Titius Justus and provided a buffer to the street as well as additional income for the household.

"Clean this up immediately!" glowered Helena. "I have guests arriving shortly, and they will not be greeted by this foul mess and your wretched backside rummaging in the gutter!"

"Yes, *domina,* immediately." Eumolpos winced, unconsciously massaging the back of his leg. Eumolpos had received his cap of freedom only last month, and the mere presence of the *domina horribilis* caused the welts on his thighs and shanks to flare up, as if anticipating her strap.

Statius hurriedly came to assist Eumolpos as Helena disappeared back into the house. "Don't let the hag terrorize you, Eumolpos. You're a *freedman*—Gaius wouldn't let her flog you now."

"Gaius is visiting his estates in Thracia, Statius, and that Numidian porter she keeps would do anything she asks. I think he enjoys thrashing fellow slaves."

"You are *not* a slave!" Statius reprimanded.

"Well, I'm little more. I'm a red-cheeked client of Gaius Titius Justus. This *taberna* is all I have, and it's barely enough. I can't afford to cross her—you know she has Gaius wrapped around her finger."

Statius's silence seemed to concede the point. They finished chasing down the last olive, whereupon Statius slapped four coins on the counter and said, "Why don't you weigh out for me a pound, Eumolpos—the green itranas."

Back in the house Helena made sure that everything would be ready for the gathering later that afternoon. The kitchen buzzed and clanked with the sounds of food preparation, slaves scampered between the tricliniums (there were two dining rooms in the *domus*) and the other rooms, cleaning and setting things in order. Although Helena was entirely ambivalent about this new religion her husband had taken up, she did enjoy the higher profile it afforded her among the locals, and even a few families of rank as well. What's more, with her husband out of town Helena had managed to transform the monthly gatherings into less dreary, much livelier affairs with a little more concern for proper Roman decorum. There was plenty of room for everyone, so why not reserve the tricliniums for the freeborn and those of status? This is a *Roman* home and that is the *Roman* way, Helena reasoned. Satisfied that all was in order, Helena took a seat in the west-facing *ala*, a small wing off the atrium peeking over a narrow lane below, and dozed beneath an image of the beautiful and horrible Medusa.

Julia waited with her door open for Phoebe and Zoe to arrive from Cenchrea. They would be traveling by litter into Corinth to attend the monthly gathering of believers, and Julia wanted to greet them in person. She had been with Zoe only once since she was sold over a month ago, and Julia's heart ached to see her again—and of course Zoe would want to see little Marky. Julia had been spending more time lately at their home in Corinth, which suited everyone quite well. The strain in her relationship with Speratus seemed less acute with several miles between them, and his frequent day trips into the city meant that they could be seen together in the forum regularly, which was important to Speratus.

"*Pax tecum*, peace be with you," said a diminutive woman peering into the open door.

"Phoebe, Zoe!" exclaimed Julia. "*Pax vobiscum*, peace be with you! Where is your litter, your slaves?"

"We left them several blocks back and proceeded on foot," replied Phoebe. "It was much quicker that way, especially as Zoe seems to know her way around the city far better than my slaves."

"Well, she would!" laughed Julia.

The women spent the better part of an hour catching up and watching Marky bounce balls and fight barbarians with his wooden gladius. Zoe was clearly thriving in Phoebe's household, and it was obvious to Julia that Phoebe had found the daughter she had always wanted.

"Well, we've probably tarried too long," announced Julia abruptly, noticing the afternoon shadows on far wall of atrium. "Your slaves can rest; I have plenty here to escort us to the *ecclesia*, the gathering. Gaius Titius Justus's home is not far."

Four stout slaves walked ahead of the trio, carrying unlit lamps for the journey home. Zoe instinctively took her place behind the women, which Julia didn't seem to notice, but which Phoebe found increasingly disconcerting. Finally, Phoebe turned around and addressed Zoe, her voice cracking with emotion: "Zoe, I know I bought you as a slave, but certainly you understand by now that I consider you to be more than just my maidservant. We are all slaves of the Master who bought us— we've *both* heard Paulus say that—and as we are all going to worship our common *Dominus*, I think we should walk *together*."

Zoe, unsure how to respond, looked hesitantly to Julia, her former mistress, who took Zoe under her arm and whispered, "Together."

It was almost a block later that Phoebe broke the silence with, "So, tell me about Gaius Titius Justus, Julia. Do you know him well?"

"No, not well at all really. I've met him, of course. He is a sweet man, nearly seventy, I'd guess—recently remarried. He was one of the first believers here in Corinth. I'm told he used to frequent the synagogue and was converted by Paulus's preaching there, before they booted Paulus out. I hear Gaius has a wonderful home."

"Oh, I assumed you had been there before," interjected Phoebe. "Where do you meet for worship and prayer?"

"With Heraclitus, the schoolmaster, and a few others in his flat above the forum. It can't hold more than a dozen of us, but I've never felt more at home. We are like a family. Stephanas is always there with his wife, Theodora, and their son Phillip; Simon, the old Syrian weaver, too, and his slave; several freedmen as well, including Timarchus, Babbius Philinus's chef. And last week one of Gallio's centurions came with Stephanas."

"I'm glad you know Stephanas," Phoebe remarked. "He and Theodora have worked hard to keep all of us connected and growing."

"Yes," agreed Julia. "It was their idea for all of us to gather together once a month."

As the party rounded the final corner and approached doorway of Titius Justus's home they were met by Stephanas, Theodora, and Phillip, accompanied by Heraclitus, who were also just arriving from the opposite direction.

"*Chairete!* Greetings!" exclaimed Stephanas, who added quickly, "Or as Paulus would say, '*Charis humin!* Grace be with you!'"

Introductions were quickly made, which essentially amounted to presenting Zoe to Stephanas's party. Phillip, who had just turned seventeen and was normally quite articulate, mumbled a confused, "Greetings be with you," as he bowed toward Zoe, which caused Julia to smirk and Heraclitus to roll his eyes in disappointment.

"Welcome, *domini et dominae*," came a deep voice from just behind them. Massinisa, Helena's *atriensis*, stood in the doorway and motioned for them to enter. Massinisa was a dark, imposing figure who took great pride in serving as the porter and steward for the household of Gaius Tititus Justus. Among his fellow slaves he was treated with due deference, and his eighth day—his day off—would be spent only with other slaves of similar rank.

Helena had given Massinisa strict instructions on the seating of guests: slaves, freedmen, and other townsfolk would remain in the atrium or the peristyle; citizens of rank would be escorted to one of the tricliniums, the dining rooms. As the party entered the atrium Massinisa pointed Zoe and Heraclitus towards the east corner of the atrium, where some fish, bread, and olives were set out on a small table. A couple dozen or so townsfolk were scattered around the room chatting and visiting. A burst of laughter came from the direction of the nearest dining room, followed by the clank of cups. Massinisa caught the attention of Stephanas, Julia, and the others and said, "This way, please," and began to escort them toward the dining room.

Stephanas paused, looking a little confused, while Phoebe clutched Zoe's hand and stood stationary. "We're *together*," she intoned, daring the massive Numidian porter to make the next move.

Momentarily taken back by this unusual breach of etiquette, Massinisa recovered his composure and replied soothingly, "*Domina*, there is hardly enough room for everyone in the triclinium, and I'm sure you would be more comfortable reclining with the lady of the house."

"Well," interrupted Phillip, "I'm perfectly happy to remain here with Zoe and Heraclitus," a note of chivalry in his voice.

"Yes, but Madame Helena has given me very explicit orders . . ."

"Did somebody mention my name?" Helena emerged from the triclinium nearest the atrium, wobbled slightly, and exclaimed, "Julia! Stephanas! Welcome! I do wish you could have arrived earlier, when the hens were just out of the oven."

Zoe couldn't believe her eyes. She recognized Helena instantly as the woman she had seen from a distance at the synagogue a month or so ago, but at the time she couldn't quite place her. Now that she stood within a few feet of her, there was no doubt. This was *Helena*: the women who raised her, flogged her almost daily, and sold her as soon as she was able to scrub floors on her own. She had obviously improved her station—and Zoe could only guess how—but the ingratiating smile, the treacle voice, and the steely eyes were still the same.

Sensing an imminent confrontation between Phoebe and Helena, Stephanas stepped into the breach. "Yes, we are a bit late—so perhaps we should all come together now for prayer." Stephanas's cheerful tone diffused the situation, though he noticed that Phoebe's eyes followed Helena as she left the atrium to assemble all the guests in the courtyard outside the larger dining room.

Helena hadn't taken any notice of Zoe.

The meeting that evening was different from what Julia, or Zoe, or Phoebe were used to. Stephanas bravely tried to lead in prayer and worship, but some of the guests had imbibed rather excessively during the meal time and kept interrupting the proceedings. One person would be praying or offering a prophetic word when somebody else would barge in with their own prayer or revelation. Crispus, who was the leader of the synagogue before he converted, tried to bring a lesson from the teaching of Moses, but several of the women kept asking questions about the characters and events in the narrative he was relating, and the end result was more confusing than helpful.

Zoe, Helena, and Phoebe had barely left the house when Phoebe burst out with, "What a disaster! I would have never imagined that one of our meetings would turn into . . . a *convivium*—some of them were drunk! And I'm not sure I trust this woman, Helena."

Zoe bit her lip. Knowing Helena as she did, Zoe was reasonably certain that she had covered her tracks well. Anything that Zoe said would be denied, and as everyone knew, slaves were liars and thieves; a slave's testimony wasn't even accepted in court. No one would believe her. Zoe thought of Phoebe and of walking together with her and Julia earlier that evening; nothing would be worse than losing Phoebe.

"Well, perhaps it wasn't a *complete* disaster," observed Julia, a smirk reappearing in the corner of her mouth. "I noticed Phillip seemed to take an interest in you, Zoe."

Zoe blushed, while Julia and Phoebe exchanged a knowing glance.

"He's a fine young man," Julia continued. "He'll inherit his father's orchards—the best in the Peloponnese I'm told."

"Enough, enough, Julia," laughed Phoebe. "I'm not quite ready to part with Zoe yet!" Squeezing Zoe's hand, she added, "Still, I suppose we should visit Corinth a little more often. Perhaps we can worship with you and Stephanas's family next time, at Heraclitus's flat."

"That is precisely what I had in mind," declared Julia, as she clasped Zoe's free hand.

THE CULTURAL CONTEXT

THE HOME

Domestic Space

There existed a variety of types of housing in the Roman world. Most urban dwellers would have lived in *tabernae* or *insulae*.[1] The *tabernae* were small two- or three-room domiciles often doubling as a workshop or storefront and were typically part of the ground floor of tenements or larger public buildings.[2] *Insulae,* the equivalent of our multifloored apartment buildings, began appearing in Rome and other population centers in the second century B.C.E. as overcrowding necessitated squeezing more and more people into the limited space within the city walls.[3] Although some of these blocks of flats contained roomy, upscale apartments on the first floor, the average room size was considerably smaller than what we would be accustomed to today, especially on upper floors.[4] These *insulae* had no running water, no central heating, and no built-in cooking facilities. The occupants relied on public latrines and chamber pots for their toilet and a small charcoal brazier for what indoor cooking they were able to do.[5] The modest homes of the almost nonexistent middle class (see City and Society: Class and Status), and the grander villas of the elite, while well excavated and amply illustrated in the literary sources,[6] constituted a tiny fraction of the housing market of an ancient city. Excavations from Rome, Pompeii, Corinth, and elsewhere reveal homes where cubicle-size rooms of perhaps 3 by 4 meters were arranged around courtyards or common reception areas (the *atrium*).[7]

> LUPERCUS, YOU NEED NOT TROUBLE YOUR SERVANT. IT IS A LONG WAY FOR HIM TO COME, AND I LIVE UP THREE FLIGHTS OF STAIRS, LONG ONES TOO.
>
> MARTIAL

Domestic Décor

The details and diversity of home décor in antiquity—styles of wall painting, typical furnishings, and so on—are not crucial for understanding the domestic context of urban Christianity in antiquity. However, as we attempt to visualize the earliest gatherings of Christians in private homes throughout the Roman world it is important to recognize the extent to which religion and mythology were integrated into the architecture and interior design of the typical Roman domicile. Although few of the poorly constructed dwellings of the lower classes have survived, the remains of larger homes, along with the literary evidence, allow us to sketch a reasonably complete picture.

Domestic shrines were a standard feature of Greek and Roman homes. The goddess of the hearth (Latin, *Vesta;* Greek, *Hestia*) was venerated in most dwellings, along with other household gods. The *penates* and the *lares* were Roman deities who watched over the pantry and the household and were commonly worshiped at shrines in the atrium[8] or the dining room.[9] A token portion of each meal was offered to the *lares* and *penates,*[10] and important family events would be accompanied a prayer to the household gods.[11] Depending on the region, other gods might also be invoked as protectors of the home. In Philippi, household shrines to the trio Liber, Libera, and Hercules seem to have been fashionable.[12] According to the Cynic epistles, the homes in Cyzicus (in Mysia, Asia Minor) all bore a dedicatory inscription to Hercules above the doorway.[13]

> IN THE CORNER OF THE ROOM I SAW A LARGE CUPBOARD CONTAINING A TINY SHRINE, WHEREIN WERE SILVER HOUSEHOLD GODS, AND A MARBLE IMAGE OF VENUS.
>
> *PETRONIUS

In addition to the common household altar were the paintings, statuary, and various household utensils that mirrored the religion, superstition, and ethics of popular culture. A visitor to an upscale home in Pompeii might pass under a protective phallus in the entryway, gaze upon a wall painting of Apollo in the atrium above the family shrine, stroll through a *peristyle* featuring Pan and the wood nymphs, and be seated in the triclinium (dining room) beneath an image of Mars fondling Venus.[14] Oil lamps, serving trays, drinking cups, and statuary frequently featured a prominent phallic element, and erotic scenes could be found on walls, vases, lamps, bowls, and mirrors—and this list is hardly exhaustive.[15] Of course, Roman homes in Pompeii and elsewhere also contained murals with scenes from nature, history, and everyday life.[16] Still, the Roman home tended to propagate the mythology and morality of the larger society, and this must have been an issue faced very early among the believers meeting in private homes in urban centers throughout the Mediterranean.

> BY THE COMMAND OF THE DEITY IS THIS ALTAR TO THE GODS LIBER AND LIBERA DEDICATED.
>
> INSCRIPTION, PHILIPPI

THE FAMILY

Like today, the family was the most basic unit of society in antiquity. However, unlike the typical household unit in contemporary Western culture, which usually comprises mother, father, and children, the so-called nuclear family, the ancient Mediterranean household was an intergenerational social unit that included other relatives and any slaves as well. A nuanced presentation of ancient families would involve careful distinctions between wealthy and poor households, urban and rural households, Greek and Roman households, and so on. The following summary attempts to crystallize the most salient features of Greco-Roman households with a view to specific NT texts and issues.

> THUS, WHOEVER DE-
> STROYS THE HUMAN
> MARRIAGE DESTROYS
> THE HOME, THE CITY,
> AND THE WHOLE
> HUMAN RACE.
>
> MUSONIUS RUFUS

Patria Potestas

The cultures of the biblical world were strongly patriarchal and male-oriented. In the Roman context, this disposition was exemplified in tradition and legislation related to *patria potestas,* "the power of the father." As the head of his family (*pater familias*), the Roman father had virtually unchecked authority over his children, grandchildren, and great-grandchildren. This authority included education, marriage, mate selection, financial transactions, and even life and death. Indeed, the most severe exercise of a *patria potestas* was the father's refusal to accept a child into his family:

> BARBAROUS, NOT
> BRAVE, IS HE WHO
> KILLS A CHILD.
>
> PUBLILIUS SYRUS

Hilarion to his wife Alis very many greetings. Know that we are still in Alexandria. Do not be anxious. I beg and entreat you, take care of the little one, and as soon as we receive our pay I will send it up to you. If by chance you bear a child, if it is a boy, let it be, if it is a girl, cast it out.[17]

The exposure of unwanted children was held in check by public opinion, though it continued until well into the Christian era, in spite of the objections of philosophers and moralists.[18]

The father's authority did not end when the child reached adulthood but continued until the death of the *pater familias.* At the death of the father, sons would become the head of their own families, and married daughters passed to the authority of their husbands. The gravity of any breach of *patria potestas* led to numerous legal and philosophical debates concerning the circumstances in which an adult son might be justified in disobeying his father.[19] The Stoics took the radical position that the pursuit of virtue through philosophy should take precedence over the will of a father. Muso-

> HE BEGAN HIS AR-
> GUMENT WITH THE
> OLD AND DISCRED-
> ITED QUESTION, "IS A
> FATHER TO BE OBEYED
> IN EVERYTHING?"
>
> SENECA THE ELDER

nius Rufus reasoned that since every father wants what is best for his son, and since philosophy offers what is best, then it is not disobedient to disobey your father if he forbids you to study philosophy.[20] Epictetus is a bit more blunt: "The good is preferred above every form of kinship. My father is nothing to me, but only the good."[21]

Household Order

Household codes in Greek, Roman, and Jewish literature describe the ideal familial relationships that ought to exist within a household. More specifically, they attempt to prescribe correct behavior and structures of authority between husbands and wives, children and parents, and slaves and masters. Arius Didymus summarizes the household hierarchy in the following way: "Connected within the house is a pattern of monarchy, of aristocracy, and of democracy. The relationship of parents to children is monarchic, the relationship of husbands to wives is aristocratic, of children to one another, democratic."[22] He goes on to argue that the husband "has the rule of this household by nature. For the deliberative faculty in a woman is inferior, in children it does not yet exist, and in the case of slaves it is completely absent."[23] As appalling as this rationale sounds to us today, some of the most enlightened minds of antiquity, including Cicero, Musonius Rufus, Dio Chyrsostom, and Philo, assumed the cognitive superiority of males over females.[24] The perspective of slaves as subhuman was also commonplace (see Household and Family: Slaves).

THAT DEPARTMENT OF PHILOSOPHY WHICH SUPPLIES PRECEPTS APPROPRIATE TO THE INDIVIDUAL CASE—HOW A HUSBAND SHOULD CONDUCT HIMSELF TOWARDS HIS WIFE, OR HOW A FATHER SHOULD BRING UP HIS CHILDREN, OR HOW A MASTER SHOULD RULE HIS SLAVE—IS ACCEPTED BY SOME AS THE ONLY SIGNIFICANT PART.

SENECA

The wife's duties involved obedience, quietness, childrearing, faithfulness, and hard work. A husband was obliged to provide for his family and treat his wife and children with respect and his slaves with patience.[25] Children and slaves were to be obedient in all things. As today, the ideal was often far removed from reality.

In spite of the fact that women could neither vote nor hold elected office in the Roman government and were subject (in theory at least) to the *pater familias,* women in the Roman world often attained high social standing. They could engage in business, own properties, and function as a benefactress.[26] Junia Theodora, a citizen of Lycia residing in Corinth, was honored by the Lycian assembly in a lengthy inscription as a "patroness" who "continuously shows her zeal and her munificence to the nation."[27] The cities of the Roman East were noteworthy for providing women with leading roles in civic religion. In Pergamum, Julia Polla held

FOR CLAUDIA METRODORA, GYMNASIARCH, WHO TWICE DISTRIBUTED OIL TO THE CITY, SUPERVISOR OF THE GAMES, QUEEN OF THE THIRTEEN CITIES OF THE IONIAN FEDERATION, PRIESTESS FOR LIFE OF THE DIVINE EMPRESS APHRODITE.

*INSCRIPTION, CHIOS

the titles of "queen of the shrines of the goddess Roma, manager of the gymnasium and high priestess."[28] Julia Polla seems to have established priestly legacy in the region. Her daughter, Julia Tyche, was also a priestess, and her later descendents are listed among the leading priestesses at Ephesus.[29] Polyaena was a "priestess of the goddess Victory" in Corinth and was honored by the high priest and the city council as "a woman of excellence."[30] This undoubtedly indicates her position as a benefactress as well as priestess. In Philippi, the temple of Augusta, wife of Augustus, contained statues of seven priestesses of the cult.[31] The inscriptions from Philippi also attest to priestesses of Diana,[32] as well as a cult of female votaries of Bacchus who funded a water supply system.[33]

> DO NOT REMAIN UN-
> MARRIED, LEST YOU
> DIE NAMELESS. GIVE
> NATURE HER DUE, YOU
> ALSO, BEGET AS YOU
> WERE BEGOTTEN.
>
> PSEUDO-PHOCYLIDES

Betrothal and Marriage

In Greek, Roman, and Jewish societies, marriage was the norm. Philosophical dissenters aside (see Household and Family: Sexual Ethics), most parents assumed their children would marry and made appropriate plans to that end—setting aside money for a dowry and selecting a suitable mate. Early in his reign, Augustus introduced legislation to encourage marriage and strengthen the traditional Roman family. The new family laws provided economic incentives to marry and produce children, while also censuring adultery and singleness, including widows and divorcees who did not remarry.[34] In some locales, this resulted in preferential treatment toward the married in municipal elections:

> C. ANTISTIUS NOMISSIA-
> NUS GAVE IN MARRIAGE
> HIS OWN DAUGHTER
> ZENARION, A VIRGIN,
> ACCORDING TO THE
> JULIAN LAW WHICH
> WAS PASSED CONCERN-
> ING THE MARRYING OF
> THE SOCIAL ORDERS
> FOR THE SAKE OF PRO-
> CREATING CHILDREN.
>
> ROMAN MARRIAGE
> CONTRACT

Where two or more candidates have the same number of votes, the magistrate in charge of the election is to prefer and declare first elected a married man to an unmarried man, and a man with children to one without children, and one with more children to one with fewer children.[35]

Girls were typically married very young, at least by modern standards. In the Roman world, most women would be married in their mid to late teens; the aristocracy married even earlier. A girl could be legally married at the age of twelve, although the betrothal could be earlier. Roman men waited till their mid to late twenties before marrying.[36] Quintilian, whose wife died at age eighteen after bearing him two sons, was in his early forties when he married.

Marriages typically involved a betrothal period and a dowry and in most cases were arranged by the fathers. The betrothal period began with an agreement between the parents and was considered legally binding, even though the marriage was not consummated. An official ceremony marked the beginning of the betrothal, which was witnessed by a magistrate. Pliny describes attendance at such as events as the routine humdrum of a senator's day: "If you ask anyone what he did that day, the answer would be, 'I was present at a coming-of-age ceremony, a betrothal, or a wedding. I was called to witness a will, to support someone in court, or to act as an assessor.'[37] The chastity of the girl was a matter of great concern to both families, particularly among the nobility,[38] which is one of the reasons why girls were betrothed so young. The family of the bride was responsible to provide funds or property as a dowry, and the larger the dowry the better the girl's prospects for marriage would be. The dowry was returned if the couple ever divorced, which provided some disincentive toward ending the marriage.

One of the most significant differences between marriage in the ancient world and marriage in the contemporary Western world is that in Greece and Rome marriages were so not much romantic partnerships as strategic alliances. While love was not completely unimportant, it was not the most crucial consideration. Marriage partners were chosen by parents on the basis of financial considerations—could the young lady bring a significant dowry into the family coffers? Or social and political advancement—was the man from a prominent family and appropriate class? While many Cynics and Stoics eschewed marriage for the sake of unhindered devotion to philosophy (see below), Epictetus defends the decision of the philosopher Crates to marry by noting that it involved the "special circumstances" of "romantic love." This, he argues, is quite different from "ordinary marriages."[39]

> FROM THIS ASSIGNMENT HE WENT TO ROME TO TAKE UP OFFICE; THERE HE MARRIED DOMITIA DECIDIANA, A WOMAN OF HIGH LINEAGE. THE MARRIAGE PROVED AT ONCE A DISTINCTION AND A STRENGTH TO HIM IN HIS UPWARD PATH.
>
> TACITUS

The exchange of vows that we are used to hearing, with promises of love, fidelity, and devotion, are a far cry from the marriage contracts of antiquity. These typically record the precise amount of the dowry, followed by the duties of both parties:

> Apollonia shall live with Philiscus, obeying him as a wife should her husband. All necessities and clothing and whatever else is proper for a wedded wife Philiscus shall supply to Apollonia. It shall not be lawful for Philiscus to bring in another wife, or concubine, or boy-lover, nor to insult or ill-treat her. If he is proved to do any of these things, Philiscus shall forthwith forfeit the dowry. In like manner, it

shall not be lawful for Apollonia to spend the night or day away from the house of Philiscus without Philiscus's consent, or to consort with another man, or to dishonor the common home or to cause Philiscus to be shamed by any act that brings shame upon a husband.[40]

> SILA IS READY TO MARRY ME ON ANY TERMS; BUT ON NO TERMS DO I WANT TO MARRY SILA. HOWEVER, WHEN SHE INSISTED I SAID, "AT OUR BETROTHAL YOU WILL GIVE ME A MILLION BY WAY OF DOWRY IN GOLD." WHAT COULD BE MORE REASONABLE?
>
> MARTIAL

To be sure, one occasionally finds a half-hearted remonstrance against this dispassionate, contractual approach to marriage,[41] but most people would have heartily concurred with Pliny's practical advice: "Certainly if one thinks of the children of the marriage . . . money must be taken into account as a factor influencing our choice."[42]

We do have examples of loving marital unions, both from literature and funerary inscriptions. One shimmering example comes from the Stoic philosopher Musonius Rufus, whose description of the ideal marriage would fit comfortably in a Christian wedding homily:

For what man is so devoted to his friend as a loving wife is to her husband? What brother to brother? What son to his parents? Who is so longed for when absent as a husband by his wife, or a wife by her husband? Whose presence would do more to lighten grief or increase joy or remedy misfortune? To whom is everything judged to be common body, soul, and possessions, except man and wife?[43]

It remains true, however, that in ancient Mediterranean society love was more the byproduct of a happy marriage than a prerequisite, and a marriage could be judged quite successful without it.

ADULTERY AND DIVORCE

Divorce was widespread in the Roman world of the first century. Also, divorce was easier and more common during the first century than the century before, despite the legislation enacted by Augustus attempting to curb the divorce rate.[44] By the NT era, either spouse could initiate divorce, though in the imperial period this was the prerogative of the husband.[45] Valerius Maximus, for example, extols the virtues of an earlier age when "wine was unknown to Roman women" and when monogamy was a virtue:

Women who had been content with a single marriage used to be honored with a crown of chastity. For they thought that the mind of a married woman was particularly loyal and uncorrupted if it knew not how to leave the bed on which she had surrendered her virginity, believing that trial of many marriages was as it were the sign of a legalized incontinence.[46]

Other first- and second-century writers (e.g., Petronius, Juvenal, Horace, Martial) further illustrate the declining marital standards, and several authors claim to have knowledge of the first Roman divorce.[47] Seneca's censure is particularly vociferous:

> Is there any woman that blushes at divorce now that certain illustrious and noble ladies reckon their years, not by the number of consuls, but by the number of their husbands, and leave home in order to marry, and marry in order to be divorced? They shrank from this scandal as long as it was rare; now, since every gazette has a divorce case, they have learned to do what they used to hear so much about. Is there any shame at all for adultery now that matters have come to such a pass that no woman has any use for a husband except to inflame her paramour? Chastity is simply a proof of ugliness.[48]

YOU ARE MARRYING YOUR LOVER, PROCULINA, AND MAKING THE ADULTERER OF YESTERDAY YOUR HUSBAND SO THAT THE JULIAN LAW CAN'T PUT A MARK AGAINST YOU. THAT'S NOT A MARRIAGE, PROCULINA, IT'S A CONFESSION.

MARTIAL

Seneca's reference to adultery as commonplace is echoed throughout the surviving literature, though much of this material issues from, and focuses on, the situation among the privileged classes in Rome.[49] It is impossible to accurately calculate a divorce rate based on such anecdotal evidence drawn mostly from upper-class literary sources. Further, it also needs to be noted that the complaint is not against divorce per se but divorce initiated by women. Most of the ancient sources we rely on were written by men and reflect their attitudes and perspectives. The chauvinistic sensibilities of the Roman male were acutely offended at the rise of liberated womanhood in the first century,[50] though in many ways their complaints serve only to further illustrate the double standard with respect to men and women in antiquity.[51]

This double standard is further illustrated in the very definition of what constituted adultery. In Roman law, adultery was defined as an illicit relationship with or by a married woman or woman of respectable rank. Sexual liaisons by

MARRIAGES AS LONG AS OURS ARE RARE—MARRIAGES ENDED BY DEATH AND NOT BROKEN BY DIVORCE.

FUNERARY INSCRIPTION

a married man with slaves, courtesans, younger boys, or women of lower social orders were legally permissible under most circumstances and involved little, if any, social stigma. After enumerating the dangers that awaited the adulterer if caught, Horace concludes, "How much safer is trafficking in the second class—with freedwomen."[52] In his "Advice to Bride and Groom," Plutarch counsels that a husband's peccadilloes and paramours should be viewed as honoring the wife, because, "it is respect for [the wife] which leads him to share his debauchery, licentiousness, and wantonness with another woman."[53] Popular novelists and poets depict men carrying on with their mistress or boy-favorite in front of their wives.[54] This comes from the realm of fiction, but as one contemporary Roman historian reminds us on this subject, "It is not probable that any humorous genre could have amused its audience without being recognizable, if exaggerated."[55]

> I WARN YOU STEP-
> CHILDREN, DON'T
> TRUST A SINGLE DISH!
> THOSE HOT PASTRIES
> ARE BLACK WITH POI-
> SON OF A MOTHER'S
> BAKING. LET YOUR
> TREMBLING TUTOR
> TAKE THE FIRST BITE!
>
> *JUVENAL

Moreover, while a husband could bring a charge against his wife as an adulteress, the law did not afford the same right to the woman.[56] In the following legal verdict rendered in 197 C.E. but citing a first-century statute, an aggrieved wife's charges of adultery are summarily dismissed by the Roman courts:

Emperors Severus and Antoninus to Cassia:

The Julian law (on adultery) declares that women do not have the right of accusation in a criminal court, . . . though they wish to complain about the violation of their own marriage. Though (the law) had offered the ability to accuse (a wife) to men by the right of the husband, it did not offer the same privilege to women.[57]

In light of this dismal state of affairs, it is perhaps not surprising that, especially among the elite, poisoning became a fashionable option for disposing of husbands, stepchildren, or fathers who stood in the way of one's inheritance.[58] Tacitus's *Annuls* records a dozen or so poisonings, or rumors of such, among the aristocracy in the first half of the first century,[59] and Juvenal claims that poisoning had become something of a status symbol: "Then up comes a lordly dame who, when her husband wants a drink, mixes toad's blood with his Calenian [wine]. . . . If you want to be anybody nowadays you must dare some crime that merits [banishment to] Gyara or a jail."[60]

> AUGUSTUS REVISED
> EXISTING LAWS AND
> ENACTED SOME NEW
> ONES, FOR EXAMPLE,
> ON EXTRAVAGANCE, ON
> ADULTERY AND CHAS-
> TITY, ON BRIBERY, AND
> ON THE ENCOURAGE-
> MENT OF MARRIAGE
> AMONG THE VARIOUS
> CLASSES OF CITIZENS.
>
> SUETONIUS

Even when one makes allowances for literary clichés, the exaggeration of satirists, and the nearly universal condemnation of adultery, the picture that emerges is one where marriage vows were often exchanged and then forgotten. Petronius captures well the tragic collision between ideal and reality among the Roman elite: "A wife should be loved like a fortune got legally. But I would not wish to love even my fortune forever."[61]

SEXUAL ETHICS

Yet while the senate and the imperial house were charged with punishing adulterers and upholding traditional Roman values, they were also engaging in all manner of vice and scandal. Augustus forced Marcus Agrippa and, when he died, Tiberius to divorce and leave their families in order to marry his daughter, Julia.[62] As Tiberius's wife, Julia was later exiled for committing "every kind of vice."[63] Meanwhile, Tiberius himself was setting up shrines on Capri as sites for deviant sexual activities.[64] And on it goes. If even half of what Suetonius records of Nero is true, his depravity was beyond description.

Nor could the common folk look to the gods as models of virtue and probity. Zeus had liaisons with women and boys and set the standard for the rest of the pantheon. Consider, for example, the cloud-gatherer's smooth approach to Hera as he attempts to coax a little romance from his divine bride:

> Come, let us take our joy bedded together in love; for never yet has desire for goddess or mortal woman so shed itself about me and overmastered the heart within my breast—not even when I was seized with love of Ixion's wife, who bore Peirithous ... nor when I was seized with love of Danaë of the fair ankles ... nor when I fell for the daughter of far-famed Phoenix ... nor in my affair with Semele, nor with Alcmene in Thebes ... nor with Demeter ... nor when I loved glorious Leto.[65]

The rest of the gods followed Zeus' lead and became known for seducing and raping the fairer of both sexes. With exemplars like these, philosophers had a difficult time enjoining ethical behavior on *hoi polloi,* so they often resorted to exhorting the people to believe in the gods but not the stories about the gods.[66]

Quite apart from the divine and imperial orders, the sexual ethics of the ancient Mediterranean world were very different from those of today. To be sure, there was nothing going on then that isn't still going on today, but it cannot be denied that fifteen hundred years of institutional Christianity has had a civilizing effect on Western society, if only to force underground what would otherwise be practiced openly.

Prostitution, for example, was not illegal in antiquity, nor was it subject to any local or imperial restrictions. According to Cicero, liaisons with courtesans were a rite of passage for Roman youths:

> However, if there is anyone who thinks that youth should be forbidden affairs even with courtesans, he is doubtless eminently austere (I cannot deny it), but his view is contrary not only to the license of this age, but also to the custom and concessions of our ancestors. For when was this not a common practice? When was it blamed? When was it forbidden? When, in fact, was it that what is allowed was not allowed?[67]

This is not to say that prostitution was considered a respectable vocation, but there was nothing criminal in it. Modern visitors to the ruins of ancient cities like Ephesus or Pompeii will find directions to the red-light district carved in stone along the main thoroughfares. The surviving graffiti from Pompeii is too explicit for a volume like this but provides ample support for Horace's disdainful summary of the main attractions of the city: "the brothel, the greasy cookshop, and the flute-playing courtesans."[68]

> AT NUCERIA, LOOK FOR NOVELLIA PRIMIGE-NIA NEAR THE ROMAN GATE IN THE PROS-TITUTE'S DISTRICT.
>
> GRAFFITO, POMPEII

Similarly, pederasty was also widely practiced and was considered an acceptable form of sexual expression between an adult male and a prepubescent teen, usually of lower social rank. A common subject for Martial's epigrammatic wit is lamenting the boy who matures and turns to heterosexual relations; other times he simply extols the delights of pederasty.[69] Indeed, in Martial's circles, pedophilia was so pervasive that he warns young men about to marry that they had better visit the prostitute's district and find someone who will train them to enjoy women.[70] As illustrated above (see Household and Family: The Family), marriage contracts often contained a stipulation against bringing a boy-lover into the home. This provides the background for the scene in the *Satyricon* where Trimalchio begins fondling a servant boy in front of his wife during dinner. His wife objects, asserting her legal rights, whereupon Trimalchio hurls a goblet at her in response.[71] To a friend who was contemplating marriage, Juvenal counsels that suicide would be a wiser option, or better yet . . .

> YOUR WIFE IS A GIRL SUCH AS A HUSBAND WOULD HARDLY ASK FOR IN HIS MOST EX-TRAVAGANT PRAYERS: RICH, NOBLE, VIR-TUOUS. YOU BURST YOUR LOINS, BASSUS, BUT YOU DO IT WITH BOYS PROCURED WITH YOUR WIFE'S DOWRY!
>
> *MARTIAL

Take some boy-bedfellow, who would never wrangle with you through the night, never ask presents of you in bed, and never complain that you took your ease and were indifferent to his solicitations![72]

Stories abound of tutors taking advantage of students in their charge, which was a perennial concern of parents.[73] In "On the Education of Children," Pseudo-Plutarch weighs the issue of whether "men who love children [romantically]" should be allowed as tutors, and answers affirmatively.[74] His rationale is based on the example of Socrates and his pupils in ancient Athens, "who sanctioned affection between males and thus guided the youth onward to learning, leadership, and virtuous conduct."[75] In Pseudo-Plutarch's view, as long as the adult's intentions are honorable, the noble philosopher "ought to have the right to kiss any fair face he sees."[76] No wonder that the first-century Jewish moralist, Pseudo-Phocylides, warns: "Guard the youthful prime of life of a comely boy, because many rage for intercourse with a man."[77]

Digging Deeper: Vice, Luxury, and Asceticism and the Philosophic Response

The ethical philosophers of the day were not unaware of the decadence of the city and the moral decay across the empire, and they crystallized their censure in the form of virtue and vice catalogs.[78] Particularly common among Stoics and Cynics, these catalogs enumerated the virtues and vices of the age in a sometimes grocery-list fashion. "The worthwhile man," writes Arius Didymus, is "affable, clever, encouraging, accommodating, charming, gracious, trustworthy, and, in addition, soothing, keen in aim, opportune, shrewd, guileless, simple, straightforward, and unaffected, while the worthless man is subject to all the opposites."[79] The counterpart to the virtuous person is described by Dio Chrysostom:

> "LOVE OF MONEY BEGAN THIS DOWNWARD SPIRAL," HE REPLIED. "IN FORMER AGES VIRTUE WAS STILL LOVED FOR HER OWN SAKE."
>
> *PETRONIUS

> Then there is the man who proclaims the orgies of Pleasure, and admires and honors this goddess. He is insatiable as to things that tickle nostril and palate, and to all that affords any pleasure to the ear, as to all things that are soothing and agreeable to the touch: warm baths—twice a day—anointings, and soft robes. He is passionately devoted to the burning madness of sexual indulgence, through intercourse both with females and males, and other unspeakable obscenities.[80]

Wealth and luxury are frequently identified as the fountainhead of all vice. Writers of the period commonly connect the wealth Rome gained through its conquests with the increase of extravagance and vice. Juvenal regards Rome's moral decline as the ironic vengeance of the plundered nations: "Luxury, more deadly than any foe, has laid her hand upon us and avenges a conquered world. Since the day when Roman poverty perished, no deed of crime or lust has been wanting to us."[81] In Tacitus's view, Rome then passed on the contagion to the tribes and peoples it conquered, spreading the disease even to the rustic Britons: "They adopted Roman ways and, little by little, they went astray, taking to the colonnades, bath-houses, and elaborate banquets that make moral failings attractive."[82]

As one would expect, the philosophers had quite a lot to say about wealth and extravagance. The Stoic-Cynic insistence on simplicity and "living according to nature" was, as we have seen (see Education, Philosophy, and Oratory: Philosophical Schools) a reaction to the opulence of the day. For Musonius, wealth led to the soul-threatening disease of indulgence: "As for my part, then, I would

> THE ORATOR WRANGLES WITH HIS OPPONENT OVER THE BOUNDARIES OF LAND, BUT THE PHILOSOPHER REBUKES THE VICES OF MANKIND AND DETERMINES BOUNDARIES OF GOOD AND EVIL.
>
> *LUCIUS APULEIUS

choose sickness rather than luxury, for sickness harms only the body, but luxury destroys both body and soul, causing weakness, impotence, lack of self-control, cowardice, injustice, and covetousness."[83]

In keeping with their rejection of creaturely comforts and their embracing of hardship as morally beneficial, some Cynic philosophers adopted a form of asceticism that rejected marriage. In the Cynic literature, marriage is deemed to be a burden that will inevitably hinder the philosopher: "One should not wed nor raise children, since our race is weak and marriage and children burden human weakness with troubles."[84] Epictetus, a Stoic-Cynic philosopher, regarded marriage as a distraction that diverted attention from serving God and humanity.[85] Likewise, sexual intercourse was considered to be a frivolous waste of time that would distract the philosopher from his calling: "As for intemperate intercourse with women, bid it farewell. For there is no spare time, either for a poor man to beg, as Plato says, nor for the person hastening on the short-cut to happiness."[86]

> IT IS FIRST NECESSARY TO OBSERVE THAT SEXUAL INTERCOURSE IS NOT FOR THE SAKE OF PLEASURE. . . . FOR THOSE WHO HAVE INTERCOURSE NOT AT ALL FOR THE SAKE OF HAVING CHILDREN DO INJUSTICE TO THE MOST REVERED SYSTEMS OF PARTNERSHIPS, AND THEIR OFFSPRING WILL BE WRETCHED AND PITIFUL, LOATHED BY THE GODS.
>
> *PSEUDO-OCELLUS LUCANUS

Most Stoics took a softer position on marriage.[87] In a discourse entitled "Is Marriage a Handicap for Philosophy?" Musonius Rufus takes issue with the hard line the Cynics took on marriage by appealing to the example of Crates of Thebes: "Crates, although homeless and completely without property, was nevertheless married. . . . How then can we, who have a home to start with and some of us even have servants to work for us venture to say that marriage is a handicap for philosophy?"[88] Musonius goes on to argue that marriage is perfectly in accord with nature, necessary for the propagation of the human race, and gives expression to the highest form of love between human beings.

Despite this difference of opinion, Stoics and Cynics, together with many others among the intelligentsia of the day, were in agreement that sexual intercourse was intended for procreation, not pleasure. Musonius was particularly insistent on this: "Men who are not wanton or immoral are bound to consider sexual intercourse justified only when it occurs in marriage and is indulged in for the purpose of begetting children . . . but unjust and unlawful when it is mere pleasure-seeking, even in marriage."[89] Although this perspective is sometimes presented as the conventional view in Greco-Roman antiquity more broadly, the enormous amount of evidence from magical papyri, inscriptions, and erotic literature gives vocal attestation to the vibrancy of *eros,* sexual passion, in antiquity.

SLAVES

The first-century world of the NT was a world brimming with slaves. Estimates vary in regard to the number of slaves in Rome and the provinces in the first century, though a conservative approximation of the slave population in Rome would be 33 to 40%.[90] Seneca relates how the senate once considered legislation that proposed distinguishing between the slave and free classes by mandating particular articles of clothing be worn by slaves. The motion was rejected when it dawned on the senators that the slaves would then be able to recognize how numerous they really were![91] Moreover, slaves were considered part of the household in antiquity, under the authority of the *pater familias,* and as such were an important and visible part of the earliest Christian house churches. Yet the economic realities of antiquity leave no doubt that most households could not afford a slave.[92] So, references in the NT suggesting the presence of slaves or owners in the local gatherings are certain indicators of the involvement of wealthy, or at least modestly successful, individuals in the early church.

> WHEN WE RECLINE AT A BANQUET, ONE SLAVE MOPS UP THE DISGORGED FOOD, ANOTHER CROUCHES BENEATH THE TABLE AND GATHERS UP THE LEFTOVERS OF THE TIPSY GUESTS. ANOTHER CARVES THE PRICELESS GAME BIRD. ANOTHER, WHO SERVES THE WINE, MUST REMAIN AWAKE THROUGHOUT THE NIGHT, DIVIDING HIS TIME BETWEEN HIS MASTER'S DRUNKENNESS AND HIS LUST.
>
> *SENECA

Occupations of Slaves

Ancient slavery differed from modern slavery—particularly that of the ante-bellum South—in some significant ways. First, slavery in the Roman world was not racially delimited. The slave population was drawn from all parts of the Roman world, regardless of ethnicity. A Roman household might have slaves who hailed from Bythinia, Syria, Numidia, and sometimes Rome itself. Another difference between slavery in the Roman world and the slavery of early American history is the range of services provided by slaves in antiquity. The largest proportion were domestic and agricultural slaves, but the occupations of slaves were as diverse as the needs of their owners—cooks, waiters, doormen, gardeners, doctors, barbers, wet nurses, entertainers, teachers, and business managers. The wealthy freedman Trimalchio, a connoisseur of grotesque extravagance, had three masseurs rubbing him down at the bath, four pages running before his hand-carried litter, a musician trotting behind, a porter at the door, an enormous array of household servants, including a trumpeter in the dining room who served as an hourly chime.[93] Trimalchio, it must be remembered, is a fictional caricature, but one that the audience could certainly correlate with real life. A matron of a wealthy Roman household getting ready for her day, Lucian tells us, was attended by "a troupe of maidservants as ugly as their mistress . . . plastering her unhappy face with a variety of medicaments."[94]

> WHY CUT YOUR SLAVE'S TONGUE OUT AND CRUCIFY HIM, PONTICUS? DON'T YOU KNOW THAT PEOPLE SPEAK OF WHAT HE CANNOT?
>
> MARTIAL

Educated slaves might serve as scribes or teachers.[95] Those who proved capable and reliable might be entrusted with more significant responsibilities, as Pseudo-Plutarch confirms was "common practice":

For some of their trustworthy slaves they appoint to manage their farms, others they make masters of their ships, others their business agent, others they make household stewards, and some even money-lenders.[96]

While the fundamental distinction between the slave and free classes was never forgotten, there were upper-strata slaves and prestigious posts that signaled status among the slave class. Dio Chrysostom illustrates both these dynamics when he mocks the ludicrous sight of slaves "quarrelling with one another over glory and preeminence."[97] Dexter, an imperial slave, included his title with pride on the wall of a pub in Pompeii: "Dexter, a slave of Caesar, ate here most agreeably and enjoyed the barmaid at the same time."[98]

Treatment of Slaves

It would be a mistake, however, to imagine that slaves were distributed evenly across the social spectrum. The vast majority were illiterate and lived at or below the subsistence level, like most others in the Roman world. Their accommodation and overall treatment depended on the disposition and largesse of the owner. Horace speaks of the "narrow cell" of the domestic slave in Rome,[99] which the archaeological record confirms.[100] Excluding the small number of slaves at the very top of the social pyramid, the conditions in which slaves were kept ranged from cruelly inhumane (particularly those working in the mines) to austere but survivable. Apuleius's grim description of slaves working in a village mill preserves a typical scene that repeated itself in countless business establishments in numerous locales throughout the Roman world:

> BUT AT THE PRESENT DAY THESE SAME LANDS ARE TILLED BY SLAVES WHOSE LEGS ARE IN CHAINS, BY THE HANDS OF MALEFACTORS AND MEN WITH A BRANDED FACE.
>
> PLINY THE ELDER

The whole surface of their skin was painted with livid welts. Their striped backs were merely shaded, not covered, by the tattered patchwork they wore: some had thrown on a tiny cloth that just covered their loins, but all were clad in such a way that you could discern them clearly through their rags. Their foreheads were branded, their heads half-shaved, and their feet chained.[101]

The welts, lacerations, and manacles borne by these slaves are indicative of the subhuman valuation of slaves in antiquity: "What? You call a slave a man?" shouts a character from one of Juvenal's satires in disbelief.[102] Slaves were chattel, property, and could be treated as their owner saw fit. Juvenal pictures the mistress of a grand household nonchalantly passing the time while slaves being beaten at her request provide the background music for her activities:

> A NOTICE WAS FAS-
> TENED ON THE
> DOORSTEP: NO SLAVE
> TO GO OUT OF DOORS
> EXCEPT BY THE MASTER'S
> ORDERS. PENALTY, ONE
> HUNDRED STRIPES.
>
> PETRONIUS

One will have a rod broken over his back, another will be bleeding from a strap, a third from the cat-o'-nine tails; some women engage their executioners by the year. While the flogging goes on, the lady will be daubing her face, or listening to her lady-friends, or inspecting the width of a gold-embroidered robe.[103]

To be sure, not all slaves were so abused (see below), but the countless, often casual, references to beatings, floggings, canings, and execution of slaves constitute a vocal witness to dark and hopeless existence of a slave in antiquity.[104] The reliance on physical punishment was due, in part, to the fact that slaves had no property that could be confiscated or money to surrender. Their bodies became the focal point of a master's discipline. As part of the ritual of emancipation, the owner would slap his soon-to-be-freed slave across the face as a symbolic expression of the master's former power over the slave's physical body. This ritual is alluded to in the narrative about Helena, when the recently freed slave Eumolpos refers to himself as a "red-cheeked client"—that is, a newly freed slave who now serves as a client to his former master.

Particularly visible were the scars left from branding, which was often done on the head and face.[105] Branding was done either for punishment or to mark slave as property. If a slave ever managed to obtain his or her freedom the marks of servitude would remain. Martial took malicious delight in exposing one such freedman who attempted to cover his branding with ornate, extravagant fashion accessories.[106] For the class-conscious Romans, no amount of wealth or success could ever erase the shame of servile origins.

> LET LYGDAMUS BE
> TORTURED, LET THE
> BRANDING IRON
> GLOW WHITE HOT
> FOR THAT SLAVE!
>
> PROPERTIUS

Particularly vulnerable were women and young boys, who were commonly used to gratify the sexual appetites of their masters. Musonius relates that many of his contemporaries view sexual relations between a male owner and his slave to be "quite without blame, since every master is held to have it in his power to use his slave as he wishes."[107] Inscribed within the basilica (civic courtroom) of Pompeii was the admonition, "Take hold of your servant-girl whenever you want to; it is your right."[108] Martial extols the frugal Linus who, rather than purchasing a handsome youth to quench his sexual thirst, beds the wives of his servants.[109] As a mere *instrumentum vocale,* a "speaking tool," the slave had little choice but to be used—and abused—as the master saw fit.

Having sketched the general picture, it is necessary to qualify this by adding that some slaves and masters had good relationships, and some masters developed real affection for their slaves—and vice versa. Slave owners like Seneca and Pliny took great pride in treating their slaves decently.[110] The poet Statius tells us of an exceptional situation in which an owner freed a slave couple and made their son his heir.[111] Martial relates the story of a slave boy by the name of Glaucius who died at the age of twelve and who was so loved by his master that he erected a sepulcher for him along the Flaminian Way, a major Roman highway.[112] More such anecdotes could be cited, but we must be careful to read the depictions of slaves and owners critically. These literary artifacts were produced by the wealthy slave-owning class and so reflect their interests and perspectives. If we were fortunate enough to discover a description of slavery from the perspective of the slave, no doubt a fuller picture would emerge.

> IF I DIE LEAVING THE PRESENT WILL, I SET FREE UNDER THE SANCTION OF ZEUS, GAIA, AND HELIOS, FOR THEIR GOODWILL AND AFFECTION, MY SLAVES PSENAMOUNIS AND APOLLONOUS AND HER DAUGHTER, AND ANOTHER SLAVE CALLED DIONYSISUS.
>
> ROMAN WILL, EGYPT

Manumission of Slaves

A slave's only hope of release from the cruelty and dehumanization of slavery was death or manumission. An owner might decide to free a faithful slave in his will, as did Epicurus.[113] The will of Gaius Longinus Castor, a Roman veteran, freed two female slaves—presumably his concubines—and made them his heirs, disinheriting all others.[114] A master might grant freedom to a slave while he lived if he were particularly fond of the slave or the slave had rendered himself or herself especially beneficial.[115] In rare circumstances a slave might manage to save or pilfer enough to purchase his or her freedom,[116] although the owner was under no obligation to manumit the slave.

In most circumstances, slaves desired freedom, though they would have to consider carefully that their situation might worsen if they were set free with few skills and no resources. The economic situation of the Roman world was so severe that it was not unheard of for a free person to sell himself into slavery to improve his lot.[117] Epictetus describes the unpleasant reality that "freedom" brought about for many:

> "If I am set free," he says, "immediately it is all happiness, I shall pay no attention to anybody, I talk to everybody as an equal." . . . Then he is emancipated, and forthwith, having no place to go and eat he looks for someone to flatter . . . next he earns a living by prostitution, and so endures the most dreadful things.[118]

Nor was the emancipated slave done with his former owner; a freedman was usually bound to his former owner as a client.[119]

> SECUNDUS, A FREED-MAN OF DEIFIED KINGS, HAD THIS HYGEIA ERECTED IN HONOR OF THE HEALING SAVIOR.
>
> INSCRIPTION, CORINTH

Yet illustrations can also be found of freedmen who achieved success and fame after their manumission. Seneca mentions Demetrius, who eventually became wealthier than Pompey, his former master.[120] Martial too—although he despises them—references freedmen who gained wealth.[121] Even Epictetus, after cataloging the misfortunes of the emancipated slave (quoted above), concedes that it is possible such a person might go on to riches and fame. The classic literary example is Petronius's Trimalchio, who, although a fictional caricature, represents the quintessential vulgar upstart freedman that the Romans loved to hate.

Success stories like these, however, are more prominent in literature than in reality. Most freedmen continued on in their master's employ; others joined the ranks of groveling clients looking for a free meal or disappeared into the masses of impoverished plebes who filled the city and countryside. Firmer evidence of freedmen who gained modest success can be found in the monuments scattered throughout the cities of the empire, in which freedmen and freedwomen honored their patrons. These honorific steles imply at least some monetary surplus. Particularly important were the *Augustales,* associations of freedmen devoted to advancing the imperial cult. Numerous inscriptions from Philippi attest to their importance in that colony, where

> WHO THEN IS FREE? THE WISE MAN WHO IS LORD OVER HIMSELF.
>
> HORACE

they were accorded special seating in the theater.[122] The *Augustales* were also active in Corinth, as were other private associations of freedmen advancing the imperial cult.

Philosophers on Slavery

The ancient economy was utterly dependent on slave labor, and society as a whole had yet to develop a moral conscience with respect to slavery. As a result, there was no serious, sustained ethical scrutiny of slavery as an institution. The philosophic response to slavery was twofold. First, we have exhortations to treat slaves humanely. The best example of this comes from the Roman Stoic, Seneca. In *Epistle* 47, Seneca argues that both slave and free are equally members of the human family and that it is mere chance that one person is free and another a slave. Moreover, circumstances can be reversed quite unexpectedly, and the free should be mindful of this. Seneca's enlightened perspective is not representative of first-century philosophy as whole, nor is his argument aimed at undermining the institution of slavery. Seneca's real concern was the moral development of the slave owner, and his argument serves to strengthen the institution of slavery through improving it. Seneca, after all, was one of the largest slaveholders in Rome.

> BUT WHAT DOES IT MATTER HOW MANY MASTERS A MAN HAS? "SLAVERY" HAS NO PLURAL; AND HE WHO HAS SCORNED IT IS FREE, NO MATTER AMID HOW LARGE A MOB OF OVER-LORDS HE STANDS.
>
> SENECA

The more common response by philosophers, Stoics in particular, was to relativize slavery and freedom by allegorizing these states as characterological attributes of the base and noble person, respectively: "Evil alone makes one a slave; virtue alone frees. . . . Even if you happen to command others who are virtuous, you yourselves are slaves on account of your evil desires, and you are ordered around by your masters."[123] This approach to dealing with slavery provides at least some evidence that Stoic conscience was not fully comfortable with the institution. The Stoics redefined freedom as self-mastery and so argued that one could be truly, inwardly free, yet outwardly a slave, and vice versa.[124]

> Therefore, the man over whom pleasure has no power, nor evil, nor fame, nor wealth, and can spit his whole paltry body into some oppressor's face and depart from this life—whose slave can he any longer be, whose subject?[125]

Because freedom is not necessary for moral progress, for the perfection of the soul, slavery was considered one of the "indifferents" (see Education, Philosophy, and Oratory: Philosophical Schools) in that virtue could be pursued by slave and free alike. This theme became a traditional topic for philosophers and is given extended treatment in essays by Epictetus, Dio Chrysostom, Horace, Philo, and others.[126] Since Stoics imagined their system to be the surest guide to moral advance and inward freedom, the only reasonable conclusion to draw, as Persius argues, is that only the Stoic is free.[127]

THE NEW TESTAMENT CONTEXT

FROM HOUSE TO HOUSE

> And Saul was there, giving approval to [Stephen's] death. On that day a great persecution broke out against the church at Jerusalem. . . . But Saul began to destroy the church. Going from house to house, he dragged off men and women and put them in prison. (Acts 8:1–3)

From his first entrance onto pages of Christian history, the apostle Paul (then, Saul) was associated with the early Christian house church. At the time, his uninvited presence at the household gatherings of Jesus worshipers in Jerusalem was intended to harass, terrorize, and, if possible, eradicate these cancerous cells from the Jewish heartland before they could infect the entire organism. Yet within a matter of months, perhaps weeks, Paul would begin spreading the faith he had sought to destroy, and according to his own testimony, the private home was one of the primary venues of his evangelistic activity: "You know that I have not hesitated to preach anything that would be helpful to you, but have taught you publicly and *from house to house*" (Acts 20:20).

> THEN PAUL LEFT THE SYNAGOGUE AND WENT NEXT DOOR TO THE HOUSE OF TITIUS JUSTUS, A WORSHIPER OF GOD. CRISPUS, THE SYNAGOGUE RULER, AND HIS ENTIRE HOUSEHOLD BELIEVED IN THE LORD.
>
> ACTS 18:7–8

It is comforting to know that at least some facts of history remain beyond dispute, and one of those facts is the crucial role that the private home played in the spread of Christianity.[128] Paul makes several specific, albeit brief, references to individuals who hosted a Christian gathering in their home:

In Rome: "Greet Priscilla and Aquila, my fellow workers in Christ Jesus. . . . Greet also the church that meets at their house." (Rom 16:3–5)

> THEY ARE RUINING WHOLE HOUSEHOLDS BY TEACHING THINGS THEY OUGHT NOT TO TEACH.
>
> TITUS 1:11

In Colossae: "To Philemon . . . and to the church that meets in your home." (Phlm 2)

In Laodicea: "Give my greetings to the brothers at Laodicea, and to Nympha and the church in her house." (Col 4:15)

In Corinth: "Gaius, whose hospitality I and the whole church here enjoy, sends you his greetings." (Rom 16:23)

In Ephesus: "The churches in the province of Asia send you greetings. Aquila and Priscilla greet you warmly in the Lord, and so does the church that meets at their house." (1 Cor 16:19)

This picture is corroborated and filled out by the book of Acts. The historical accounts in Acts do not dwell on house churches as such, but they provide
enough information to allow us to get a general picture of Paul's missionary
strategy. In Philippi, Thessalonica, Berea, Corinth, and Ephesus, Paul used the
local synagogue as a starting point for his evangelistic work, which in most cases
led to the ministry continuing through the hospitality of local residents. At the
proseuchē in Philippi, a Jewish place of worship, Paul met a retailer of purple
fabric named Lydia, who persuaded Paul and his companions to stay at her
home (Acts 16:14–15). Later, when Paul and Silas were released from prison,
he returned to Lydia's house, "where they met with the brothers and encouraged them" (16:40). The entire household of the Philippian jailor was also baptized (16:29–34), and presumably a Christian fellowship began there as well. In
Thessalonica, Jason becomes the host of the Christian assembly (17:1–9), and
in Corinth it was Titius Justus who became Paul's host (18:7). In addition to
Gaius and Titius Justus (if the two are to be distinguished), strong arguments
can be marshaled demonstrating the likelihood of house churches in the homes
of Stephanas (1 Cor 16:15–16) and Erastus as well (Rom 16:23).[129] In any
event, from Paul's wording in 1 Cor 14:23 and Rom 16:23 we can be reasonably
certain that several house churches existed in Corinth. In both passages Paul
speaks of "the whole church" coming together, which is a distinctly different
expression from the one he uses in the passages above when he is referring to
"the church in so-and-so's house" (*hē kat' oikon* + possessive pronoun).[130] Romans 16:23 provides the added detail that it is in the residence of a presumably
wealthy Corinthian by the name of Gaius where "the whole church" in Corinth is able to assemble.
We can reasonably infer that Gaius's home was large enough to accommodate all the members of
the various house churches in Corinth.[131]

> GAIUS, WHOSE HOS-
> PITALITY I AND THE
> WHOLE CHURCH HERE
> ENJOY, SENDS YOU
> HIS GREETINGS.
>
> ROMANS 16:23

Apart from Acts 20:8, which mentions a
gathering of believers in an upstairs room, we are
given no information on the types of residential
structures used by the first generation of Christians for their meetings. As noted
above, there is evidence to suggest that at least one Christian in Corinth had a
home with ample space for a larger assembly, and we can assume that Erastus,
an aedile and Corinthian benefactor, possessed a similarly well-suited domicile
for gatherings. But Paul informs us that the majority of the believers in Corinth
were from the lower social orders: "Not many of you were wise, influential, or of
noble birth. Rather, God has chosen the foolish, the weak, the lowly, the despised"
(1 Cor 1:26–28, abbreviated). These demographic data correlate well with the
socio-economic profile of the society as a whole and indicate the probability that
a variety of domestic settings were employed for communal gatherings, including
small flats in *inuslae* and residences located above shops and *tabernae*.

For example, it is not likely that Priscilla and Aquila, working-class artisans, would have been able to afford anything more than a very simple domicile. Murphy-O'Connor has conjectured that they probably operated a shop on the ground floor of an *insula* and hosted their church in their rented flat above.[132] Based on excavations of small shops east of the theater in Corinth, David Horrell engages in some "disciplined imagination" and suggests that these common business-residential structures could well have accommodated Christian gatherings.[133]

> WHEN SHE AND THE MEMBERS OF HER HOUSEHOLD WERE BAPTIZED, SHE INVITED US TO HER HOME. "IF YOU CONSIDER ME A BELIEVER IN THE LORD," SHE SAID, "COME AND STAY AT MY HOUSE." AND SHE PERSUADED US.
>
> ACTS 16:15

The use of private homes for Christian gatherings was sensible and pragmatic and had a formative influence on early Christian identity. The image of the church as a family or household was more than just a productive metaphor; it became a defining paradigm for Christian relationships and ethics. But the the use of invidual home and the appropriation of household imagery was not entirely unproblematic; it presented both challenges and opportunities. We can only imagine how the early Christians dealt with the vestiges of pagan religion and morality present in the furnishings and décor of their domestic gatherings, but we have firmer information related to other matters. Paul eagerly incorporates the familial ethos of the household setting into his vision of Christian community, but how should these house groups be organized and led, especially as the movement grew? If the church is a family, what are the implications for providing for destitute family members. And what if social customs relevant to the domestic setting contravened important Christian principles and values? In what follows we will explore these issues, as well as other matters directly related to the Greco-Roman household and the domestic setting of the primitive Jesus movement.

> ALTHOUGH I HOPE TO COME TO YOU SOON, I AM WRITING YOU THESE INSTRUCTIONS SO THAT, IF I AM DELAYED, YOU WILL KNOW HOW PEOPLE OUGHT TO CONDUCT THEMSELVES IN GOD'S HOUSEHOLD.
>
> 1 TIMOTHY 3:14–15

THE CHURCH AS A FAMILY

The private home not only gave believers in Jesus a convenient place to assemble but also helped foster a new identity among this odd assortment of Jews and Gentiles, slaves and free who gathered to worship a common savior: the church as a family.[134] The person most responsible for nurturing and promoting the familial identity of the earliest followers of Jesus would be, without a doubt, the apostle Paul.

Paul's favorite designation for fellow believers was *adelphoi,* "brothers," a term he uses more than 130 times in his letters to include both male and female members of the Christian household gatherings. In Paul's view, when believers gathered in homes it was as a family, "a household of faith" (Gal 6:10). While God is the ultimate father of this great family (Rom 1:7; 1 Cor 8:6), Paul is not opposed to claiming that role himself when referring to those he personally converted (Phlm 10) or mentored (1 Tim 1:18; Titus 1:4) or when his protective instincts were aroused: "I am not writing this to shame you, but to warn you, as my dear children. Even though you have ten thousand guardians in Christ, you do not have many fathers, for in Christ Jesus I became your father through the gospel" (1 Cor 4:15; cf. Gal 4:19). During his involuntary separation from the Thessalonians, Paul wrote to them to remind them of his parental affection, and in the space of ten verses he employs nearly the entire gamut of familial relations to make his point: "You remember when I was with you I was like an *infant,* and I nursed you like a *mother,* and exhorted you like a *father* does with his *children,* and now that we are separated, *brothers,* I feel like an *orphan!*" (summarizing 1 Thess 2:8–17).[135] Sociologists often refer to this kind of imagery as "fictive kinship" language, though Paul would have bristled at the word "fictive." The phrase tends to imply that the only real kinship is biological kinship, and anything else is somewhat fictional. Paul would hotly contest such a notion. Spiritual kinship, he would argue, is not less real than biological kinship; it is more real. Paul's experience, as recounted by Luke, attests to this fact and probably helps explain the abundance of familial language in his letters. The first words that Luke records Paul heard after his conversion—from someone he had never met—were, "Saul, *brother*" (Acts 9:17; cf. 22:13). Paul's earliest experience of the Christian community was that of a family, and this formative influence reverberates throughout his life and letters.

> ENCOURAGE AN OLDER MAN AS YOU WOULD YOUR FATHER, YOUNGER MEN AS BROTHERS, OLDER WOMEN AS MOTHERS, AND YOUNGER WOMEN AS SISTERS.
>
> 1 TIMOTHY 5:1–2
> AUTHOR'S TRANSLATION

> YES, OF COURSE, WE ARE RIDICULED FOR CALLING EACH OTHER BROTHER.
>
> TERTULLIAN, APOLOGY 39.8

LOVE AND MARRIAGE

In keeping with the image of the church as a family, Paul employs the familiar household code to depict the proper relationships that ought to exist within believing households—husbands and wives, children and parents, slaves and masters.[136] Much of Paul's advice is in accord with conventional expectations and may have been aimed at silencing the rumors of outsiders who were suspicious of this new religious sect springing up in their towns and cities.[137] This seems to be the case by the time of the writing of Titus, where three times Paul appends a rationale for his exhortations that consists of making the gospel appealing to those outside the faith (Titus 2:5, 8, 10).

Yet Paul does not endorse uncritically the family values of his age. In particular, Paul seems to be concerned to introduce mutuality and love into the authoritarian and contractual conception of the husband/wife relationship that prevailed in his day. In each of the passages where Paul articulates his vision of relationships within the Christian household by means of the traditional household code, marital love is affirmed as the ideal that a husband and wife should embody. That this was a somewhat novel idea to Paul's readers is evident in his instructions to Titus that the young women need to be "taught" to love their husbands (Titus 2:4). The highest expression of this ideal is found in Ephesians, where Paul repeatedly admonishes husbands to love their wives (Eph 5:25, 28, 33), to cherish them (5:29), and to give themselves sacrificially on their behalf. Clearly Paul expects a deep affection to be present, but equally clearly this involves more than mere feelings of romantic emotion. Paul commands husbands to act toward their wives as Christ acted toward the church: Christ laid down his life for the church, and Paul expects husbands to do the same for their wives (Eph 5:28–30). Similarly, Paul's advice to married couples regarding sexual intercourse (1 Cor 7:1–5) indicates that both partners have conjugal rights and that each partner should consider the needs of the other. In other words, mutuality.

Pastoral exhortations to spousal affection are always appropriate and relevant, but given the dominant marital paradigm of the first century—duties, rights, obligations, and consequences—Paul's recurring emphasis on mutual love in marriage likely represents deliberate rejection of the sterile alliances that typified Greco-Roman marriages and reveals a calculated determination to offer an alternative paradigm for marriage: the self-sacrificing love of Christ.

> HUSBANDS, LOVE YOUR WIVES AND DO NOT BE HARSH WITH THEM.
>
> COLOSSIANS 3:19

> DO NOT BRING A WIFE INTO YOUR HOME AS A BAD AND WEALTHY WOMAN, FOR YOU WILL BE A SLAVE OF YOUR WIFE BECAUSE OF HER DOWRY. WE SEEK NOBLE HORSES AND STRONG-NECKED BULLS, YET WE FOOLS DO NOT STRIVE TO MARRY A GOOD WIFE.
>
> PSEUDO-PHOCYLIDES

Yet in spite of Paul's lofty vision of marital union as the living embodiment of Christ's sacrificial love, the apostle never married, and his candid opinion on the subject was that he wished everyone were like him—single (1 Cor 7:7–8).[138] How can we explain this contradiction?

MARRIAGE AND CELIBACY

First Corinthians 7 represents Paul's only extended discussion of marriage, celibacy, and related matters, and in this chapter Paul is remarkably frank about his personal preference for singleness. Moreover, Paul's rationale for celibacy so clearly echoes the perspective of the Stoics (at points) that one could be forgiven for thinking that it was written by Musonius.

> I ASKED THE ANGEL, "SIR, IF A MAN HAS A WIFE WHO BELIEVES IN THE LORD, AND HE FINDS HER IN SOME ADULTEROUS SITUATION, DOES THE MAN SIN IF HE CONTINUES TO LIVE WITH HER?"
>
> *SHEPHERD OF HERMES

Crucial for properly understanding this passage is recognizing that 1 Cor 7 is not a treatise on marriage per se. That is, Paul is not offering a comprehensive, orderly, systematic theology of marriage. Rather, his comments are directed toward a certain set of problems in Corinth and need to be read in that light. Like so much of Paul's theological argumentation in his letters, his advice here is occasioned by specific circumstances in a particular locale. In fact, if these problems had not arisen, we would be left in the dark regarding Paul's perspective on a number of important matters related to marriage, divorce, and singleness. In this respect we can be thankful that the early churches had so many problems that Paul needed to address. The difficulty for us is that we are not given a full description of the problems Paul is addressing, and so some of his answers are obscure and difficult to interpret.

The impetus for this entire chapter is specific questions the Corinthians had addressed to Paul regarding marriage, singleness, and divorce. Paul directs his response to different groups (married, unmarried, widows) and different scenarios (those with unbelieving spouses, those engaged), and in the process a strikingly familiar picture is revealed: married couples negotiating sexual intimacy (vv. 2–5), singles and engaged couples struggling with desire and self-control (vv. 8–9; 36–39), husbands and wives contemplating divorce (vv. 10–11), and marriages in which one partner is not a believer (vv. 12–16). In some ways life in the first-century church was not all that different from life in the twenty-first-century church.

The initial question that Paul deals with relates to the propriety of sexual relations: "Now concerning your questions: 'It is good for a man not to touch a woman,' as you say. However, to avoid sexual immorality, each man should have his own wife, and each woman her own husband" (7:1 author's translation).[139] Essentially, some among the Corinthians had come to believe that celibacy was the optimum way of life for a person, and from Paul's comments in verses 2–5, we learn that some of these people were married. To most of us, it probably seems inconceivable that such a proposition would be seriously entertained, yet, as we have seen, this is precisely what the Cynics, and many of the Stoics, argued. It must be remembered that these philosophers consciously adopted an austere lifestyle as a protest against luxury and vice, and in this regard we should be able to sympathize with their cause. In fact, Paul seems sympathetic as well.

As has been convincingly argued by Will Deming,[140] Paul's comments in 1 Cor 7 correspond to a large extent to the position of the moderate Stoics. This group of philosophers accepted that marriage was allowable for the sage in some circumstances but that in general the philosopher's obligation is to a life of reflection and ethical admonition and this rendered marriage a luxury that he could not afford. Epictetus, the Stoic-Cynic philosopher, explains:

> DIOGENES THE CYNIC DID NOT HAVE TO GO ANYWHERE FOR HIS SEXUAL GRATIFICATION BUT, AS HE HUMOROUSLY PUT IT, FOUND APHRODITE EVERYWHERE. WHEN THE CROWD DOUBTED HIS BOAST, HE SERVICED HIMSELF IN FRONT OF THEM ALL, SAYING THAT IF MORE MEN WERE LIKE HIM, TROY WOULD NEVER HAVE BEEN SACKED.
>
> *DIO CHRYSOSTOM

> But in such an order of the things as the present, which is like a battlefield, it is a question, perhaps, if the Cynic ought to be free from distraction, wholly devoted to the service of God, not tied down by the private duties of men. For the [married] man must show certain services to his father-in-law, to the rest of his wife's relatives, to his wife herself; finally he is driven from his profession [as a philosopher] to act as a nurse in his own family. In short, he must get a kettle to heat water for the baby, wool for his wife when she has a baby, oil, a cot, utensils—not to speak of the rest of his business and his distraction.[141]

Later on in this discourse Epictetus describes "passionate love" as one of the special circumstances warranting marriage, and elsewhere he accepts that marrying for love is allowable but may not be the "better" option.[142] The parallels with 1 Cor 7 are striking:

> Because of the present crisis, I think it is good for you who are virgins to remain as you are . . . but if you do marry you do not sin. (7:26, 28)

> Those who marry will face many troubles in this life, and I want to spare you this. (7:28)

> I would like you to be free from concern. An unmarried man is concerned about the Lord's affairs—how he can please the Lord. But a married man is concerned about the affairs of this world—how he can please his wife, and his interests are divided. (7:32–34)

> So then, he who marries the virgin does right, but he who does not marry her does even better. (7:38)

Paul's advice concerning marriage in 1 Cor 7 has been a source of embarrassment for theologians and pastors, especially given the apostle's more lofty evaluation of marriage in Eph 5, and the larger biblical portrayal of marriage, which is decidedly positive. Moreover, while it is true that Paul's advice is given in light of some kind of "present crisis" (v. 26),[143] it is also true that he places this event, along with decisions like when and if to marry, in an eschatological framework of apocalyptic expectation: "the times have been shortened . . . the present form of this world is passing away" (7:29, 31).

> GREET PRISCILLA AND AQUILA, MY FELLOW WORKERS IN CHRIST.
>
> ROMANS 16:3

Often overlooked in discussions of 1 Cor 7, but crucial for making sense of Paul's perspective in this chapter, is the first statement Paul makes on the topic of marriage versus singleness: "Each has his own gift from God; one has this gift [marriage], another has that [singleness]" (7:7). Paul makes it clear at the outset that God is the one who ultimately determines whether one marries or remains single, and this represents a very different position from that of the Stoics and Cynics. For these philosophers, singleness and abstinence represented a higher calling for the noble sage but was not expected of the average person. Paul heartily affirmed marriage as an appropriate way of life for church leaders (1 Tim 3:2, 12; Titus 1:6) and apostles (1 Cor 9:5) and even referred to Andronicus and Junia (probably a husband and wife team like Priscilla and Aquila) as "foremost among the apostles" (Rom 16:7).[144]

> FOR AMONG THESE CHRISTIANS ARE BOTH MEN AND WOMEN WHO REFRAIN FROM CO-HABITATING ALL THEIR LIVES, AND WHO, IN SELF-DISCIPLINE AND SELF-CONTROL IN FOOD AND DRINK, AND IN THEIR KEEN PURSUIT OF JUSTICE, HAVE ATTAINED A STANDARD NOT INFERIOR TO THAT OF GENUINE PHILOSOPHERS.
>
> GALEN

More significantly, Paul also disagreed with the Stoics and the intelligentsia of his day in affirming that erotic love was appropriate within marriage and inappropriate outside of marriage. In advising the unmarried and the widows to "marry rather than burn [with passion]" (7:8–9), Paul assumes that marital affection was expressed, in part, through the consummation and relief of physical desire. Although single—and happily so—Paul understood that pleasureless intercourse (the Stoics) was not the kind of marital intimacy God designed. Furthermore, Paul takes for granted that to be unmarried was to either control one's sexual desire or to "burn" with no outlet for sexual expression. This would have been considered oppressively restrictive by Paul's contemporaries.

The truly remarkable feature of 1 Cor 7 is that while Paul acknowledges that God is the one who "gifts" people for either marriage or singleness (with continence), he then goes on to argue why he thinks singleness is preferable. In essence, Paul seems to be saying, "I wish God saw things my way on this matter, but he doesn't."

So, was Paul an ascetic? Some think so. In fact, Calvin Roetzel calls Paul "the model ascetic" and argues, based largely on 1 Cor 7, that "for Paul, marriage was an intermediate position between *enkrateia,* or self-control and *porneia,* or immorality."[145] Such an appraisal, however, hardly does justice to Paul's comments elsewhere on marriage (e.g., Eph 5:22–32), and fails to appreciate Paul's insistence that both marriage and singleness are gifts from God (1 Cor 7:7). For a person called to marriage, singleness would represent a betrayal of God's calling, not a higher spirituality—and vice versa.

Yet while Paul's theoretical stance was that both marriage and singleness were divine callings, he was also a man focused on a singular mission: advancing Christ's kingdom. Similar to the Stoics, Paul saw himself as a soldier on the battlefield (Phil 2:27–28; Eph 6:10–18; 2 Tim 2:3–4) and married life as a distraction. His enthusiastic if one-sided representation of the single life as "better" (1 Cor 7:38) and "undistracted" (7:32, 35) needs to be understood in light of his broader teaching on marriage and the sober dictum that prefaced this entire discussion: "But each one has his own gift from God" (7:7).

ORGANIZATION AND LEADERSHIP IN THE HOUSE CHURCHES

In the course of this description of the social setting of the early Jesus movement, we have examined synagogue life, voluntary associations, philosophical schools, and Greco-Roman households. Each of these important socio-religious institutions may be regarded as potentially influential on the structure and leadership of the primitive Christian assemblies. In fact, each has its supporters among historians of Christian origins, and, although no consensus has emerged, the issue has occupied a prominent place in recent scholarship.[146] In this section we will tie together these various threads from previous chapters and situate the Pauline house churches in the broader context of similar social institutions. We are fortunate to have important primary sources to draw on (Paul's letters and Acts), and in what follows we will make ample use of this data. The primary questions that concern us here are: Were the Pauline communities modeled, consciously or unconsciously, after one of these groups? What organizational patterns or strategies can we discern from our primary sources, Paul's letters and the book of Acts? What would the early house churches have looked like to members of the surrounding communities? In other words, how would outsiders have classified this new phenomenon? It is important to remember that primitive Christianity was a social movement as well as a religious movement, and a consideration of its structure and organization will help us better understand the rise of one of the most significant phenomena of antiquity. Intrinsic to any discussion of Christianity in the Greco-Roman world is the character of these early communities, their leadership, communal organization, and rituals. Before examining more closely patterns of leadership in the early church, it will be useful to highlight significant elements of continuity and discontinuity between the Christian gatherings and some of these first-century counterparts.[147]

The Household as a Missional Base

Although we can take for granted the crucial function of the household in the spread of Christianity throughout the Aegean basin, we are on firmer ground in emphasizing the importance of the private home as a platform for the advance of the gospel rather than a model for the organization of ecclesia itself.[148] The household contributed to the vital familial ethos of the Pauline communities, but in terms of the structure and activities of the early church—worship, teaching, evangelism, social welfare—the Greco-Roman household offers only the faintest correspondence. Kinship language and household imagery applied to the church in the NT has more to do with identity formation and demarcation than function and organization.

> THEN THEY SPOKE THE WORD OF THE LORD TO HIM AND TO ALL THE OTHERS IN HIS HOUSE. . . .THE JAILOR WAS FILLED WITH JOY BECAUSE HE HAD COME TO BELIEVE IN GOD—HE AND HIS WHOLE FAMILY.
>
> *ACTS 16:32–34

In addition to a sense of intimate community, the use of individual homes afforded relative privacy, which may have been important in some locales and was an extremely efficient mechanism for the quick establishment and rapid expansion of Christianity. The venues for the gatherings were immediately available at no cost and were already embedded in a network of social relations that could be parlayed into further expansion. The use of the private home added a certain agility and resiliency to the early Jesus movement which, from the perspective of the Roman government, rendered it difficult to track and control, let alone eradicate. The modern reader is probably correct to discern a note of exasperation in Pliny's letter to Trajan (ca. 108 C.E.) as he describes the proliferation of Christians (*chrsitiani*) in his province:

> The question [of how to deal with Christians] seems to me to be worthy of your consideration, especially in view of the number of persons endangered; for a great many individuals of every age and class, both men and women are being brought to

trial [as Christians], and this is likely to continue. It is not only the towns, but villages and rural districts too which are infected through contact with this wretched cult. I think though, it is possible for it to be checked.[149]

Although Pliny is remembered for his sobriety and good judgment, he miscalculated with respect to his confidence that this "wretched cult" (*superstitio*) could be checked.

First-century Analogies

As we look for ancient analogies to the primitive church—first-century movements that may have furnished a paradigm for the church's organization and operation—it is striking that each of the previously mentioned groups offers at least some parallel to what we see taking place in the Pauline communities, though none appear to provide a comprehensive blueprint.

The synagogue was obviously critical to the formation of the Christian assemblies in the Hellenistic cities where Paul evangelized.[150] Paul often began his outreach in the context of the local synagogue or *prosueché*. In Corinth, the synagogue leader was converted, and the new messianic assembly that formed next door might appear to outsiders as a synagogal splinter group (Acts 18:5–8). Further, the Scriptures that were taught in the house churches and quoted by Paul were the Jewish Scriptures that proclaimed a Jewish messiah. The central pillars of the new movement hailed from Jerusalem and, like the synagogues of the Diaspora, members of the Christian assemblies understood themselves to be part of a larger, translocal religious movement. However, Paul seems to intentionally adopt distinct nomenclature for his congregations: *ecclesia,* not synagogue or *prosueché*.[151] And while many facets of worship were similar between the churches and the synagogues—readings from Scripture, hymns, prayer—there are also differences.[152] For example, considerably more freedom was allowed to women in the churches Paul founded,[153] although Paul does impose limitations in some matters (1 Tim 2:8–15). Women could prophesy in the public assembly (1 Cor 11:3–10), and Paul lists women as his co-workers in the spread of the gospel (Phil 4:3), as deacons (Rom 16:1), and in one instance as a fellow apostle (Rom 16:7).[154] It is reasonable to suppose that Jewish communal organization would have influenced the structure of the early church in certain circumstances and in particular locations. However, if Lee Levine's conclusions regarding the relative diversity of synagogue structures and leadership patterns across the Mediterranean are sound,[155] it may well be that variation and adaptation were the primary lessons Paul learned from his involvement in Palestinian and Hellenistic synagogues.

> WHEN THE CONGREGATION WAS DISMISSED, MANY OF THE JEWS AND DEVOUT CONVERTS TO JUDAISM FOLLOWED PAUL AND BARNABAS.
>
> ACTS 14:43

Likewise, voluntary associations offer several intriguing parallels to the Christian assemblies: their membership drew largely from the lower strata of society; they sometimes met in homes; there was a clear religious orientation, in that each had a patron deity who was honored at the meetings and offered the members protection. Most importantly, voluntary associations often assembled around a communal meal where the officers would often receive a double portion of the provisions (cf. 1 Tim 5:17).[156] Evidently, in the early second century at least some Christian groups understood that they resembled a voluntary association; in Bithynia the Christians stopped gathering for their evening communal meal when Trajan issued a ban on voluntary associations.[157]

> THIS MADE ME DE-
> CIDE IT WAS ALL THE
> MORE NECESSARY TO
> EXTRACT THE TRUTH
> BY TORTURE FROM
> TWO SLAVE-WOMEN
> THESE CHRISTIANS
> CALL "DEACONESSES."
>
> *PLINY TO TRAJAN

However, voluntary associations had no intrinsic translocal connections, nor were they known for promoting ethical behavior. Their penchant for hierarchies of officers contrasts sharply with the ethos of the Pauline communities—even the later developments of the Pastoral Epistles. The strongest link between Christianity and voluntary associations is the communal meal, yet this was a feature of most religious, social, and political groups, including the synagogues.[158]

As for the philosophical schools, their clearest correspondence to the early Christian movement relates not to community organization and leadership but to the methods and message of the philosopher and the sometimes dramatic response of conversion that accompanied his preaching (see Education, Philosophy, and Oratory: Conversion). Dio Chrysostom, a Stoic philosopher-sophist and younger contemporary of Paul, provides a fruitful comparison. He traveled around cities of the Mediterranean preaching on ethical, religious, and social themes. He exhorted his listeners to pursue virtue, reject vice, endure hardship, and honor the gods. At points Paul sounds a lot like Dio. Philosophers like Dio would speak to large assemblies as invited guests (cf. Acts 17:19), in private homes, and in public squares, or perhaps they would settle in rented facilities for daily lectures and instruction in philosophy. Paul's pattern of ministry was similar, and in Ephesus, after leaving the synagogue, he sets up shop in the "lecture hall of

> RESOLVED: THE PERSON
> IN THIS ASSOCIATION
> ENTRUSTED WITH THE
> OFFICE OF QUINQUIN-
> NALES WILL BE EXEMPT
> FROM ALL DUES AND
> WILL RECEIVE A DOU-
> BLE PORTION FROM
> PROVISIONS [AT THE
> APPOINTED BANQUETS].
>
> STATUTE FROM A VOLUNTARY
> ASSOCIATION, LANUVIUM

Tyrannus," where he continued teaching daily for two years (Acts 19:9–10). The passerby hearing Paul argue and reason from the Jewish Scriptures might think this was some kind of Jewish philosophy being propagated. Galen, a second-century physician and critic of Christianity and Judaism, pours contempt on those who have "come into the school of Moses and Christ," using a term (*diatribēn*) that designates a philosophical or rhetorical school.[159]

> . . . JUST AS NOW WE SEE THE PEOPLE CALLED CHRISTIANS DRAWING THEIR FAITH FROM PARABLES AND MIRACLES, YET ACTING IN THE SAME WAY AS THOSE WHO PHILOSOPHIZE. FOR THEIR CONTEMPT OF DEATH AND OF ITS SEQUEL IS PATENT TO US EVERY DAY.
>
> GALEN

What this quick survey illustrates is that, while the communities Paul established can be helpfully compared to many first-century clubs, organizations, and movements, Paul does not appear to be consciously adopting the format of any group in particular.[160] This initial impression will be reinforced as we turn to consider leadership structures in the Pauline churches.

House Church Leadership

The question of leadership structures in the early house churches is fraught with difficulties. There are those who insist that there was never any formally appointed leadership in the churches Paul founded, while others are equally adamant that Paul's letters, and the NT as a whole, consistently and uniformly attest a singular model of ecclesiology. The former often regard the elders, overseers, and deacons of the Pastoral Epistles to be a post-Pauline development as the Spirit-led, egalitarian ethos of the early Christian communities degenerated into institutionalized hierarchies. The latter sometimes appear to superimpose modern ecclesial structures on the NT texts, while ignoring data and texts not congenial to their model.

> . . . SO IN CHRIST WE WHO ARE MANY FORM ONE BODY, AND EACH MEMBER BELONGS TO ALL THE OTHERS. WE HAVE DIFFERENT GIFTS. . . . IF A MAN'S GIFT IS PROPHESYING, LET HIM USE IT IN PROPORTION TO HIS FAITH. IF IT IS SERVING, LET HIM SERVE; IF IT IS TEACHING, LET HIM TEACH . . . IF IT IS LEADERSHIP, LET HIM GOVERN DILIGENTLY.
>
> ROMANS 12:5–8

Another assumption that many NT scholars make is that the host of the Christian assembly, the owner of the house, would have been the de facto, or at least provisional, leader of the church that met in his or her home.[161] This is not an unreasonable hypothesis, although the link is not explicitly made by Paul, and it may be slightly at odds with other data from Paul's letters. Paul's letters describe spiritually endowed leadership ("first apostles, then prophets, then teachers," 1 Cor 12:28), those "who instruct in the word" (Gal 6:6), and those "who labor, lead, and admonish" (1 Thess 5:12), and we should not assume that all this was done by the householder. It may well be that in many cases the householder was the host of the assembly and little more. We should at least be prepared to reckon with more than one type of leader in the early household assemblies.

DURING THIS TIME
SOME PROPHETS CAME
DOWN FROM JERUSA-
LEM TO ANTIOCH.

ACTS 11:27

As we approach this subject and begin analyzing the relevant NT texts, we should not assume that a uniform picture will emerge, but neither should we be opposed to such a conclusion. We must take seriously the fragmentary nature of the evidence and be willing to ascribe levels of certainty to our conclusions. The data may render some conclusions certain, others probable, and still others possible but far from certain. We will look first at Acts, then turn to Paul's earlier letters, and conclude by considering 1 Timothy, 2 Timothy, and Titus, the Pastoral Epistles.

Acts

The Book of Acts introduces nearly all of the significant types of leaders in the first decades of the Jesus movement: apostles, prophets, teachers, evangelists, pastors, overseers, elders, and perhaps deacons as well.[162] In terms of visible community organization, Jerusalem is noteworthy for a having a council of "apostles and elders" (Acts 15:2, 4, 6, 22, 23; 16:4) overseeing the ministry there. The jurisdiction of the leadership in Jerusalem extended beyond Jerusalem itself. The decision reached by the apostles and elders concerning the Mosaic law was considered binding on the Gentile churches founded by Paul and Barnabas (Acts 15:22–29), and Gal 2 records their direct intervention in table fellowship at Antioch.

Especially significant is the emerging prominence of James among the elders and apostles in Jerusalem. It is James who rendered the final judgment at the Jerusalem Council in Acts 15 (vv. 13–21),

JAMES, SURNAMED "THE
JUST" BY EVERYONE,
RECEIVED THE GOVERN-
MENT OF THE CHURCH
WITH THE APOSTLES.

*HEGESIPPUS, ACCORDING
TO EUSEBIUS

and when Paul returns from his third missionary tour he reported, as Luke tells it, "to James— and all the elders were present" (Acts 21:18; cf. 12:17).[163] Luke presents James as working in concert with the other apostles and elders but occupying an acknowledged position of eminence. In keeping with this, the delegation from the Jerusalem church sent to Antioch to monitor the open table fellowship between Jewish and non-Jewish believers is described by Paul as "men from James" (Gal 2:12). According to Josephus, when the Jewish authorities in Jerusalem decided to crack down on the followers of Jesus, it was "James, and some others" who were executed.[164] Lightfoot's description of James as "the earliest bishop" may overstate the matter, but not wildly so.[165]

Luke sketches a very different kind of leadership structure operating in Antioch, where Paul and Barnabas were ministering. In contrast to Jerusalem's "apostles and elders," taking the lead in Antioch were "prophets and teachers":

> In the church at Antioch there were prophets and teachers: Barnabas, Simeon called Niger, Lucius of Cyrene, Manaen (who had been brought up with Herod the tetrarch) and Saul. While they were worshiping the Lord and fasting, the Holy Spirit said, "Set apart for me Barnabas and Saul for the work to which I have called them." So after they had fasted and prayed, they placed their hands on them and sent them off. (Acts 13:1–3)

Luke makes no mention of apostles or elders or overseers in Antioch. Although his comments are concise, there appears to be no leading figure giving direction and oversight; guidance comes not from strategic planning sessions but is given directly by the Holy Spirit in the context of worship, prayer, and fasting. It is within this environment that Paul labored with Barnabas for more than a year (Acts 11:26). As a closer look at Paul's letters will demonstrate, this ecclesial setting would prove formative for the apostle's conception of Christian communal experience.

A third strand of material to consider from Acts relates to the churches Paul established during his missionary work. Paul and his companions made several extensive tours of Asia Minor and Greece, doing evangelistic work in numerous cities. In some places his stay was very short (e.g., Iconium, Acts 14), in others, like Thessalonica, he stayed several weeks (Acts 17:2). In Corinth and Ephesus, Paul managed to take up residence and work for a much longer period: eighteen months in Corinth (Acts 18:11) and two years in Ephesus (Acts 19:10).[166]

In one instance, and only one, Luke tells us that Paul and Barnabas appointed elders. This occurs during Paul's first missionary journey as he and Barnabas double back through some of the cities they had previously visited, Lystra, Iconium, and Antioch: "Paul and Barnabas appointed elders for them in each church and, with prayer and fasting, committed them to the Lord in whom they had put their trust" (Acts 14:23). By "church" Luke does not mean that elders were appointed in each individual house church but that each locale had at least one elder in place. Luke consistently uses "church" to refer to all the believers in a particular area or city; for example, the church "in Jerusalem" (Acts 8:31) or the church "throughout Judaea" (Acts 9:31), meaning all the household assemblies in these geographical

> THEN THE CHURCH THROUGHOUT JUDEA, GALILEE AND SAMARIA ENJOYED A TIME OF PEACE.
>
> ACTS 9:31

locales.[167] Luke's intention is clarified by Paul's explicit instructions to Titus that he is to appoint elders "in every town" (Titus 1:5). Some infer from in Acts 14:23 that Paul routinely appointed elders in all of the towns where he established churches, throughout his missionary career.[168] These interpreters point to Paul's later letters, the Pastoral Epistles, where Paul gives detailed instruction on the appointment of church officers, and to Acts 20, where we hear of elders in the church at Ephesus during Paul's final visit there.

However, several arguments weigh against drawing such an inference from this single reference in Acts 14:23. First, Luke does not indicate that this was a routine feature of Paul's evangelistic work. He mentions the appointment of elders in three cities that Paul has the opportunity to revisit, leaving the impression that the other churches that Paul did not revisit on this journey did not have appointed leaders. If it were Paul's normal procedure to appoint elders, it is surprising that Luke makes no further reference to this as he chronicles Paul's subsequent journeys and church-planting activity. Second, we know from Paul's letters to Corinth and Thessalonica (see below) that in these churches—Corinth certainly, and Thessalonica probably—Paul did not appoint elders. The evidence of Acts 20 demonstrates only that Paul may have appointed leaders under certain circumstances, especially as the church in a specific locale grew, not that he did this as a matter of course from the start. By the time Paul wrote the Pastorals (discussed below), he seems to regard designated leaders as an important part of the ultimate survival of the church in a given locale, though perhaps not crucial in the initial stages of a newly formed Christian assembly (Titus 1:5).

Paul's Early Letters

Turning now to Paul' early letters, three in particular (1 Corinthians, 1 Thessalonians, and Philippians) are worth considering more closely to learn what they reveal about the organization of the early Pauline communities.

We know more about the Christian assemblies in Corinth than any other church of the NT era—their demographics, their problems, and their worship. Given the length of these letters and the variety of topics Paul addresses, this should come as no surprise. It is also no secret that the Corinthians were Paul's wayward children in many respects. In the course of 1 Corinthians the apostle censures their value system (chs. 1–4), their ethics (ch. 5),

> IF SOMEONE'S GIFT
> IS LEADERSHIP, LET
> THEM LEAD.
>
> ROMANS 12:8

their squabbling (ch. 6), their worship (chs. 11–14), and their theology (ch. 15). In 2 Corinthians we read of a painful visit in which Paul was humiliated (2:1; 12:21), a tearful letter of rebuke (2:4), a joyful reconciliation (7:5–13), more opponents (chs. 10–13), and an ominous threat that the apostle "will spare no one" if he has to return with a rod (13:2, 10). One thing we hear nothing of is officially appointed leaders—elders, overseers, and deacons. How could Paul deal with so many dire matters and never once appeal to, or make reference to, his apostolically sanctioned leadership team (cf. Phil 4:2)? The only conclusion one can draw is that, for whatever reason, Paul did not appoint leaders in Corinth.[169] If there were any doubts about this, Paul removes them when he closes 1 Corinthians by urging his errant children to "submit to the household of Stephanas" on the grounds that they were the first converts in Achaia and because *they have appointed themselves* to the service of the saints" (1 Cor 16:15–16 author's translation and emphasis). If Paul had appointed elders and other leaders in Corinth, it is inconceivable that he would fail to commend them here. Paul clearly approves of this initiative on the part of Stephanas, and he encourages others along this line by adding, "and submit to any such as these and to every coworker and laborer" (1 Cor 16:16). It is equally clear, however, that these are locally generated, Spirit-prompted leaders.[170] The grounds Paul offers for following these leaders is not apostolic appointment but maturity ("the first converts") and a proven record of service.[171]

> WE HAVE DIFFERENT GIFTS, ACCORDING TO THE GRACE GIVEN US.
> ROMANS 12:6

Yet Corinth is not devoid of leaders. In addition to the hosts/leaders of the house churches and motivated self-starters like Stephanas, Paul envisions an ordered hierarchy of divinely appointed men and women who serve the community:

> Now you are the body of Christ, and each of you is a part of it. And in the church God has appointed first of all apostles, second prophets, third teachers, then workers of miracles, also those having gifts of healing, those able to help others, those with gifts of administration, and those speaking in different kinds of tongues. (1 Cor 12:27–28)

In these verses Paul offers us a programmatic statement of his vision for the church. This may not represent the sum total of Paul's ecclesiology, but it does indicate that the core and foundation of Paul's conception of the church consists of Spirit-endowed individuals playing their role in the body. This does not negate the legitimacy of other ecclesial offices (elder, overseer), nor does it exclude hierarchy ("first apostles, second prophets"), but it does serve to relativize and subordinate office to gifting. The order that Paul lays out in 1 Cor 12:28 is fleshed out two chapters later as Paul describes what he desires to see in operation when the church gathers:

> DO NOT QUENCH THE SPIRIT BY DESPISING PROPHECY.
> 1 THESSALONIANS 5:19–20

> When you come together, everyone has a hymn, or a word of instruction, a revelation, a tongue or an interpretation. All of these must be done for the strengthening

of the church. If anyone speaks in a tongue, two—or at the most three. . . . Two or three prophets should speak, and the others should weigh carefully what is said. . . . For you can all prophesy in turn so that everyone may be instructed and encouraged. (1 Cor 14:26–31)

This important glimpse into Paul's vision for a Christian gathering reveals a charismatically governed community where Spirit-filled prophets and teachers guide the assembly, as opposed to elders, overseers, or a senior pastor. What we see here seems to reflect the Antioch model of Christian communal experience, which was so crucial during Paul's formative early years. We would be wrong to assume that the ideal that Paul describes is taking place in Corinth (see 1 Cor 11:17), but we can at least observe what Paul would like to see happening in the assemblies in Corinth.

First Thessalonians is probably Paul's earliest correspondence. As in 1 Corinthians, Paul concludes this letter by urging deference to leaders in the community:

Now we ask you, brothers [and sisters], to respect those who work hard among you, who are over you in the Lord and who admonish you. Hold them in the highest regard in love because of their labor [work]. (1 Thess 5:12–13)

The picture here corresponds to 1 Cor 16. Once again, there is no reference to appointed leadership in 1 Thessalonians or 2 Thessalonians, even in this closing admonition where it would be most appropriate. The Greek construction Paul uses indicates that "those who work . . . those who are over you . . . those who admonish you" refer to one group of people[172] and emphasizes their function. The leaders in this community are evident by their service, not their appointment to office, and Paul's concern is that this Spirit-generated leadership be followed.[173]

> YOU MUST FOLLOW THE BISHOP, AS JESUS CHRIST FOLLOWED THE FATHER, AND FOLLOW THE PRESBYTERY AS YOU WOULD THE APOSTLES; RESPECT DEACONS AS THE COMMANDMENT OF GOD.
>
> IGNATIUS

It is in Philippians that we encounter the only certain reference in the early letters of Paul to officers.[174] By the time of the writing of Philippians (59–61 C.E.), nearly a decade after Paul's initial visit to the city, the household assemblies in Philippi had both overseers and deacons: "Paul and Timothy, servants of Christ Jesus, to all the saints in Christ Jesus at Philippi, together with overseers and deacons" (Phil 1:11). It is unconvincing to disregard this reference to overseers and deacons as a later gloss[175] or to dilute it to the point that it contains no connotation of recognized groups of leaders.[176] Only a prejudicial determination not to find designated leadership in Paul's letters can account for such maneuvers. The most natural reading of Phil 1:1 is to see it as evidence of emerging ecclesial organization and to recognize a trajectory of development in the Pauline churches.[177] We are not told if each house church had overseers and deacons or if these leaders represent the Christian community as a whole. Nor are we told anything about the function of these leaders—and one must be careful not read into mid-first-century Philippi later ecclesiastical responsibilities. We are also told nothing of how these leaders were selected. Given the circumstances of Paul's initial ministry in Philippi (his arrest, abrupt departure), we can be reasonably certain that this did not occur during the visit described in Acts 16. Whether Paul had a hand in leadership selection during a subsequent visit[178] or whether the Philippians organized themselves as they saw fit,[179] we have clear evidence of ecclesial organization and leadership, "officers," in the earlier letters of Paul, and the apostle evinces no hesitation in affirming this development.

> THESE, THEN, ARE THE THINGS YOU SHOULD TEACH. ENCOURAGE AND REBUKE WITH ALL AUTHORITY. DO NOT LET ANYONE DESPISE YOU.
>
> TITUS 2:15

The Pastoral Epistles

The Pastoral Epistles, 1 Timothy in particular, reflect a degree of organizational maturity not clearly evident in Paul's earlier letters, but not surprising given this later phase of the Christian movement. In about 63 C.E., Paul writes to Timothy in Ephesus, where Timothy has been sent by Paul to oversee the ministry that began some ten to twelve years earlier (Acts 18). We will look at the growing complexity of this ministry in our discussion of the widows, but for the moment we will focus attention on the importance Paul places on the selection and qualifications of elders/overseers,[180] deacons, and deaconesses.[181] At this stage the situation has developed to the extent that procedures need to be in place for selecting (1 Tim 3:1–13; Titus 1:5–10), disciplining (1 Tim 5:20), and even compensating (1 Tim 5:17–18) some leaders. Paul's instructions also imply a significant pool of individuals from which the candidates are selected (1 Tim 3:1). Equally noteworthy is that Timothy and Titus are invested with authority from the apostle to carry out their tasks (Titus 2:15), which, structurally speaking, sets them over the elders and deacons as Paul's apostolic representatives. It is true that Timothy and Titus are only temporarily assigned to Ephesus and Crete, respectively, but there is strong evidence that Paul envisions the position they occupy to be permanent. According to 2 Tim 4:12 and Titus 3:12, these two apostolic

> THEREFORE, APPOINT FOR YOURSELVES OVERSEERS AND DEACONS. . . . DO NOT DESPISE THEM, FOR THEY ARE HONORED MEN, ALONG WITH THE PROPHETS AND TEACHERS.
>
> DIDACHE 15.1–2

delegates are to return to Paul only after their replacements have arrived, Artemas and Tychicus.[182]

When we add to this basic sketch the fact that Paul is directing matters in Ephesus and Crete from a distance, working from a different locale, we perceive another early precedent for the translocal authority structures that would emerge in subsequent centuries. What emerges from 1 Timothy and Titus is a kind of hierarchical arrangement approximated in the following diagram:

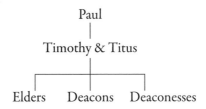

In the final analysis, it is clear that leadership and organization are important to Paul and are present throughout the churches he established. It is also clear that in Paul's mind, Spirit-endowed leadership is fully compatible with organization and ministerial offices. In the Pastoral Epistles, they walk hand in hand:

> **FOR GOD IS NOT A GOD OF DISORDER BUT OF PEACE.**
>
> 1 CORINTHIANS 14:33

Until I come, devote yourself to the public reading of Scripture, to preaching and to teaching. Do not neglect your gift, which was given you through a prophetic message when the body of elders laid their hands on you. (1 Tim 4:13–14; cf. 2 Tim 1:6, 14)

It is less clear, however, that Paul had a single ideal organizational model in mind as he evangelized and planted churches. As the ministry expanded, so too did its organization and administration. This becomes especially apparent in Paul's instructions to Timothy regarding the widows in Ephesus.

THE WIDOWS

As we detailed in chapter 3, the ancient Mediterranean world was characterized by grinding poverty and social inequities on a grand scale (see City and Society: Population Density as well as City and Society: Urban Unrest as well as City and Society: Class and Status). Particularly exposed were those at the bottom of the social pyramid, a group that included widows. Paul's instructions concerning the care of widows in Ephesus (1 Tim 5:3–16) represent the first programmatic attempt of the early church to address this social evil and reveals a community vitally situated in this socio-economic context. The problem that

Paul and Timothy are attempting to deal with in Ephesus reflects a concrete instantiation of the bleak economic reality of the first-century urban milieu and illustrates how the organizational resources of the early church were brought to bear on this issue. As we learn from 1 Tim 5, the familial ethos of the Jesus movement necessitated extending care to those who had lost all earthy familial relations.

> HONOR WIDOWS WHO ARE TRULY IN NEED. BUT IF A WIDOW HAS CHILDREN OR GRAND-CHILDREN, THESE SHOULD LEARN FIRST OF ALL TO PUT THEIR RELIGION INTO PRAC-TICE BY CARING FOR THEIR OWN FAMILY.
>
> 1 TIMOTHY 5:4

In the earliest days of Paul's evangelistic work the structure and administration of the local assemblies was relatively simple. The most urgent concern would have been to find an acceptable meeting place, a home or homes adequate for worship, breaking bread, and so on. Identifying leaders was the next priority, although, as we have seen, it would appear that Paul did not appoint leaders as a matter of course in every church he established. Initially, elders or overseers were selected (Acts 14:23; Titus 1:5, 7). As the needs of the believing community grew, an order of deacons (Phil 1:1; 1 Tim 3:8–10, 12–13) and deaconesses (Rom 16:1; 1 Tim 3:11) was added. Alongside these officially commissioned leaders were charismatically endowed individuals engaged in teaching, prophesying, contributing financially, leading, and performing other necessary acts of service (Rom 12:6–8; 1 Cor 12:4–11). By the time of the writing of 1 Timothy, perhaps in the early 60s,[183] the situation in Ephesus had grown considerably more complex. In addition to elders (who receive a stipend, 1 Tim 5:17–19), deacons, and deaconesses, we have an apostolic delegate, Timothy, on long-term assignment overseeing the expanding—albeit struggling—ministry,[184] and we find a charitable foundation in place for the permanent maintenance of one of the most vulnerable classes of people in the ancient world, the widow. In fact, although 1 Timothy is most widely read for its teaching on church order and the selection of elders and deacons, the topic that receives the longest sustained treatment in this letter relates to caring for the widows in the community (1 Tim 5:3–16).

> NOTE WELL THOSE WHO HOLD HERETI-CAL OPINIONS ABOUT THE GRACE OF JESUS CHRIST. . . . THEY HAVE NO CONCERN FOR LOVE, NONE FOR THE WIDOW, NONE FOR THE ORPHAN, NONE FOR THE OPPRESSED.
>
> IGNATIUS

The social circumstances that gave rise to the problems addressed in 1 Tim 5 are not difficult to surmise. In a society where girls were married very young and often to men considerably older (see Household and Family: The Family), the inevitable outcome was a lengthy widowhood or remarriage for a significant portion of the female population. Beyond the daily distribution of bread (the dole), there were no government-sponsored welfare programs. So, it is not surprising that one of the standard subjects for ancient artists and sculptors was the stooped old woman who begged in the marketplace. Wearing a tattered shawl, hunched over with pleading eyes and hands outstretched, this tragic figure was a familiar sight in the forums and on the temple steps.

Among the wealthy, the woman's dowry was her primary insurance policy. Upon the death of her husband, a widow could return to her parents' home with her dowry.[185] If she had children, she might remain with them in her deceased husband's home, with her eldest son or another male in charge of the dowry, as stipulated by the deceased husband's will. There were laws concerning the repayment of the dowry that protected the widow from unscrupulous guardians.[186]

> **IF ANY WOMAN WHO IS A BELIEVER HAS WIDOWS IN HER FAMILY, SHE SHOULD HELP THEM AND NOT LET THE CHURCH BE BURDENED WITH THEM, SO THAT THE CHURCH CAN HELP THOSE WIDOWS WHO ARE REALLY IN NEED.**
>
> 1 TIMOTHY 5:16

From 1 Tim 5 we learn that the leaders in Ephesus had constructed a registry of widows that it supported financially (v. 9), but the ministry had grown beyond the capacity of the church to support it. Apparently, some less deserving widows had been enrolled (vv. 11, 17) and were siphoning valuable resources away from those in desperate need (v. 17). Paul's advice is a balanced mixture of compassion and common sense. His primary concern is that "real widows" (vv. 3, 5, 16)—that is, truly destitute widows—be properly cared for. He advises Timothy to exclude younger widows who could remarry, and those with family members who could support them. He is not saying these groups should never receive any support but that they should not be included on the list of those receiving permanent maintenance. Paul further stipulates that the widow should be a deserving widow, one whose life was characterized by godliness and service, not self-indulgence (5:5–6, 10). Again, these restrictions are aimed at ensuring that the church is able "to care for those who are truly destitute" (5:16).

The decision of the church in Ephesus to offer financial support to its widows represents another example of early Christian social concern (see City and Society: Paul and Poverty) and continues a prominent theme of the Old Testament, God as the protector of the widow: "A father to the fatherless, a defender of widows, is God in his holy dwelling. God sets the lonely in families" (Ps 68:5–6; cf. Deut 10:18; 27:19; Exod 22:22–24). Although Paul was primarily an evangelist called to proclaim Jesus among the Gentiles, his concern for the "truly destitute"—be they the poor in Jerusalem or the widows in Ephesus—represents a vibrant witness to the apostle's vision of how the gospel should affect society.

THE COMMUNITY GATHERED

Worship in the House Church

Although we lack anything resembling a detailed order of service for the early communal gatherings of Christians, we have enough information scattered throughout Paul's letters in the NT to construct a rough sketch. In many respects, the basic elements of worship have changed little in two thousand years, though the configuration of these components would be different from today and varied from location to location; again, very much like the contemporary setting.

> WE MEET IN A GATHERING AND APPROACH GOD IN PRAYER—FOR THE EMPEROR, FOR PEACE. WE MEET TO READ THE BOOKS OF GOD. THERE IS ALSO EXHORTATION, REBUKE, DIVINE CENSURE.
>
> *TERTULLIAN

Prayer and Singing

In 1 Tim 2:8 Paul expresses his desire that "men in every place should pray, lifting up holy hands without anger or disputing." The unusual expression "in every place" (*en panti topō*) indicates that Paul is specifically addressing the household gatherings in Ephesus and commanding that sincere prayer, free of partisan bickering, be practiced in every meeting.[187] Paul's frequent exhortations to be vigilant in prayer (Rom 12:2; 15:26; 2 Cor 13:7; Eph 6:17) and his numerous reminders that he prays daily for each congregation (Rom 1:9; Eph 1:16–17; Phil 1:4; 1 Thess 1:2; 2 Tim 1:3) confirm the picture presented in Acts that when believers gathered prayer was central (4:31; 12:12; 14:23; 20:36).

Equally prominent in community worship was music and hymnody. Paul expects that edification will take place through "singing psalms, hymns, and spiritual songs" (Col 3:16; cf. Eph 5:19; 1 Cor 14:15), and it is likely that hymns or portions of hymns are woven into some of his letters (e.g., Rom 11:33–36; Phil 2:6–11).[188]

> THEREFORE, APPOINT FOR YOURSELVES OVERSEERS AND DEACONS. . . . DO NOT DESPISE THEM, FOR THEY ARE HONORED MEN, ALONG WITH THE PROPHETS AND TEACHERS.
>
> DIDACHE 15:1-2

Instruction

Edification through teaching took many forms among first-century Christians. As we have already seen, in Corinth a process of mutual instruction took place as each member employed his or her gift: "When you come together, everyone has a hymn, or a word of instruction, a revelation, a tongue or an interpretation. All of these must be done for the strengthening of the church" (1 Cor

14:26). Here we see prophecy, tongues, and instruction (perhaps by the "teachers" mentioned in v. 28) all done for the strengthening of the body.

> THE ELDERS WHO DIRECT THE AFFAIRS OF THE CHURCH WELL ARE WORTHY OF DOUBLE HONOR, ESPECIALLY THOSE WHOSE WORK IS PREACHING AND TEACHING.
>
> 1 TIMOTHY 5:17

Teaching in the more formal sense also took place in the household gatherings, as Acts and Paul's letters amply illustrate. Paul's practice of teaching "from house to house" (Acts 20:20) established a pattern and a priority for the early churches as they sought to grow in the knowledge of their faith and relate it to the world in which they lived. In Troas, Luke tells us, Paul taught the believers who had gathered in a local home till past midnight (Acts 20:7). One of the qualifications for an elder is that he be "able to teach" (1 Tim 3:2; Titus 1:9), which takes for granted that teaching was a regular feature of communal worship. In the same way, Paul's frequent exhortations to Timothy and Titus to teach, instruct, encourage, command, and rebuke (1 Tim 1:3; 4:6, 11; 6:17; 2 Tim 4:2; Titus 2:1–15), along with his emphasis on sound doctrine (1 Tim 3:9; 4:16; 2 Tim 1:13–14; Titus 1:9; 2:1), underscores the importance of formal instruction in the community. The content of the teaching would have been based on the Old Testament Scripture (2 Tim 3:16) and Paul's letters (Col 4:16; 1 Tim 3:15–16; 2 Tim 2:14), along with recollection of Paul's apostolic proclamation of Christian traditions (1 Cor 11:23–25; 15:3).

Offering

There is also evidence that as churches became established, resources were collected and pooled for needs in the community.[189] This is fairly explicit in the case of the support given to the widows in Ephesus and with the remuneration offered to elders (1 Tim 5:17–18). Paul's instructions to the Romans that they are to "contribute to the needs of the saints" (Rom 12:13) may also indicate regular monetary support for the needy. We are not told how such collections would have been made, but it is reasonable to use Paul's instructions concerning the collection for the poor in Jerusalem as a pattern: "Now about the collection for God's people: Do what I told the Galatian churches to do. On the first day of every week, each one of you should set aside a sum of money in keeping with his income, saving it up" (1 Cor 16:1–2).

The Lord's Supper

Perhaps the most noteworthy feature of early Christian worship is the celebration of the Lord's Supper (*kuriakon deipnon*), a meal patterned after Jesus' final meal with his disciples described in the Gospels (Matt 26:17–30; Mark 14:12–26; Luke 22:7–38). It is not clear if this meal was a part of every Christian gathering or if it was reserved for special gatherings. According to Pliny's account from the early second century, the believers in Bythinia gathered early for singing and mutual exhortation and then later for a meal, which was probably a celebration of the Lord's Supper. This passage is worth citing in full because it gives us an independent account of ancient Christian worship practices:

> ON THE LORD'S OWN DAY GATHER TOGETHER AND BREAK BREAD, HAVING FIRST CONFESSED YOUR SIN SO THAT YOUR SACRIFICE MAY BE PURE.
>
> DIDACHE 14:1

They [the Christians] also declared that the sum total of the guilt or error amounted to no more than this: They had met regularly before dawn on a fixed day to chant verses alternately among themselves in honor of Christ as if to a god, and to bind themselves by oath, not for any criminal purpose, but to abstain from theft, robbery and adultery, to commit no breach of trust, and not to deny a deposit when called upon to restore it. After this ceremony it had been their custom to disperse and reassemble later to take food of an ordinary harmless kind.[190]

Paul's vision for this celebration was for it to be a visual representation of the unity of the church (1 Cor 10:17). In Corinth, however, it had become something very different indeed.

Class Distinctions at the Lord's Table

Can you imagine going to church on Sunday, being sized up by an usher at the door who, observing your frayed hem and scuffed shoes, rolls his eyes as he shunts you off to a corner room to fellowship with those of your own social standing? This may sound incredible—I hope it does—but something close to this scenario was occurring at the celebration of the Lord's Supper in Corinth. Paul seems genuinely mortified at what he has heard from Chloe's servants:

> IF YOU'RE POOR, YOU'RE A JOKE, ON EACH AND EVERY OCCASION. . . . POVERTY'S GREATEST CURSE IS THAT IT MAKES MEN OBJECTS OF MIRTH, RIDICULED, EMBARRASSED.
>
> JUVENAL

In the following directives I have no praise for you, for your meetings do more harm than good! First, I hear that when you come together as a church, there are divisions among you. . . . This is not the Lord's supper! For when you eat, each of you goes ahead with his own meal. Some remain hungry, others get drunk. . . . Do you despise the church of God and humiliate those who have nothing? What do you want me to say to this? Should I praise you? Of course not! (1 Cor 11:17–21 author's translation)

The problem can be boiled down to divisions, which defeat the purpose of the gathering and lead to some eating plenty and drinking too much, while others eat little, with the result that those who have nothing are humiliated. As bizarre as this sounds, what Paul is describing is nothing more than the normal protocols of Roman dining being applied in the setting of the Christian communal meal.[191] From what we know of practices common among many of the elite (serving less important guests lower-quality food and in smaller amounts, see City and Society: Class and Status), it would appear that the meals that Paul is referring to took place in the home of one of the upper strata of Corinthian society. When Paul remarks at the beginning of 1 Corinthians that "not many of you are of noble birth" (1 Cor 1:26), he implies that at least a few were. Erastus was part of the local aristocracy and would have had a home large enough to host a gathering of this nature. So too would have Gaius, mentioned in Rom 16:23 as someone who did play host to "the whole church" in Corinth; apparently all the local house assemblies could gather in his home.

Excavations in Corinth have revealed several elegant Roman villas, and we can assume that Corinth would have had its share of *insulae, tabernae,* and other types of standard accommodation that have been uncovered in places like Rome and Pompeii.[192] The *triclinium* (dining room) of an upscale home was designed to accommodate twelve people (three or four per couch), though it has been suggested that as many as twenty could be squeezed in a pinch. Naturally, following Roman meal etiquette, guests of higher social standing would be admitted into the *triclinium,* while others would been left in the *atrium* or escorted to the courtyard. Estimates on the size of the church in Corinth at the time of the writing of Paul's first epistle to that church range from 50 to 100, meaning that a significant number of celebrants would have been segregated from the privileged minority in the main dining room.[193]

RANK MUST BE PRESERVED!

*CICERO

Close attention to Paul's account of what had essentially become a Corinthian *convivium,* along with his subsequent admonition, reveal another class-related issue: the timing of the meals was such that the leisured classes consumed most of the food and drink before the working class arrived. In 1 Cor 11:20–21 Paul notes that "when you come together . . . each goes ahead with his own meal." In his concluding remarks he advises, "So, my brothers and sisters, when you come together to eat, wait for each other." As we recall (see City and Society: Urban Landscape and Environment), the typical workday for the Roman gentleman ended around 1:00 p.m., which was followed by a visit to the baths and then dinner by 3:00 p.m. The lower orders, however, were not so fortunate. Their workday might not end till after sunset, which explains Paul's insistence that those who arrived earlier should wait for the others. Otherwise, as Paul explains, "it is not the Lord's supper" but rather "your own meal."

Paul's pastoral strategy takes two forms: practical and theological. In terms of the practical, he addresses the issue of inconsiderate timing by commanding the privileged to wait for the others, "those who have nothing" (11:22, 33). He speaks to the matter of unequal consumption of food by telling those who arrived first to "eat at home, if you are hungry" (11:22, 34). The problem of space limitations is not so easily solved, and Paul may have this in mind when he concludes with, "about other matters, I will give instructions when I come" (1 Cor 11:34). Paul's theological reflection consists of a reminder of the meaning and symbolism of the Lord's Table (11:23–26), followed by a sober warning against partaking unworthily, without serious self-examination (11:28) and with no thought to the larger body (11:29): "It is because of this that many among you are weak and ill, and some have died" (11:30 author's translation). In Paul's view, the connection between the spiritual body and the physical body cannot be severed; to thoughtlessly injure the corporate body is to unwittingly harm one's own body.[194]

> I MEANT TO CONGRATU-
> LATE YOU ON THE WAY
> YOU PRESERVE THE
> DISTINCTIONS IN CLASS
> AND RANK; ONCE THESE
> ARE THROWN INTO
> CONFUSION AND DE-
> STROYED, NOTHING IS
> MORE UNEQUAL THAN
> SO-CALLED EQUALITY.
> PLINY

Paul's vision of the Lord's Table is spelled out in 1 Cor 10:17: "Because there is one loaf, we who are many are one body." The horrible irony of the abuses occurring in Corinth was that the very celebration intended to represent unity and community instead became emblematic of discord and division. The ceremony designed to eliminate distinctions in status was tragically distorted to reinforce distinctions in status. What Paul envisioned was not too different from the leveling of the social order that occurred during the feasts of Saturnalia:

> Every order eats at one table: children, women, plebes, equestrian, senator. Freedom has relaxed reverence. . . . Now everyone, be he rich or poor, boasts of dining with the leader.[195]

For the Romans, this suspension of the social hierarchy was a ridiculous parody, tolerable for an evening or two. For Paul, this was the new order.

SLAVERY

"In Christ," Paul told the Galatians, "there is neither Jew nor Greek, slave nor free, male nor female, for you are all one in Christ Jesus" (Gal 3:28; cf. 1 Cor 12:13; Col 3:11). This verse is one of many that attests to the presence of slaves in the churches Paul established,[196] while also revealing Paul's vision of a new kind of community, one where external markers of status differentiation became null and void. Yet in spite of this bold and even subversive language, Paul never says a word against the institution of slavery as such, nor does he permit slaves to shirk their obligations to their owners. Rather, slaves must be obedient "in everything" (Titus 2:9), in both attitude and action (Eph 6:5–9). The book of Philemon is no exception. In returning the slave Onesimus to his master, Philemon, Paul is clearly pressuring Philemon to free Onesimus (vv. 15–17, 20–21),[197] but his rationale—at least as far as it is explicit in the letter—is not based on opposition to slavery but because of Paul's affection for Onesimus (vv. 12, 16), and Onesimus's usefulness in Paul's ministry (vv. 11, 13).

> PERHAPS THE REASON HE WAS SEPARATED FROM YOU FOR A LITTLE WHILE WAS THAT YOU MIGHT HAVE HIM BACK FOR GOOD—NO LONGER AS A SLAVE, BUT BETTER THAN A SLAVE, AS A DEAR BROTHER.
>
> PHILEMON 15–16

In many respects, Paul's approach to slavery corresponds to that of his Stoic contemporaries (see Household and Family: Slaves). First, Paul urges masters to treat their slaves kindly (Eph 6:9; Col 4:1; Phlm 16–17). Second, he regards slavery as a matter of "indifference" as far as progress in the Christian life is concerned. The key passage here is 1 Cor 7:21–22:

> Were you a slave when you were called? Don't let it trouble you—although if you can gain your freedom, do so. For he who was a slave when he was called by the Lord is the Lord's freedman; similarly, he who was a free man when he was called is Christ's slave.

This passage is notoriously difficult to translate, but the rendering of the NIV cited above gets the message right.[198] Slaves are not disadvantaged with respect to the Christian life or God's favor, so in that regard they needn't worry about being slaves.

Third, as 1 Cor 7:22 also illustrates, Paul could relativize and spiritualize slavery and freedom, although with a slightly different twist than the Stoics. In Paul's view, the Christian slave is now a freedman of the Lord (hence, obligated to the Lord as to his patron), and the Christian free-born are now the Lord's slaves (hence, obligated to the Lord as his servants).

> IF I WERE STILL TRYING TO PLEASE MEN, I WOULD NOT BE A SLAVE OF CHRIST.
>
> GALATIANS 1:10

Paul's metaphorical use of slave/master imagery is rich and varied,[199] with his most jarring image occurring at the end of Galatians. In Gal 6:17 he warns the troublemakers in Galatia that they would be wise to leave him alone since he bears on his body the "brands" (*stigmata*) of Jesus. The Greek word Paul uses, *stigma,* indicates the kind of branding done to cattle, criminals, captive soldiers, and, as we have seen, especially slaves.[200] Attaching the possessive "brands of Jesus" indicates that the metaphor is related to slavery and that Paul is depicting the wounds he received in the service of the gospel as proof of Christ's ownership. Having begun Galatians by portraying himself as a "slave of Christ" (Gal 1:10), Paul returns to this metaphor as he signs off, bringing the argument full circle. Although we know nothing of Paul's physical appearance, this verse indicates that his body visibly displayed his commitment to his master and Lord.

> PAUL, A SLAVE OF
> GOD AND APOSTLE
> OF JESUS CHRIST.
> TITUS 1:1

Finally, again like the Stoics, Paul also referred to slavery and freedom as a moral sphere, metaphorically related to vice and virtue:

> Don't you know that when you offer yourselves to someone to obey him as slaves, you are slaves to the one whom you obey—whether you are slaves to sin, which leads to death, or to obedience, which leads to righteousness? But thanks be to God that, though you used to be slaves to sin, you wholeheartedly obeyed the form of teaching to which you were entrusted. You have been set free from sin and have become slaves to righteousness. (Rom 6:16–18)

Slavery in the Roman world was perhaps the most pernicious and pervasive social evil facing the early church, and modern Christians are right to be concerned that slavery was not "pinged" by the moral radar of the earliest Christians.[201] Yet there are also clear indicators that the Christian faith as articulated by Paul and other NT writers could not coexist with the institution of slavery. Paul's vision of the church as a community in which "slave and free" were obsolete categories (Gal 3:28) was not conducive to the institution of slavery. To the extent that this vision of humanity affected the larger society—and it did—slavery would become increasingly untenable. We have hints of this already occurring in the later epistles of Paul, specifically, 1 Tim 6:2. Here we read of Christian slaves who were being disrespectful to their masters because they were fellow believers. It is not difficult to surmise the circumstance prompting this behavior: the sense of equality fostered within the *ecclesia* was absent outside the *ecclesia,* and some Christian slaves were beginning to find the disjunction between the ideal and reality difficult to accept. Moreover, while it is true that Paul's letter to Philemon contains no explicit denunciation of slavery, it is also true, as F. F. Bruce comments, that this letter effectively "brings us into an atmosphere in which the institution [of slavery] could only wilt and die."[202]

> HERE THERE IS NO
> GREEK OR JEW,
> CIRCUMCISED OR UNCIR-
> CUMCISED, BARBARIAN
> SCYTHIAN, SLAVE OR
> FREE, BUT CHRIST IS
> ALL, AND IS IN ALL.
> COLOSSIANS 3:11

FURTHER READING

Primary Sources

Seneca (first century C.E.), *Epistle* 47, offers an enlightened rationale for treating slaves well and contains informative comments on the treatment of slaves in his day. Available in the LCL.

Dio Chrysostom (late first, early second century C.E.) is typical of the Stoic rationalization of slavery and freedom as inward moral dispositions. His two essays "On Slavery and Freedom I, II" (*Or.* 14, 15) represent excellent examples of the Stoic approach. Available in the LCL.

The Greco-Roman consensus on what a well-ordered household looked like can be found in Arius Didymus, *Concerning Household Management*. This essay provides a useful point of comparison between the NT household codes and those found in nonbiblical sources. See David L. Balch, "Household Codes," in the bibliography.

Several ancient writers have informative treatments of marriage and sexuality. Plutarch's "Advice to Bride and Groom" sheds light on the patriarchal worldview of Roman society and on the duties of both husband and wife. Musonius Rufus critiques rampant promiscuity in *Discourse* 12, while offering the Stoic vision of marriage in *Discourses* 13A, 13B, and 14. Both are first-century writers. Plutarch is available in the LCL. Musonius's *Discourses* have been translated by Cora E. Lutz in *Musonius Rufus: The Roman Socrates* (New Haven: Yale University Press, 1947).

Tertullian's *Apology* (second century C.E.) is crucial reading for understanding the developments of Christianity in the second century. In this work, Tertullian defends Christianity against the criticisms and accusations of wary—and often uniformed—Romans. In the process he gives an insider's view of the practices of the church in his day.

Secondary Sources

Robert J. Banks. *Going to Church in the First Century: An Eyewitness Account.* Auburn, Maine: Christian Books, 1990.

Keith R. Bradley. *Slavery and Society at Rome.* Cambridge: Cambridge University Press, 1994.

Will Deming. *Paul on Marriage and Celibacy: The Hellenistic Background of 1 Corinthians 7.* Grand Rapids, Mich.: Eerdmans, 2004.

Simon P. Ellis. *Roman Housing.* London: Duckworth, 2000.

Roger W. Gehring. *House Church and Mission: The Importance of Household Structures in Early Christianity.* Peabody, Mass.: Hendrickson, 2004.

Kevin Giles. *Patterns of Ministry among the First Christians.* Melbourne: Collins Dove, 1989.

Joseph H. Hellerman. *The Ancient Church as Family*. Minneapolis: Fortress, 2001.

Mary R. Lefkowitz and Maureen B. Fant. *Women's Life in Greece and Rome*. Baltimore: Johns Hopkins University Press, 1982.

Carolyne Osiek and Margaret Y. MacDonald, with Janet H. Tulloch. *A Woman's Place: House Churches in Earliest Christianity*. Philadelphia: Fortress, 2006.

Vincent L. Wimbush. *Paul, the Worldly Ascetic: Response to the World and Self-Understanding according to 1 Corinthians 7*. Macon, Ga.: Mercer University Press, 1987.

EPILOGUE

WHY CHRISTIANITY?

The story of the spread of Christianity in the Roman world is, in many ways, the story of the improbable achieving the impossible. The exponential growth of the Jesus movement in the first few centuries after the crucifixion of its founder continues to puzzle and fascinate scholars and in recent years has spawned a new generation of literature exploring the topic.[1] It is tempting to say that Christianity succeeded because God was in it, but a complete answer to the question also needs to examine conditions and causation on the human plane. What social and political factors enabled the followers of Jesus to propagate their faith and win converts? On the level of the individual, what was the appeal of the Christian message? What needs did it meet? What problems did it solve? Here we are asking about the plausibility basis of the Christian message, which Gerd Theissen defines as "the social conditions and factors which allow a conviction to seem obviously tenable."[2]

Some may find this line of inquiry disturbing, as if I am trying to explain religious phenomena (personal faith, remarkable church growth) solely in terms of nonreligious and nonsupernatural factors; treating theological beliefs as if they were the product of prevalent social conditions and nothing more. That is not my intention. Explaining religious faith as merely the byproduct of social factors would be akin to saying that it is water that generates fish, which is silly. However, where there is no water, there are no fish, because water is the necessary environment for marine life. In the same way, religious beliefs flourish in certain kinds of environments and not in others. When Jesus said, "It is easier for a camel to go through the eye of a needle than for a rich person to enter the kingdom of God" (Luke 18:25), he was identifying an important socioeconomic factor that inhibits receptivity to the gospel.

PAX ROMANA

Looking first through a panoramic lens, it is true that events on the international scene created a context in which religious movements like Christianity could disseminate their message and multiply. The advance of Hellenistic culture in the preceding centuries—and with it the Greek language—meant that Paul, a Jew, could preach and write letters in Greek to such diverse locales as Galatia and Rome (and everywhere in between) and fully expect to be understood. With the rise of Rome and the establishment of a superpower came roads that connected all parts of the empire. Paul, and other Christian preachers, evangelists, prophets, and tradesmen, used these roads to great effect. The Augustan peace led to a mobility in society previously unknown in the ancient world. It is one of the great ironies of history that the system of roads built by Rome to strengthen its empire and rapidly deploy its military might would ultimately prove crucial for the ascendency of a religious movement it had attempted to eradicate.

ORGANIZATIONAL EFFICIENCY

Organizational efficiency is a mantra of the corporate world because efficiency breeds success. Paul's strategy of expansion—if I can extend the corporate metaphor—was both shrewd and practical; it leveraged existing religious institutions (synagogues), along with private residences and volunteer leaders, to create a religious movement that was self-sustaining and self-propagating. Paul's first stop in the cities he evangelized was the local synagogue. In this Jewish house of worship Paul would teach, preach, make contacts, and win converts, if possible. He would also meet sympathetic Greeks and Romans who frequented the synagogue, "God-fearers," to use Luke's term. Acts records several instances where churches were formed directly from synagogue contacts: Pisidian Antioch, Philippi, Berea, and Corinth.

Once Paul had worn out his welcome at the synagogue, he moved his base of operations to the homes of key people who had converted. This was a bold stroke. As noted in chapter 4, the house-church movement was nimble, flexible, and able to expand and adapt to new situations. Households were also imbedded in larger social networks that would inevitably be affected when a household converted. Numerous sociological studies of conversion among deviant religious groups—as Christianity would have been considered in the first century—have demonstrated that relational bonds are crucial in gaining converts.[3] We can imagine the scene described in Acts 10:24 as Cornelius prepares to hear Peter's message repeating itself many times in the next few decades: "The following day Peter and the brothers arrived in Caesarea. Cornelius was expecting them and had called together his relatives and close friends." When the gospel reached a household, it also reached a community.

The house-church movement also involved considerably less overhead than the Olympian deities. Even a modest temple required state support, wealthy benefactors, a paid staff, and so on.[4] Tertullian's censure of the priests of Mars (the Salli) and other pagan cults is telling:

> The Salli cannot have their feast without going into debt; you must get the accountants to tell you what the tenths of Hercules and the sacrificial banquets cost; the choicest cook is appointed for the Apaturia, Dionysia, the Attic mysteries; the smoke from the banquet of Serapis will call out the firemen.[5]

Tertullian (160–220 C.E.) is not unbiased, but his account of the expense of pagan feasts and temple life could easily be deduced from the remains of pagandom still visible today.

EVANGELISTIC ENTREPRENEURS

No account of the advance of Christianity would be complete without considering the importance of pioneer evangelists who risked their lives, their livelihood, and their reputation telling other people the good news of the death and resurrection of Jesus. This is one of the distinctive elements of Christianity when compared with other religions and cults of the Roman world. The closest analogy to the missional work of early Christian preachers would be the Stoics and Cynics, who preached moral reform and living simply. Yet there is no concern among the Stoics and Cynics to establish communities, nor is there any discernable interest beyond individual reform.

Paul was the quintessential evangelistic entrepreneur and the most important figure in the spread of Christianity in the first century. We get a glimpse of his missional mindset in Rom 15:19–23, as he describes his calling and his strategy: "So, from Jerusalem all the way around to Illyricum, I have fully proclaimed the gospel of Christ. It has always been my ambition to preach the gospel where Christ was not known . . . and now there is no more work for me in these regions." In saying that he has "fully proclaimed" the gospel from Jerusalem to Illyricum (the western portion of the Balkans, north of present-day Macedonia), Paul refers to a vast swath of the Roman world that contained many cities, municipalities, and regions with no gospel presence. Apparently, Paul's strategy was to proclaim Christ extensively, in as many regions as possible—not intensively, to every town in a particular region. We might say that Paul's approach was to drop glowing hot embers throughout as many provinces as he could reach and then allow the Spirit to fan these into a conflagration.

Yet while Paul was critical in spreading the faith, he was by no means alone. In the accounts of Acts and the writings Paul we also hear of people like Barnabas, Phillip, Apollos, Priscilla and Aquila, Andronicus and Junia, and many more—to say nothing of the other apostles. When Paul writes to Rome, the city already has a significant Christian presence, complete with problems that need to be addressed (Rom 14), yet we have no idea who carried the embers to the capital.

CARING COMMUNITY

The spectacular growth of Christianity was not simply the result of resourceful, opportunistic visionaries working in an optimal political climate; there was something attractive about this new religious movement. In the narrative introducing chapter 4, Julia expresses the sentiment that her house group, meeting in Heraclitus's little flat above the forum, felt like a family. As we learned in chapter 4, the familial ethos was intentionally fostered by Paul among the communities he founded. Establishing a family dynamic in the house churches served to reconfigure personal identities, individual loyalties, and social alliances, while giving expression to a nurturing, loving community. Kinship language and a familial ethos continued to characterize Christianity in the second and third century, as evidenced by Tertullian's comments defending Christians from pagan ridicule on this point:

> Yes, their indignation at us for using among ourselves the name of "Brothers" must really, I take it, come from nothing but the fact that among them every kind of kinship so far as affection goes is false and feigned. But we are your brothers too, by right of descent from the one mother, Nature—even if you fall short of being men because you are bad brothers. But how much more fitting are those both called brothers and treated as brothers . . . who from one womb of common ignorance have come with wonder to the one light of truth![6]

In important ways, Christian communities were fundamentally countercultural in the classless, egalitarian ideals that they sought to actualize. Membership was not based on rank, or ethnicity, or gender, or wealth. Slaves worshiped beside city magistrates, and former prostitutes beside aristocratic matrons. Those of us who have grown up with the ideals of modern Western democracies cannot fully appreciate how radical, even subversive, this mentality appeared to the status-obsessed Roman society. When Paul admonishes the believers in Rome, "Do not be proud, but be willing to associate with people of low position" (Rom 12:16), his words betray a concern that the deeply engrained Roman scruples regarding rank and status could undermine the true *communitas* of the Christian gatherings.

The Christian community was also a place where needs were met. Elders laid hands on the sick and prayed for them. Widows were cared for. The poor were supplied with provisions. An important concern for Paul was the believers' care for the physical needs of other believers (Rom 15:25–26; 2 Cor 8–9; 1 Tim 6:17–18), and this conviction vitally informed Paul's theology of work: "He who has been stealing must steal no longer, but must work, doing something useful with his own hands, that he may have something to share with those in need" (Eph 4:28). In Paul's view, the goal of work was not wealth accumulation but wealth dissemination, "sharing with those in need." The emphasis on charitable collections and providing for the destitute continued to characterize the church of Tertullian's day:

> Even if there is a money chest of a sort, it is not made up of money paid in entrance fees, as in pagan temples, as if religion were a matter of contract. Every man once a month brings some modest coin—or whenever he wishes, and only if he does wish, and if he can; for nobody is compelled, it is a voluntary offering. You might call them the trust funds of piety, for they are not spent upon banquets or drinking parties, nor thankless eating houses, but to feed the poor and to bury them, for boys and girls who lack property and parents, and then for slaves too old to work, and shipwrecked mariners; and any who may be in the mines, islands, or prisoners. . . . Such work of love—for so it is—puts a mark upon us in the eyes of some. "Look," they say, "how they love one another."[7]

Other, less tangible, but equally important, needs were also satisfied by the message of the gospel and the experience of Christian community. Zoe, for example, who is being sexually exploited by her master, wonders silently in the opening narrative what it would be like to be Selena, the lunar goddess, with the power to make herself new. The message proclaimed by Paul not only leveled the ground socially but also declared that everyone in Christ was newly created, the slate was wiped clean, "all things have become new" (2 Cor 5:17). Zoe, at the bottom of the social pyramid, a slave and a woman, longed for dignity and a sense of belonging that she had never known but that the gospel offered her freely. Surely this was an appealing element of the Christian message for someone in Zoe's position.

Another deeply felt psychological need the gospel addressed relates to the afterlife and what comes next. As we saw in the chapter City and Society, there was an enormous variety of contradictory notions on life after death, and in 1 Thessalonians Paul refers to the grief of those "who have no hope" (4:13). The message of judgment and eternal life provided assurances of justice for those living in an unjust world and hope of rest for those toiling and moiling to make ends meet every day. In other words, it was not simply the practices of the early church that attracted converts; its theology and worldview carried its own appeal as well.

EMBODIED VIRTUE

In a recent book purporting to explain "why Christianity happened," James Crossley sets out to answer this question "without recourse to theological reasons." Crossley attempts a purely secular and sociological explanation for Christian origins that eschews theologizing as illegitimate in historical enquiry. In Crossley's view, Christianity was not "in any way superior to any other movement." Crossley's book is carefully argued, and he is to be commended for guarding against Christian triumphalism in its various forms. As I have made clear, sociological analysis is crucial in accounting for the rise of Christianity, or any social movement. The fallacy of Crossley's method, however, is that it is one-dimensional. A full, multidimensional description of Christianity's stunning growth must accept in principle that its ideas, its worldview, its theology might indeed have contained elements that pagans found attractive, even superior. In fact, the sense of community and equality described above, along with the early church's social concerns—feeding the poor, providing for widows and orphans—did not arise in an ideological vacuum but were the manifestation of deeply held theological beliefs. The worldview Christianity offered may not have been the primary reason why people converted, but it cannot be dismissed as irrelevant.

The mythology of the ancient world abounds with tales of the gods doing vindictive things to humans—seducing, deceiving, and killing. At several points in the preceding chapters we discussed the problems these stories posed for thoughtful denizens of the mortal realm: Can these stories really be believed? How can the gods serve as guides to moral conduct? Are the gods for me or against me? The Stoics, as we have seen, re-created god(s) in line with their own ideals and ignored popular mythology when it contradicted their view of ultimate reality. Christianity offered something different. In the Christian stories, God exemplified the ethic he enjoined on humanity; he embodied, through Jesus, the virtues he expected of his followers. Even the call for sacrificial generosity is grounded by Paul in the example of Christ: "For you know the grace of our Lord Jesus Christ, that though he was rich, yet for your sakes he became poor, so that you through his poverty might become rich" (2 Cor 8:9).

The figure of Jesus was an oddity in the religious smorgasbord of antiquity. The person the Christians called "Lord" didn't live in a cloud on Mount Olympus, coming down to earth once in a while only to seduce a fair maiden. Jesus walked, sweated, cried, suffered, and died, just like us; a Jewish peasant killed by Rome but vindicated by God. This story must have exited the imagination in a way that the feeble frivolities of the gods could not.

More than this, however, Jesus' sacrificial death on the cross was held out as a paradigm that believers were called to emulate in their daily lives: "This is how we know what love is: Jesus Christ laid down his life or us. And we ought to lay down our lives for our brothers and sisters" (1 John 3:16). The logic of the cross demands a life lived for others. One of the appeals of the gospel, I suggest, was not that it was easy but that it was difficult and entailed hardship and sacrifice. It appealed to humanity's higher instincts and deeper intuition, which understands that a life consumed with self is a life that consumes itself. This was also the appeal of Stoicism, but the Stoics lacked a personal divine embodiment of sacrificial love, which rendered their message somewhat hollow.

In the final analysis, there were many reasons why Christianity succeeded in the Roman world, including the fact that God was in it. Success alone, however, is hardly decisive proof of divine favor. More telling in this regard is the fact that Christianity, the story of the death and resurrection of Jesus of Nazareth, changed lives. This is the most compelling feature of the gospel, both in the Roman world and in the modern world.

ENDNOTES

NOTES TO INTRODUCTION

1. The research is compiled by Ken Bain in *What the Best College Teachers Do* (Cambridge, Mass.: Harvard University Press, 2004), 37–42.

2.*Plutarch, *Mor.* 737A, Table Talk.

3. Strabo, 8.6.23; 17.3.15.

4. Jerome Murphy-O'Connor, *St. Paul's Corinth: Texts and Archaeology* (3d rev. and exp. ed.; Collegeville, Minn.: Liturgical Press, 2002), 55–57; Steven M. Baugh, "Cult Prostitution in New Testament Ephesus: A Reappraisal," *JETS* 42 (1999): 443–60.

5. In Acts 18:3, Paul is called a *skēnopoios,* which is sometimes translated as "tentmaker." The Greek term, however, refers more broadly to an artisan who produced a wide variety of leather goods. See further discussion at City and Society: Paul the Leatherworker.

6. I accept the hypothesis of Goodspeed that "Gaius," who Paul describes as a host to the whole church in Corinth (Rom. 16:23) is the praenomen (first name) of Titius Justus, who hosted the church according to Acts 18:7. See E. J. Goodspeed, "Gaius Titius Justus," *Journal of Biblical Literature* 69 (1950): 382–83.

NOTES TO PART 1: RELIGION AND SUPERSTITION

1. Unlike Judeo-Christian monotheism, the polytheism of the ancient world could offer no *a priori* metaphysical objection to a new god emerging in the heavens. Yet Greeks and Romans were intuitively suspicious of any new religion or deity; the antiquity of a religious belief was considered a powerful argument for its legitimacy. However, as long as a new cult offered no threat to the moral order and other venerated religious traditions, it could eventually gain acceptance in the Roman world.

2. See Precatio Omnium Herbarum; Precatio Herbarum; Aetna 340–48, in *Minor Latin Poets,* LCL 284.

3.*Juvenal, *Sat.* 13.45–53. In Greek mythology Ixion made advances toward Zeus' wife, Hera, and was sentenced to eternity in Tartarus bound to a wheel spinning in all directions. Sisyphus was the legendary founding king of Corinth who was assigned an equally dismal fate in the underworld: to roll a stone up a hill, only to watch it continually roll back on him. Tityus' punishment for rape was to be stretched out in Hades with two ravenous vultures feeding on his entrails—eternally. The Furies were the goddesses of vengeance who tortured mercilessly any wrongdoer.

4. Origen, *Against Celsus* 8.2.

5. Pilhofer, 321/L77.

6. Apuleius, *Defense* 55.

7. Victor Tcherikover, *Hellenistic Civilization and the Jews* (Peabody, Mass.: Hendrickson, 1999), 292–95.

8. Philo, *Embassy* 214, 245, 281–83; *Against Flaccus* 43, 45–46; *Moses* 2.232; Josephus, *Ant.* 11.133; 14.115; 17.300; Josephus, *J.W.* 7.43; 7.445; 1 Macc 15:13–24; *Sib. Or.* 3.271–272.

9. Cited by Josephus, *Ant.* 14.115.

10. A full survey is given by John M. G. Barclay, *Jews in the Mediterranean Diaspora: From Alexander to Trajan (323 B.C.E.–117 C.E.)* (Edinburgh: T&T Clark, 1996).

11. Josephus, *J.W.* 7.46–53.

12. Pilhofer, 132/L303.

13. Cited in G. H. R. Horsley, *New Documents Illustrating Early Christianity* (9 vols. edited by G. H. R. Horsley and S. R. Llewelyn; Grand Rapids, Mich.: Eerdmans, 1987), 4.113.

14. See, for example, Martial's complaints of the smell of Jewish women fasting (4.4) or his sarcastic references to circumcision (7.3). The pejorative term "superstition" is used by many to describe Judaism: Apuleius, *Flor.* 6; Horace, *Sat.* 1.5.100; Plutarch, *Mor.* 167C, Superstition. See also the uncomplimentary descriptions in Cicero, *Flac.* 69; Tacitus, *Hist.* 5:1–13; Juvenal, *Sat.* 3:10–16, 269; 6:153–160; 14.96–106.

15. Dio Cassius, *Rom. Hist.* 67.14.2.

16. Juvenal, *Sat.* 14.97.

17. Petronius, *Poems* 24; cf. Tacitus, *Hist.* 5.4.

18. Juvenal, *Sat.* 14.105; Tacitus, *Hist.* 5.4.

19. Shaye J. D. Cohen, "Crossing the Boundary and Becoming a Jew," *HTR* 82 (1989): 14–33.

20. E.g. Cicero, *Nature of the Gods* 2.35–62; Dio Chrysostom, *Or.* 32.15; Epictetus, *Disc.* 2.8.

21. Obscene from our vantage point. Priapus was a god of fertility and protection commonly stationed in fields and gardens. He is typically portrayed as a small and comically misshapen fellow with enormous genitalia—standing at full attention. In inscriptions he is known as "the rigid god."

22. Persius, *Sat.* 2.31–37. Crassus was a Roman aristocrat known for his vast wealth.

23. Plutarch, *Mor.* 153A, Dinner of the Seven Wise Men.

24. Pseudo-Heraclitus, *Epistle 8.1.*

25. Apuleius, *Defense* 43, 64.

26. Diogenes Laertius, *Lives* 1.110; Pausanias, *Descr.* 1.1.4; 5.14.8; cf. Acts 17:23.

27. Cited in Hans-Josef Klauck, *The Religious Context of Early Christianity: A Guide to Graeco-Roman Religions* (Minneapolis: Fortress, 2003), 191.

28. Horace, *Saec.* 13–16; cf. *Sat.* 2.6.20–23.

29. A question directed to an oracle: *P. Oxy. 1477 (*Select Papyri,* #195). See also Ramsay MacMullen, *Paganism in the Roman Empire* (New Haven: Yale University Press, 1981), 90.

30. P. Oxy. 1382 (second century), cited from MacMullen, *Paganism,* 178.

31. Pliny the Elder, *Nat. Hist.* 32.113.

32. Horace, *Art of Poetry* 470–72.

33. This is the response of Trimalchio, the garish nouveau-riche freedman in Petronius, *Satyr.* 70. He also marks lucky and unlucky days on his calendar and insists that his guests cross the threshold of his dining room with the right foot; entering with the left is a bad omen (*Satyr.* 30).

34. Cicero, *Nature of the Gods* 1.117; 2.71–72.

35. Horace, *Sat.* 2.281–95.

36. Plutarch, *Mor.* 166A, Superstition 166A.

37. Juvenal, *Sat.* 6.610–14.

38. Pliny, *Ep.* 20.

39. See his *Alexander the False Prophet; The Lover of Lies; The Ship; Menippus, or Descent into Hades,* and scattered references throughout his writings.

40. Valerius Maximus, *Memorable Doings and Sayings* 2.6.7c.

41. *Jub.* 12:20.

42. 1QH 4:24.

43. *4Q544.

44. See *Jub.* 17:16; 18:12; 49:2–4; 48:9.

45. *1 En.* 8:1–2.

46. *1 En.* 10:4–9.

47. *Apoc. Zeph.* 6:11–17.

48. 1QM 9:15–16.

49. *T. Ab.* 13:11.

50. *Jos. Asen.* 15:7–10.

51. 4Q230, 4Q231.

52. E.g., *4 Ezra; Apoc. Mos.* 13; *3 Bar.* 1:1–8.

53. E.g., *Jubilees, 1 Enoch,* and many texts from Qumran, including 4Q387–390 and especially 1QM, "The War Scroll."

54. Philo, *Dreams* 1.141.

55. 1 Cor. 10:20–21; cf. *1 En.* 19; *L.A.B.* 25:9; 2Q23 Frag. 1:7; Ps. 95:5 (LXX).

56. As did Apuleius, recounted in his *Defense.*

57. Horace, *Sat.* 1.111–15.

58. Horace, *Sat.* 1.8.17–22.

59. Philo, *Spec. Laws* 3.101.

60. Suetonius, *Aug.* 31.1; Horace, *Epodes* 17:4–5.

61. *PGMT* 3.495–500.

62. *PGM* LXXII.24–26.

63. Valerius Maximus, *Memorable Doings and Sayings,* 3.3–4; Juvenal, *Sat.* 6.542–47; Lucian, *Gout* 171–73; Celsus in Orgien's *Against Celsus* 1.26.

64. 4Q560; 11Q11 5.4; 4Q444; 4Q561; 4Q186; 4Q318. But the scrolls also contain injunctions against divination and sorcery: CD 12.5; 11Q19 60.18.

65. Juvenal, *Sat.* 6.582–86.

66. See especially 1.4–6 of his *Memorable Doings and Sayings.* As a proud Roman, Valerius Maximus's idealogical agenda is to promote and defend Roman values and imperial policies.

67. Dio Chrysostom, *Or.* 1.52.

68. Horace, *Sat.* 1.9.30–34.

69. See J. B. Ward-Perkins and Amanda Claridge, *Pompeii A.D. 79: Treasures from the National Archaeological Museum, Naples, and the Pompeii Antiquarium* (Boston: Boston Museum of Fine Arts, 1978).

70.*Pseudo-Diogenes, *Epistle 38.2.*

71. Pausanius, *Descr.* 9.39.5–14.

72. Valerius Maximus, *Memorable Doings and Sayings* 1.5.4.

73. Plutarch, *Mor.* 159A, Dinner of the Seven Wise Men.

74. Plutarch, *Mor.* 635E, Table Talk.

75. Pliny, *Ep.* 1.18.1, quoting Homer, *The Iliad* 1.63.

76. Martial, *Ep.* 7.54; 11.49.

77.*P. Par. 47 (*Select Papyri,* #100).

78. Augustine, *Christian Instruction* 2.20.31. Celsus, the second-century opponent of Christianity, argued that a sneeze was sure proof of a prophetic divinity within (Origen, *Against Celsus* 4.94).

79.*Tacitus, *Ann.* 12.64. Similar enumerations are found at 12.43 and 15.47.

80. Suetonius, *Tib.* 69. Josephus also comments on Tiberius's devotion to astrology in *Ant.* 18.216.

81. Our word "mathematics" comes from the Latin word (borrowed from Greek) for astrologer, *mathematicus.*

82. Manilius, *Astr.* 3.47–66.

83. Manilius, *Astr.* 4.114–16.

84. Petronius, *Satyr.* 39.

85. Cicero, *Divination* 2.90.

86. Cicero, *Nature of the Gods* 1.43.

87. Valerius Maximus, *Memorable Doings and Sayings* 1.8 ext. 8.

88. Juvenal, *Sat.* 13.34; see also 2.149–52.

89. Petronius, *Poems* 3.

90. MacMullen, *Paganism,* 62.

91. Dio Chrysostom, *Or.* 12.29; cf. 12.60; 3.51–52.

92. Cicero, *Nature of the Gods* 1.2.

93.*Epictetus, *Disc.* 1.16.15–17.

94. Lucian, *Demonax* 11; Dio Chrysostom, *Or.* 43.11; 75.5; Apuleius, *Defense*; *Mart. Pol.* 12.

95. Gerd Theissen, *Social Reality and the Early Christians: Theology, Ethics, and the World of the New Testament* (Minneapolis: Fortress, 1992), 187.

96. Clinton E. Arnold, "'I Am Astonished That You Are So Quickly Turning Away!' (Gal 1.6): Paul and Anatolian Folk Belief," *NTS* 51 (2005): 429–49.

97. Collected by Georg Petzl in *Die Beichtinschriften Westkleinasiens*, Epigraphica Anatolica 22 (1994), hereafter *BWK*. Analysis is offered by Hans-Josef Klauck, "Die kleinasiatischen Beichtinschriften und das Neue Testament," in *Geschichte—Tradition—Reflexion: Festschrift für Martin Hengel zum 70. Geburtstag: Frühes Christentum* (Tübingen: Mohr Siebeck, 1996).

98. *BWK* 76.

99.*BWK* 34.

100. *BWK* 41. This inscription is dated to 81/82 C.E.

101. Arnold, "Astonished," 440–41.

102. Ibid., 448–49.

103. This is the unanimous witness of the ancient church and remains the most reasonable conclusion from the evidence. See Ben Witherington, *The Acts of the Apostles: A Socio-Rhetorical Commentary* (Grand Rapids, Mich.: Eerdmans, 1998), 51–64; David John Williams, *Acts* (NIBC; Peabody, Mass.: Hendrickson, 1990), 2–11. On the testimony of the ancient church, see C. K. Barrett, *A Critical and Exegetical Commentary on the Acts of the Apostles,* Vol. 1, *I–XIV* (ICC; Edinburgh: T&T Clark, 1994), 30–48.

104. For other contrasts, see Hans-Josef Klauck and Brian McNeil, *Magic and Paganism in Early Christianity: The World of the Acts of the Apostles* (Minneapolis: Fortress, 2003), 17–23.

105. Literally, "son of Jesus." The name Jesus was the Hellenized form of the Hebrew and Aramaic Yeshua (Joshua) and was a common Jewish name.

106. Following Klauck and McNeil, *Magic,* 48.

107. Suetonius, *Tib.* 13, 69; *Nero* 36, 41; *Otho* 6; *Dom.* 15; See also Tacitus, *Ann.* on Otho (1.2) and Vespasian (2.78).

108. Josephus, *Ant.* 20.142.

109. For more on Sergius Paulus and archaeological finds possibly mentioning him, see Rainer Riesner, *Paul's Early Period: Chronology, Mission Strategy, Theology* (Grand Rapids, Mich.: Eerdmans, 1998), 137–46.

110. The term Luke uses for this "place of prayer," *prosuchē,* could refer to a synagogue or simply to a place of prayer.

111. The phrase "[God] Most High," or its equivalent, occurs nearly one hundred times in the Greek version of the OT (e.g., Gen 14:18; Num 24:16; Ps 78:35; Dan 5:18).

112. See Paul Trebilco, "Paul and Silas: 'Servants of the Most High God' (Acts 16:16–18)," *JSNT* 36 (1989): 51–73; Peter Pilhofer, *Die Erste Christliche Gemeinde Europas* (WUNT 87; Tübingen: Mohr, 1995), 182–86; Richard S. Ascough, *Paul's Macedonian Associations: The Social Context of Philippians and 1 Thessalonians* (WUNT 2.161; Tübingen: Mohr Siebeck, 2003), 158, 195–200; Witherington, *Acts,* 494–95.

113. Pilhofer, *Gemeinde,* 184; Colin H. Roberts, T. C. Skeat, and Arthur Darby Nock, "The Guild of Zeus Hypsistos," *HTR* 29 (1936): 72.

114. Cited in Pilhofer, *Gemeinde,* 186.

115. See especially Clinton E. Arnold, *Ephesians, Power and Magic: The Concept of Power in Ephesians in Light of Its Historical Setting* (Cambridge: Cambridge University Press, 1989); Paul Trebilco, "Asia," in *The Book of Acts in Its Graeco-Roman Setting* (ed. David Gill and Conrad Gempf; Grand Rapids, Mich.: Eerdmans, 1994).

116. On the *Ephesia Grammata,* see John G. Gager, ed., *Curse Tablets and Binding Spells from the Ancient World* (New York: Oxford University Press, 1992), 5–7.

117. See Marvin W. Meyer and Richard Smith, *Ancient Christian Magic: Coptic Texts of Ritual Power* (San Francisco: Harper, 1994).

118. Pliny the Younger, *Ep.Tra.* 10.96.

119. Paul uses this language to refer to the demonic realm also in Rom 8:38; 1 Cor 15:24; Eph 3:10; Col 1:16; 2:10, 15. Some would also include 1 Cor 2:6–8, but this text more likely refers to the human authorities responsible for Jesus' crucifixion (v. 8).

120. The Greek word Paul uses, *ekstasis* (cf. "ecstasy") refers to "a state of being in which consciousness is wholly or partially suspended" (BDAG, s.v.).

121. Here I draw on Christian Dietzfelbinger, *Die Berufung Des Paulus Als Ursprung Seiner Theologie* (Neukirchen-Vluyn: Neukirchener, 1985), 64–75.

122. Following Bernhard Heininger, *Paulus Als Visionär: Eine Religionsgeschichtliche Studie* (New York: Herder, 1996).

NOTES TO PART 2: EDUCATION, PHILOSOPHY, AND ORATORY

1. For example, Pakistan has a literacy rate of 49%, Chad 26%, and Niger 14%, as reported by UNESCO (unesco.org, accessed October 1, 2008). It should be noted, however, that most informed observers believe that even these rates are optimistic, being based solely on the reporting of the country itself.

2. For more detailed discussion, consult William V. Harris, *Ancient Literacy* (Cambridge, Mass.: Harvard University Press, 1989), 3–24.

3. Pliny, *Ep.* 4.13. Comum was Pliny's home town and frequently benefited from his generosity.

4. Apuleius, *Flor.* 20.

5. For a complete description of education in the Roman world, see Stanley F. Bonner, *Education in Ancient Rome: From the Elder Cato to the Younger Pliny* (London: Methuen, 1977) and Henri Irénée Marrou, *A History of Education in Antiquity* (Wisconsin Studies in Classics; Madison: University of Wisconsin Press, 1982). My brief presentation here relies on their detailed analyses.

6. Suetonius, *Gramm.* 7, 17; Pliny, *Ep.* 3.3. Quintilian (*Inst.* 1.2) offers a lengthy protest against the practice of hiring a private tutor, which is some attestation to its prevalence.

7. Martial, *Ep.* 10.68.

8. Suetonius, *Gramm.* 15; Dio Chrysostom, *Or.* 20.9–10.

9. Pseudo-Diogenes, *Epistle 8.*

10. See Suetonius, *Gramm.* 12, and 9, respectively.

11. See Suetonius, *Gramm.* 18, 22, and 23, respectively.

12. Petronius, *Satyr.* 58–59; 75, citing 46.

13. Or so Suetonius reports (*Gramm.* 23). Large classes are implied in the remarks of Pliny, *Ep.* 2.18, and Juvenal, *Sat.* 7.150–55, 240–41.

14. Suetonius, *Gramm.* 8, 9, 20, 11, respectively.

15. *Greek Anthology* 9.169. The opening line of *The Iliad,* the primary textbook of the *grammaticus,* begins with the line "Sing, goddess, of the wrath of Achilles!" For other writers, see Martial, *Ep.* 10.60, and the examples cited in Bonner, *Education,* 131–32.

16. A concise treatment can be found in Ronald F. Hock, "Paul and Greco-Roman Education," in *Paul in the Greco-Roman World: A Handbook* (ed. J. Paul Sampley; Harrisburg, Pa.: Trinity Press International, 2003), 201–4.

17. *Greek Anthology* 11.322.

18. *Greek Anthology* 11.138. See also 11.321, 347.

19. Suetonius, *Gramm.* 22. The epic poets fared no better; see Aulus Gellius, *Attic Nights* 2.6; 2.16.

20. Pliny, *Ep.* 2.18.

21. Horace, *Sat.* 1.1.25–26. Similarly, Suetonius refers to the *grammaticus* Marcus Antonius Gnipho as "kind and good natured" (*Gramm.* 7).

22. Horace, *Ep.* 2.1.70.

23. Quintilian, *Inst.*1.3.15–18.

24. Apuleius, *Flor.* 12.

25. This image is reproduced in Bonner, *Education,* 118.

26. Martial, *Ep.* 9.68.1–5; cf. 8.3.15–16; 9.29.7.

27. *Greek Anthology* 11.279, alluding again to *The Iliad.*

28. Seneca (the Younger), *Ep.* 94.9.

29. A full discussion of the *progymnasmata* can be found in George A. Kennedy, *A New History of Classical Rhetoric* (Princeton: Princeton University Press, 1994), 201–29. A more concise treatment is offered by Hock, "Education," 204–8.

30. So Vipstanus Messala in Tacitus's *Dialogue on Oratory* 35: "Two kinds of subject-matter are dealt with by the rhetoricians, the persuasive [*suasoriae*] and the controversial [*controversiae*]. The persuasive, being comparatively easy and requiring less skill, is given to boys."

31. Seneca the Elder, *Suas.* 1.

32. Seneca the Elder, *Suas.* 2.

33. Seneca the Elder, *Suas.* 7.

34. Dio Chrysostom, *Or.* 11, "The Trojan Discourse."

35. Suetonius, *Rhet.* 1.

36. Seneca the Elder, *Contr.* 1.6. For a more optimistic appraisal of the practical legal issues underlying the *controversiae,* see Bonner, *Education,* 309–27.

37.*Quintilian, *Inst.* 2.10.8; similar comments at 2.20.1–5.

38.*Petronius, *Satyr.* 1. See also Tacitus, *Dial.* 35; Juvenal, *Sat.* 7.150–70.

39. Bonner, *Education,* 310.

40. *Greek Anthology* 11.41; cf. 11.42–44; Martial, *Ep.* 6.19; Persius, *Sat.* 1.83–98; Lucian, *A Professor of Public Speaking* 16. Favorinus leveled a similar criticism at orators who used archaic terminology merely to impress their hearers, according to Aulus Gellius, *Attic Nights* 1.10.

41. Although criticism of the sophists and sophism is scattered throughout Plato's *Dialogues* and *The Republic,* particularly important are *Phaedrus, Meno, Euthydemus, Protagoras, Gorgias,* and *Sophist.* For a concise summary of Plato's critique, see Duane Litfin, *St. Paul's Theology of Proclamation: 1 Corinthians 1–4 and Greco-Roman Rhetoric* (SNTSMS 79; Cambridge: Cambridge University Press, 1994), 49–59.

42. Plato, *Meno* 92A; Plato, *Protag.* 309D; Plato, *Euthyd.* 305D. In *Euthydemus,* Socrates sarcastically refers to the sophists Euthydemus and Dionysodorus as "absolutely omniscient" (271C).

43. Plato, *Soph.* 217C; Plato, *Phaedr.* 274C–277A; Plato, *Protag.* 334C–338E.

44. Plato, *Protag.* 310D; *Meno* 91B–E.

45. Litfin, *Proclamation,* 52–53.

46. Plato, *Phaedr.* 271D.

47. Plato, *Phaedr.* 273E.

48. Plato, *Phaedr.* 270E.

49. The best treatment of the Second Sophistic remains that of G. W. Bowersock, *Greek Sophists in the Roman Empire* (Oxford: Clarendon, 1969).

50. Philostratus, *Vit. soph.* 181.

51. Dio Chrysostom, *Or.* 4.14.

52. Philo, *Agriculture* 143.

53. Tacitus, *Dial.* 5.

54. Lucian, *A Professor of Public Speaking* 1.

55. Philostratus, *Vit. soph.* 488. See also his comments on Nicetes and Nero (512), Scopelian and Domitian (520), Polemo and Hadrian (531), Aristides and Marcus Aurelius (582–83), and so on. Dio Chrysostom was not a sophist per se but was such an eloquent philosopher that he struggled to distinguish himself from this group. He would not have approved of Philostratus including him in his biography of the sophists (*Vit. soph.* 487–488).

56. Described by Philostratus in *Vit. soph.* 489.

57. Plutarch, *Mor.* 543E–543F, On Praising Oneself Inoffensively; cf. 45A–C, F, On Listening to Lectures.

58. Apuleius, *Flor.* 18.

59. Apuleius, *Flor.* 9.

60. Apuleius, *Flor.* 9.

61. In Dio Chrysostom, *Or.* 37.26.

62. Plato, *In Defense of Oratory* 193.

63. Philostratus, *Vit. soph.* 616.

64. Persius, *Sat.* 1.96–97.

65. Epictetus, *Disc.* 3.23.26. That sophistry is the intended target of this has been established by Bruce W. Winter, *Philo and Paul among the Sophists: Alexandrian and Corinthian Responses to a Julio-Claudian Movement* (2d ed.; Grand Rapids, Mich.: Eerdmans, 2002).

66. Epictetus, *Disc.* 3.32.7.

67. Epictetus, *Disc.* 3.23.30–32. The philosopher as physician was a common image: Musonius Rufus, *Disc.* 1; Dio Chrysostom, *Or.* 8.5; 32.10; 33:6; Seneca (the Younger), *Ep.* 75; 123.17; Epictetus, *Disc.* 3.23.27–32; Horace, *Ep.* 1.1.33–40.

68. Epictetus, *Disc.* 3.23.16.

69. Epictetus, *Disc.* 3.23.38.

70. Epictetus, *Disc.* 3.23.19–20, 23–24.

71. Philostratus, *Vit. soph.* 582.

72. Epictetus, *Disc.* 3.23.19.

73. Pliny, *Ep.* 2.14.4–8.

74. Epictetus, *Disc.* 3.23.29; cf. 1.23.37. Similar sentiments are found in Musonius Rufus, *Disc.* 48, 49, and Seneca (the Younger), *Ep.* 52.9.

75. Epictetus, *Disc.* 3.23.34–35.

76. Compare Musonius Rufus, *Disc.* 19 and 21 on the same subject.

77. Epictetus, *Disc.* 3.1.1.

78. Epictetus, *Disc.* 3.1.14, 27–35.

79. Tacitus, *Dial.* 26.

80. Lucian, *A Professor of Public Speaking* 16.

81. Lucian, *A Professor of Public Speaking* 15.

82. Apuleius, *Flor.* 3. Compare his description of the sophist Hippias, who arrived at the Olympian games "in raiment that was remarkable to the eye," including spectacular jewels, gold rings, a colorful belt imported from Babylon, and an exquisite gown and undershirt (*Flor.* 9).

83. Dio Chrysostom, *Or.* 12.5.

84. Juvenal, *Sat.* 7.145.

85. Apuleius, *Defense* 4–6, 13. Philostratus tells the story of the shabby Aristocles who, upon converting from philosophy to sophistry, became a veritable Beau Brummel (*Vit. soph.* 567).

86. Seneca (the Younger), *Ep.* 108.7.

87. Apuleius, *Flor.* 11, concerning poverty, and *Flor.* 20, concerning wealth.

88. Apuleius, *Flor.* 9, 16, 18, and 20.

89. Philostratus, *Vit. soph.* 607.

90. Tacitus, *Dial.* 26. Similarly, Plutarch contrasts the sober instruction of the philosopher with the theatrical manner of the sophist and warns, "Students must remember they have not come to a theater or a musical hall, but to a school" (*Mor.* 42A, On Listening to Lectures).

91. Plutarch *Mor.* 7A, The Education of Children.

92. Pliny, *Ep.* 3.15.3–4. Dio Chrysostom makes the same criticism of sophists in *Or.* 12.9–11, though more pointedly and in greater detail.

93. Plutarch, *Mor.* 42E, On Listening to Lectures.

94. Plutarch, *Mor.* 41D, On Listening to Lectures.

95. "Sophistry," "Sophist," *Merriam-Webster's Collegiate Dictionary*, 10th ed., 1993.

96. In Aulus Gellius, *Attic Nights* 1.6.4.

97. E.g., Epictetus, *Disc.* 1.27, 3.8, 4.5; Lucian, *The Runaways* 10–11; *A Professor of Public Speaking* (passim); Dio Chrysostom, *Or.* 3.27, 4.33, 6.21–24; Valerius Maximus, *Memorable Doings and Sayings* 1.8. ext. 8; Apuleius, *Flor.* 18; Plutarch, *Mor.* 41B, On Listening to Lectures; 158B, Dinner of the Seven Wise Men.

98. Philo, *Cherubim* 9. cf. *Worse* 72.

99. Philo, *Posterity* 101.

246   Notes to Pages 81–85

100. Philo, *Worse* 71–74; *Dreams* 2.40; *Posterity* 86.

101. Philo, *Questions on Genesis* 2.27; 3.33; *Moses* 2.212; *Husbandry* 159; *Heir* 246; *Names* 10; *Worse* 71.

102. Philo, *Allegorical Interpretation* 3.232; *Contemplative Life* 31; *Posterity* 86; *Migration* 72.

103. Philo, *Creation* 46; *Cherubim* 9; *Questions on Genesis* 3.33; *Worse* 73.

104. See, respectively, Philo, *Cherubim* 9; *Worse* 71; *Allegorical Interpretation* 3.232; *Migration* 76 (cf. 82–85); *Husbandry* 96.

105. Philo, *Heir* 85.

106. Philo, *Questions on Genesis* 2.27.

107. Philo, *Husbandry* 136.

108. Philo, *Husbandry* 159; cf. *Posterity* 101; *Migration* 76; *Cherubim* 9.

109. Philo, *Dreams* 2.40; cf. *Names* 240.

110. Lucian, *The Double Indictment* 6. See also Lucian's *The Runaways, Philosophies for Sale, The Carousal, or the Lapiths,* and *The Dead Come to Life, or the Fisherman.*

111. Diogenes Laertius's *Lives of Eminent Philosophers* provides a useful ancient account of the history and development of the philosophical schools. A more accessible summary is found in Everett Ferguson, *Backgrounds of Early Christianity* (3d ed.; Grand Rapids, Mich.: Eerdmans, 2003), 319–95.

112. Persius, *Sat.* 5.104. Similarly Musonius Rufus: "how to lead good lives, which is precisely the study of philosophy" (*Disc.* 3).

113. Plutarch, *Mor.* 7DE, Education of Children.

114. Apuleius, *Defense* 16.

115. Seneca (the Younger)'s *Letters to Lucillius* are the quintessential example of the philosopher as psychagogue.

116. Musonius Rufus, *Disc.* 4.

117. A. A. Long, "Roman Philosophy," in *The Cambridge Companion to Greek and Roman Philosophy* (ed. D. N. Sedley; Cambridge: Cambridge University Press, 2003), 192.

118. Seneca (the Younger), *Ep.* 13.15.

119. Tertullian, *The Soul* 20.

120. Jerome, *Adversus Jovinianum* 1.49.

121. This belief was reinforced by a collection of spurious letters between Paul and Seneca that circulated widely in the early centuries of the Christian era.

122. Seneca (the Younger), *Ep.* 44.2–3.

123. A. A. Long, "Socrates in Hellenistic Philosophy," in *Stoic Studies* (Berkeley: University of California Press, 2001), 1–34.

124. Dio Chrysostom, *Or.* 51.1, 8.

125. Epictetus, *Disc.* 4.5.1.

126. Epictetus, *Disc.* 3.24.40.

127. Cicero, *Nature of the Gods* 2.22, 30, 47, spoken by Lucilius Balbus, Cicero's Stoic spokesman.

128. One scholar uses the phrase "emerging monotheistic pantheism" to describe Stoicism of the Hellenistic and Roman eras. See Paul Wendland, *Die Hellenistisch-Römische Kultur in Ihren Beziehungen Zu Judentum Und Christentum. Die Urchristlichen Literaturformen* (Tübingen: Mohr, 1912), 111.

129. Epictetus, *Ench.* 53.

130. Epictetus, *Disc.* 4.7.15.

131. Dio Chrysostom, *Or.* 8.15; cf. Epictetus, *Disc.* 30.2–3.

132. Arius Didymus, *Epitome* 5a.

133. Seneca (the Younger), *Ep.* 92.11.

134. E.g., Arius Didymus, *Epitome* 5b1; 5b3, 5b5; Musonius Rufus, *Disc.* 14, 17, 19; Epictetus, *Disc.* 1.4.14, 18; 1.11; 1.15; 3.3.1–10; 3.24.1–8.

135. Epictetus, *Disc.* 2.19.23–24.

136. "Stoic," *Merriam-Webster's Collegiate Dictionary,* 10th ed., 1993.

137. Diogenes Laertius, *Lives* 7.116.

138. Seneca (the Younger), *Ep.* 9.

139. Seneca (the Younger), *Ep.* 116.1, 3. See also *Ep.* 85.

140. Epictetus, *Disc.* 1.11.

141. Epictetus, *Disc.* 3.24.14.

142. Epictetus, *Disc.* 3.24.18–19, slightly paraphrased.

143. Seneca (the Younger), *Ep.* 104.11; see also *Ep.* 63.

144. Epictetus, *Disc.* 4.1.

145. Juvenal says of Stoics and Cynics that "they differ only by a shirt" (*Sat.* 13.121–22), referring to the Cynics' practice of going without a tunic.

146. Lucian's Cynic spokesman in *Demonax,* 23.

147. Versions of this meeting can be found in Plutarch, *Alexander* 13.1–3; Diogenes Laertius, *Lives of Eminent Philosophers* 6.38; Pseudo-Diogenes, *Epistle 33.*

148. Pseudo-Diogenes, *Epistle 44.*

149. *Pseudo-Diogenes, *Epistle 26;* cf. ibid., *Epistles 10, 36;* Pseudo-Heraclitus, *Epistle 4;* Pseudo-Socrates, *Epistle 28.* Lucian's wry caricature of the Cynic's admiration of Herakles hits the mark: *Philosophies for Sale 7–8.*

150. *Greek Anthology 11.155. See also Dio Chrysostom's description of Diogenes in *Or.* 6.17–20. The milder Cynics would not have approved of lewd or crass behavior in public.

151. Pseudo-Diogenes, *Epistle 10.*

152. *Greek Anthology,* 11.153; cf. 11:154, 156; Martial, *Ep.* 4.53.

153. Epicurus, *Letter to Menoeceus,* in Diogenes Laertius, *Lives* 10.128.

154. Diogenes Laertius, *Lives* 10.137.

155. Diogenes Laertius, *Lives* 10.137.

156. Epicurus, *Letter to Menoeceus,* in Diogenes Laertius, *Lives* 10.129.

157. Epicurus, *Letter to Menoeceus,* in Diogenes Laertius, *Lives* 10.130–32.

158. Dio Chrysostom, *Or.* 12.36. Cf. Cicero, *Nature of the Gods* 1.113; Cicero, *Red. sen.* 14–15; Horace, *Ep.* 1.4.56–66; Lucian, *Philosophies for Sale* 19; Petronius, *Satyr.* 132.

159. Philodemus, *Epig.* 13. Sexual desire, which Philodemus calls "madness" (*mania*), is a constant theme of these epigrams. See Philodemus and David Sider, *The Epigrams of Philodemos* (New York: Oxford University Press, 1996).

160. Philodemus, *Epig.* 6.

161. Epicurus, *Letter to Herodotus* in Diogenes Laertius, *Lives* 10.81; *Principal Doctrines* 11–13 in Diogenes Laertius, *Lives* 10.142–43.

162. Cicero, *Nature of the Gods* 1.123. See also Lucian, *Philosophies for Sale* 19; Dio Chyrsostom, *Or.* 12.37; Epictetus, *Disc.* 2.20.22–23.

163. Epicurus, *Principal Doctrines* 2 in Diogenes Laertius, *Lives* 10.139.

164. See Ferguson, *Backgrounds*, 299–371.

165. Lucian, *Nigrinus* 35. It is unclear if this depiction is autobiographical or if Lucian's use of the first person is a literary device.

166. See, for example, Pseudo-Diogenes, *Epistle 31*; ibid., *Epistle 38.25*; Musonius Rufus, *Disc.* 16, 18–20; Lucian, *Philosophies for Sale* 9; *Double Indictment* 6; Epictetus, *Disc.* 3.3.5–10; Suetonius, *Gramm.* 18.

167. Apuleius, *Flor.* 14; Pseudo-Diogenes, *Epistle 9*.

168. Epictetus, *Disc.* 3.22.38–49; 3.24.58–77; Lucian, *Nigrinus* 1–4; Seneca (the Younger), *Ep.* 37.3–4; Dio Chrysostom, *Or.* 13.13; Horace, *Ep.* 1.1.106.

169. Lucian, *The Downward Journey, or The Tyrant* 24.

170. Seneca (the Younger), *Ep.* 6.1.

171. Valerius Maximus, *Memorable Doings and Sayings* 3.3 ext. 1.

172. Horace, *Ep.* 1.1.33–37.

173. For more detail see Cohen, "Crossing the Boundary," 14–33.

174. *Jos. Asen.* 8:9.

175. Apuleius, *Metam.* 11.21.

176. Apuleius, *Metam.* 11.25.

177. On which see E. Randolph Richards, *Paul and First-Century Letter Writing: Secretaries, Composition, and Collection* (Downers Grove, Ill.: InterVarsity Press, 2004).

178. On the form of Paul's letters, see M. Luther Stirewalt, *Paul, the Letter Writer* (Grand Rapids, Mich.: Eerdmans, 2003), who argues that Paul intentionally adapted the official administrative letter format.

179. In the Mishnah, a third-century compilation of earlier Jewish traditions, Gamaliel is one of the leading authorities commonly cited.

180. Martin Hengel and Roland Denies lay out the evidence for a basic level of rhetorical training in the Hellenistic synagogues of Jerusalem in *The Pre-Christian Paul* (Philadelphia: Trinity Press International, 1991), 56–72.

181. Bruce W. Winter, "Rhetoric," in *Dictionary of Paul and His Letters* (ed. Gerald F. Hawthorne, Ralph P. Martin, and Daniel G. Reid; Downers Grove, Ill.: InterVarsity Press, 1993), 820–22.

182. This speech is passed down to us under Dio Chyrsostom's name. See Dio Chrysostom, *Or.* 37.27.

183. Philostratus, *Vit. soph.* 481.

184. Pliny, *Ep.* 1.22.23.

185. Herodes Atticus, the famous second-century orator and student of Favorinus, donated the theater. The orators mentioned in the inscriptions from Corinth include Herodes Attiicus, Publius Aelius Sospinus, Maecius Faustinus, Marcus Valerius Taurinus, and Poseidonius. See Kent nos. 128, 226, 264, 268, 269, 307.

186. Dio Chrysostom, *Or.* 8.9.

187. Maxiums of Tyre, *Disc.* 36, cited in Abraham J. Malherbe, *Moral Exhortation: A Greco-Roman Sourcebook* (Philadelphia: Westminster Press, 1986), 73–79.

188. Plutarch, *Mor.* 45E, On Listening to Lectures. For numerous examples of the picayune nature of this criticism peruse the essays of Aulus Gellius in *Attic Nights.*

189. Martial, *Ep.* 10.65. In addition to his dress, his deliberately affected speech, which Martial mocks, is further indication that Charmenion is an orator.

190. Juvenal, *Sat.* 8.111–15.

191. Cited in John Piper, *The Supremacy of God in Preaching* (Grand Rapids, Mich.: Baker, 1990), 55.

192. In the Cynic epistles, for example, we find the belief that souls wander the earth after death (Pseudo-Diogenes, *Epistle 25;* ibid., *Epistle 39.2*), that the evil are punished in the afterlife (Pseudo-Diogenes, *Epistle 45*), and that some philosophers, notably Socrates, attain blissful immortality among the stars (Pseudo-Socrates, *Epistle 25.1;* cf. ibid., *Epistle 14.6–7.*

193. Valerius Maximus, *Memorable Doings and Sayings* 2.6.10.

194. For example, banquet scenes (Pilhofer, 510/G213), the deceased as a horseman (Thracian rider) ascending to immortality (Pilhofer 029/G215; 555/G518; 597/G211), or references to the deceased joining the divinized "heros" (Pilhofer 390/G571; 538/G529; 547/G524).

195. On burial practices in Roman Corinth, see Mary E. Hoskins Walbank, "Unquiet Graves: Burial Practices of the Roman Corinthians," in *Urban Religion in Roman Corinth: Interdisciplinary Approaches* (ed. Daniel N. Schowalter and Steven J. Friesen; Cambridge, Mass.: Harvard University Press, 2005), 249–80; Christine M. Thomas, "Placing the Dead: Funerary Practice and Social Stratification in the Early Roman Period at Corinth and Ephesos," in *Urban Religion in Roman Corinth: Interdisciplinary Approaches* (ed. Daniel N. Schowalter and Steven J. Friesen; Cambridge, Mass.: Harvard University Press, 2005), 281–304.

196. Petronius, *Satyr.* 71.

197. Apuleius, *Metam.* 6.5. Elysium or the Elysian fields is a mythical paradise where noble souls reside after death.

198. Pliny the Elder, *Nat. Hist.* 7.189–190.

199. E.g., Ignatius, *To the Smyrneans* 3; *2 Clem.* 9.1–3; Tatian, *To the Greeks* 6; Theophilus, 1.13; Athenagoras, *On the Resurrection;* Tertullian, *On the Resurrection.*

200. Cited in Ramsay MacMullen, "Two Types of Conversion in Early Christianity," *Vigiliae Christianae* 37 (1983): 182.

201. Philo, *Creation* 135; Wis 3; 4 Macc 18:23.

202. Cf. Matt 17:22–23; 1 Cor 15:12–58; 2 Macc 7:14; *2 Bar.* 49–51.

203. Pliny, *Ep.* 1.12.13.

204. For example, Dio Chrysostom, *Or.* 16, "On Pain and Distress of Spirit;" Musonius Rufus, *Disc. 7*, "That One Should Disdain Hardship"; Epictetus, *Disc.* 1. 24, "How Should We Struggle against Difficulties"; Seneca (the Younger), *On Constancy; Ep.* 62, "On Ill-health and the Endurance of Suffering"; *Ep.* 96, "On Facing Hardship," etc.

205. Arius Didymus, *Epitome* 11.g.

206. Musonius Rufus, *Disc.* 9.

207. Epictetus, *Disc.* 1.1.8–13; Musonius Rufus, *Disc.* 3; Seneca (the Younger), *Ep.* 124.

208. Seneca (the Younger), *Ep.* 124.

209. Epictetus, *Disc.* 2.18.8.

210. Dio Chrysostom, *Or.* 32.16.

211. Epictetus, *Ench.* 5.

212. Epictetus, *Disc.* 1.11.37; cf. 4.1.68–75.

213. Epictetus, *Disc.* 2.2.39.

214. Epictetus, *Disc.* 4.1.111–112.

215. Epictetus, *Disc.* 2.18.19–23; cf. Seneca (the Younger), *Ep.* 37.

216. Epictetus, *Disc.* 2.25.

217. Seneca (the Younger), *Ep.* 9.8.

218. Epictetus does hint at the prospect of divine help in moral progress (e.g., *Disc.* 2.8.1; 2.18.29), but the idea plays no real role in his philosophy of spiritual development.

219. E.g., *The Republic; Protagoras; Crito.* On the cardinal virtues of Hellenistic philosophy and the priority of justice, see Troels Engberg-Pedersen, "The Relationship with Others: Similarities and Differences between Paul and Stoicism," *Zeitschrift für die neutestamentliche Wissenschaft und die Kunde der Älteren Kirche* 96 (2005): 35–60.

220. As noted earlier (see Education, Philosophy, and Oratory: Philosophical Schools), while Socrates founded no school of philosophy, the Stoics claimed him as their patron saint and believed their philosophy most faithfully represented the Socratic tradition.

221. This portrait of Socrates' death is presented by Plato in *The Apology* and *Crito.* It is frequently developed by first-century Stoics and Cynics: Epictetus, *Disc.* 1.9.23–26; 3.1.19–23; Seneca (the Younger), *Ep.* 24.4; 70.9; 104.27–28; Dio Chrysostom, *Or.* 31.9–10; Pseudo-Socrates 21.3.

222. Musonius Rufus, *Disc.* 28, 29, 35; Seneca (the Younger), *Ep.* 70; 61.2; cf. Publillius Syrus, *Sententiae* 63, 95, 96, 105, 243, etc.

223. Epictetus, *Disc.* 4.1; Seneca (the Younger), *Ep.* 24.4.

224. The Greek word Paul uses, *dikaiosunē*, is normally translated "righteousness" but is the same word used for "justice" in Greek philosophy.

NOTES TO PART 3: CITY AND SOCIETY

1. Both C. H. Dodd, *New Testament Studies* (1st ed.; Manchester: Manchester University Press, 1967), 70–73, and Wayne A. Meeks, *The First Urban Christians: The Social World of the Apostle Paul* (New Haven: Yale University Press, 1983), 9–10, come to similar conclusions.

2. Virgil, *Aeneid* 6.790; see also his *Eclogue* 4.

3. From a decree issued by the Provincial Assembly of Asia (9 B.C.E.); cited in Frederick C. Grant, *Ancient Roman Religion* (New York: Liberal Arts, 1957), 174.

4. On brigandage in the New Testament era, see Ramsay MacMullen, *Enemies of the Roman Order: Treason, Unrest, and Alienation in the Empire* (Cambridge, Mass.: Harvard University Press, 1967), 255–68.

5. Epictetus, *Disc.* 3.13.9. Cf. Philo, *Embassy* 145–47.

6. Epictetus, *Disc.* 4.1.91–92. According to the Cynic epistles, Socrates' guiding spirit protected him from roads where robbers lurked (Pseudo-Socrates, 1.16–35).

7. Plutarch, *Mor.* 165D, On Superstition.

8. Petronius, *Satyr.* 80; cf. Josephus, *J.W.* 2.125.

9. Lionel Casson, *Travel in the Ancient World* (Baltimore: Johns Hopkins University Press, 1994), 179.

10. Ibid., 181.

11.*Horace, *Sat.* 1.6.100–104.

12. F. F. Bruce, "Travel and Communication: The New Testament World," in *Anchor Bible Dictionary* (ed. David Noel Freedman; Garden City, N.Y.: Doubleday, 1992), 50.

13. Horace, *Sat.* 5; Plutarch (*Mor.* 148A, Dinner of the Seven Wise Men) mentions travelers using a tent when necessary.

14. See Petronius, *Satyr.* 16–20 (promiscuity); 21, (thievery), 94–96 (brawling); Valerius Maximus, *Memorable Doings and Sayings,* 1.7 ext. 10 (murder). See Casson, *Travel,* 197–218.

15. Summarized by Casson, *Travel,* 207–13.

16. *CIL* 4.4957; cf. Casson's more graphic rendering in *Travel,* 209.

17. Josephus, *Ant.* 12.276; cf. Martial, *Ep.* 1.56; 3.57.

18. P. Oxy. 292 (*Select Papyri* no. 106), about 25 c.e.

19. Pseudo-Diogenes, *Epistle 48;* cf. Pseudo-Socrates, *Epistle 2.*

20. Full details on seafaring in antiquity can be found in Lionel Casson, *Ships and Seamanship in the Ancient World* (Baltimore: Johns Hopkins University Press, 1995); more briefly in Casson, *Travel,* 149–62.

21. Horace, *Sat.* 5.14–17.

22. The NIV translation of Acts 27:30 mentions the lowering of a lifeboat, which is a misleading rendering. The Greek term *skaphē* denotes a dinghy or skiff used for a variety of purposes but not primarily as a lifeboat in the modern sense. See Casson, *Ships,* 329–43.

23. Dio Chrysostom, *Or.* 7.2; Acts 27:39.

24. Josephus, *Life* 13–15; Acts 27:43–44.

25. *Greek Anthology* 6.166; cf. 6.164.

26. Petronius, *Poems* 31; Plutarch, *Mor.* 165D–E, Superstition; Horace, *Sat.* 1.1.6–8; *Ps. Sol.* 6.3; Horace, *Art of Poetry* 20–21.

27. Seneca (the Younger), *Ep.* 59.51; Persius, *Sat.* 1.86–92; Publilius Syrus, *Sententiae* 331; Petronius, *Poems* 14, 19; Juvenal, *Sat.* 14.298–302.

28. Juvenal, *Sat.* 14.295–97.

29. Petronius, *Poems* 15.

30. Petronius, *Satyr.* 103; Plutarch, *Mor.* 664C, Table Talk.

31. Philodemus, *Epig.* 34.

32. *OGIS* 74 (in *New Documents,* 4.26).

33. Craig Steven De Vos, *Church and Community Conflicts: The Relationships of the Thessalonian, Corinthian, and Philippian Churches with Their Wider Civic Communities* (Atlanta: Scholars Press, 1999), 109–10.

34. A. H. M. Jones, *The Greek City from Alexander to Justinian* (Oxford: Clarendon, 1998), 170–73.

35. De Vos, *Church and Community Conflicts,* 110; John E. Stambaugh and David L. Balch, *The New Testament in Its Social Environment* (Library of Early Christianity; Philadelphia: Westminster Press, 1986), 20.

36. Apuleius, *Metam.* 10.18 (see 4.13–14).

37. Kent no. 232.

38. Especially enlightening in this regard is Ramsay MacMullen, *Paganism in the Roman Empire* (New Haven: Yale University Press, 1981), 34–48.

39. Pilhofer, 022/G220.

40. Cicero, *Nature of the Gods* 1.82, in Cotta's critique of Epicureanism. See also Horace, *Sat.* 1.3.16–17; Juvenal, *Sat.* 14.261–62; Pseudo-Heraclitus, *Epistle 4,* 1; ibid., *Epistle 7,* 4; ; Lucian, *Toxaris.* 28; *SIG* 997 (*New Documents* 4.25).

41. Juvenal, *Sat.* 14.256–60; *P. Oxy.* 269; 91 (*Select Papyri* 69; 79).

42. Dio Chrysostom, *Or.* 2.34–35.

43. His *Descriptions of Greece* spans ten volumes. Almost as useful in depicting the artwork of ancient temples is Pliny the Elder's *Natural History,* book 35, which describes painting and portraiture in antiquity.

44. In *Toxaris* 6, Lucian demonstrates the educational value of religious artwork in temples. Pausanias's description of the ivory, bronze, and gold statuary of the temple of Poseidon near Corinth suggests it was intended as a mere display of the wealth (*Descr.* 1.7–9).

45. On libraries associated with temples, see Horace, *Ep.* 1.3.15–17; 2.2.90–92. Apuleius describes a temple scribe of Isis in *Metam.* 11.17. On poets reciting at temples, see Horace, *Sat.* 1.10.36–39; Petronius, *Satyr.* 90.

46. Pliny the Elder, *Nat. Hist.* 28.3.10.

47. Erich Lessing and Antonio Varone, *Pompeii* (Paris: Terrail, 2000), 44–45.

48. *I. Eph.* 1a. 10 (in *New Documents* 4.25).

49. Lucian, *The Dance* 15–16.

50. Ignatius, *Rom.* 2.2.

51. MacMullen, *Paganism,* 36–37, and notes.

52. A full *triclinium* (dining room) was nine guests, three per couch (Horace, *Sat.* 1.4.85–90); Cicero suggests that four or five guests per couch constituted a crowded party (*Pis.* 27.67). Both references, however, refer to homes of the upper classes with separate dining rooms. Most domiciles were far more modest.

53. Pausanius, *Descr.* 2.32.1.

54. James Wiseman, "Corinth and Rome I: 228 B.C.–A.D. 267," *Aufstieg und Niedergang der Römischen Welt* 2.7.1 (1979): 509–11.

55. Groves and gardens attached to temples are common (e.g., Pliny the Elder, *Nat. Hist.* 16.213; Martial, *Ep.* 1.12; Horace, *Art of Poetry,* 14–20; Pausanias, *Descr.* 2.27.1), and Wiseman suggest this likelihood for the temple of Demeter and Kore on the Acrocorinth ("Corinth and Rome," 509).

56. Pausanius, *Desc.* 2.27.1.

57. *New Documents* 1.5. The Thoereion was probably a banquet room connected to the temple of Isis or Serapis.

58. Dio Chrysostom, *Or.* 27.6.

59. Plutarch, *Mor.* 169D, Superstition.

60. See John Fotopoulos, *Food Offered to Idols in Roman Corinth: A Social-Rhetorical Reconsideration of 1 Corinthians 8:1–11:1* (WUNT 2.151; Tübingen: Mohr Siebeck, 2003), 158–78.

61. Quintilian, *Inst.* 1.2.

62. E.g., Martial, *Ep.* 1.27; 3.88; 5.78.

63. Pseudo-Heraclitus, *Epistle 7,* 5–8; Aulus Gellius, *Attic Nights* 19.9.1–5; Petronius, *Satyr.* 17, 21, 67; Philodemus, *Epig.* 6.

64. Depicted in Katherine M. D. Dunbabin, *The Roman Banquet: Images of Conviviality* (New York: Cambridge University Press, 2003), plates I–III.

65. Pseudo-Diogenes, *Epistle 28.4.*

66. Kent no. 155.

67.*In Barbara Levick, *The Government of the Roman Empire: A Sourcebook* (2d ed.; New York: Routledge, 2000), no. 14.

68.*Pilhofer 241/L466.

69.*In Levick, *Government,* no. 102.

70. First-century inscription from Baetica (southern Spain), in Levick, *Government,* no. 28.

71. In Levick, *Government,* no. 123. These particular honors were refused by Tiberius.

72. Dio Chrysostom, *Or.* 3.6.

73. Martial, *Ep.* 2.91.

74. An inscription from Asia Minor cited in Grant, *Ancient Roman Religion,* 174.

75. Gaius Caligula and Domitian openly encouraged divine associations. On the former, see Philo, *Embassy* 75–114; on the latter, Suetonius, *Dom.* 13.2.

76. As a part of the religious environment of the first century a discussion of the worship of the emperor would have fit comfortably in chapter 1, Religion and Superstition. I have decided to treat it here in order to highlight its political and social dimensions, without intending to reduce it to merely politics.

77. E.g., Statius hails Domitian as divine (*Silvae* 1.1.74–81), as does Martial, *Ep.* 5.3 and 5.8 ("our lord and god"). The historian Valerius Maximus makes the claim of Tiberius (preface to book 1 of *Memorable Doings and Sayings*).

78. Siculus, *Eclogue* 1.42–43. The *Eclogues* depict the rejuvenation of nature under the emperors.

79. Siculus, *Eclogue* 4.142–46, slightly abbreviated.

80. S. R. F. Price, *Rituals and Power: The Roman Imperial Cult in Asia Minor* (Cambridge: Cambridge University Press, 1984), 146–56.

81. *Inscriptiones latinae selectae* 6914, cited in Levick, *Government,* no. 130.

82. Pilhofer, 250/L374.

83. Nancy Bookidis, "Religion in Corinth: 146 B.C.E. to 100 C.E.," in *Urban Religion in Roman Corinth: Interdisciplinary Approaches* (ed. Daniel N. Schowalter and Steven J. Friesen, Harvard Theological Studies 53; Cambridge, Mass.: Harvard University Press, 2005), 156.

84. See *Ara Pacis*; Levick, *Government,* no. 124, etc.

85. See Price, *Rituals,* 133–69.

86. A letter from Claudius to the magistrates in Alexandria approves their request to celebrate "Augustus Day." See Levick, *Government,* no. 124.

87. Translation adapted from Grant, *Ancient Roman Religion,* 174.

88. Matt 12:9; 13:57; Mark 6:2; Luke 4:16; 6:5; John 18:20; Acts 13:14; 14:1; 17:1, 10, etc.

89. Stephen K. Catto. *Reconstructing the First-Century Synagogue: A Critical Analysis of Current Research* (Library of New Testament Studies 363; New York: T&T Clark, 2007), 52–61.

90. Philo, *Embassy* 132.

91. Tacitus, *Hist.* 5.5; Catto, *First-Century Synagogues,* 38. Philo also uses "temple" in place of synagogue on occasion (e.g., *Deus* 7–9).

92. The data is helpfully surveyed and assessed by Catto, *First-Century Synagogue,* 52–61.

93. *Inscriptiones Judaicae Orientis,* vol. 1, *Eastern Europe* (D. Noy, A. Panayotou, H. Bloedhorn, eds.; TSAT 101; Tübingen: Mohr Siebeck, 2004), Macedonia, inscription #1, cited in Catto, *First-Century Synagogue,* 104.

94. *CIJ* 1404, cited in Tessa Rajak and David Noy, "*Archisynagogoi:* Office, Title, and Social Status in the Greco-Jewish Synagogue," *JRS* 83 (1993): 91.

95. So, Lee I. Levine, *The Ancient Synagogue: The First Thousand Years* (New Haven: Yale University Press, 2000), 401–2.

96. James Tunstead Burtchaell conjectures that the *archons,* which he translates as "the notables," in many instances were a subset of the elders: *From Synagogue to Church: Public Services and Offices in the Earliest Christian Communities* (Cambridge: Cambridge University Press, 1992), 233–37.

97. Levine, *Synagogue,* 407.

98. Ibid., 407.

99. Ibid., 426–27.

100. Anders Runeson, *The Origins of the Synagogue: A Socio-Historical Study* (Stockholm: Almqvist & Wiksell International, 2000), 193–231; Catto, *First-Century Synagogue,* 116–25; Levine, *Synagogue,* 135–42.

101. Josephus, *Ag. Ap.* 2.175.

102. Philo, *Good Person* 81–82.

103. *Jewish Inscriptions of Western Europe* (ed. D. Noy; 2 vols.; Cambridge: Cambridge University Press, 1993–1995), 1.13, cited in (and discussed by) Catto, *First-Century Synagogue,* 59–60.

104. 4Q291, 4Q292, 4Q293, 4Q408, 4Q409, 4Q448, 4Q503, 4Q504, 4Q506, 4Q507, 4Q508, 4Q509, etc. An analysis is offered by Daniel K. Falk, "Prayer in the Qumran Texts," in *The Cambridge History of Judaism,* vol. 3, *The Early Roman Period* (ed. W. Horbury, W. D. Davies, and John Sturdy; Cambridge: Cambridge University Press, 2001), 852–76.

105. Philo, *Against Flaccus* 121–122.

106. Levine, *Synagogue,* 128–31.

107. Josephus, *Ant.* 14.213–214.

108. Josephus, *Ant.* 14.235.

109. Discussed by Hanswulf Bloedhorn and Gil Hüttenmeister, "The Synagogue," in *The Cambridge History of Judaism,* vol. 3, *The Early Roman Period* (ed. W. Horbury, W. D. Davies, and John Sturdy; Cambridge: Cambridge University Press, 2001), 295–96; Levine, *Synagogue,* 128–34; 357–86.

110. Mark 13:9; Matt 10:17–18; Luke 21:12; cf. Matt 22:24; Luke 12:11.

111. 2 Cor 11:24; Acts 22:19; cf. Gal 1:13.

112. Pausanius, *Descr.* 2.3.5.

113. Fikret K. Yegül, *Baths and Bathing in Classical Antiquity* (Cambridge, Mass.: Architectural History Foundation; MIT Press, 1992), 30.

114. Jérôme Carcopino, *Daily Life in Ancient Rome: The People and the City at the Height of the Empire* (ed. Henry T. Rowell; trans. E. O. Lorimer; New Haven: Yale University Press, 1966), 254.

115. See Martial's summary of the typical day for an urban Roman in *Ep.* 4.8, along with frequent references to bathing before the evening meal: Valerius Maximus, *Memorable Doings and Sayings* 9.5.3; Petronius, *Satyr.* 130; Pliny, *Ep.* 3.1.7–8; Juvenal, *Sat.* 6.419–26.

116. See the descriptions of Martial, *Ep.* 2.78; 6.42; Statius, *Silvae* 1.5; Pliny, *Ep.* 2.17.10–13; 3.1.5–10; 3.14.2; Petronius, *Satyr.* 73 (fictional).

117.*Lucian, *Hippias,* or *The Bath* 5–6.

118. Clients were especially eager to procure an invitation to dinner at the baths. See Martial, *Ep.* 2.14; 12.82 and more in Garrett G. Fagan, *Bathing in Public in the Roman World* (Ann Arbor: University of Michigan Press, 2002), 27.

119. Martial, *Ep.* 3.25, 44; Horace, *Sat.* 1.4.70–77.

120. Seneca (the Younger), *Ep.* 56.2.

121. The practice of mixed bathing, and the (somewhat) conflicting evidence from antiquity is judiciously summarized by Fagan: "The best solution is . . . to accept that in all likelihood mixed bathing varied from region to region or even from establishment to establishment. . . . Whether one went to a mixed bath or not was a matter of personal choice." See Fagan, *Bathing in Public,* 34–36, on sexual activity at the baths.

122. Martial, *Ep.* 3.57, 72, 87; 11.47.

123. In *Ep.* 1.96 Martial tells of unwanted advances from other men at the baths. See also 1.23; 9.33; 11.63, 95.

124. Fagan, *Bathing in Public,* 34–36, on the sexual activity at the baths.

125. *PGM*² 36.69–75, cited in Fagan, *Bathing in Public,* 35, who also refers to *PGM*² 127.1–12.

126. Clement of Alexandria, *The Instructor* 3.5.

127. Clement of Alexandria, *The Instructor* 3.9.

128. At least, I have yet to find any references to prison facilities in Pausanias.

129. Brian Rapske, *The Book of Acts and Paul in Roman Custody,* vol. 3 of *The Book of Acts in Its First Century Settings* (Grand Rapids, Mich.: Eerdmans, 1994), 21–22, on the Tullianum in Rome; 123 on the prison in Philippi.

130. Sallust, *Bellum catilinae* 55.3, as cited in Rapske, *Roman Custody,* 22.

131. Cicero, *Verr.* 2.5.23. See also Seneca the Elder, *Contr.* 1.6.1. See also Tertullian, *Mart.* 2; *Martyrdom of Perpetua and Felicitas* 3.

132. Citing Lucian, *Toxaris* 29 and Tertullian, *Mart.* 2, respectively.

133. Lucian, *Toxaris* 29.

134. Lucian, *Toxaris* 30. According to Petronius, "long dirty hair" was characteristic of prisoners (*Satyr.* 105).

135. Rapske, *Roman Custody,* 20–35.

136. *Martyrdom of Perpetua and Felicitas* 7.9.

137. Lucian, *Toxaris* 29.

138. Philostratus, *Vita Apoll.* 7.36.

139. Seneca the Elder, *Contr.* 1.6.2.

140. Tacitus, *Ann.* 14.14, 16; 15.33; Seutonius, *Nero* 23–25.

141. Kent no. *153.

142. Kent nos. 72–73.

143. Kent no. 30.

144. Kent no. 158.

145.*Dio Chrysostom, *Or.* 8.15.

146. John S. Kloppenborg, "*Collegia* and *Thiasoi*: Issues in Function, Taxonomy and Membership," in *Voluntary Associations in the Graeco-Roman World* (ed. John S. Kloppenborg and S. G. Wilson; New York: Routledge, 1996), 18–23.

147. See Richard S. Ascough, *Paul's Macedonian Associations*, 15–46.

148. Philo, *Against Flaccus* 136; cf. *On Drunkenness* 22–25, 29; *Spec. Laws* 1.323.

149. From Lanuvium, southeast of Rome, dated at 136 C.E., cited in Robert Louis Wilken, *The Christians as the Romans Saw Them* (New Haven: Yale University Press, 1984), 38–39, slightly abbreviated.

150. Meeks, *Urban Christians,* 134.

151. Kent no. 62, dated to Hadrian's reign.

152. Statistics are drawn from 2000 U.S. Government census data available online at www.census.gov, accessed April 2, 2007.

153. Rome: John Stambaugh, *The Ancient Roman City* (Ancient Society and History; Baltimore: Johns Hopkins University Press, 1988), 337. Antioch: Rodney Stark, "Antioch as the Social Situation for Matthew's Gospel," in *Social History of the Matthean Community: Cross-Disciplinary Approaches* (ed. David L. Balch; Minneapolis: Fortress, 1991), 192. Jerusalem: M. Broshi, "Estimating the Population of Jerusalem," *Biblical Archaeology Review* 4 (1978): 10–15. Ostia: James E. Packer, "Housing and Population in Imperial Ostia and Rome," *JRS* 57 (1967): 80–95. In some instances I have converted the original figures from hectares to acres.

154. Juvenal, *Sat.* 3.245–48.

155. Plutarch, *Mor.* 146D, Dinner of the Seven Wise Men. Although this narrative is set in pre-Socratic Greece, these picturesque details are certainly drawn from Plutarch's own time period, the late first or early second century.

156. *CIL* 4.10488.

157. *CIL* 4.7716.

158. *CIL* 4.10619, from neighboring Herculaneum.

159. Ramsay MacMullen, *Roman Social Relations, 50 B.C. to A.D. 284* (New Haven: Yale University Press, 1974), 62–67.

160. For more detail on bustle and crowds of ancient urban centers see MacMullen, *Social Relations*, 57–87.

161. Examples of such etchings have been found in numerous ancient cities. See ibid., 170 n. 22.

162. Dio Chrysostom, *Or.* 32.30.

163. Following S. J. Friesen,"Poverty in Pauline Studies: Beyond the So-Called New Consensus." *JSNT* 26.3 (2004): 323–61 (2004). Scheidel, however, places this group at only 1%; Walter Scheidel, "Stratification, Deprivation, and Quality of Life," in

Poverty in the Roman World (ed. E. M. Atkins and Robin Osborne; Cambridge: Cambridge University Press, 2006), 42.

164. See S. J. Friesen, "Injustice or God's Will: Explanations of Poverty in Proto-Christian Communities," in *Christian Origins: A People's History of Christianity.* (ed. R. A. Horsley; Minneapolis: Fortress, 2005), 240–60, see 241–43; Justin Meggitt estimates that fully 99% of the population could expect little more from life than "abject poverty": *Paul, Poverty and Survival* (Edinburgh: T&T Clark, 1998), 50.

165. Apuleius, *Metam.* 4.14.

166. Following Friesen, "Injustice," 242.

167. MacMullen, *Social Relations,* 88–99.

168. Horace, *Ep.* 1.10.39–41; Suetonius, *Gramm.* 21; Martial, *Ep.* 2.53; Petronius, *Satyr.* 117.

169.*Horace, *Sat.* 6.4–6.

170. Plutarch, *Mor.* 1B, The Education of Children.

171. Siculus, *Eclogue* 7.25–27. Scattered references to reserved seating: Suetonius, *Aug.* 44; Martial, *Ep.* 5.8; 5.12; 5.24; 5.27; 5.41; Valerius Maximus, *Memorable Doings and Sayings* 2.4.3; Juvenal, *Sat.* 3.147–55; Horace, *Sat.* 1.6.40–43.

172. Pilhofer 145/L763 and 146/L764.

173. Aulus Gellius, *Attic Nights* 2.2.

174. Persius, *Sat.* 1.30–40. See also Plutarch, *Mor.* 148F, Dinner of the Seven Wise Men; Lucian, *On Salaried Posts* 26; Juvenal, *Sat.* 5.12–15; Petronius, *Satyr.* 38 (note the "place of the freedman" at Trimalchio's feast).

175. Pliny, *Ep.* 2.6.1–2, slightly abbreviated.

176. See Martial, *Ep.* 1.20, 3.49, 3.60, 3.82, 4.68, 4.85, 6.11, etc. Musonius Rufus, *Disc.*18B; Plutarch, *Mor.* 154C–D, Dinner of the Seven Wise Men; Horace, *Sat.* 2.2.65–69; Lucian, *On Salaried Posts* 26; Juvenal, *Sat.* 5.

177. Juvenal, *Sat.* 5.9–10.

178. Kent no. 21.

179. Dio Chrysostom, *Or.* 18.3.

180.*Pilhofer 348/G56.

181. On Greco-Roman gift-giving conventions, see Peter Marshall, *Enmity in Corinth: Social Conventions in Paul's Relations with the Corinthians* (WUNT 2.23; Tübingen: J. C. B. Mohr, 1987).

182. See the literature cited by Richard S. Ascough, *What Are They Saying about the Formation of Pauline Churches?* (New York: Paulist, 1998), 92.

183. Pilhofer 535/G207.

184. Martial, *Ep.* 5.59.

185. Pliny curtailed his evening activities on account of his pre-dawn callers: *Ep.* 3.12.2.

186. Juvenal, *Sat.* 1.101.

187. Martial, *Ep.* 6.88.

188. Martial, *Ep.* 2.54; 2.74.

189. Publilius Syrus, *Sententiae* 61; cf. 93.

190. Martial, *Ep.* 11.77.

191. Horace, *Art of Poetry* 419–437; Martial, *Ep.* 2.27; 3.46; 6.47.

192. Martial, *Ep.* 3.36; Juvenal, *Sat.* 1.46, 7.142; Seneca the Elder, *Contr.* 5.2.

193. Horace, *Ep.* 1.17; 1.18.

194. Plutarch, *Mor.* 48F–74E.

195. Martial, *Ep.* 11.66.

196. Cicero, *De officiis* 1.150.

197. See Lucian's *The Dream.*

198.*Dio Chrysostom, *Or.* 7.114; cf. Horace, *Sat.* 1.6.

199. Especially Musonius Rufus, *Disc.* 1; 3; 9; 11; 19.

200. Similar observations are made by Ben Witherington, *Conflict and Community in Corinth: A Socio-Rhetorical Commentary on 1 and 2 Corinthians* (Grand Rapids, Mich.: Eerdmans, 1995), 209, and Timothy B. Savage, *Power through Weakness: Paul's Understanding of the Christian Ministry in 2 Corinthians* (SNTSMS 86; Cambridge: Cambridge University Press, 1996), 85–86.

201. Calpurnius Siculus, *Eclogue,* 4.5–9, slightly abbreviated.

202. Cited in Grant, *Ancient Roman Religion,* 76.

203. Cited in J. R. Harrison, "Paul and the Imperial Gospel at Thessaloniki," *JSNT* 25/1 (2002): 90.

204. Horace, *Odes* 4.15.

205. Aristides, *Or.* 65.

206. Price, *Rituals,* xxv.

207. Ibid., 101–21. See Levick, *Government,* nos. 131–33, for illuminating primary sources.

208. V. Ehrenberg and A. H. M. Jones, *Documents Illustrating the Reigns of Augustus and Tiberius* (ed. D. L. Stockton; Oxford: Clarendon, 1976), 102, slightly adapted from Levick, *Government,* no. 123.

209. Lukas Bormann, *Philippi: Stadt und Christengemeinde zur Zeit des Paulus* (Leiden: Brill, 1995), 46.

210. Kent no. 210, and notes.

211. Bormann, *Philippi,* 48–50, who cites Quintilian, *Res Ges.* 25.

212. See Bormann, *Philippi,* 49. The military oaths are amply illustrated by Tacitus, *Hist.* 1.12, 36, 55; 2.55, 73, 79; 4.31, 37, etc.

213. Ehrenberg and Jones, *Documents Illustrating,* 315, cited in Levick, *Government,* no. 141.

214. Pliny, *Ep.* 10.52; cf. 10.102.

215. Ehrenberg and Jones, *Documents Illustrating,* 102, from Levick, *Government,* nos. 131–133.

216. Kent no. 158; see also nos. 151–156; 159–163.

217. This issue of Erastus and the oath of office is treated briefly by Bruce W. Winter in *Seek the Welfare of the City: Christians as Benefactors and Citizens* (Grand Rapids, Mich.: Eerdmans, 1994), 192–95. Winter notes the evidence of certain Jewish public officials in the second and third century being excused from this duty and speculates that Erastus might have been treated accordingly.

218. *SIG* 695, cited in Richard S. Ascough, "The Completion of a Religious Duty: The Background of 2 Cor. 8:1–15," *NTS* 42 (1996): 597.

219. First Corinthians 10 address two related issues: participating in pagan sacrifices (1–22) and eating meat sold in the marketplace that has been offered in such a sacrifice (23–30).

220. Tacitus, *Ann.* 15.44. Tertullian also defends against the charge (*Apology* 35–37).

221. My assumptions regarding the Corinthians' prior knowledge of, and desire to participate in, the collection are based on the way Paul introduces this topic, "Now concerning the collection . . ." This is Paul's manner of replying to questions the Corinthians have asked him (e.g., 7:1, 25; 8:1; 12:1), and from his response (16:1–4) their question was something like, "How should we go about collecting money for the destitute in Jerusalem?"

222. Pliny, *Ep.* 9.30.2.

223. See Louis William Countryman, *The Rich Christian in the Church of the Early Empire: Contradictions and Accommodations* (New York: Mellen, 1980), 105–8, and Roman Garrison, *Redemptive Almsgiving in Early Christianity* (Journal for the Study of the New Testament Supplement Series; Sheffield: JSOT Press, 1993), 38–45.

224. Dio Chrysostom, *Or.* 1.84.

225. My analysis closely follows Ronald F. Hock, *The Social Context of Paul's Ministry: Tentmaking and Apostleship* (Philadelphia: Fortress, 1980).

226. Hock, *Social Context*, 21–22.

227. 1 Cor 4:12–13; 9:3–18; 2 Cor 11:7–12; 12:15–16.

228. For a fuller presentation of this view, see Marshall, *Enmity in Corinth.*

229. For the view that Paul refused support primarily to model a life of self-imposed poverty before the materialistic Corinthians, see Savage, *Power through Weakness,* 80–99.

230. Hock, *Social Context,* 27.

231. My observations here rely on Robert J. Banks, "'Walking' as a Metaphor of the Christian Life: The Origins of a Significant Pauline Usage," in *Perspectives on Language and Text* (ed. Francis I. Andersen, Edgar W. Conrad, and Edward G. Newing; Winona Lake, Ind.: Eisenbrauns, 1987).

232. It is found once in Mark, Acts, and Hebrews. John uses it ten times, mostly in the epistles.

233. E.g., Ps. 84:12, "walking blamelessly"; see Banks, "Walking," 305–6.

234. Banks, "Walking," 306–9.

235. See, for example, the comments on these episodes in the commentaries of Conzelmann and Haenchen: Hans Conzelmann, *Acts of the Apostles: A Commentary on the Acts of the Apostles* (trans. Eldon Jay Epp and Christopher R. Matthews; Philadelphia: Fortress, 1987); Ernst Haenchen, *The Acts of the Apostle: A Commentary* (Philadelphia: Westminster Press, 1971).

236. The best available treatment of the subject is found in MacMullen, *Enemies of the Roman Order,* 163–91.

237. Cicero, *Dom.* 12.

238. Pseudo-Socrates, *Epistle, 14.*

239. Petronius, *Satyr.* 90. Although fictional, the *Satyricon* preserves numerous memorable scenes from everyday life, and the author's casual reference to passersby lobbing stones at Eumolpus is presented as an unremarkable occurrence.

240. Lucian, *Peregrinus* 15, 19; *Alexander the False Prophet,* 45.

241. Apuleius, *Metam.* 2.27; Lucian, *Dialogues of the Dead* 375; Pseudo-Diogenes, *Epistle 20.*

242. Suetonius, *Claud.* 18.

243. Plutarch, *Mor.* 580A, Sign of Socrates.

244. Dio Chrysostom, *Or.* 32.23.

245. Dio Chrysostom, *Or.* 34.33.

246. E.g., Epictetus, *Disc.* 1.1.22–25; 3.15.11–12; Dio Chrysostom, *Or.* 32.11–34; 34.33; 38.6–7; 43.3; Horace, *Sat.* 1.3.130–134; Lucian, *Demonax* 11, 16; *Anarchasis or Athletics,* 39; Pseudo-Diogenes, *Epistles 20, 34, 45;* Philostratus, *Vit. soph.* 526; Philo, *Against Flaccus* 33–34.

247. Petronius, *Poems* 31.

248. Dio Chrysostom, *Or.* 32.11.

249. Dio Chrysostom, *Or.* 32.23, citing an unnamed poet.

250. Pseudo-Phocylides, 95–96.

251. Philo, *Embassy* 67.

252. Citing Apulieus, *Metam.* 4.14 and Dio Chrysostom, *Or.* 7.36.

253. Similar incidents occur in Lystra (Acts 14:19) and Berea (Acts 17:13).

NOTES TO PART 4: HOUSEHOLD AND FAMILY

1. John Stambaugh, *The Ancient Roman City* (Baltimore: Johns Hopkins University Press, 1988), 157–82; James E. Packer, "Housing and Population in Imperial Ostia and Rome," *JRS* 57 (1967): 80–95.

2. Simon P. Ellis, *Roman Housing* (London: Duckworth, 2000), 78–79; John Stambaugh, "Social Relations in the City of the Early Principate: State of Research," in *Society of Biblical Literature 1980 Seminar Papers* (ed. P. J. Achtmeier; Chico, Calif.: Scholars Press, 1980), 74–78.

3. Karl P. Donfried and Peter Richardson, *Judaism and Christianity in First-Century Rome* (Grand Rapids, Mich.: Eerdmans, 1998), 132.

4. Consult the dimensions and plans scattered throughout Stambaugh, *The Ancient Roman City,* and Ellis, *Roman Housing.*

5. Stambaugh, *The Ancient Roman City,* 178.

6. For example, Pliny, *Ep.* 2.17.2; Statius, *Silvae* 1.3; Aulus Gellius, *Attic Nights* 1.2.2.

7. In addition to Stambaugh (*The Ancient Roman City*) and Ellis (*Roman Housing*), see Michele Geroge, "*Servus* and *Domus*: The Slave in the Roman House," in *Domestic Space in the Roman World: Pompeii and Beyond* (ed. Ray Laurence and Andrew Wallace-Hadrill; Portsmouth, R.I.: Journal of Roman Archaeology, 1997), 15–24; Roger W. Gehring, *House Church and Mission: The Importance of Household Structures in Early Christianity* (Peabody, Mass.: Hendrickson, 2004), 313–20; and Jerome Murphy-O'Connor, *St. Paul's Corinth: Texts and Archaeology* (3d rev. and exp. ed.; Collegeville, Minn.: Liturgical Press, 2002), 178–85.

8. See the scene described in Petronius, *Satyr.* 29.

9. Horace, *Sat.* 2.6.65–67.

10. Horace, *Sat.* 2.5.10–17.

11. Ken Dowden, *Religion and the Romans* (Classical World Series; London: Bristol Classical, 1992), 25–30.

12. See Pilhofer 332/L777; 338/L333; 339/L338; 340/L589; cf. 341/L267; 342/L292.

13. Pseudo-Diogenes, *Epistle 36.1–2*. The *Cynic epistles* are fictitious philosophical essays, and so it is unclear if this depiction represents the actual situation in Cyzicus. In either case, the *Cynic epistles* portray common scenes that are broadly representative of Greco-Roman society and culture.

14. See the images in Erich Lessing and Antonio Varone, *Pompeii* (Paris: Terrail, 2001).

15. See the images and commentary in Michael Grant et al., *Eros in Pompeii: The Erotic Art Collection of the Museum of Naples* (New York: Stewart, Tabori & Chang, 1997).

16. See Lessing and Varone, *Pompeii*.

17.*P. Oxy. 744 (Select Papyri* no. 105). A similar command is given by a father in Apuleius, *Metam.* 10.23.

18. Musonius Rufus, *Disc.* 15; Epictetus, *Disc.* 1.23; Publilius Syrus, *Sententiae* 123.

19. For the legal discussion see Seneca the Elder, *Contr.* 1.1; 1.6; 2:1; 2.3, summarized by Aulus Gellius, *Attic Nights* 2.7. Musonius Rufus treats the subject in *Disc.* 16.

20. Musonius Rufus, *Disc.* 16.

21. Epictetus, *Disc.* 3.3.5.

22. Arius Didymus, *Concerning Household Management* 148.14–18 in David L. Balch, "Household Codes," in *Greco-Roman Literature and the New Testament: Selected Forms and Genres* (ed. David E. Aune; Atlanta: Scholars Press, 1988).

23. Arius Didymus, *Concerning Household Management* 149.5–8 in Balch, "Household Codes."

24. Cicero, *Mur.* 12.27; Musonius Rufus, *Disc.* 12; Dio Chrysostom, *Or.* 3.70; Josephus, *Ag. Ap.* 2.201.

25. See, for example, Musonius Rufus, *Disc.* 3, 12, 13A, 13B, 14; Pseudo-Plutarch, *Mor.* 7E, 13–14, *Education of Children*; Pliny, *Pan.* 83.4–7; Arius Didymus in Balch, "Household Codes." The Greco-Roman household codes can be traced to Aristotle, *Politics* 1.2.1–3, 11–15; 1.5.6. For the Jewish equivalent, see Josephus, *Ag. Ap.* 2.199–208; Philo, *Decalogue* 165–67; Pseudo-Phocylides, 175–227.

26. For a fuller and more nuanced picture of women in antiquity, see Mary R. Lefkowitz and Maureen B. Fant, *Women's Life in Greece and Rome* (Baltimore: Johns Hopkins University Press, 1982).

27. Texts, translations, and commentary in Rosalinde A. Kearsley, "Women in Public Life in the Roman East: Iunia Theodora, Claudia Metrodora and Phoebe, Benefactress of Paul," *TynBul* 50 (1999): 189–211.

28. *IGR* 4.1687 (=*MDAI.A,* no. 25).

29. *Inschr. von Ephesos* 3.980. For this connection and the previous reference to Julia Polla, I am indebted to a presentation by L. Michael White at the 2003 annual meeting of the Society of Biblical Literature.

30. Kent no. 199.

31. Pilhofer 266/L344.

32. Pilhofer 451/L158.

33. Pilhofer 340/L589.

34. Eva Marie Lassen, "The Roman Family: Ideal and Metaphor," in *Constructing Early Christian Families: Family as Social Reality and Metaphor* (ed. Halvor Moxnes; London: Routledge, 1997).

35. M. McCrum and A. G. Woodhead. *Select Documents of the Principates of the Flavian Emperors including the year of Revolution, AD 68–96* (Cambridge: Cambridge University Press, 1961), 454 from Baetica (modern Spain) dated from 82–84 C.E. Cited in Barbara Levick, *The Government of the Roman Empire: A Sourcebook* (2d ed.; New York: Routledge, 2000), no. 29.

36. Judith Evans Grubbs, *Women and the Law in the Roman Empire: A Sourcebook on Marriage, Divorce, and Widowhood* (New York: Routledge, 2002), 88.

37. Pliny, *Ep.* 1.9.2.

38. Pliny, *Ep.* 1.14.8. Pseudo-Phocylides, 215–216.

39. Epictetus, *Disc.* 3.22.7.6.

40.*P.Tebt. 104 (*Select Papyri,* no. 2). Further example, with commentary, can be found in Grubbs, *Women*, 122–35.

41. E.g., Pseudo-Plutarch, *Mor.* 141C–D, *Advice to Bride and Groom*; Musonius Rufus, *Disc.* 13B; Juvenal, *Sat.* 6.200–231; Pseudo-Phocylides, 199–206.

42. Pliny, *Ep.* 1.14.9.

43. Musonius Rufus, *Disc.* 14, "Is Marriage a Handicap for the Pursuit of Philosophy."

44. Suetonius, *Aug.* 14.

45. Grubbs, *Women*, 187.

46. Valerius Maximus, *Memorable Doings and Sayings* 2.1.3.

47. Valerius Maximus, *Memorable Doings and Sayings* 2.1.4; Plutarch, *Mor.* 267B–C, *Roman Questions*; Aulus Gellius, *Attic Nights* 4.3.2.

48. Seneca (the Younger), *Ben.* 3.15.2–3.

49. Amy Richlin, "Approaches to the Sources on Adultery at Rome," in *Reflections of Women in Antiquity* (ed. Helene P. Foley; New York: Gordon and Breach Science, 1981).

50. On the "liberation" of women in the first century and the rise of the "new woman" in the Roman world, see Bruce W. Winter, *Roman Wives, Roman Widows: The Appearance of New Women and the Pauline Communities* (Grand Rapids, Mich.: Eerdmans, 2003).

51. For more on this double standard, see G. W. Peterman, "Marriage and Sexual Fidelity in the Papyri, Plutarch, and Paul," *TynBul* 50:2 (1999): 163–72.

52. Horace, *Sat.* 1.2.47.

53. Plutarch, *Mor.* 140B, Advice to Bride and Groom.

54. E.g., Petronius, *Satyr.* 74 ; Martial, *Ep.* 11.23; 11:43.

55. Richlin, "Adultery," 393.

56. Grubbs, *Women*, 63–64.

57. Codex justinianus 9.9.1, cited in Grubbs, *Women*, 63.

58. L. Cilliers and F. P. Retif, "Poisons, Poisoning and the Drug Trade in Ancient Rome," *Akroterion* 45 (2000): 88–100.

59. E.g., Tacitus, *Ann.* 1.5; 2.88; 3.13–14; 4.8–12; 6.32–33; 12.66–67; 13.15–17; 15.45.

60. Juvenal, *Sat.* 1.69–74; cf. 6.133; 7.169; 14.250–255.

61. Petronius, *Poems* 5.

62. Suetonius, *Aug.* 63.

63. Suetonius, *Aug.* 65; *Tib.* 11.

64. Suetonius, *Tib.* 43.

65.*Homer, *Iliad* 14.313–328.

66. Pseudo-Heraclitus, *Epistle 4;* Cicero, *Nature of the Gods* 1.42–43.

67. Cicero, *Cael.* 48.

68. Horace, *Ep.* 1.14.20–30.

69. Martial, *Ep.* 3.65; 4.42; 6:34; 7.29; 11.6; 11.22; 11.26; 11.43; 11.56; 12.75; 12.96.

70. Martial, *Ep.* 11.78

71. Petronius, *Satyr.* 74; cf. Martial, *Ep.* 7.43, on a wife complaining of her husband's affairs with young boys. Included among Lucian's writings is a lengthy dialog, *Affairs of the Heart,* weighing the pros and cons of man-boy relations versus man-woman relations.

72. Juvenal, *Sat.* 6.34–37.

73. Petronius, *Satyr.* 85–87; Lucian, *Philosophies for Sale* 15; Suetonius, *Gramm.* 5, 6; Juvenal, *Sat.* 10.224–225; Pliny, *Ep.* 3.3–4; Quintilian, *Inst.* 1.2.4–5; 3.17.

74. Plutarch, *Mor.* 11D–F, The Education of Children. See also Pseudo-Lucian, *Affairs of the Heart,* which is devoted to weighing the pros and cons of heterosexual love versus man-boy relations.

75. Plutarch, *Mor.* 11E–F, The Education of Children.

76. Plutarch, *Mor.* 11F, The Education of Children, citing Plato, *Republic* 468B.

77. Pseudo-Phocylides, 213–214.

78. A few examples: Apuleius, *Flor.* 11; 22; Pseudo-Heraclitus, 4; 7; Dio Chrysostom, *Or.* 3.39–41; Epictetus, *Disc.* 2.18.8; Horace, *Ep.* 1.1.33–40; *Sat.* 2.3; Musonius Rufus, *Disc.* 3, 4, 16; Philo, *Virtues; Sacrifices* 32.

79.*Arius Didymus, *Epitome of Stoic Ethics* 11m.

80. Dio Chrysostom, *Or.* 4.102, abbreviated.

81. Juvenal, *Sat.* 290.

82. Tacitus, *Agr.* 21; cf. Tacitus, *Ann.* 3.53–54.

83.*Musonius Rufus, *Disc.* 20, "On Furnishings."

84. Pseudo-Diogenes, *Epistle 47.*

85. Epictetus, *Disc.* 3.22.69–76.

86. Pseudo-Diogenes, *Epistle 44.* This letter goes on to advocate masturbation in place of marriage and intercourse, which was a common Cynic theme: Pseudo-Diogenes, 35, 42; Dio Chrysostom, *Or.* 6.16–20.

87. See Will Deming, *Paul on Marriage and Celibacy: The Hellenistic Background of 1 Corinthians 7* (2d ed.; Grand Rapids, Mich.: Eerdmans, 2004).

88. Musonius Rufus, *Disc.* 14.

89. Musonius Rufus, *Disc.* 12; cf. 13A, 13B; see also Pseudo-Diogenes, *Epistle 21;* Pseudo-Ocellus Lucanus, *On the Nature of the Universe* 43b–51 (cited in Deming, *Paul on Marriage,* 231–37).

90. Keith R. Bradley, *Slavery and Society at Rome* (Cambridge: Cambridge University Press, 1994), 30.

91. Seneca (the Younger), *Clem.* 1.24.1

92. David C. Verner, *The Household of God: The Social World of the Pastoral Epistles* (Society of Biblical Literature Dissertation Series 71; Chico, Calif.: Scholars Press, 1983), 61.

93. Petronius, *Satyr.* 26–30.

94. *Amores* 39 (possibly not written by Lucian).

95. Cicero, *Att.* 11.22 (a scribe); Suetonius, *Gramm.* 13 (a teacher).

96. Plutarch, *Mor.* 4A, On the Education of Children.

97. Dio Chrysostom, *Or.* 34.51.

98. *CIL* 4.10677 (edited for graphic language).

99. Horace, *Sat.* 1.8.8.

100. Geroge, *Domestic Space,* 3.

101. Apuleius, *Metam.* 9.12.

102. Juvenal, *Sat.* 4.222.

103. Juvenal, *Sat.* 6.479–482.

104. Martial, *Ep.* 2.82; 3.21; Horace, *Ep.* 1.16.44–45; 2.2; Dio Chrysostom, *Or.* 10.1–2; Seneca (the Younger), *Ep.* 47.5; Juvenal, *Sat.* 14.15–23.

105. Petronius, *Satyr.* 103.

106. Martial, *Ep.* 2.29.

107. Musonius Rufus, *Disc.* 12, "On Sexual Indulgence."

108. *CIL* 4.1863.

109. Martial, *Ep.* 4.66.

110. Seneca (the Younger), *Ep.* 47; Pliny, *Ep.* 1.4

111. Statius, *Silvae* 2.1.70–100.

112. Martial, *Ep.* 6.28–29.

113. Diogenes Laertius, *Lives* 10.21. Cf. Persius, *Sat.* 3.88–106, which references the "cap of freedom" which a manumitted slave wore.

114. BGU 326, *Select Papyri* no. 85.

115. Statius, *Silvae* 2.1.70–100. See also Martial, *Ep.* 6.28–29; Persius, *Sat.* 5.73–82.

116. Suetonius. *Gramm.* 13; Petronius, *Satyr.* 57.

117. Martial, *Ep.* 2.53, 58; Horace, *Ep.* 1.10.39–41; Petronius, *Satyr.* 117; Suetonius, *Gramm.* 13, 21.

118. Epictetus, *Disc.* 4.34–35.

119. Martial, *Ep.* 1.101; Pliny, *Ep.* 2.6; Pilhofer 282/L370.

120. Seneca, *On Tranquility* 8.6.

121. Martial, *Ep.* 2.29; 5.13; 11.37.

122. Pilhofer 146/L763 (theater seating); other references: 037/L037; 256/L444; 267/L376; 410/G258.

123. Pseudo-Heraclitus, *Epistle 9,* 5.

124. Arius Didymus, *Epitome* 11i.

125. Epictetus, *Disc.* 3.24.71.

126. Philo, *Good Person*; Dio Chrysostom, "On Slavery and Freedom" (*Or.* 14 and 15); Epictetus, *Disc.* 4.1; Horace, *Sat.* 2.7.

127. The subject of Persius, *Sat.* 5. Arius Didymus (*Epitome* 11i) summarizes the Stoic position in a similar fashion, while Horace (*Sat.* 2) mocks the Stoics on this point.

128. For the most recent and most thorough treatment, see Gehring, *House Church*. For less technical and more concise summaries, see Robert J. Banks, *Paul's Idea of Community* (rev. ed.; Peabody, Mass.: Hendrickson, 1994), esp. 26–36; Arthur G. Patzia, *The Emergence of the Church: Context, Growth, Leadership and Worship* (Downers Grove, Ill.: InterVarsity Press, 2001), 188–93.

129. Gehring, *House Church*, 134–42.

130. Wayne A. Meeks, *The First Urban Christians: The Social World of the Apostle Paul* (New Haven: Yale University Press, 1983), 75.

131. Gehring, *House Church*, 139.

132. Jerome Murphy-O'Connor, "Prisca and Aquila," *Bible Review* (December 1992): 49–50.

133. David G. Horrell, "Domestic Space and Christian Meetings at Corinth. Imagining New Contexts and the Buildings East of the Theatre," *NTS* 50 (2004): 349–69. Robert Jewett draws similar conclusions regarding the Christian meetings in Thessalonica: "Tenement Churches and Communal Meals in the Early Church: the Implications of a Form-Critical Analysis of 2 Thessalonians 3:10," *Biblical Research* 38 (1993): 23–43.

134. For a full exploration, see Joseph H. Hellerman, *The Ancient Church as Family* (Minneapolis: Fortress, 2001); more concisely, Banks, *Community*, 47–57.

135. Emphasis author. Infant (v. 7, which many versions render "gentle," following a later and less reliable manuscript tradition), mother (v. 7), father (v. 11), children (v. 11), orphan (v. 17, from the Greek verb *aporphanizō*, rendered by many translations "torn away").

136. Eph 5:22–6:9; Col 3:18–4:1; Titus 2:1–9.

137. David L. Balch, "'Let Wives Be Submissive . . .': The Origin, Form and Apologetic Function of the Household Duty Code (Haustafel) in I Peter" (Thesis, Yale University, 1974).

138. Murphy-O'Connor argues that, as a Pharisee, Paul must have married and that he probably had children as well. He further conjectures that Paul never mentions his family because they "perished in an accident so traumatic that he sealed off their memory forever. It was too painful to be revisited." This is simply fanciful speculation. See Jerome Murphy-O'Connor, *Paul: His Story* (Oxford: Oxford University Press, 2004), 14–15.

139. With the NLT, NRSV, ESV, NET, NJB, and most commentaries, I take 7:1 to be a citation or summary of a point made by the Corinthians that Paul provisionally concedes and then significantly qualifies. This is a frequent strategy of Paul in 1 Corinthians: e.g., 6:13; 8:1, 4; 10:23.

140. Deming, *Paul on Marriage*. See also Vincent L. Wimbush, *Paul, the Worldly Ascetic: Response to the World and Self-Understanding according to 1 Corinthians 7* (Macon, Ga.: Mercer University Press, 1987).

141. Epictetus, *Disc.* 3.22.69–72, abbreviated.

142. Epictetus, *Disc.* 3.22.76; 4.1.176.

143. The most plausible attempt to determine the precise nature of the crisis comes from Bruce Winter, who finds evidence for widespread famines in the latter half of the first century. See Bruce W. Winter, *After Paul Left Corinth: The Influence of Secular Ethics and Social Change* (Grand Rapids, Mich.: Eerdmans, 2001), 215–68. The chief drawback of this interpretation is that it cannot fully explain 7:29–35, where Paul portrays the crisis in much broader, eschatological terms: living in the final phase of the present age (7:29, 31). Yet Winter's proposal may be partly true, as Thiselton observes: "famine could well provide *a concrete instantiation of the eschatological question mark which stands over against the supposed stability, security, or permanence of lifestyles available in mid first-century Roman society* (his emphasis). See Anthony C. Thiselton, *The First Epistle to the Corinthians: A Commentary on the Greek Text* (NIGTC; Grand Rapids, Mich.: Eerdmans, 2000), 573.

144. The recent work of Bauckham and Epp has established beyond doubt that Junia was a female name, not a shortened form of a man's name, and that Andronicus and Junia are listed by Paul as "prominent *among* the apostles" (as opposed to "well known to the apostles"). See Richard Bauckham, *Gospel Women: Studies of the Named Women in the Gospels* (Grand Rapids, Mich.: Eerdmans, 2002), 165–80, Eldon Jay Epp, *Junia: The First Woman Apostle* (Minneapolis: Fortress, 2005).

145. Calvin J. Roetzel, *Paul: The Man and the Myth* (Minneapolis: Fortress, 1999), 147.

146. A full survey and helpful bibliography is found in Ascough, *What Are They Saying?*

147. For a full comparison, see the following: Meeks, *Urban Christians,* 75–84; Ekkehard Stegemann and Wolfgang Stegemann, *The Jesus Movement: A Social History of Its First Century* (Minneapolis: Fortress, 1999), 273–84; Ascough, *What Are They Saying?* passim; Stambaugh and Balch, *Social Environment,* 138–45.

148. Gehring, *House Church.*

149. Pliny the Younger, *Ep. Tra.* 10.96.9.

150. Burtchaell, *From Synagogue to Church*; Howard Clark Kee, *Who Are the People of God? Early Christian Models of Community* (New Haven: Yale University Press, 1995).

151. Meeks, *Urban Christians,* 81.

152. A useful summary of worship practices in the synagogue is found in Catto, *First-Century Synagogue,* 106–51.

153. William Horbury notes that the inscriptions that record women as occupying offices in the synagogue date from the second to the sixth century C.E. and are probably honorific: William Horbury, "Women in the Synagogue," in *The Cambridge History of Judaism,* vol. 3, *The Early Roman Period* (ed. William Horbury, W. D. Davies, and John Sturdy; Cambridge: Cambridge University Press, 1999), 388–401.

154. On the apostolic status of Junia, see Epp, *Junia;* Bauckham, *Gospel Women,* 165–80; Linda L. Belleville, "Ιουνίαν . . . ἐπίσημοι ἐν τοῖς ἀποστόλοις: A Re-Examination of Romans 16.7 in Light of Primary Source Materials," *NTS* 51/2 (2005): 231–49.

155. Lee I. Levine, *The Ancient Synagogue: The First Thousand Years* (New Haven: Yale University Press, 2000), 426–27.

156. Drawn from Richard S. Ascough, *Paul's Macedonian Associations*, 15–109. On the double portion at meals in connection with the "double honor" due to elders, see Georg Schoellgen, "Die διπλῆ τιμή von 1 Tim. 5:17," *ZNW* 80 (1989): 232–39.

157. Pliny, *Ep.* 10.96.7; 10.34.

158. Summarizing the assessments of Stambaugh and Balch, *Social Environment*, 141; Meeks, *Urban Christians*, 78–80; Stegemann and Stegemann, *The Jesus Movement*, 281. For an informative and spirited defense of the role of voluntary associations in the formation of the churches in Philippi and Thessalonica, see Ascough, *Paul's Macedonian Associations*.

159. Galen, *De Pulsum Differentiis* 2.4, cited in Richard Walzer, *Galen on Jews and Christians* (London: Oxford University Press, 1949), 14. A valuable discussion of Galen's comments can be found in Robert Louis Wilken, *The Christians as the Romans Saw Them* (New Haven: Yale University Press, 1984), 68–93.

160. So, too, Meeks, *Urban Christians*, 84.

161. E.g., Gehring, *House Church*, 193–96.

162. Many point to Acts 6 as the establishment of the diaconate, but on very slender grounds. The men appointed to oversee the distribution of food are not called "deacons," and some of them (Stephen and Philip) are engaged with teaching and preaching like the apostles and later elders of 1 Timothy (Patzia, *Emergence*, 167). The argument in favor of relating Acts 6 to the deaconate runs like this: Although the noun "deacon" is not used in Acts 6, the verbal form, *diakoneō*, is used to describe the work of this ministry; The seven are chosen to minister to the material needs of the community, which is presumably how deacons functioned; Luke lingers on this incident in a way that emphasizes it as important, and it can be assumed that he is providing the historical background for the important office of deacon. See J. B. Lightfoot, *Saint Paul's Epistle to the Philippians* (London: Macmillan, 1890), 187–91.

163. On James' prominence in Jerusalem, see Lightfoot, *Philippians*, 197–98, and C. K. Barrett, *Acts of the Apostles*, 2:729.

164. Josephus, *Ant.* 20.200.

165. Lightfoot, *Philippians,* 197.

166. The dates provided by Luke may not be inclusive of Paul's entire ministry in these cities, which may have been longer.

167. Kevin Giles, "Luke's Use of the Term *Ekklēsia* with Special Reference to Acts 20:28 and 9:31," *NTS* 31 (1985): 135–42.

168. Alexander Strauch, *Biblical Eldership: An Urgent Call to Restore Biblical Church Leadership* (Littleton, Colo.: Lewis & Roth, 1995), 101–17, esp. 113.

169. James D. G. Dunn, *The Theology of Paul the Apostle* (Grand Rapids, Mich.: Eerdmans, 1998), 584–85; Kevin Giles, *Patterns of Ministry among the First Christians* (Melbourne: Collins Dove, 1989), 32–35. By the time Paul wrote Romans several years later (57–58 c.e.) we hear of a deaconess named Phoebe from nearby Cenchreae (Rom 16:2). Some (e.g., Banks, *Community*, 143–44) argue that the word *diakonos* used of Phoebe should not be understood as designating an official of the church but should be translated "servant." For the counter arguments, see Douglas J. Moo, *The Epistle to the Romans* (NICNT; Grand Rapids, Mich.: Eerdmans, 1996), 913–14.

170. So most commentaries, including Gordon D. Fee, *The First Epistle to the Corinthians* (NICNT; Grand Rapids, Mich.: Eerdmans, 1987), 829–30; C. K. Barrett, *The First Epistle to the Corinthians* (Peabody, Mass.: Hendrickson, 1993); Thiselton, *First Corinthians*, 1338–39; Ben Witherington, *Conflict and Community in Corinth: A Socio-Rhetorical Commentary on 1 and 2 Corinthians* (Grand Rapids, Mich.: Eerdmans, 1995), 319.

171. Especially insightful are the comments of Wolfgang Schrage, *Der Erste Brief an Die Korinther: 1 Kor 15,1 – 16,24* (4 vols.; Zurich: Neukirchener, 2001), 4.452–55.

172. One definite article governs all three participles (*tous kopioōntas . . . prosistamenous . . . nouthetountas*), indicating one group is in view.

173. This interpretation represents the consensus among New Testament scholars, e.g., F. F. Bruce, *1 and 2 Thessalonians* (WBC 45; Waco, Tex.: Word, 1982), 118–19; Charles A. Wanamaker, *The Epistles to the Thessalonians: A Commentary on the Greek Text* (NIGNT; Grand Rapids, Mich.: Eerdmans, 1990), 191–94; Abraham J. Malherbe, *The Letters to the Thessalonians: A New Translation with Introduction and Commentary* (AB 32B; New York: Doubleday, 2000), 313. Fee, however, assumes that *hoi proistamenoi* ("those over you") represents an alternative designation for what would later become known as overseers and deacons (Phil 1:1) and that these individuals were appointed by Paul: Gordon D. Fee, "Reflections on Church Order in the Pastoral Epistles, with Further Reflections on the Hermeneutics of *Ad Hoc* Documents," *JETS* 28 (1985): 147. However, it seems more likely that the second and third designations qualify the first ("those who labor by leading and admonishing"), rather than ascribing to the middle term an almost titular sense. Further, the same term (*proistamenos*) is used by Paul in Rom 12:8 in a list of divinely imparted spiritual gifts: service, teaching, exhorting, comforting, generosity, leading, and showing mercy. There is no compelling reason to regard this as designating an apostolically appointed office.

174. On Phoebe (Rom 16:1), see note 169.

175. As Schrenk attempts in *Die Philipperbriefe des Paulus: Kommentar* (Stuttgart: W. Kohlhammer, 1984), 78–82. The words are not omitted anywhere in the manuscript tradition.

176. As does Banks, *Community*, 144.

177. On developing patterns of organization, see Giles, *Patterns of Ministry*, 27–48; Patzia, *Emergence*, 152–82; I. Howard Marshall and Philip Towner, *A Critical and Exegetical Commentary on the Pastoral Epistles* (ICC; Edinburgh: T&T Clark, 1999), 171–81.

178. In 2 Cor 1:16; 2:13; 7:5, Paul mentions visits, or intended visits, to Macedonia. Acts 20:3 also mentions a visit to the province. Presumably Philippi would have been on the itinerary.

179. So John Reumann, "Church Office in Paul, Especially in Philippians," in *Origins and Method: Towards a New Understanding of Judaism and Christianity: Essays in Honour of John C. Hurd* (ed. John Coolidge Hurd and Bradley H. McLean; Sheffield: JSOT Press, 1993), 87–88; Andrew D. Clarke, *A Pauline Theology of Church Leadership* (London: T&T Clark, 2008), 83–85, with reference to Thessalonica and Corinth.

180. With many, I find compelling the case made long ago by Lightfoot that "elder" and "overseer" are alternative designations for the same office. Particularly important is that both Titus 1:5–7 and Acts 20:28 appear to use the terms interchangeably. See Lightfoot, *Philippians*, 95–99. See Marshall and Towner, *A Critical and Exegetical Commentary*

on the Pastoral Epistles, 171–81; William D. Mounce, *Pastoral Epistles* (WBC 46; Nashville: Thomas Nelson, 2000), 389–90; George W. Knight, *The Pastoral Epistles: A Commentary on the Greek Text* (NIGTC; Grand Rapids, Mich.: Eerdmans, 1992), 290–91.

181. Titus, overseeing a new work on the island of Crete, is charged only with appointing elders/overseers, not deacons, or other officers. This is further evidence that ministry positions expanded as the ministry itself expanded. We can presume that other leadership positions were put in place in the churches on Crete as need arose.

182. The operative verb in 1 Tim 4:12 is an epistolary aorist, as in 1 Cor 4:17: "I am sending..." See Mounce, *Pastoral Epistles*, 591.

183. On the possibility of dating these letters within the lifetime of Paul or shortly after (Marshall), see the introductory material in the commentaries of William Mounce, Luke Timothy Johnson, and I. Howard Marshall.

184. The church was infiltrated by false teachers: 1 Tim 1:3–11; 4:1–5; 6:3–10.

185. Bruce W. Winter, "Widows and Legal and Christian Benefactions," in *Seek the Welfare of the City: Christians as Benefactors and Citizens* (Grand Rapids, Mich.: Eerdmans, 1994), 64–65.

186. Ibid., 65.

187. Luke Timothy Johnson observes, "The phrase 'in every place' is somewhat odd, unless we think of the Ephesian church as consisting of several meetings or assemblies"; see *The First and Second Letters to Timothy: A New Translation with Introduction and Commentary* (AB 35A; New York: Doubleday, 2001), 198. So too the commentaries of Gordon D. Fee (*1 and 2 Timothy, Titus* [NIBC; Peabody, Mass.: Hendrickson, 1988], 71) and Knight, *The Pastoral Epistles*, 128.

188. Ralph P. Martin, *Worship in the Early Church* (Grand Rapids, Mich.: Eerdmans, 1981).

189. Patzia, *Emergence*, 213–14.

190. Pliny, *Ep.* 10.96.6–7. See also Tertullian, *Apology* 39.1–7.

191. Following Jerome Murphy-O'Connor's widely accepted analysis: "House Churches and the Eucharist," in *St. Paul's Corinth*. I am not, however, in agreement with every detail of O'Connor's essay. In particular, when he describes the Corinthian villa at Anaploga as "a typical house" (178), he is surely mistaken, unless he means a typical house of the aristocracy. I am also indebted to the analysis of Christian Strecker, *Die liminale Theologie des Paulus: Zugänge zur paulinischen Theologie aus kulturanthropologischer Perspektive* (Göttingen: Vandenhoeck & Ruprecht, 1999), 320–34.

192. No *insulae* have yet been discovered in Corinth, though the remains of Corinth are poorly preserved and the excavations there have been confined to the central forum area. Lower-class housing like *insulae* rarely leave an archaeological footprint.

193. The scenario sketched here is the most plausible, in my view, and is advocated by, for example, Fee and Thisleton in their major commentaries. However, we should keep in mind that Paul does not mention the room in which the food is being served, and there were larger spaces than the *triclinium* available in most upper-class homes. Some villas contained very spacious courtyards (the *peristyle*) that could have comfortably accommodated eighty or so. See Carolyn Osiek and David L. Balch, *Families in the New Testament World: Households and House Churches* (Louisville, Ky.: Westminster John Knox, 1997), 201–3.

194. Strecker, *Liminale Theologie*, 330.

195. Statius, *Silvae* 1.6.43–50. This leveling of the social hierarchy is perhaps the only aspect of the saturnalian celebrations that Paul would have found commendable.

196. See also 1 Cor 7:20–24; Phlm; Eph 6:5–9; 1 Tim 6:1–2; Titus 2:9–10. In addition to Philemon, other passages may also refer to slaves in the Christian community, particularly texts with the expression "those of so-and-so's household" (Rom 16:10–11; 1 Cor 1:11; Phil 4:22).

197. The decisive evidence comes from verse 21, where Paul expresses his confidence that Philemon will do "more than what I ask." On this see F. F. Bruce, *The Epistles to the Colossians, to Philemon, and to the Ephesians* (New International Critical Commentary; Grand Rapids, Mich.: Eerdmans, 1984), 216–21; James D. G. Dunn, *The Epistles to the Colossians and to Philemon: A Commentary on the Greek Text* (Grand Rapids, Mich.: Eerdmans, 1996), 345; Markus Barth and Helmut Blanke, *The Letter to Philemon: A New Translation with Notes and Commentary* (Grand Rapids, Mich.: Eerdmans, 2000), 492.

198. See also the ESV, NASB, NTL, NET. The difficulty in translating this verse issues from the fact that Paul does not explicitly complete his thought. Literally it reads, "If you can gain your freedom, rather, use it." Use what? Their opportunity for freedom or their present servitude? Paul probably does not intend to prohibit slaves from gaining their freedom. This would contradict verse 23, where he forbids making oneself a slave to others. In defense of the NIV's rendering, see Fee, *First Corinthians*, 315–22. Thiselton, however, offers a judicious alternative. He translates the clause, "Even if there is a possibility that you might come to be free, rather, start to make positive use of the present." In Thisleton's view, Paul is not forbidding slaves from taking advantage of manumission if the opportunity should arise; rather, he is simply encouraging them to make the most of their present situation and not to be obsessed with gaining freedom. See Thiselton, *First Corinthians*, 553–62.

199. Paul refers to himself as Christ's slave (e.g., Rom 1:1, Phil 1:1) and a slave of "all" (e.g., 1 Cor. 3:5; 2 Cor 4:5). He refers to Christ taking the form of slave (Phil 2:6–11). Other images related to slavery, masters, and manumission abound: Rom 3:24; 7:14; 2 Cor 2:14; Gal 5:1; 1 Tim 1:10.

200. O. Betz, "Στίγμα," in *TDNT* 7:657–64. Betz also notes that in some provinces later in the imperial period it was also used to mark soldiers.

201. It should be pointed out, however, that the biblical material related to slavery represents a higher ethic and standard of treatment vis-à-vis the surrounding cultures, both in terms of the ancient Near East and the Greco-Roman world. On this see William J. Webb, *Slaves, Women, and Homosexuals: Exploring the Hermeneutics of Cultural Analysis* (Downers Grove, Ill.: InterVarsity Press, 2001), 401.

202. F. F. Bruce, *Paul, Apostle of the Heart Set Free* (Grand Rapids: Eerdmans, 2000), 401.

NOTES TO EPILOGUE

1. James G. Crossley, *Why Christianity Happened: A Sociohistorical Account of Christian Origins (26–50 C.E.)* (Louisville, Ky.: Westminster John Knox, 2006); Jack T. Sanders, *Charisma, Converts, Competitors: Societal and Sociological Factors in the Success of Early Christianity* (London: SCM, 2000); Rodney Stark, *Cities of God: The Real Story of How Christianity Became an Urban Movement and Conquered Rome* (New York: HarperCollins, 2007); Rodney Stark, *The Rise of Christianity: A Sociologist Reconsiders History* (Princeton: Princeton University Press, 1996); Michael F. Bird and James G. Crossley, *How Did Christianity Begin? A Believer and Non-Believer Examine the Evidence* (Peabody, Mass.: Hendrickson, 2008).

2. Gerd Theissen, *Social Reality and the Early Christians: Theology, Ethics, and the World of the New Testament* (Minneapolis: Fortress, 1992), 187.

3. The literature is surveyed in Stark, *The Rise of Christianity*, 15–18.

4. For more detail, consult Ramsay MacMullen, *Paganism in the Roman Empire* (New Haven: Yale University Press, 1981), 128–30.

5. Tertullian, *Apology* 39.15, cited in Stark, *The Rise of Christianity*, 198.

6. Tertullian, *Apology* 39.8–9.

7.*Tertullian, *Apology* 39.6–7.

GLOSSARY

aedile   A magistrate chiefly responsible for overseeing the markets and forums

agonothete, agnothetes   The official supervising the public games

agora, agorai   A public market

amphora   A vessel used for carrying or storing oil, grain, and other goods

Asklepion   The sanctuary of the god Asklepios

atriensis   A household slave with responsibilities similar to a porter

atrium   A large open central court in a Greco-Roman home

augur   A priest who interpreted the will of the gods by studying flight of birds

Augustales   A priesthood dedicated to the imperial house, usually composed of freedmen

Charon   The mythological ferryman of Hades who carried the souls of the dead across the river Styx

clunis   The Latin word for buttocks

communitas   A Latin noun indicating a strong sense of community, equality, and relational connectedness

consul   The highest elected Roman official, chiefly responsible for presiding over the senate

convivium   A roman banquet or dinner party

Craneum   A district in Roman Corinth

cubiculum (cubicula)   A room(s) in a Roman house

cursus honorum   The "ladder of success"—a succession of honors

daemones, daimonia   A spirit

Decurion   A member of the city council

demos   The population of a Greek city-state, or a public assembly of citizens

denarius, denarii   A Roman coin

diaspora   From the Greek word meaning "scattered," diaspora refers to Jews living outside of the Jewish heartland

dignitas   Personal honor

Divi Filius   "son of a god"

dole   The free supply of grain to the poor in Rome

domina domi   The "Lady of the house"; a woman presiding over a home

domina horribilis   "Horrible mistress"

domini et dominae   "Lords and Ladies," referring to men and women of rank

Dominus, Domine   "Lord," or "Master"

domus   Latin for "home"

duovir, duoviri, duumviri   Chiefs of the city council

duovirate   Pertaining to the office of the duumvir

fides   "Faith," "trust"

fortuna   Goddess of luck and fortune

freedman, freedwoman   A former slave freed by his/her master

genius   Guardian spirit

gladius   A small Roman sword

grammaticus, grammatici   A teacher of elementary reading, math, and literature

haruspicy   A type of divination based on examining the entrails of animals

Hellenization   A term describing the spread of Hellenic (Greek) culture

horoscopus   Latin for "horoscope"

hoi polloi   Greek for "The many," that is, the average person

imperial cult   The religious system dedicated to venerating Caesar and the imperial family

impluvium   A sunken portion of the floor of the atrium of a Greco-Roman home for catching rainwater

insula, insulae   A multi-story apartment building(s), often poorly built and intended to house the lower ranks of Roman society

iure dicundo   A Latin phrase meaning "speaking for the law," used as part of a magistrate's title

kurios, kurie   Greek for "lord," or "master"

lararium   A shrine for the guardian spirits of a Roman household

lares   Spirits protecting the home

Meum mel   A Latin term of affection: "My sweet," "Dearest"

mos maijorum   The customs of the ancients; honored tradition

narcissus   A flower

obol   A Greek coin

ordo decurionum   The city council

palaestra   An exercise courtyard, often attached to a gymnasium in the Roman era

pantheon   The chief deities of Greek and Roman religion, or a temple dedicated to these deities

pater familias   "Father of the family"; the oldest living male member of a household

patria potestas   "The power of the Father"; the authority of the *pater familias* over his family

Pax Romana   Modern term for a long period of relative peace under Roman rule

penates   Roman deities protecting the home

peplum   A Greek garment worn by women

peristyle   A courtyard surrounded by columns

peroration   A rhetorically crafted speech

pietas   A Latin word denoting one's religious duties

plebe   A member of the lower classes

pontifex   A priest

prætor   A city magistrate, or a military commander

prefect   A high ranking Roman official

principate   The period of Roman history in which emperors were the head of state

psychagogue   A spiritual guide, mentor

quaestor, quaestores   A mid-level Roman magistrate often charged with financial oversight

quaestorship   The office of quaestor

quinquennalis(-es), quinquennial   Referring to an office lasting for five years, or occurring every five years

salutatio   The early morning greeting of a patron by a client

Salve   A Latin greeting, "Health to you!"

Selena   A lunar goddess

sestercius, sesterces   A Roman coin

shaman, shamanism   Shamanism encompasses a broad variety of religious beliefs relating to communicating with the spiritual realm; shamans are the "priests" of this type of folk-religion

sistrum   A small musical instrument similar to a rattle

sophist   A public orator

stola   An overgarment worn by Roman women

strigil   A small, hooked, metal instrument used to scrape dirt and sweat from the body

Styx   A mythical river separating the realm of the living from the realm of the dead

superstitio   A derogatory term used by Latin writers of non-Roman religious systems

sybil   A female oracle or prophetess

taberna, tabernae   A small retail shop

tablinum   A room in a Roman house usually connected to the atrium

testimonia   Testimonies

tetrastoa   A hall with four columns, an atrium

Thanatos   Greek god associated with death

timbrel   A small musical instrument

tintinnabuli   A kind of wind chime used to ward off evil

toga candida   Latin for "bright toga"; it was worn by candidates for public office

toga trabea   A colorful toga with scarlet and purple stripes worn by priests and religious functionaries

toga virilis   The white toga worn by adult male Roman citizens

Tribune   A military or civil magistrate with varying respsonsibilities

tribunician   Of or related to a Tribune, especially with regard to the powers of the office

triclinium   The dining room of a Greco-Roman home

trident   A three-pronged spear often used in gladiatorial contests

Via Egnatia   An important Roman road connecting Rome to its eastern provinces

votaries of Bacchus   Devotees of the god Bacchus

wolfsbane   A poisonous herb

BIBLIOGRAPHY

Arnold, Clinton E. *Ephesians, Power, and Magic: The Concept of Power in Ephesians in Light of Its Historical Setting*. Cambridge: Cambridge University Press, 1989.

———. " 'I Am Astonished That You Are So Quickly Turning Away!' (Gal 1.6): Paul and Anatolian Folk Belief." *NTS* 51 (2005): 429–49.

Ascough, Richard S. "The Completion of a Religious Duty: The Background of 2 Cor. 8:9–15," *NTS* 42 (1996): 597.

———. *Paul's Macedonian Associations: The Social Context of Philippians and 1 Thessalonians*. WUNT 2.161. Tübingen: Mohr Siebeck, 2003.

———. *What Are They Saying about the Formation of Pauline Churches?* New York: Paulist, 1998.

Bain, Ken. *What the Best College Teachers Do*. Cambridge, Mass.: Harvard University Press, 2004.

Balch, David L. "Household Codes." Pages 25–50 in *Greco-Roman Literature and the New Testament: Selected Forms and Genres*. Edited by David E. Aune. Atlanta: Scholars Press, 1988.

———. "'Let Wives Be Submissive . . .': The Origin, Form and Apologetic Function of the Household Duty Code (Haustafel) in 1 Peter." Thesis, Yale University, 1974.

Banks, Robert J. *Going to Church in the First Century: An Eyewitness Account*. Auburn, Maine: Christian Books, 1990.

———. *Paul's Idea of Community*. Rev. ed. Peabody, Mass.: Hendrickson, 1994.

———. "'Walking' as a Metaphor of the Christian Life: The Origins of a Significant Pauline Usage." Pages 303–13 in *Perspectives on Language and Text*, edited by Francis I. Andersen, Edgar W. Conrad, and Edward G. Newing. Winona Lake, Ind.: Eisenbrauns, 1987.

Barclay, John M. G. *Jews in the Mediterranean Diaspora: From Alexander to Trajan (323 B.C.E.–117 C.E.)*. Edinburgh: T&T Clark, 1996.

Barrett, C. K. *A Critical and Exegetical Commentary on the Acts of the Apostles.* 2 vols. ICC. Edinburgh: T&T Clark, 1994, 1998.

———. *The First Epistle to the Corinthians.* Peabody, Mass.: Hendrickson, 1993.

Barth, Markus, and Helmut Blanke. *The Letter to Philemon: A New Translation with Notes and Commentary.* Grand Rapids, Mich.: Eerdmans, 2000.

Bauckham, Richard. *Gospel Women: Studies of the Named Women in the Gospels.* Grand Rapids, Mich.: Eerdmans, 2002.

Baugh, Steven M. "Cult Prostitution in New Testament Ephesus: A Reappraisal." *JETS* 42 (1999): 443–60.

Belleville, Linda L. " Ιουνίαν . . . ἐπίσημοι ἐν τοῖς ἀποστόλοις: A Re-Examination of Romans 16.7 in Light of Primary Source Materials." *NTS* 51 (2005): 231–49.

Bloedhorn, Hanswulf, and Gil Hüttenmeister. "The Synagogue." Pages 267–97 in *The Cambridge History of Judaism.* Vol. 3, *The Early Roman Period.* Edited by William Horbury, W. D. Davies, and John Sturdy. Cambridge: Cambridge University Press, 2001.

Bonner, Stanley F. *Education in Ancient Rome: From the Elder Cato to the Younger Pliny.* London: Methuen, 1977.

Bookidis, Nancy. "Religion in Corinth: 146 B.C.E. to 100 C.E." Pages 141–64 in *Urban Religion in Roman Corinth: Interdisciplinary Approaches.* Edited by Daniel N. Schowalter and Steven J. Friesen. Cambridge, Mass.: Harvard University Press, 2005.

Borman, Lukas. *Philippi: Stadt und Christengemeinde zur Zeit des Paulus.* Leiden: Brill, 1995.

Bowersock, G. W. *Greek Sophists in the Roman Empire.* Oxford: Clarendon, 1969.

Bradley, Keith R. *Slavery and Society at Rome.* Cambridge: Cambridge University Press, 1994.

Broneer, Oscar. *Ancient Corinth: A Guide to the Excavations.* 4th edition. American School of Classical Studies at Athens. Athens: Hestia, 1947.

Broshi, M. "Estimating the Population of Jerusalem." *Biblical Archaeology Review* 4 (1978): 10–15.

Bruce, F. F. *1 and 2 Thessalonians.* WBC 45. Waco, Tex.: Word, 1982.

———. *The Epistles to the Colossians, to Philemon, and to the Ephesians.* New International Critical Commentary. Grand Rapids, Mich.: Eerdmans, 1984.

———. *Paul, Apostle of the Heart Set Free.* Grand Rapids, Mich.: Eerdmans, 2000.

———. "Travel and Communication: The New Testament World." Pages 648–53 in *Anchor Bible Dictionary.* Edited by David Noel Freedman. Garden City, N.Y.: Doubleday, 1992.

Burtchaell, James Tunstead. *From Synagogue to Church: Public Services and Offices in the Earliest Christian Communities.* Cambridge: Cambridge University Press, 1992.

Carcopino, Jérôme. *Daily Life in Ancient Rome: The People and the City at the Height of the Empire.* Edited by Henry T. Rowell. Translated by E. O. Lorimer. New Haven: Yale University Press, 1966.

Casson, Lionel. *Ships and Seamanship in the Ancient World.* Baltimore: Johns Hopkins University Press, 1995.

———. *Travel in the Ancient World.* Baltimore: Johns Hopkins University Press, 1994.

Catto, Stephen K. *Reconstructing the First-Century Synagogue: A Critical Analysis of Current Research.* Library of New Testament Studies 363. London: T&T Clark, 2007.

Cilliers, L., and F. P. Retif. "Poisons, Poisoning and the Drug Trade in Ancient Rome." *Akroterion* 45 (2000): 88–100.

Clarke, Andrew D. *A Pauline Theology of Church Leadership.* London: T&T Clark, 2008.

Cohen, Shaye J. D. "Crossing the Boundary and Becoming a Jew." *HTR* 82 (1989): 14–33.

Conzelmann, Hans. *Acts of the Apostles: A Commentary on the Acts of the Apostles.* Translated by Eldon Jay Epp and Christopher R. Matthews. Philadelphia: Fortress, 1987.

Countryman, Louis William. *The Rich Christian in the Church of the Early Empire: Contradictions and Accommodations.* New York: Mellen, 1980.

Crossley, James G. *Why Christianity Happened: A Sociohistorical Account of Christian Origins (26–50 C.E.).* Louisville, Ky.: Westminster John Knox, 2006.

Davis, William Stearns. *Readings In Ancient History II : Rome And The West.* New York: Agmatiallyn and Bacon, 1913. Repr., n.p.: Yoakum, 2007.

De Vos, Craig Steven. *Church and Community Conflicts: The Relationships of the Thessalonian, Corinthian, and Philippian Churches with Their Wider Civic Communities.* Atlanta: Scholars Press, 1999.

Deming, Will. *Paul on Marriage and Celibacy: The Hellenistic Background of 1 Corinthians 7.* 2d ed. Grand Rapids, Mich.: Eerdmans, 2004.

Dietzfelbinger, Christian. *Die Berufung Des Paulus Als Ursprung Seiner Theologie.* Neukirchen-Vluyn: Neukirchener, 1985.

Dodd, C. H. *New Testament Studies.* 1st Edition. Manchester: Manchester University Press, 1967.

Donfried, Karl P., and Peter Richardson. *Judaism and Christianity in First-Century Rome.* Grand Rapids, Mich.: Eerdmans, 1998.

Dowden, Ken. *Religion and the Romans.* Classical World Series. London: Bristol Classical, 1992.

Dunbabin, Katherine M. D. *The Roman Banquet: Images of Conviviality*. New York: Cambridge University Press, 2003.

Dunn, James D. G. *The Epistles to the Colossians and to Philemon: A Commentary on the Greek Text*. Grand Rapids, Mich.: Eerdmans, 1996.

———. *The Theology of Paul the Apostle*. Grand Rapids, Mich.: Eerdmans, 1998.

Ehrenberg, V., and A. H. M. Jones. *Documents Illustrating the Reigns of Augustus and Tiberius*. Edited by D. L. Stockton. Oxford: Clarendon, 1976.

Ellis, Simon P. *Roman Housing*. London: Duckworth, 2000.

Engberg-Pedersen, Troels. "The Relationship with Others: Similarities and Differences between Paul and Stoicism." *Zeitschrift für die neutestamentliche Wissenschaft und die Kunde der Älteren Kirche* 96/1 (2005): 35–60.

Epp, Eldon Jay. *Junia: The First Woman Apostle*. Minneapolis: Fortress, 2005.

Fagan, Garrett G. *Bathing in Public in the Roman World*. Ann Arbor: University of Michigan Press, 2002.

Fee, Gordon D. *1 and 2 Timothy, Titus*. NIBC. Peabody, Mass.: Hendrickson, 1988.

———. *The First Epistle to the Corinthians*. NICNT. Grand Rapids, Mich.: Eerdmans, 1987.

———. "Reflections on Church Order in the Pastoral Epistles, with Further Reflections on the Hermeneutics of *Ad Hoc* Documents." *JETS* 28 (1985): 141–51.

Ferguson, Everett. *Backgrounds of Early Christianity*. 3d ed. Grand Rapids, Mich.: Eerdmans, 2003.

Fotopoulos, John. *Food Offered to Idols in Roman Corinth: A Social-Rhetorical Reconsideration of 1 Corinthians 8:1–11:1*. WUNT 2.151. Tübingen: Mohr Siebeck, 2003.

Friesen, S. J. "Injustice or God's Will: Explanations of Poverty in Proto-Christian Communities," Pages 240–60 in *Christian Origins: A People's History of Christianity*. Edited by R. A. Horsley. Minneapolis, Fortress Press, 2005.

———. "Poverty in Pauline Studies: Beyond the So-Called New Consensus." *JSNT* 26.3 (2004): 323–61.

Gager, John G. *Curse Tablets and Binding Spells from the Ancient World*. New York: Oxford University Press, 1992.

Garrison, Roman. *Redemptive Almsgiving in Early Christianity*. Journal for the Study of the New Testament Supplement Series. Sheffield: JSOT Press, 1993.

Gehring, Roger W. *House Church and Mission: The Importance of Household Structures in Early Christianity*. Peabody, Mass.: Hendrickson, 2004.

Geroge, Michele. "*Servus* and *Domus*: The Slave in the Roman House." Pages 15–24 in *Domestic Space in the Roman World: Pompeii and Beyond*. Edited by Ray Laurence and Andrew Wallace-Hadrill. Portsmouth, R.I.: Journal of Roman Archaeology, 1997.

Giles, Kevin. "Luke's Use of the Term *Ekklēsia* with Special Reference to Acts 20:28 and 9:31." *NTS* 31 (1985): 135–42.

———. *Patterns of Ministry among the First Christians*. Melbourne: Collins Dove, 1989.

Goodspeed, E. J. "Gaius Titius Justus." *Journal of Biblical Literature* 69 (1950): 382–83.

Grant, Frederick C. *Ancient Roman Religion*. New York: Liberal Arts, 1957.

Grant, Michael, et al. *Eros in Pompeii: The Erotic Art Collection of the Museum of Naples*. New York: Stewart, Tabori & Chang, 1997.

Grubbs, Judith Evans. *Women and the Law in the Roman Empire: A Sourcebook on Marriage, Divorce, and Widowhood*. London: Routledge, 2002.

Haenchen, Ernst. *The Acts of the Apostles: A Commentary*. Philadelphia: Westminster Press, 1971.

Harris, William V. *Ancient Literacy*. Cambridge, Mass.: Harvard University Press, 1989.

Harrison, J. R. "Paul and the Imperial Gospel at Thessaloniki." *JSNT* 25 (2002): 71–96.

Hawthorne, Gerald F., Ralph P. Martin, and Daniel G. Reid, eds. *Dictionary of Paul and His Letters*. Downers Grove, Ill.: InterVarsity Press, 1993.

Heininger, Bernhard. *Paulus Als Visionär: Eine Religionsgeschichtliche Studie*. Freiburg: Herder, 1996.

Hellerman, Joseph H. *The Ancient Church as Family*. Minneapolis: Fortress, 2001.

Hengel, Martin, and Roland Deines. *The Pre-Christian Paul*. London: Trinity Press International, 1991.

Hock, Ronald F. "Paul and Greco-Roman Education." Pages 198–227 in *Paul in the Greco-Roman World: A Handbook*. Edited by J. Paul Sampley. Harrisburg, Pa.: Trinity Press International, 2003.

———. *The Social Context of Paul's Ministry: Tentmaking and Apostleship*. Philadelphia: Fortress, 1980.

Horbury, William. "Women in the Synagogue." Pages 358–401 in *The Cambridge History of Judaism*. Vol. 3, *The Early Roman Period*. Edited by William Horbury, W. D. Davies, and John Sturdy. Cambridge: Cambridge University Press, 1999.

Horsley, G. H. R, and S. R. Llewelyn. *New Documents Illustrating Early Christianity*. 9 vols. North Ryde: The Ancient History Documentary Research Centre, Macquarie University, 1981.

Hubbard, Moyer V. *New Creation in Paul's Letters and Thought*. SNTSMS 119. Cambridge: Cambridge University Press, 2002.

Johnson, Luke Timothy. *The First and Second Letters to Timothy: A New Translation with Introduction and Commentary*. AB 35A. Garden City, N.Y.: Doubleday, 2001.

Jones, A. H. M. *The Greek City from Alexander to Justinian.* Oxford: Clarendon, 1998.

Kearsley, Rosalinde A. "Women in Public Life in the Roman East: Iunia Theodora, Claudia Metrodora and Phoebe, Benefactress of Paul." *TynBul* 50 (1999): 189–211.

Kee, Howard Clark. *Who Are the People of God? Early Christian Models of Community.* New Haven: Yale University Press, 1995.

Kennedy, George A. *A New History of Classical Rhetoric.* Princeton: Princeton University Press, 1994.

Kent, John Harvey. *Corinth: The Inscriptions, 1926–1950.* Vol. 8, part 3. Princeton, N.J.: American School of Classical Studies at Athens, 1966.

Kittel, Gerhard, and Gerhard Friedrich, eds. *Theological Dictionary of the New Testament.* Translated by Geoffrey W. Bromiley. 10 vols. Grand Rapids, Mich.: Eerdmans, 1964–76.

Klauck, Hans-Josef. "Die kleinasiatischen Beichtinschriften und das Neue Testament." Pages 63–87 in *Geschichte—Tradition—Reflexion: Festschrift für Martin Hengel zum 70. Geburtstag: Frühes Christentum.* Tübingen: Mohr Siebeck, 1996.

———. *The Religious Context of Early Christianity: A Guide to Graeco-Roman Religions.* Minneapolis: Fortress, 2003.

Klauck, Hans-Josef, and Brian McNeil. *Magic and Paganism in Early Christianity: The World of the Acts of the Apostles.* Minneapolis: Fortress, 2003.

Kloppenborg, John S. "*Collegia* and *Thiasoi*: Issues in Function, Taxonomy and Membership." Pages 16–30 in *Voluntary Associations in the Graeco-Roman World.* Edited by John S. Kloppenborg and S. G. Wilson. New York: Routledge, 1996.

Knight, George W. *The Pastoral Epistles: A Commentary on the Greek Text.* NIGTC. Grand Rapids, Mich.: Eerdmans, 1992.

Lassen, Eva Marie. "The Roman Family: Ideal and Metaphor." Pages 103–20 in *Constructing Early Christian Families: Family as Social Reality and Metaphor.* Edited by Halvor Moxnes. New York: Routledge, 1997.

Lefkowitz, Mary R., and Maureen B. Fant. *Women's Life in Greece and Rome.* Baltimore: Johns Hopkins University Press, 1982.

Lessing, Erich, and Antonio Varone. *Pompeii.* Paris: Terrail, 2001.

Levick, Barbara. *The Government of the Roman Empire: A Sourcebook.* 2d ed. New York: Routledge, 2000.

Levine, Lee I. *The Ancient Synagogue: The First Thousand Years.* New Haven: Yale University Press, 2000.

Lightfoot, J. B. *Saint Paul's Epistle to the Philippians.* London: Macmillan, 1890.

Litfin, Duane. *St. Paul's Theology of Proclamation: 1 Corinthians 1–4 and Greco-Roman Rhetoric.* SNTSMS 79. Cambridge: Cambridge University Press, 1994.

Long, A. A. "Socrates in Hellenistic Philosophy." Pages 1–34 in *Stoic Studies*. Berkeley: University of California Press, 2001.

MacMullen, Ramsay. *Enemies of the Roman Order: Treason, Unrest, and Alienation in the Empire*. Cambridge, Mass.: Harvard University Press, 1967.

———. *Paganism in the Roman Empire*. New Haven: Yale University Press, 1981.

———. *Roman Social Relations, 50 B.C. to A.D. 284*. New Haven: Yale University Press, 1974.

———. "Two Types of Conversion in Early Christianity." *Vigiliae Christianae* 37 (1983): 174–92.

Malherbe, Abraham J. *The Cynic Epistles: A Study Edition*. SBLSBS 12. Atlanta: Scholars Press, 1977

———. *The Letters to the Thessalonians: A New Translation with Introduction and Commentary*. AB 32B. New York: Doubleday, 2000.

———. *Moral Exhortation: A Greco-Roman Sourcebook*. Philadelphia: Westminster Press, 1986.

Marrou, Henri Irénée. *A History of Education in Antiquity*. Wisconsin Studies in Classics. Madison: University of Wisconsin Press, 1982.

Marshall, I. Howard, and Philip Towner. *A Critical and Exegetical Commentary on the Pastoral Epistles*. ICC. Edinburgh: T&T Clark, 1999.

Marshall, Peter. *Enmity in Corinth: Social Conventions in Paul's Relations with the Corinthians*. WUNT 2.23. Tübingen: Mohr Siebeck, 1987.

Martin, Ralph P. *Worship in the Early Church*. Grand Rapids, Mich.: Eerdmans, 1981.

McCrum, M., and A. G. Woodhead. *Select Documents of the Principates of the Flavian Emperors including the year of Revolution, AD 68–96*. Cambridge: Cambridge University Press, 1961.

McKnight, Scot. *A Light among the Gentiles: Jewish Missionary Activity in the Second Temple Period*. Minneapolis: Fortress, 1991.

Meeks, Wayne A. *The First Urban Christians: The Social World of the Apostle Paul*. 2d ed. New Haven: Yale University Press, 2003.

Meyer, Marvin W., and Richard Smith. *Ancient Christian Magic: Coptic Texts of Ritual Power*. San Francisco: Harper, 1994.

Moo, Douglas J. *The Epistle to the Romans*. NICNT. Grand Rapids, Mich.: Eerdmans, 1996.

Mounce, William D. *Pastoral Epistles*. WBC 46. Nashville: Thomas Nelson, 2000.

Murphy-O'Connor, Jerome. *Paul: His Story*. Oxford: Oxford University Press, 2004.

———. *St. Paul's Corinth: Texts and Archaeology*. 3d rev. and exp. ed. Collegeville, Minn.: Liturgical Press, 2002.

Oakes, Peter. *Philippians: From People to Letter*. Cambridge: Cambridge University Press, 2001.

Osiek, Carolyn, and David L. Balch. *Families in the New Testament World: Households and House Churches*. Louisville, Ky.: Westminster John Knox, 1997.

Packer, James E. "Housing and Population in Imperial Ostia and Rome." *JRS* 57 (1967): 80–95.

Patzia, Arthur G. *The Emergence of the Church: Context, Growth, Leadership, and Worship*. Downers Grove, Ill.: InterVarsity Press, 2001.

Peterman, G. W. "Marriage and Sexual Fidelity in the Papyri, Plutarch, and Paul." *TynBul* 50 (1999): 163–72.

Philodemus, and David Sider. *The Epigrams of Philodemos*. Oxford: Oxford University Press, 1996.

Pilhofer, Peter. *Die Erste Christliche Gemeinde Europas*. WUNT 87. Tübingen: Mohr Siebeck, 1995.

———. *Katalog der Inschriften von Philippi*. WUNT 119. Tübingen: Mohr Siebeck, 2000.

Piper, John. *The Supremacy of God in Preaching*. Grand Rapids, Mich.: Baker, 1990.

Price, S. R. F. *Rituals and Power: The Roman Imperial Cult in Asia Minor*. Cambridge: Cambridge University Press, 1984.

Rajak, Tessa, and David Noy. "*Archisynagogoi*: Office, Title, and Social Status in the Greco-Jewish Synagogue." *JRS* 83 (1993): 75–93

Rapske, Brian. *The Book of Acts and Paul in Roman Custody*. Vol. 3 of *The Book of Acts in Its First Century Setting*. Grand Rapids, Mich.: Eerdmans, 1994.

Reumann, John. "Church Office in Paul, Especially in Philippians." Pages 83–91 in *Origins and Method: Towards a New Understanding of Judaism and Christianity: Essays in Honour of John C. Hurd*. Edited by John C. Hurd and Bradley H. McLean. Sheffield: JSOT Press, 1993.

Richards, E. Randolph. *Paul and First-Century Letter Writing: Secretaries, Composition, and Collection*. Downers Grove, Ill.: InterVarsity Press, 2004.

Richlin, Amy. "Approaches to the Sources on Adultery at Rome." Pages 379–404 in *Reflections of Women in Antiquity*. Edited by Helene P. Foley. New York: Gordon and Breach Science, 1981.

Riesner, Rainer. *Paul's Early Period: Chronology, Mission Strategy, Theology*. Grand Rapids, Mich.: Eerdmans, 1998.

Roberts, Colin H., T. C. Skeat, and Arthur Darby Nock. "The Guild of Zeus Hypsistos." *HTR* 29 (1936): 39–88.

Roetzel, Calvin J. *Paul: The Man and the Myth*. Minneapolis: Fortress, 1999.

Runeson, Anders. *The Origins of the Synagogue: A Socio-Historical Study*. Stockholm: Almqvist & Wiksell International, 2000.

Sanders, Jack T. *Charisma, Converts, Competitors: Societal and Sociological Factors in the Success of Early Christianity*. London: SCM, 2000.

Savage, Timothy B. *Power through Weakness: Paul's Understanding of the Christian Ministry in 2 Corinthians*. SNTSMS 86. Cambridge: Cambridge University Press, 1996.

Scheidel, Walter. "Stratification, Deprivation, and Quality of Life." Pages 40–59 in *Poverty in the Roman World*. Edited by E. M. Atkins and Robin Osborne. Cambridge: Cambridge University Press, 2006.

Schenk, Wolfgang. *Die Philipperbriefe des Paulus: Kommentar*. Stuttgart: W. Kohlhammer, 1984.

Schoellgen, Georg. "Die διπλῆ τιμή von 1 Tim. 5:17." *ZNW* 80 (1989): 232–39.

Schrage, Wolfgang. *Der Erste Brief an Die Korinther*. 4 vols. Zurich: Neukirchener, 2001.

Sedley, D. N. *The Cambridge Companion to Greek and Roman Philosophy*. Cambridge: Cambridge University Press, 2003.

Stambaugh, John. *The Ancient Roman City*. Ancient Society and History. Baltimore: Johns Hopkins University Press, 1988.

———. "Social Relations in the City of the Early Principate: State of Research." Pages 75–90 in *Society of Biblical Literature 1980 Seminar Papers*. Edited by P. J. Achtmeier. Chico, Calif.: Scholars Press, 1980.

Stambaugh, John E., and David L. Balch. *The New Testament in Its Social Environment*. Library of Early Christianity. Philadelphia: Westminster Press, 1986.

Stark, Rodney. "Antioch as the Social Situation for Mathew's Gospel." Pages 189–210 in *Social History of the Matthean Community: Cross-Disciplinary Approaches*. Edited by David L. Balch. Minneapolis: Fortress, 1991.

———. *Cities of God: The Real Story of How Christianity Became an Urban Movement and Conquered Rome*. New York: HarperCollins, 2007.

———. *The Rise of Christianity: A Sociologist Reconsiders History*. Princeton: Princeton University Press, 1996.

Stegemann, Ekkehard, and Wolfgang Stegemann. *The Jesus Movement: A Social History of Its First Century*. Minneapolis: Fortress, 1999.

Stirewalt, M. Luther. *Paul, the Letter Writer*. Grand Rapids, Mich.: Eerdmans, 2003.

Strauch, Alexander. *Biblical Eldership: An Urgent Call to Restore Biblical Church Leadership*. Littleton, Colo.: Lewis & Roth, 1995.

Tcherikover, Victor. *Hellenistic Civilization and the Jews*. Peabody, Mass.: Hendrickson, 1999.

Theissen, Gerd. *Social Reality and the Early Christians: Theology, Ethics, and the World of the New Testament*. Minneapolis: Fortress, 1992.

Thiselton, Anthony C. *The First Epistle to the Corinthians: A Commentary on the Greek Text*. NIGTC. Grand Rapids, Mich.: Eerdmans, 2000.

Thomas, Christine M. "Placing the Dead: Funerary Practice and Social Stratification in the Early Roman Period at Corinth and Ephesos." Pages 281–304 in *Urban Religion in Roman Corinth: Interdisciplinary Approaches*. Edited by Daniel N. Schowalter and Steven J. Friesen. Cambridge, Mass.: Harvard University Press, 2005.

Trebilco, Paul. "Asia." Pages 291–376 in *The Book of Acts in Its Graeco-Roman Setting*. Edited by David Gill and Conrad Gempf. Grand Rapids, Mich.: Eerdmans, 1994.

———. "Paul and Silas: 'Servants of the Most High God' (Acts 16:16–18)." *JSNT* 36 (1989): 51–73.

Verner, David C. *The Household of God: The Social World of the Pastoral Epistles*. Society of Biblical Literature Dissertation Series 71. Chico, Calif.: Scholars Press, 1983.

Walbank, Mary E. Hoskins. "Unquiet Graves: Burial Practices of the Roman Corinthians." Pages 249–80 in *Urban Religion in Roman Corinth: Interdisciplinary Approaches*. Edited by Daniel N. Schowalter and Steven J. Friesen. Cambridge, Mass.: Harvard University Press, 2005.

Walzer, Richard. *Galen on Jews and Christians*. London: Oxford University Press, 1949.

Wanamaker, Charles A. *The Epistles to the Thessalonians: A Commentary on the Greek Text*. NIGTC. Grand Rapids, Mich.: Eerdmans, 1990.

Ward-Perkins, J. B., and Amanda Claridge. *Pompeii A.D. 79: Treasures from the National Archaeological Museum, Naples, and the Pompeii Antiquarium*. Boston: Boston Museum of Fine Arts, 1978.

Webb, William J. *Slaves, Women, and Homosexuals: Exploring the Hermeneutics of Cultural Analysis*. Downers Grove, Ill.: InterVarsity Press, 2001.

Wendland, Paul. *Die Hellenistisch-Römische Kultur in ihren Beziehungen zu Judentum und Christentum. Die urchristlichen Literaturformen*. Tübingen: Mohr, 1912.

Wilken, Robert Louis. *The Christians as the Romans Saw Them*. New Haven: Yale University Press, 1984.

Williams, David John. *Acts*. NIBC. Peabody, Mass.: Hendrickson, 1990.

Wimbush, Vincent L. *Paul, the Worldly Ascetic: Response to the World and Self-Understanding according to 1 Corinthians 7*. Macon, Ga.: Mercer University Press, 1987.

Winter, Bruce W. *After Paul Left Corinth: The Influence of Secular Ethics and Social Change*. Grand Rapids, Mich.: Eerdmans, 2001.

———. *Philo and Paul among the Sophists: Alexandrian and Corinthian Responses to a Julio-Claudian Movement*. Grand Rapids, Mich.: Eerdmans, 2002.

———. *Roman Wives, Roman Widows: The Appearance of New Women and the Pauline Communities*. Grand Rapids, Mich.: Eerdmans, 2003.

―――. "Widows and Legal and Christian Benefactions." Pages 61–78 in *Seek the Welfare of the City: Christians as Benefactors and Citizens.* Grand Rapids, Mich.: Eerdmans, 1994.

Wiseman, James. "Corinth and Rome I: 228 B.C.–A.D. 267." *Aufstieg und Niedergang der Römischen Welt* 2.7.1 (1979): 438–548.

Witherington, Ben. *The Acts of the Apostles: A Socio-Rhetorical Commentary.* Grand Rapids, Mich.: Eerdmans, 1998.

―――. *Conflict and Community in Corinth: A Socio-Rhetorical Commentary on 1 and 2 Corinthians.* Grand Rapids, Mich.: Eerdmans, 1995.

Yegül, Fikret K. *Baths and Bathing in Classical Antiquity.* Cambridge, Mass.: Architectural History Foundation; MIT Press, 1992.

INDEX OF MODERN AUTHORS

INDEX OF SUBJECTS

Index of Ancient Sources

Index of Callouts

Page	Source of Callout
39.2	Common Roman Coin
39.3	Musonius Rufus, *Disc.* 9
40.1	Plutarch, *Mor.* 1102A, Epicurus
41.1	Pausanias, *Descr.* 2.3.3
42.1	Tacitus, *Hist.* 5.5
43.1	*BWK* 72
43.2	*BWK* 51
44.1	*PGM* 410–423
45.1	*Didache* 11:4–6
46.1	Seneca the Elder, *Suas.* 4.2
47.1	Valerius Maximus, *Memorable Doings and Sayings* 1.8.10
47.2	Cited in Pilhofer, *Erste Christliche Gemeinde,* 185
48.1	Cited in Ascough, *Macedonian Associations,* 158
48.2	Tacitus, *Annals* 15.32.2
49.1	The Suda, under Ἐφέσια γράμματα Cited from http://www.stoa.org/sol/ accessed 8/12/09
50.1	Cited in Meyer and Smith, *Ancient Christian Magic,* 208
50.2	Cited in Horsley, *New Documents,* 4.1
51.1	Pliny, *Ep.*10.96.5–6
51.2	Acts 23:9
52.1	2 Cor 2:10–11
52.2	2 Thess 3:3
53.1	Ezek 36:26–27
53.2	Jer 17:9
54.1	2 Cor 12:1
55.1	2 Cor 12:3
55.2	Gal 2:1–2
56.1	Acts 23:9
68.1	*P.Oxy.* 275
68.2	*Cynic Ep.* Socrates 8
68.3	Pliny the Elder, *Nat. Hist.* 25.6
69.1	Phil 2:22
69.2	*The Augustan History,* Pertinax 1.4–2, 11
70.1	Horace, *Ep.* 1.20.18
72.1	Dio Chrysostom, *Or.* 18.8
72.2	*Greek Anthology* 11.139
73.1	Cited in Bonner, *Education,* 174
73.2	Cited in Bonner, *Education,* 118
74.1	Tacitus, *Dial.* 35
75.1	Seneca, Cited in Carcopino, *Daily Life,* 120
75.2	Plato, *Phaedrus* 260A
76.1	Horace, *Ep.* 1.6.19
76.2	Dio Chrysostom, *Or.* 12.5
77.1	Kent no. 128
77.2	Plutarch, *Mor.* 41F–42A, On listening to Lectures
78.1	Aulus Gellius, *Attic Nights* 1.9.10
78.2	Seneca the Elder, *Contr.* 1 preface 8
79.1	Persius, *Sat.* 1.85–87

Page	Source of Callout
120.2	2 Cor 3:1
121.1	Pilhofer 388/L566
121.2	Plutarch, *Mor.* 147C, Dinner of the Seven Wise Men
122.1	Pseudo-Phocylides, 25
123.1	Cited in Levick, *Roman Government,* no. 28
124.1	Pausanius, *Descr.* 2.4
124.2	*BWK* 22
125.1	Pausanius, *Descr.* 4.21.4
125.2	Pausanius, *Descr.* 10.32.14
126.1	Pseudo-Lucian, *Affairs of the Heart* 12
127.1	Livy, *Germania* 18–19
128.1	West no. 68
129.1	Kent no. 32
129.2	Common Roman Coin
130.1	Cited in Levick, *Roman Government,* no. 119
131.1	Merritt no. 111
132.1	Philo, *Embassy* 156
132.2	*CIJ* 744, Cited in Rajak and Noy, 92
133.1	*CIJ* 264, Cited in Rajak and Noy, 88
134.1	Acts 15:21
134.2	1Q33 [War Scroll] 15.4–5
135.1	Aelius Aristides, Cited in Fagan, *Bathing* 41
136.1	Cited in Carcopino, *Daily Life,* 263
137.1	*Martyrdom of Perpetua and Felicitas* 3
137.2	Plutarch, *Mor.* 165D–E, On Superstition
137.3	Pseudo-Cyprian, *De Spect.* 4
138.1	Merritt no. 14, lines 60–67
140.1	Cited in Levick, *Roman Government,* no. 199
140.2	Pilhofer 166/L007
141.1	Martial, *Ep.* 1.86
142.1	Juvenal, *Sat.* 3.274–277
143.1	*CIL* VI.6.1
143.2	Pilhofer 357/L120
144.1	Martial, *Sat.* 2.46
144.2	Lucian, *Runaways* 17
145.1	Cited in Levick, *Roman Government,* no. 124
145.2	Juvenal, *Sat.* 3.153–155
146.1	Martial, *Ep.* 3.60
146.2	Cited in Levick, *Roman Government,* no. 148
147.1	Pseudo-Socrates, *Ep.* 6.3
147.2	Seneca, *Ep.* 19.4
148.1	Martial, *Ep.* 2.27
149.1	Aulus Gellius, *Attic Nights* 1.12.1–6
150.1	Halicarnassus, Cited in Grant, *Roman Religion,* 174–75
151.1	Common Roman Coin
151.2	Cited in Grant, *Roman Religion,* 175
152.1	Pliny, *Pan. 68.4*
153.1	Pilhofer 395/L789

Page	Source of Callout
197.2	Titus 1:11
198.1	Rom 16:23
199.1	Acts 16:15
199.2	1 Tim 3:14–15
200.1	1 Tim 5:1–2
200.2	Tertullian, *Apol.* 39.8
201.1	Col 3:19
201.2	Pseudo-Phocylides 199–203
202.1	Shepherd of Hermes, *Mand.* 41.4
203.1	Dio Chrysostom, *Or.* 6.17
204.1	Rom 16:3
204.2	Galen, Cited from Walzer, *Galen* 14
206.1	Acts 16:32–34
207.1	Acts 14:43
208.1	Pliny, *Ep.*10.96.8
208.2	Cited in Schoellgen, 237
209.1	Galen, Cited from Walzer, *Galen* 15
209.2	Rom 12:5–8
210.1	Acts 11:27
210.2	Hegesippus, Cited by Eusebius, *Ecclesiastical History* 23.4
211.1	Acts 9:31
212.1	Rom 12:8
213.1	Rom 12:6
213.2	1 Thess 5:19–20
214.1	Ignatius, *Smyrn.* 8.1
215.1	Titus 2:15
215.2	*Didache* 15.1–2
216.1	1 Cor 14:33
217.1	1 Tim 5:4
217.2	Ignatius, *Smyrn.* 6.2
218.1	1 Tim 5:16
219.1	Tertullian, *Apol.* 175
219.2	*Didache* 15.1–2
220.1	1 Tim 5:17
221.1	*Didache* 14:1
221.2	Juvenal, Cited in Worth, *Seven Cities,* 41
222.1	Cicero, *Pro Cnaeo Plancio* 15
223.1	Pliny, *Ep.* 9.5.3
224.1	Phlm 15–16
224.2	Gal 1:10
225.1	Titus 1:1
225.2	Col 3:11